Governing in Black Africa

Governing in Black Africa

Revised Edition

Edited by
Marion E. Doro
and
Newell M. Stultz

Africana Publishing Company
a division of Holmes & Meier
New York   London

Published in the United States of America 1986 by
Africana Publishing Company, a division of
Holmes & Meier Publishers, Inc.
30 Irving Place
New York, N.Y. 10003

Great Britain:
Pindar Road
Hoddedson, Hertsfordshire EN11 0HF
England

First edition published 1970. Revised edition 1986.

Book design by Ellen Foos

Library of Congress Cataloging-in-Publication Data
Main entry under title:

Governing in Black Africa.

  Includes bibliographies.
   1. Africa—Politics and government—1960— —
Addresses, essays, lectures.   2. States, New—Addresses,
essays, lectures.   I. Doro, Marion E.   II. Stultz,
Newell Maynard.
DT30.5.G68 1986   320.96   85-24959
ISBN 0-8419-0997-0
ISBN 0-8419-0998-9 (pbk.)

Manufactured in the United States of America

Affectionately dedicated
to three people
who made a difference

Jeffrey Butler
Gwendolen Carter
Marian D. Irish

Contents

Preface

This is the second edition of a reader in African politics that we originally published in 1970. We quoted Pliny at that time—*ex Africa semper aliquid novi*—out of Africa, always something new. Nearly fifteen years later, new—if somewhat predictable—things continue to "come out" of Africa. Since 1970 five more African states have achieved independence,[1] while two others continue to struggle to establish theirs.[2] Fifteen states have experienced one or more coups d'état.[3] Between 1970 and mid-1985 nine of Africa's founding presidents have died (six of natural causes, three as a consequence of military coups) and one has announced his pending retirement.[4] The continent's total population has nearly doubled since 1970, and in three-quarters of the states the rate of population growth has been greater than the rate of increase in the Gross Domestic Product (GDP). Fully half the new black African states have renamed themselves since independence, symbolically shedding their colonial past.[5] These events and others, both major and minor, mark changes of substance and style that Africanist scholars continue to follow with interest and concern.

In this second edition, our goal is much the same as it was in the first: "to present evidence which is relevant to contemporary Africa as a supplement to the materials that Africanists ingeniously gather for their courses." We suspect now, as we did then, that instructors may not all agree that these are necessarily the best selections, and that some will want to construct other patterns of organization with the articles in this volume. Moreover, now as earlier, even the two of us have sometimes disagreed concerning which are the "best" selections, or the categories in which they belong. But we underscore our conviction that the present collection represents a continuing tradition "of excellence in African studies." We are, of course, grateful to all our contributors and their publishers for allowing us this opportunity to make their work available to a wider audience.

We reviewed several hundred articles for this revision, identified initially from listings in the *International Political Science Abstracts* for the years 1970–1984. This current bibliography indexes a wide range of scholarly journals, it appears sufficiently often to stay abreast of scholarly productivity, and it provides abstracts that are useful guides for preliminary judgments. Some of the other sources we used are listed in the bibliographic section at the end of this book. From a quantitative point of view, we found this time an appreciable increase in the number of journals devoted exclusively to African affairs, as well as an increase in the number of articles on Africa in generalist and disciplinary journals. We also found that more women and more Africans are now contributing to Africanist scholarship than was true in the late 1960s. And while most of the authors of articles in the 1970 edition continue as major contributors in the field, it is apparent that a new generation of Africanist scholars is emerging, as indeed one would expect.

We note a number of changes in the state of the art of Africanist social science writing since the late 1960s. More articles are genuinely comparative and fewer focus on just one country; also, micro studies are now relatively rare. Current Africanist scholarship is more commonly theoretical and more sophisticated, indicating not only an increase in the amount and level of evidence available since the 1960s but also more rigorous intellectual examination of that evidence. At the same time, Africanist social science is still largely impressionistic, offering arguments that are basically persuasive rather than statistical, although use of statistical methodologies and computers is increasing. The early work of the 1960s was essentially pioneering, often "behavioralist" (focused on observable behavior), and usually optimistic in outlook. This has been followed by extensive application of "dependency theory" and much subsequent pessimism.

It is relatively easy to account for the transition from hope to gloom in forecasts about the future of African politics. In the latter half of the 1960s, both African politicians and Africanist observers, on the whole, were optimistic about the future of the new states because of the recent successes of nationalism and the end of colonialism. Ex-colonial civil servants often did not share this view, but they were generally ignored when they predicted that the new African leaders would not be able to match their states' performance to their own rhetoric. For their parts, the new leaders were confident that they could overcome the problems of "ignorance, poverty, and disease," and despite the ferocity with which independence elections were waged, there was a surprisingly high level of certainty not only that competitive party systems were a permanent feature on the African political scene, but also that nationalism would override political and ethnic differences in the postindependence period as effectively as it had during the anticolonial era. While most African politicians were realistic about the enormity of the problems that lay ahead, the experience over the past two decades of trying to deal with them has inevitably had a sobering effect, and at least privately many of these leaders have now lowered the level of their expectations concerning what can be achieved. This, of course, has not quite the same meaning for the proverbial "man on the street." His expectations have continued to be high, and although tempered by government failures, the rise of single-party states, the persistence of ethnic politics, coups and countercoups, his hopes for a better life have not been dashed. Nonetheless, a mixture of impatience and cynicism now characterizes the political orientations of many Africans, and this appears especially true for those individuals who have come of age since independence.

As observers of the African scene began to record and analyze government failures, conspicuous consumption and corruption among public servants, the collapse of competitive party systems, and the destructive consequences that followed many military coups, they too became increasingly doubtful about the ability of African governments to promote economic development and political stability. Many analysts of the 1960s generation who were "present at the creation" were disappointed and disillusioned by what they later saw and acknowledged that they had not previously given sufficient heed to limited authority, fragmented influences, and the low level of political consensus that accompanied the launching of the new states. Scholars of the mid and late 1970s who arrived on the scene after the halcyon days of the immediate pre- and post-independence eras were of course less influenced by the optimism and hope that the end of colonialism spawned. It was thus easier for them to be deeply impressed (or depressed) by the economic legacy that nearly all of the new states inherited. These observers became pessimistic, not so much because things seemed to "fall apart" as because of their conviction that none of the African states was likely to resolve its political and economic problems until it rid itself of its dependence on the former colonial masters, other countries, and multinational companies alike.

These changes on the African political scene, and subsequently on the content of Africanist scholarship, are reflected in the content and organization of this revised edition of *Governing in Black Africa*. For the most part, we have selected articles that are primarily comparative in scope, rather than focussed on a specific country. And we have given priority to authors whose analyses are based on a theory or paradigm that can be used as a model to test behavior in a variety of different settings. Our hope is that students will go beyond analyzing African politics as current events and instead see it as illustrating political behavior in general. With one exception, the topical arrangement of the original reader remains. Space considerations have required a reduction in the total number of articles, but we hope this affects only the number of illustrations of issues we can offer and not the overall usefulness of the volume.

In the original reader the "Determinants of Political Behavior" section dealt mainly with historical and traditional influences—

e.g., national integration, political culture, and African nationalism; the present version is concerned with factors that are currently more directly relevant to the African scene, particularly the continuing importance of ethnicity and patterns of political change. We have converted the original "Agencies of Mobilization" section into "Political Participation," taking note in so doing of the decline of *mass* participation and the emergence of popular involvement in politics in new forms, such as trade unions. In the section "Structures and Processes of Government," we look at various modes and consequences of executive dominance rather than concentrating as before on constitutions and formal political structures.

We omit altogether this time the unit "National Integration" and note that this topic is substantially subsumed in articles appearing in other units. The section "Development" is geared indirectly to economic growth rather than as before to social and political development, and takes into account "dependency theory," ethnic competition, and one of Africa's most compelling economic problems—food production. Finally, in the section "International Affairs" we emphasize the ways African states achieve a role on the international level, as well as the extent to which they are still subject to external intervention.

Some of the evidence and reasoning contained in the fifteen articles that follow may, we suppose, incline the reader to pessimistic conclusions about the future possibilities for economic growth and political stability on the African continent. For our part as editors, we suggest that such a conclusion is probably as erroneous or misleading as the tendency of earlier Africanist literature to advance decidedly optimistic projections concerning black Africa's future. In the end, we have come to share the recent pragmatic outlook of our friend and disciplinary colleague, Professor Ali A. Mazrui. In a book that he coauthored in 1984 with Michael Tidy, Mazrui responds to an appreciation of widespread economic stagnation in Africa by recommending (with Tidy) six strategies for effecting Africa's economic "liberation."[6] Each of these, including the last, which urges "domestic

austerity," is essentially a specific *pragmatic* response to an element of Africa's present economic subordination. Mazrui and Tidy recommend, for example, that far from isolating themselves from the world's "citadels of power," African states should follow the example of the OPEC countries, and where possible "interpenetrate" them. Similarly, our own view is that while black African states cannot escape their history altogether, their individual futures need not be wholly determined by present circumstances either. But which of these three outlooks—pessimism, optimism, or "pragmatism"—will most influence future African political and economic behavior (as well as academic and other reporting of it) remains to be seen. What is clear is that each perspective will continue to be hotly debated.

NOTES

1. Angola (1975); Dijbouti (1977); Guinea-Bissau (1974); Mozambique (1975); and Zimbabwe (1980).

2. Western Sahara/Saharan Arab Democratic Republic (SADR), and Namibia.

3. Benin (Dahomey); Burundi; Central African Republic; Chad; Equatorial Guinea; Ethiopia; Ghana; Liberia; Mauritania; Niger; Nigeria; Rwanda; Sudan; and Uganda. This does not account for numerous abortive coups, as in The Gambia, Kenya, The Seychelles, Tanzania, Swaziland, and Cameroon, to name a few.

4. Jomo Kenyatta, Kenya, 1978; Sir Seretse Khama, Botswana, 1980; Antonio Agostinho Neto, Angola, 1979; Kwame Nkrumah, Ghana, 1972 (in exile); King Sobhuza II, Swaziland, 1982; Sèkou Touré, Guinea, 1984; Francisco Macias Nguema, Equatorial Guinea, executed following 1979 coup; Emperor Haile Selassie, Ethiopia, 1975, died under mysterious circumstances while imprisoned following 1974 coup; François Tombalbaye, Chad, killed during 1975 military coup. In 1984, Julius Nyerere of Tanzania announced he would not run for re-election in 1985.

5. For example, at its independence in 1980, Africans renamed Rhodesia Zimbabwe, and the capital Salisbury as Harare; in late 1984, President Thomas Sankara of Upper Volta renamed the country Burkina Faso.

6. *Nationalism and New States in Africa* (London: Heinemann, 1984), pp. 340–42.

Unit I

DETERMINANTS OF POLITICAL BEHAVIOR

Politics is ultimately the political behavior—albeit frequently the collective political behavior—of individuals. Individuals are not only the smallest unit of political analysis; they are, in a sense, the *only* unit. Why individuals behave as they do politically is thus a central question for political scientists, as it has been for both philosophers and pragmatists from time immemorial.

One finds a variety of methods of inquiry that link human nature and political behavior. One of these methods is the Marxist approach, which is one of the two "schools of thought" that Nelson Kasfir examines in this section. This approach is based on a class analysis of politics and presumes that individuals are primarily concerned with their material self-interest. According to the Marxist view people tend to act in a manner calculated to maximize their economic and social positions. Another approach examines the significance of an individual's "role" by analyzing how perceptions of one's place in the overall political process affect one's role performance. How, for example, does a legislator's conception of his or her position affect that individual's performance as a legislator? In what ways are African civil servants affected by their perceptions of the roles of former white colonial administrators?

Yet a third approach turns on the extent to which aspects of an individual's personality affect or mold political behavior. Some analysts argue that individual personalities are a combination of nature and nurture, that our behavior is shaped by organic foundations that determine our reflexes, intelligence, drives, etc., and by the cultural context in which we are socialized. When comparing or contrasting large groups of people, or whole populations (e.g., Kenyans with Italians), the observer must assume that the organic foundations of personality are similar and provide no explanation at all for differences in the political behavior of the groups or populations. Such "organic" explanations are possible only in the analysis of the behavior of specific individuals, as illustrated in Erik Erikson's well-known studies of Martin Luther and Mahatma Gandhi.[1] Politically relevant differences in personality between large groups of people then must be

1

attributed to cultural variables, although this approach can be used to explore the behavior of individuals as well.

In fact, social scientists have devoted considerable energy to identifying environmentally rooted personality traits that are relevant to political behavior, and the sum of these characteristics is conceptualized as "political culture." This refers to the attitudes, beliefs, and values which, being broadly distributed through a population, give special public meaning to events and provide the premises that underlie political behavior in that society. In recent decades, political scientists have given considerable attention to the question of political culture in North America and Western Europe. In large measure this work has been motivated by an interest in the distinctive psychological attributes of publics in stable democracies, characteristics now summarized under the rubric "civic culture." By comparison, little work has been done on the political cultures of non-Western countries, or on the process of "political socialization" through which a political culture is shaped, maintained, or transformed. Our selection by Brownsberger in Unit III is thus particularly interesting for its contention that a source of widespread official corruption in Nigeria, and by inference in the Third World generally, is a pervasive culture of materialism that, the author argues, is a result of a particular moment in the developmental process.

Political culture rests upon the collective history of a political community as well as the life experiences of its individual members. Nearly every African state experienced some form of colonial rule, and Ruth Berins Collier argues in her contribution to this collection that differences between British and French colonial experience, in part at the level of norms and democratic expectations, have had an important impact on patterns of political change in present-day Africa. As a major social institution throughout black Africa, tribes have an even more fundamental place in the life histories and political experience of a great majority of contemporary Africans. Tribes differ, of course, in such matters as their internal structures and their social values, and these differences can be important in explaining variations in political behavior, as, for example, in adapting to the modernizing process. But it may also be said that the traditionalism of tribal affinities does tend to promote common orientations that govern the choices Africans make as individuals. Put in terms of Talcott Parsons's well-known "pattern variables," these orientations may be said to promote (1) collectivism rather than individualism; (2) a concern with objects less in terms of their universal attributes than in terms of their particular relationship with self or group; (3) deference to the ascribed rather than to the objective or performance qualities of persons or objects; and (4) involvement with objects that is general and diffuse, rather than limited and specific.

Translated into contemporary political practices in Africa, these orientations suggest normatively neutral, cultural explanations for what Westerners may see as corrupt and undemocratic decision making. If tradition in Africa required giving gifts to those in authority, then the processes of modernity may well entail the giving and taking of "bribes"; and if tribal authority was structurally or functionally undifferentiated, then it may not matter whether civilian or military leaders command ultimate authority. Rhoda Howard's article that we include here notes, however, that traditional norms of particularistic, ascriptive behavior can be used "as a cover for gross violations of principles of both modern and traditional morality."

Yet any attempt to evaluate political culture in Africa must account as well for modern influences on political life, such as tensions between intellectuals and the uneducated, urbanization and pressures for economic development, and the differential effects of colonialism. In populations that are still largely illiterate, it should perhaps be expected that the educated will feel that they have a special role to play, and indeed many writers have commented on such *elitism* among African university graduates in general. Similarly, *statism*, i.e., acceptance of the primacy of the state in the process of modernization, is an understandable dimension of the perceptions of many African leaders, who grew up in societies wherein the colonial bureaucracy was virtually the only public institution that mattered.

Obviously, such conclusions can be dangerous if they are overgeneralized. The availability of evidence on the subjective dimensions of African politics is not only incomplete, but frequently it only reflects the orientations of specific groups within the political community. We are thus compelled to agree with Richard Dawson and Kenneth Prewitt, who wrote in 1969 that African states still lack "a general, systematic pattern of political norms which can be adopted by the average citizen."[2] But it is also important to point out that this condition stems in some measure from the accumulation of conflicting and different values that Africans have inherited from their own cultures as well as those imposed on them by colonialism and westernization. This situation forces upon Africans ideological and moral choices concerning the worth of the traditional and modern values that coexist in contemporary African society. Ali Mazrui illustrated this dilemma when he commented in his 1979 BBC Reith Lectures: "What is corrupt and what is not is sometimes a function of competing moral systems in the same society."[3]

The articles we included in this section relate to three of these compelling determinants of behavior: ethnicity, with contrasting interpretations drawn from antithetical intellectual traditions (Kasfir); general economic and social conditions that affect official attitudes and behavior regarding the treatment of individuals (Howard); and experiences during the colonial and decolonizing periods that can be seen, as we have said, to have shaped later modes of behavior (Collier). These analytic commentaries indicate that each African state is still in the process of *creating* its own national political culture out of its unique combination of subcultures, needs, and circumstances. Nevertheless, this process in itself offers insights into current political behavior in Africa, for it can be argued that the fragmented or incipient character of African political cultures is one explanation of the confusion, insecurity, and fluctuations that unfortunately characterize contemporary politics in many of these states.

NOTES

1. Erik H. Erikson, *Young Man Luther* (New York: Norton, 1958), and *Gandhi's Truth on the Origins of Militant Nonviolence* (New York: Norton, 1969).

2. Richard E. Dawson and Kenneth Prewitt, *Political Socialization* (Boston: Little, Brown and Co., 1969), p. 35.

3. Ali A. Mazrui, *The African Condition* (London: Heinemann, 1980), p. 119.

Explaining Ethnic Political Participation

Nelson Kasfir

Far too many explanations of the role of ethnicity in political behavior, particularly in Africa, vastly understate or overstate its relevance. For every writer who insists that "tribalism is Africa's natural condition, and is likely to remain so for a long time to come,"[1] another will assert that "tribalism is not an explanation but an ideology, one which itself needs to be explained."[2] That observers of these matters—whether they be liberal modernization theorists or Marxists—are so often wide of the mark poses an interesting question about unrecognized biases hidden within Western social science. The conclusions of Marxist writers and of students of modernization usually conflict because their analyses begin from opposite assumptions. It is the restrictiveness of each set of assumptions that prevents an accurate assessment of ethnicity in particular political situations.

The concept of ethnicity developed here comprises both schools of thought. By converting the assumptions of both approaches into empirical questions, a more subtle and useful inquiry into the political force of ethnicity can be articulated. The essential feature that underlies this conjunction is the observer's acceptance that ethnic identity is both fluid and intermittent. Thus it is one of many possible identities that could become the motivation for political action. The political situation— both the present moment and its historic development—contains the causal factors impelling an individual to prefer a particular social identity. The individual's choice may be fundamentally ethnic, class, religious, or—it is worth stressing—a combination of these identities. This choice may be constant or it may change from one situation to another. Indeed, even when an ethnic identity is preferred, an individual may, within limits, change from one ethnic category to another. This choice is a political resource over which individuals have varying degrees of control.

When political participation is based on ethnicity, individuals are necessarily constrained (though to a greater or lesser degree) by those objective indicators of common ancestry thought to be especially salient—culture, myths, language, or territory. Whether these objective indicators are the product of a history of traditional usage or the result of recent manipulation, subjective perception by others involved in the same political situation is essential for credible political participation. Shared perception permits, but does not necessarily create, sufficient social solidarity to turn individuals assigned to an ethnic category into an active ethnic group. Even then, the likelihood of social solidarity being channeled into participation depends on the opportunities created by the specific political situation.

Each of the foregoing steps introduces a new set of empirical questions that take the place of the starting assumptions of the modernization and Marxist schools. The research task created as a result is immeasurably more complicated than most observers of ethnicity realize. However, it permits the observer to develop a more sophisticated explanation of the different possibilities and changing interrelationships between ethnicity and class in political action. The assumptions concerning politicized ethnicity common to writers on modernization, and those of Marxist or radical analysts, are presented below. The utility in combining these pos-

From *World Politics*, vol. 31, no. 3 (April 1979). Copyright © 1979 by Princeton University Press. Excerpts, pp. 365–78, 385–88, adapted by permission of Princeton University Press.

tulates to resolve various empirical issues is then demonstrated. In the final section, the tendency toward reification of the role of ethnicity in explanations based on cultural pluralism and consociationalism is highlighted by applying the situational notion of ethnicity in politics.

Political participation, understood in its broadest sense, includes any form of political involvement from voting to rioting, from nepotism to revolution. It may or may not be based to some measure on ethnic considerations.[3] When two cases of ethnic political participation are compared, differences almost always emerge—not only in the kind of political involvement, but also in the nature of ethnicity espoused.

Before examining the conflict in assumptions between the two approaches, it is worth noting the points on which there is some agreement. First, ethnic political participation is concerned with actions of a group or an individual arising from the imputation of common ancestry to themselves or to others. It makes little difference whether that ancestry is genealogically factual or fictitious. Where common ancestry is not at least indirectly implied, ethnicity is not involved and the roots of political action must be sought elsewhere. Second, for Africa in particular, there is an important difference between "tribe" in the precolonial sense of a small, remote, culturally distinctive, and self-sufficient unit, and "tribalism," involving certain political actions taken in the colonial or independence periods.[4] To the extent that tribalism is taken to refer to the act of a tribesman who is defined in the former sense, it has virtually disappeared from Africa. Few Africans are so untouched by outside influences that they can be considered members of the tribes that social anthropologists have attempted to reconstruct. Third, ethnicity and tribalism refer to the same political actions. Unfortunately, the latter term suggests that political behavior in Africa is not only qualitatively different from ethnic participation elsewhere, but also inferior.[5] Although "tribalism" is in constant popular usage in Africa, wider generalizations and less emotional discussion are more likely to result if "ethnicity" is the operative term.

OPPOSING SETS OF ASSUMPTIONS

Anyone wishing to discuss ethnicity as a political variable has to consider the following questions: (1) Is ethnicity to be regarded as a characteristic of the mental state of the political actor or of the social milieu in which he lives? (2) Are the advocates of ethnicity those of high position within society, or those without power, wealth, or status? (3) Is the decision to act on ethnic motives based on rational calculation or deeply held values? Each of these questions has been stated in "either-or" terms to focus attention on the assumptions that analysts often make, usually implicitly, on each of these themes. A more comprehensive notion of ethnicity requires, however, that each of these themes be treated as an empirical continuum on which instances of politicized ethnicity can be placed according to the characteristics of each case studied.

The restrictiveness of basic assumptions are illustrated by the dominant view on ethnicity in the late colonial period, particularly in the British colonies.[6] Fortified by acceptance of the proposition that all people move in a unilinear, irreversible path from tradition to modernity, observers took ethnicity to be a set of primordial values growing out of the coincidence of culture, political organization, language, and territory. As people were educated in schools with a Western curriculum, converted to a Western religion, or entered the cash sector by growing new crops or taking wage employment, they were believed to be shedding the trappings of tradition and embracing the modern (that is, the colonial) world. The growth of African cities was regarded as evidence of this shift, which came to be called "detribalization." Behind this point of view were three assumptions: (1) that ethnicity was based on objective indicators (2) which produced values held deeply (3) primarily by the masses—that is, those who had not gained elite status by entering the colonial cash economy.

A variety of difficulties afflict this point of view, even though it probably remains the most widely held conception of ethnicity today. The survival and intermixture of tradition and outside influences raise serious questions about the notion that social change leads ineluctably to an easily specified modernity. The coincidence between culture, political organization, language, and territory was questionable before colonial rule began; it was increasingly distorted afterwards. Seeing ethnicity as a primordial value meant overlooking the fact that new ethnic groups were suddenly appearing under colonial rule—sometimes in rural areas, but more inexplicably, in the towns.

The older perspective has recently also been subjected to a thoroughgoing attack by analysts influenced by Marxist modes of inquiry.[7] In their view, it is economic relationships that carry critical political importance. The economic factors that shaped the colonial situation permitted those who acquired control over one or another aspect of the means of production to use new forms of ethnicity as weapons to mystify peasants and workers. In this sense, members of disadvantaged classes who enter politics to pursue ethnic goals are the victims of "false consciousness." At the root of this point of view are the three assumptions (1) that ethnicity is subjective (since it is the direct consequence of ideology rather than of economic material relationships), (2) that its political uses can frequently be traced to members of the recently formed middle classes who (3) advocate ethnic demands as a consequence of their rational calculations in pursuit of desired resources. These assumptions, of course, are the polar opposites of those adopted by the writers on modernization.

The basic problem with the radical approach is the willingness of its proponents to "throw out the baby with the bathwater." False consciousness is still consciousness, whether or not the actor recognizes his "true" interests. Where his life is in danger on the basis of an ethnic threat, it would be foolish to expect him to ignore ethnic considerations. To dismiss all manifestations of politicized ethnicity as irrelevant is to ignore a range of motives many of which will, on empirical examination, turn out to be strongly felt. Even where ethnic symbols are merely the façade for economic grievances, they often structure the political situation and thus affect the outcome.

A More Comprehensive Notion of Ethnicity

By accepting that a combination of the assumptions in both perspectives may sometimes explain an aspect of ethnic politics, we may examine how these different factors can vary from one case to another. It is useful, though, to begin with the issue of whether ethnicity is the product of subjective perception or whether it is an objective indicator, because we may then ask how pervasively ethnicity occurs in political participation. Or, to put a closely related question, when ethnicity is put forward to explain political participation, are other variables—notably class, but also religion and status—automatically ruled out?

Because ethnicity implies common ancestry, kinship is the most obvious objective indicator of membership in an ethnic group. Since many people cannot trace their genealogy through more than three generations, however, language, culture, and territory become more useful signs of membership in a larger group. The central difficulty—as in the case of using objective indicators to demonstrate affiliation with economic classes—is that the individual's perception of the group in which he considers himself a member may differ substantially from the group in which he would be classed on the basis of his first language, customs, or place of birth. The consequences for explaining his political participation are likely to be equally significant.

Thus, the subjective alternative—that an individual is a member of a group when he so thinks of himself—seems more attractive. However, political action is the result not only of an individual's beliefs (presuming for the moment that he acts on the basis of those beliefs), but also of the reaction of others to his assertion. Insiders may classify him as an outsider despite his desire to join their ethnic category. This is particularly apparent where a person who bears the objective indicators of a low-prestige ethnic unit attempts to become a member of a more desirable category. The problem is parallel to that which faces analysts who infer class membership solely from class consciousness.

The solution is to take objective indicators as well as subjective perceptions into account without assuming that they will be combined in precisely the same way in every ethnic group. There are, so to speak, standard paraphernalia that each ethnic group must display in order to make a political claim that will be taken seriously. A traditional history that stretches back many centuries or a standard language that is widely spoken will give plausibility to the assertion of group identity. But, where these are missing, they can often be constructed—as many local cultural enthusiasts and political entrepreneurs set out to do during the colonial period. The question then is whether these indicators are matched by equally widespread perceptions of ethnic membership. It may seem unduly restrictive to require both insiders *and* outsiders to share a perception of ethnic membership before labeling participation as ethnic. But since self-perception and external perception affect one another in most instances, widespread agreement can often be achieved on membership boundaries. Where it is not, the political value of ethnic assertion will be dubious.

The combination of subjective perception and objective indicators shared by insiders and outsiders may be related, either closely or distantly, to the traditional heritage of particular individuals. The work of urban anthropologists has shown how much ethnic identities can change as people migrate to the city and find that new skills and new associations are necessary, first for survival, and then for economic advancement.

Many of the newly defined urban ethnic groupings brought together migrants whose traditional homes in the countryside were close to each other and whose languages were closely related, but who had never previously thought of each other as possessing the same ethnic identity. These new groupings often developed intense social solidarities and then became the successful vehicles of political entrepreneurs. Sometimes, consciousness of the enlarged group seeped back to the countryside, where it stimulated the basis of political unity of much larger rural groupings. Relatively small ethnic units thus coalesced into much larger ethnic groups during the colonial period, creating the Ibo, Yoruba, Bagisu, Iteso, and Kikuyu as we know them today. On the other hand, a new ethnic consciousness created in the city might be resisted in the countryside. The urban migrant would then develop two ethnic identities: one that was appropriate for his urban life, and a different set of loyalties that was activated whenever he returned to the countryside. A third possibility, typical of "target workers," was to import one's traditional lifestyle into the city and avoid new loyalties as much as possible.[8] Finally, some migrants chose to break their ties to their rural ethnic units when they moved to the city.

Because of the changes created in ethnic loyalties by colonial influences, particularly urbanization (and too often we overlook the changes in ethnic identities that occurred in the precolonial period), the problem of the "proper" ethnic label for the people one met, for one's friends, and for one's self became immensely complicated, especially in the cities. The solution, as in any complex social situation, was to stereotype by creating a small number of ethnic categories. Social distance and relative prestige have been shown to be important elements in constructing these categories on the Zambian copperbelt, for instance,[9] though the elements undoubtedly vary from one place to another and often also involve differences in economic position. Ethnic categories imposed by others may also become the basis of self-definition—at least in situations in which those categories are regarded as relevant.[10]

The categories themselves are not necessarily stable. They may vary over time, depending upon the degree to which they are reinforced. S. R. Charsley builds on Mitchell's work in a useful manner by treating ethnic categories as proposals by the identifier that may be accepted or rejected by the person so identified. If the "transaction" is not completed (that is, if the proposal is rejected), the parties must find a new category—not necessarily ethnic—or fail to interact.[11]

If ethnic categories are understood to be subjective and changeable, there are several implications for the observer of political behavior. First, the relationship between traditional culture and ethnicity is empirical and variable, rather than definitional and constant.[12] Thus, any demand for a political solution to satisfy an economic grievance or bolster local prestige on the basis of ethnicity will not necessarily involve primordial customs, though some sort of objective indicators must be asserted to make the appeal credible. Second, identifying someone as a member of an ethnic category at a particular time and in a particular place does not mean that, for political purposes, he will continue to hold that identity in other places and at other times. Again, the question must be decided empirically. Third, if categories are fluid, identity may shift dramatically not only from one ethnic category to another, but from ethnicity to class or religion. Fourth, and most important, by accepting that the identities people assume are both multiple and intermittent, the researcher must consider the situation that activates the particular identity the individual chooses.[13]

The identity chosen may be rationally selected by calculating costs and benefits, or it may be conditioned by deeply held values. Threats to personal survival because of membership in a particular ethnic group are likely to cause a potential victim to think in terms of his ethnic identity when objective indicators (characteristic scarification, for example) make it impossible for him to escape this label. The same individual may, in another situation (for example, where a strike is called to demonstrate against a government-ordered wage freeze), perceive himself and be perceived by others solely in terms of his class. Both cases point to the necessity for empirical research to establish how the choice of a particular identity, however constructed, is activated in the pursuit of a particular goal.

In taking this approach, it would be a mistake to assume that all social action must be reduced to fluctuating individual perceptions. A variety of factors help to stabilize political situations that reduce the choices open to an individual over a period of time. The possibilities of migration, economic opportunities, and social stratification may not change rapidly. The presence of entrepreneurs who assert a cultural identity by reinforcing traditional values or creating new ones may establish a mass consciousness among the relevant public that firmly stabilizes an ethnic label accepted by insiders and outsiders. J. S. La Fontaine describes the process by which members of the "Bagisu-to-become" created an "ideology of unity" by standardizing the dialects spoken by several smaller groups to create a single language, and by emphasizing that everyone should carry out particular ceremonies, especially those involving circumcision.[14] A "tribal" welfare association was founded, and new administrative boundaries demarcating "Bagisu" land were claimed in colonial and postcolonial arenas.

The most important factor in the political situation in Uganda that stimulated the formation of the Bagisu, as well as other large ethnic units containing people who were conscious of the political advantages of a shared identity, was the favored position of the Baganda.[15] Others emulated the Baganda, both to avoid cultural and political domination and to improve their own share of economic rewards. Political mobilization took place when the process of ethnic formation so dominated the consciousness of people who might otherwise have chosen other identities that it became the basis of strong feelings of social solidarity. The vigorous Bagisu response to the Mbale dispute (in which two recently created ethnic groups were involved in disturbances in the late 1950s and early 1960s over "control" of a town) shows the intense passions that even newly created ethnic loyalties can arouse.[16]

The concept of ethnicity so far developed can be summarized in four steps:

(1) Particular objective indicators associated with common ancestry
(2) become the focus of subjective per-

ceptions both by members within the unit and by non-members

(3) through social solidarity created by a resurgence, or the fictive creation, of traditional unity

(4) so that in certain situations political participation will occur.

The creation of social solidarity in response to a situation turns the members of an ethnic *category* into an ethnic *group*. Political mobilization may occur at the same time, thus producing ethnic political participation. However, the third step may also be bypassed where individual ethnic political action occurs in the absence of social solidarity. (An example would be a client-patron relationship based on personal loyalty.) A much debated issue—whether the ethnic group is the small subgroup or the larger coalition into which the subgroups have united—can easily be resolved in this framework. By examining the political situation, the boundaries of the politically active ethnic group can be determined. For purposes of participation no other group matters.

We can now more directly consider the opposition between ethnic and economic explanations of political action. By analyzing the second and third set of opposed assumptions in liberal and Marxist discussions, we come to a more complex perspective than the simple presumption that class and ethnicity are antithetical. Political action stemming from economic class may be conceived along the same lines as those just developed for ethnicity. There are objective indicators of class (occupation, salary, place of residence, education, and even language and culture) which may or may not be the focus of subjective perceptions of those within them, and of outsiders. Consider, for example, the members of the bourgeoisie who organize proletarian action, or members of the fallen petite bourgeoisie who intensely oppose the workers. The formation of social solidarity (shared class consciousness) *may* lead to political mobilization in response to particular situations. There is a peculiar blindness among some Marxist writers who presume that, when they have demonstrated a common objective class membership, they have proved that political action will occur on the basis of class.[17]

Political situations that evoke participation along class lines may appear and disappear just as they do for participation along ethnic lines. A well-known example involves the Nigerian workers who participated in a general strike in June 1964, only to vote along ethnic lines the following December.[18] Robin Cohen correctly argues that "class and class consciousness have a partial manifestation that may be activated in certain conditions and in certain measure."[19] It is a short step to recognizing that class and ethnicity may involve the same political participants in different situations, and that both may be involved in the same situation. In the latter case, class motives may either conflict with or reinforce ethnic motives.

By conceiving the relationship of ethnicity and class in this manner, we recognize a subtle variation in the possible answers to the questions whether political action is based on rational calculation or deeply held primordial values, and whether the active agents are leaders or followers. Where the persistence of ethnic groups can be directly attributed to the desire to acquire the fruits of the modernization process,[20] rational calculations are probably more important than long-held fundamental values. Thus, "tribal" unions were often willing to pay for the education of those possessing the same objective indicators of ethnicity in hope of gaining tangible benefits for their members when these men achieved professional status or political office. Abner Cohen provides a case in point in his study of "retribalization" of the Hausa in Ibadan who maintained their separation from their co-religionists among the Yoruba in order to protect their control over an economic speciality.[21]

On the other hand, the traditional values that form the basis for an ideology of unity may not be a recent fabrication, but the product of a long cultural history. Threats to their kingdom, the cultural inheritance of several centuries, have evoked deep responses among many Baganda—whether rich or poor, educated or illiterate. Of course, particular Baganda often have manipulated this response to their own economic advantage. For ethnic groups to persist, their members must rally to a shared set of definitions of common ancestry. The legitimacy and enrichment provided by a historical culture may (or may not) underlie the group's political coherence. Despite the stress Abner Cohen places on rational calculations in his account of the Ibadan Hausa mentioned above, he appropriately insists that explanations of ethnicity depending solely on maximizing self-interest are "one-sided and *cannot account for the potency of the normative symbols* which the individual manipulates in his struggle for power. An ethnic group is not simply the sum total of its individual members, and its culture is not the sum total of the strategies adopted by independent individuals."[22]

As Cohen goes on to argue, a political entrepreneur who attempts to advance himself by manipulating ethnic beliefs is necessarily *constrained* by the symbolic implications and cultural participation that make these beliefs meaningful to those whom he intends to persuade. The transaction between the entrepreneur and others receptive to these symbols occurs in the creation or reinforcement of the ethnic group. This transaction limits the choices open to the entrepreneur, no matter how disingenuous his motives may be. To understand this behavior, it is important to recognize that there may be differences in motives among those claiming membership. But in no way is it logically contradictory to recognize that some will respond to rational calculations and others to primordial values, while all intensely assert their ethnic membership.

Of course, any empirical examination of subjective perceptions that is carried out by means of Western techniques of social science will run the risk of substituting explanations of motives that are familiar to foreigners for those held by the actors. In Malaysia, for example,

in some contexts where westerners would perceive class and party divisions, the Malaysian will see ethnic divisions so that the ethnic unit supports similar functions and ideology as does class in western society. . . . This is particularly noticeable in relations of greatest social distance and antipathy.[23]

The danger is greatest where the researcher is so eager to find either objective cultural or economic consequences for political participation that he presumes that the motives of the actors were determined by these consequences.

On the issue whether leaders or followers (or members of the middle or lower classes) are the active agents in ethnic political participation, there is a range of possibilities that are more useful than the opposed assumptions of those who adopted the tradition-to-modernity proposition in the late colonial period or of the Marxists who wrote approximately fifteen years later. Elites and masses cannot exist without each other. An ethnic group may evolve in response to frustration on the part of unemployed urban migrants unable to break into an ethnically stratified labor market, or to threats felt by poor villagers fearing domination from another group whom they perceive in terms of *its* ethnic charter. Or an ethnic group may be carefully constructed by an upwardly mobile entrepreneur looking for a political base, or by introducing ethnic disputes into the civil service or university. The educated man, lamented Kenneth Dike in July 1966, is "the worst peddler of tribalism in Nigeria."[24]

However, examination of either type usually reveals a complicated mixture of motives, often by self-designated leaders and their followers. Members of the political elite, for example, may find themselves at least temporarily outflanked by their followers or by marginal men eager to raise their own status. The Kabaka of Buganda and his (well-to-do) advisors took full advantage, and ultimately full control, of the *Kabaka Yekka* (the "King Alone") movement which swept all opposition in the kingdom's elections of 1962 with an extraordinary display of intense ethnic unity. But two years earlier, with ferment growing over Buganda's place in an independent Uganda, a wildcat anti-Asian boycott organized by low-level Baganda politicians and traders had succeeded for a time in taking the initiative from the Kabaka's hands. In eastern Nigeria, on the other hand, the rise in "Ibo consciousness" among peasants, which facilitated the creation of Biafra, was to a large degree the work of academics and civil servants who fled to the East following the massacres of 1966.[25]

In some cases, class or ethnicity alone may explain political action. For example, in 1968 the *Egbe Agbekoya* (the "Farmers are Suffering") movement in western Nigeria was a protest carried out by rural peasants who took violent action over several months, responding to peasant leaders from their own villages rather than to members of an elite or an urban bourgeoisie.[26] Aside from the apparently liberal use of traditional magic (which provided some ethnic reinforcement within the movement), this was basically a class action. The massacres of Ibos in May and September of 1966, in which the victims were chosen on the basis of objective indicators of ethnicity, on the other hand, were primarily ethnic political actions. Even here, however, elements of class motivation were involved. To many Hausa-Fulani and Middle Belt peoples, the Ibos symbolized exploitation and, after the January 1966 coup d'état, humiliation. Dudley finds that in both massacres the participants were predominantly petty hawkers and urban unemployed.[27] In Uganda the agitation—soon after Amin's coup in 1971—for the return of the Kabaka's body for a funeral and for the coronation of his son as the new Kabaka seems primarily to have been an ethnic response—the release of long repressed cultural sentiments. Yet, members of the Baganda elite surely recognized that recapture of a strong political and economic position within Uganda would have been promoted by a resurgent Buganda.

Alternatively, both ethnicity and class may be organizing principles of equal fundamental importance within the same political situation. The two may be in conflict where, for example, migrants of rising economic status are involved in political disputes with indigenous inhabitants of a town—as occurred in Port Harcourt, Ibadan, and Kampala. Or, ethnicity and class may reinforce each other, as in the case of Ibo and Hausa-Fulani in pre–civil war northern Nigeria, where "conflict of any sort—whether over jobs or markets or political office—threatened an all-out communal struggle."[28] Differential modernization during colonial rule created similar cases in virtually every African country. In each of these four types of situations—class alone, ethnicity alone, class and ethnicity in conflict, and class and ethnicity in concert—the research problem is to untangle and assess the mixture of motives held by the actors.[29] In every case, the observer must seek the causes in the political situation that stimulate people to think of (and organize) themselves in class, ethnic, or other terms—or some combination of them.

* * *

REIFICATION OF ETHNICITY IN THEORIES OF CULTURAL PLURALISM AND CONSOCIATIONALISM

In terms of the concept of ethnicity articulated here, the use of ethnic groups in theories relating cultural pluralism and consociationalism to political stability or instability should be reconsidered, since the logic of these theories requires that ethnic groups be conceived as separate communities. These theories therefore cannot cope with ethnic groups that are fluid and intermittent in character. Imposing false concreteness on the boundaries of ethnic solidarity produces a generous measure of unreality.

The concepts of cultural pluralism and consociationalism were developed to explain political and social relations in societies presumed to be deeply divided. They begin from opposite starting points. Cultural pluralists assert that the institutions into which people are segmented are deeply and rigidly unequal so that political stability is ensured through domination.[30] Consociationalists argue that the leaders of institutions from each segment can form an elite cartel that makes political decisions satisfactory to members of all segments, so that political stability is ensured through accommodation.[31] There is not necessarily a contradiction here, since cultural pluralists have focused primarily on authoritarian societies containing highly stratified racial or cultural groups such as colonies in Asia and Africa and countries like South Africa, while the consociationalists have directed their attention to European democracies which exhibit pronounced cleavages.

The danger in relying upon the notion of ethnicity developed to support the concept of cultural pluralism is vividly illustrated by two sophisticated uses of aggregate data analysis based on information from 32 black African countries. Both test the proposition that an increase in cultural pluralism is positively correlated with greater political instability. In one case, a positive correlation was found; in the other, no correlation (with one limited exception) could be discerned.[32] Since both studies drew on the same data bank, the differences in the conclusions are somewhat distressing. The test variables are constructed somewhat differently, however, which may explain the variation in findings.

But no statistical measure can do better than the concepts on which it is based. The data used to construct the concept of cultural pluralism in both studies were differences in cultural traits of groups identified in national censuses and in the ethnographic literature. As a result, the authors of both articles include distortions caused by (1) colonial governmental definitions of ethnic units for census purposes, and (2) idealized accounts by social anthropologists attempting to reconstruct a precolonial description of cultural practices "purified" of colonial influence. In addition, these two analyses based on cultural pluralism assume that in all cases *traditional* cultural traits (which may never have been practiced by contemporary ethnic advocates) somehow "explain" participation in *current* violence or coups d'état. And the writers argue this despite the fact that they cite the literature dealing with the situational nature of ethnicity!

Consociational procedures, on the other hand, have been suggested as an appropriate instrument of government in ethnically divided societies. Arend Lijphart, for example, speaks of separate "subcultures" and makes references to Lebanon, Cyprus, and Nigeria (when those countries were under parliamentary rule).[33] The notion of subculture remains an unexplored concept

for Lijphart except where he finds it necessary to elaborate it to develop his theory. To support consociationalism, subcultures must have distinct boundaries on the basis of which the political cleavages of the society rest; they must also possess a high degree of political cohesion, permitting their leaders to strike compromises with each other without losing their status within the subculture.[34]

Although Lijphart's model was constructed as an alternative to pure majoritarian rule in a typology of *democratic* governments, the concept—in principle—might be used to explain national decision making where democratic institutions are absent.[35] Thus, consociationalism has been taken up with enthusiasm in certain heterogeneous societies in which governments have insisted upon separation of ethnic communities as a matter of policy. In South Africa, for example, a radio commentator recently went so far as to cite Lijphart in support of the principle that it was more important to guard the rights of different communities than to preserve majority rule in order to protect what he called "democratic rights."[36] But the South African notion of separate development, or *apartheid*, is strictly based on the *government*'s definitions of ethnic units and their appropriate boundaries. In view of the immense inequalities that have been legitimated on this basis, this use of the term consociationalism amounts to nothing more than a fashionable façade to hide white domination.

Brian Barry presents a more general argument against the extension of consociationalism to ethnic cleavage; but it is based on the inadequate assumption that ethnic groups are continuous political units.[37] He argues that ethnicity, unlike other cleavages, is not manageable through bargaining by group representatives. In his view, "gross inhumanity" is more likely to occur in ethnic conflicts than in disagreements based on other cleavages. Organizations, and therefore leaders, have less relevance for ethnic groups than they have for religious or class conflict. Ethnic definitions of issues permit greater clarity of goals sought, and thereby reduce the ability of leaders to bargain. Thus, ethnic leaders have a more difficult time agreeing to compromises in the elite cartels that consociationalism requires. Finally, ethnic issues often raise the question of secession, but class and religious issues do not.[38] Thus, Barry insists that ethnic cleavages are too intense for consociational arrangements. But he can succeed in this argument only by assuming (contrary to the analysis presented above) that ethnic groups are necessarily based on deeply held primordial values against which rational calculations are unavailing.

The most serious theoretical problem for most proponents of cultural pluralism and consociationalism is their insistence that ethnic categories be treated as self-contained communities. Any useful concept of ethnicity must embody the possibility that situations evoking ethnic identity may stabilize over a period of time and may give birth to reinforcing institutions. Long-term racial domination is a case in point. But racial attitudes may change, and ethnic identity may turn out to be too evanescent a basis to support political institutions that are separate and parallel, and also durable. The fact that polarization of ethnic identities may in some situations create civil strife does not necessarily mean that ethnic identities have stabilized. Political solutions which remove the factors that evoke ethnic identification may produce greater stability than those which explicitly build upon and reinforce such identification. One of the great mysteries of the post–civil war period in Nigeria is what has happened to Ibo ethnic solidarity. No one would argue that ethnicity is absent from Nigeria now, but the creation of 12 states in 1967, increased to 19 in 1976 (dividing into two the so-called heartland identified with the Ibos), has certainly reduced its political relevance.[39]

The central point of any situational analysis of ethnicity is that the range of possible degrees and duration of ethnic group coalescence should not be converted into a rigid assumption of presence or absence of a continuous subculture. If comparative analysis based on cultural pluralism, or the creation of consociational solutions for ethnic problems, must therefore be narrowly constricted or abandoned, that may be the price that must be paid in order to stay in touch with the complexities of social reality.

NOTES

1. Colin Legum, "Tribal Survival in the Modern African Political System," *Journal of Asian and African Studies*, v (January–April 1970), 102.
2. Mahmood Mamdani, *Politics and Class Formation in Uganda* (New York and London: Monthly Review Press 1976), 3.
3. The concept of participation is analyzed in Kasfir, *The Shrinking Political Arena: Participation and Ethnicity in African Politics with a Case Study of Uganda* (Berkeley and Los Angeles: University of California Press 1976), 5–14; six ethnic case studies from Uganda are presented, 119–52.
4. Aidan Southall, "The Illusion of Tribe," *Journal of Asian and African Studies*, v (January–April 1970), 28.
5. An explicit comparison showing the similarity of "nationalist" movements in Europe and "tribal" movements in Africa can be found in W. J. Argyle, "European Nationalism and African Tribalism," in P. H. Gulliver, ed., *Tradition and Transition in East Africa: Studies of the Tribal Element in the Modern Era* (London: Routledge & Kegan Paul 1969), 41–58.
6. For example, see Daniel F. McCall, "Dynamics of Urbanization in Africa," *The Annals of the American Academy of Political and Social Science*, No. 298 (March 1955); and Clifford Geertz, "The Integrative Revolution: Primordial Sentiments and Civil Politics in the New States," in Geertz, ed., *Old Societies and New States: The Quest for Modernity* (New York: Free Press 1963).
7. For example, see Archie Mafeje, "The Ideology of 'Tribalism,'" *Journal of Modern African Studies*, ix (August 1971); and Ken Post, "'Peasantization' and Rural Political Movements in Western Africa," *Archives européenes de Sociologie*, xiii, No. 2 (1972).
8. For a discussion of the varieties of responses by migrants to the city, see David Parkin, "Tribe as Fact and Fiction in an East African City," in Gulliver (fn. 5), 286–92.
9. The argument was originally developed by J. C. Mitchell, *The Kalela Dance*, Rhodes-Livingstone Institute, No. 27 (Manchester: Manchester University Press 1956).
10. In his research, Mitchell used objective indicators (based on *rural* criteria) to establish the ethnic units whose social distance he then measured in an *urban* area by asking respondents to classify *others*. Both the uncritical reliance on objective indicators and the use of rural definitions in the urban setting make his findings du-

bious, though the conceptual implications greatly advanced the study of ethnicity. Mitchell rediscusses his own work, though without reference to these difficulties, in "Perceptions of Ethnicity and Ethnic Behavior: An Empirical Exploration," in Abner Cohen, ed., *Urban Ethnicity* (London: Tavistock Publications 1974).

11. Charsley, "The Formation of Ethnic Groups," in Cohen, *ibid.*, 360–61.

12. The point is developed by Frederick Barth, "Introduction," in Barth, ed., *Ethnic Groups and Boundaries: The Social Organization of Culture Difference* (London: George Allen & Unwin 1969).

13. For valuable analyses articulating this point, see Crawford Young, *The Politics of Cultural Pluralism* (Madison: University of Wisconsin Press 1976), 41–44, 64–65, and particularly 140–62; Robert Melson and Howard Wolpe, "Modernization and the Politics of Communalism: A Theoretical Perspective," *American Political Science Review*, Vol. 64 (December 1970).

14. La Fontaine, "Tribalism among the Gisu: An Anthropological Approach," in Gulliver (fn. 5).

15. Kasfir (fn. 3), 104–113.

16. For a brief account of this controversy, see *ibid.*, 139–41. In some ways, the "Bakedi," the opponents of the Bagisu, are a more extreme case because they had no basis on which to build a homogeneous "traditional" culture due to the extraordinary variation in local customs. The "Bakedi" were merely disparate groups who found themselves in a single administrative district. This circumstance did not prevent them from acting as if they were an ethnic group, and even demanding a traditional head like the Kabaka at the time of Uganda's independence.

17. For a typical example, despite careful attention to definitional problems, see V. L. Allen, "The Meaning of the Working Class in Africa," *Journal of Modern African Studies*, x (July 1972), 177–78.

18. Melson and Wolpe (fn. 13), 1127.

19. Robin Cohen, "Class in Africa: Analytical Problems and Perspectives," in Ralph Miliband and John Savile, eds., *The Socialist Register 1972* (London: Merlin Press 1972), 243.

20. Robert Bates, "Ethnic Competition and Modernization in Contemporary Africa," *Comparative Political Studies*, vi (January 1974).

21. Abner Cohen, *Custom and Politics in Urban Africa: A Study of Hausa Migrants in Yoruba Towns* (London: Routledge & Kegan Paul 1969).

22. "Introduction: The Lesson of Ethnicity," in Cohen (fn. 10), xiii; emphasis added.

23. Judith Nagata, "The Status of Ethnicity and the Ethnicity of Status: Ethnic and Class Identity in Malaysia and Latin America," *International Journal of Comparative Sociology*, xvii (September–December 1976), 251.

24. Quoted in Robin Luckham, *The Nigerian Military: A Sociological Analysis of Authority and Revolt* (Cambridge: Cambridge University Press 1971), 278.

25. B. J. Dudley flatly states that "it was the academics who spearheaded the movement for secession." *Instability and Political Order: Politics and Crisis in Nigeria* (Ibadan: Ibadan University Press 1973), 195n.

26. C. E. F. Beer, *The Politics of Peasant Groups in Western Nigeria* (Ibadan: Ibadan University Press 1976), 179–205.

27. Dudley (fn. 25), 132–33 (May); 166 (September).

28. Melson and Wolpe (fn. 13), 1116.

29. See Cohen (fn. 19), 250–52. It seems unnecessary to accept his additional categories of class structure within ethnic groups and of interethnic hostility within a class, as these can be adequately handled within the four types of situations identified here.

30. For a recent statement, see the essays in Leo Kuper and M. G. Smith, eds., *Pluralism in Africa* (Berkeley and Los Angeles: University of California Press, 1969).

31. See the useful collection of articles in Kenneth D. McRae, ed., *Consociational Democracy: Political Accommodation in Segmented Societies* (Toronto: McClelland and Stewart, Carleton Library 1974).

32. The positive correlation is argued in D. G. Morrison and H. M. Stevenson, "Cultural Pluralism, Modernization, and Conflict: An Empirical Analysis of Sources of Instability in African Nations," *Canadian Journal of Political Science*, v (March 1972). The absence of correlation (with the exception of the relationship of "ethnic pluralism" and instability when controlling for the category of "civil servants/wage earners") is asserted in Walter L. Barrows, "Ethnic Diversity and Political Instability in Black Africa," *Comparative Political Studies*, ix (July 1976). Indeed, Barrows (pp. 161–62) concludes from the lack of statistical association that researchers ought to examine other variables instead of ethnicity in studying instability.

33. Lijphart, "Consociational Democracy," in McRae (fn. 31), 70–89. For one appeal in support of extending this particular approach to ethnically divided societies, see Young (fn. 13), 527–28.

34. Lijphart (fn. 33), 82–84.

35. Cf. Ian Lustick, "Stability in Deeply Divided Societies: Consociationalism versus Control," *World Politics*, xxxi (April 1979), 334.

36. "South Africa's Answer to the World," Johannesburg Radio broadcast, October 5, 1977, British Broadcasting Corporation, *Summary of World Broadcasts*, Part 4B, ME/5634/B/1–2, October 7, 1977. In an extremely interesting paper,

"Consociational Authoritarianism: Incentives and Hindrances toward Power Sharing and Devolution in South Africa and Namibia," John Seiler reviews efforts by Afrikaner intellectuals to make use of consociationalism. American Political Science Association Conference, Washington, D.C., September 1977, pp. 21–22.

Lijphart left himself open to this sort of interpretation by referring approvingly to "a kind of voluntary *apartheid* policy as the best solution for a divided society," in his argument that separation of subcultures may reduce conflict (fn. 33), 83.

37. Barry, "Political Accommodation and Con-

sociational Democracy," *British Journal of Political Science*, v (October 1975), 502–3.

38. Oddly, Barry insists (*ibid.*, 504) that political parties in Northern Ireland are ethnically (rather than religiously) based. In so arguing, he appears to plant the seeds of a tautology by implying that all cleavages too intense to be amenable to consociational solutions are ethnic.

39. There is evidence that political disagreements produced demands among those objectively identified as Ibos that the 1975 panel considering the number of new states divide the old East Central state into *four* new ones. *Daily Times* (Lagos), June 27, 1977, p. 3.

The Dilemma of Human Rights in Sub-Saharan Africa

Rhoda Howard

THE PROBLEM

The question of human rights in the Third World is one of the central humanitarian issues of the last quarter of the twentieth century. In this essay, I intend to address the issue by examining English-speaking African countries in an historical and comparative context. English-speaking African states have a common colonial heritage, sharing an official language and institutional structure. Moreover, the ruling élites of these countries were generally educated in Britain or the United States, where in many cases they developed a commitment to the democratic ideals of the Western world. Thus in sub-Saharan English-speaking nations a body of Third World countries can be identified which, at least in their ideals, resemble Western democracies, yet which in their practice do not seem able to attain the degree of civil and political liberty to which they ostensibly aspire. This suggests that there may be social, economic, or historical impediments to an implementation of their ideals; in other words, that structures limit the realization of values. It is the task of the scholar to investigate these impediments.

Implicit in such an investigation is the belief that all individuals *ought* to have certain fundamental human rights. Defenders of Third World régimes, however, often maintain that such beliefs are ethnocentric and that the freedoms with which Western liberals are concerned are not suitable to developing, formerly colonized economies. I cannot investigate theories of

human nature, human "need," and human rights in this paper.[1] It is my belief, however, that all human beings need a certain sense of dignity or autonomy. To achieve such dignity, each individual needs a certain amount of order, physical security, and personal freedom. Order is rarely problematic in a nation-state, since it benefits the governors as well as the governed, but rights to freedom and security not only may be mutually contradictory but also may threaten the state structure by making demands upon it which it cannot fulfil. Moreover, there is no necessary connection between individual dignity and the types of civil and political freedoms which exist in Western democracies. Dignity may be as realizable through an assigned, acknowledged work role in an ordered society based upon ascriptive status as through the rights of citizenship in a "free" competitive society.

This essay will discuss different interpretations of human rights in the West and in Africa, and the ideological and structural context of the conflict between citizen and state over the allocation of rights in English-speaking sub-Saharan countries.

THE UNITED NATIONS, BRITISH RULE, AND HUMAN RIGHTS IN AFRICA

The Universal Declaration of Human Rights, passed by the General Assembly of the United Nations in 1948, is generally used as a standard by which to measure human rights. The declaration is a statement of principles and objectives which was hammered out of conflicting interpretations of human rights advocated by three

Reprinted from *International Journal*, vol. 35, no. 2 (Spring 1980), 724–47, by permission of the Canadian Institute of International Affairs.

competing factions: the Soviet bloc, the liberal democratic states of North America and Western Europe, and the independent "underdeveloped" countries of Latin America, Asia, and the Near East. In accepting the declaration as a standard it is essential to remain aware of the political disagreements which it masks.

The Universal Declaration[2] in fact encompasses two levels of human rights. The first is what can in general be called social and economic rights, including the rights to social security, to work, to education, and to free participation in the community's cultural life (articles 22–27). Within the United Nations, the Soviet bloc and the Third World bloc have consistently stressed economic and social rights more strongly than has the United States or the United Kingdom.[3] The second level of human rights embodied in the Universal Declaration is that of civil and political rights (articles 3–21). These include those rights to a fair trial embodied in the British judicial system, the right to protection from slavery, servitude, and torture, the basic freedoms of thought, religion, movement, assembly, and participation in government, and the rights to marry and have a family and to have a nationality.

Independent African nations have in general been strong supporters of the Universal Declaration of Human Rights. The declaration is included as a principal concern of the Organization of African Unity (OAU), and by 1969 twenty-nine African constitutions made reference to it.[4] However, within the United Nations African members have concentrated more on economic, social, and cultural rights than on civil and political rights; the only cases in which they have consistently insisted on investigating the latter have been with regard to forced labour in the former Portuguese African colonies and to apartheid in South Africa.[5] Abuses of civil and political rights in independent black African nations have been consistently ignored. During the late 1960s the OAU refused to consider violations of the right to life of Biafrans on the grounds that the civil war in Nigeria was a purely internal affair. When the expulsion of Ugandan Asians was brought before the United Nations in 1972, Nigeria argued that it was not "a mat-ter related to human rights." Similarly Kenya has denied that its policy of gradually expelling Asians is a form of racial discrimination, violating article 2 of the Universal Declaration.[6]

In considering why African states do not grant those civil and political liberties common in the West, it is critical to avoid the pitfall of assuming that independent African states have "regressed" from a state of comparative civil and political freedom under colonialism.[7] The administrators of African colonies were products of their own times, and they certainly did not consider establishing rights in the colonies which did not exist in their own societies. Thus, those rights of women which are incorporated into the Universal Declaration by virtue of its prohibition against discrimination on the basis of sex (article 2), such as the right to equal pay for equal work, and the right to marry freely and to have equal rights during marriage and marital dissolution, were at best a very vulnerable part of Western liberal ideology during the period of colonialism. When independent African states attempt to implement these rights, they are trying to do so at the same time as are the Western democracies to whom these are also "new" rights.

Moreover, whatever the ideologies of the colonial powers in Africa were, actual human rights in the colonies were very limited. It took two years of discussion before the United Nations accepted the principle in article 2 of the Universal Declaration that no distinction (as to human rights) was to be made "on the basis of the political, jurisdictional or international status of the country or territory to which a person belongs, whether it be independent, trust, non-self-governing or under any other limitation of sovereignty." The United Kingdom consistently opposed this clause because it meant in effect that it was obliged to extend human rights to its colonies. Its ostensible reason for opposing the clause was rather ironic: it argued that "many of its territories [had] a large measure of self-government and that it would wish to consult the legislative organs of these territories to ascertain whether the treaty should apply to them."[8] In Africa, there was a very limited measure of indigenous participation in colonial legislatures and no self-government at all. In Ghana, the most advanced colony in this respect (with the exception of white settler representation in Kenya), a few Africans were appointed to the local Legislative Council, but they were always outweighed by government representatives, and in any case local decisions could be overruled by the Colonial Office in London. The British maintained that they ruled in cooperation with indigenous chiefs, yet many chiefs were arbitrarily deposed because they refused to collaborate. In other cases, as among the Ibo of Nigeria, the British imposed "warrant" chiefs, persons warranted to become chiefs in the absence of an indigenous hierarchical structure which could be relied upon to produce individuals who would collaborate. Thus if African nation-states are not democracies in 1980, it is not because they have abandoned a colonial heritage of democracy; at best, the colonial régime was a benevolent dictatorship.

In the social and economic fields as well, human rights were absent in the British African colonies. Racial discrimination was widespread. In Zambia, Kenneth Kaunda, now president, led a struggle against racial discrimination as late as the 1950s.[9] The first international conventions on human rights were conventions of labour rights in the 1920s under the auspices of the International Labour Organization (ILO). The ILO strengthened international edicts against slavery and forced labour; it may be partly as a result of this that Britain ceased forced labour in northern Ghana, which had been practised from about 1906.[10] However, the British managed to coerce Africans in Kenya to labour for European settlers by the simple expedient of depriving them of their land and giving the land to Europeans to start the very farms which would then employ the landless Africans. Other labour rights were endorsed by the ILO, including the rights to strike, to join trade unions, and to have the freedom to choose or leave a job. The British opposed extending the ILO's field of jurisdiction to the colonies, where labour relations were regulated by the Masters and Servants Act, under which it was illegal, among other things, for a worker to leave his job, to be slack on the job, to be rude to his master, or to arrive drunk on the job.

On the whole, then, the citizen of an English-speaking sub-Saharan African country has more human rights now than he did under colonialism. He is no longer forced to work against his will, and he sometimes has the right to form trade unions. He has had, sporadically, the right to vote in either multiparty or one-party elections. Furthermore, his government has made a commitment to provide him with basic socio-economic rights such as universal medical care, universal literacy, and a decent standard of living; these were never commitments of the British colonial governments. Nevertheless, the historical and social context is such that independent African governments have not been able to implement the complete set of human rights endorsed by the Universal Declaration.

HUMAN RIGHTS IDEOLOGY IN AFRICA

Civilian leaders of most of the independent English-speaking African states do accept, at least publicly, the Western ideals of civil and political freedom, but in so doing they often stress the unique African context of these ideals. President Kaunda of Zambia, for example, calls himself an African humanist:

> . . . African humanism stems from the structure of the traditional society and its effects upon African psychology. . . . The tribal community was a *mutual* society. It was organised to satisfy the basic human needs of all its members, and, therefore, individualism was discouraged. . . . Human need was the supreme criterion of behaviour . . . social harmony was a vital necessity.[11]

Julius Nyerere, president of Tanzania, is known as one of the great humanists of Africa. On two occasions, as a result of his humanistic beliefs, he has contravened the principle, which both the United Nations and the OAU uphold, that the domestic jurisdiction of individual countries should not be violated. In 1969 Nyerere recognized the government of secessionist Biafra.[12] Ten year later, Tanzanian troops assisted exiled Ugandans in overthrowing Idi Amin.

Yet, "even humanists like Nyerere or Kaunda have put [their] opponents in preventive detention."[13] In 1976 Kaunda jailed students and lecturers from the University of Zambia for protesting his decision to permit Zambian planes to carry South African arms to rebel forces in Angola.[14] The fact that even very strongly held ideals seem destined to give way to Realpolitik in Africa needs to be analysed from the point of view both of whether politicians do more than profess such ideals and of whether implementation of such ideals is possible, given structural constraints.

Claude Ake, a Nigerian scholar, suggests that African politicians merely make a pretence of liberalism or humanism because such a pretence is politically useful,[15] insofar as it serves both as a means of mobilizing liberal support in the "mother country" for decolonization and as a mask for the continued economic disparities of contemporary African societies. He discounts the professed ideologies of African politicians: for him, it is not merely the socio-historical context which impedes their honest implementation of their ideals; rather, their own class interests make a mockery of this imitation of Western ideology.

Other theorists take professions of liberal ideology to be an "inauthentic"[16] stage in the thought of African politicians. For these commentators, the humanists among African leaders are still intellectually colonized. Christian Africans are criticized for accepting the very religion which helped to open up Africa to European conquest by undermining African religion and culture and teaching converts to accept the authority of the white man. These theorists assume that a completely free African will move towards a new ideology which is informed by a return to indigenous African styles of thought. It is therefore perhaps worthwhile to investigate the argument that indigenous African concepts of social organization, especially indigenous concepts of freedom, are both authentic and unique.

The first contention to be considered here is that the African conception of freedom is radically at odds with Western conceptions in the sense that whereas Western Enlightenment thought stressed the freedom of the individual and his right to *detach* himself from the group, African thought stresses precisely the opposite, the right of the individual to become *part* of the group. Suzanne Miers and Igor Kopytoff contend that in traditional African society there was a continuum between being a member of the family and being a stranger, outsider, or indeed a slave, and that the aim of every individual was to become incorporated into a kingroup or family, that is, to become a non-stranger.[17] But the Western idea of freedom is the freedom of the individual to detach himself from the group. Conceptions of freedom in Western society stem from eighteenth-century protests by the rising capitalist class against feudal restrictions on commercial activities. Simultaneous with the rise of the new capitalist class was the rise of Protestantism. Max Weber argued that the two coincided because Protestantism stressed the individual and his works; that is, the belief that what one achieved was more important than one's ascribed (feudal) status.[18] By contrast, in African societies, the traditional emphasis upon one's status and its concomitant role (as elder or young man, male or female) is still strong. The value placed on status comes into conflict with the values of Westernized, Christianized Africans who wish to be released from traditional constraints and to be judged by their achievements in the modern African market place.

Following from this it is argued that the indigenous African legal system contains precepts very different from those which guide the legal systems of the West. In Western societies, law takes precedence over morality. Someone may commit an act which the community as a whole considers to be manifestly wrong; nevertheless, if there is no law against it, it is not a crime. In traditional African societies, however, morality, based upon an implicit community consensus, takes precedence over formal rules of law. Legal decisions are made not through an adversary process but rather through the judgments of the politico-religious elders, who consider both the evidence and the needs of the community.

The idea of law being based upon the

consensus of opinion of religious leaders is reinforced in Africa wherever Islamic law is practised. Islam is the dominant religion in northern Nigeria, but Muslims can also be found in other English-speaking countries in both East and West Africa. The difference between modern Western law and Islamic law is twofold. Whereas Western law is essentially proscriptive, that is, concerned with specific areas of behaviour which are not permitted, Islamic law is prescriptive, that is, concerned with all of human behaviour and thus defining what may be done, not merely what may not be done.[19] This difference stems from the more fundamental opposition of the two systems of law; whereas Western law is perceived as manmade, Islamic law is divine. Islamic law is "imposed on society from above," and changes can only be made if they are "in conformity with the accepted dictates of the revealed will of Allah."[20] This system of law reinforces traditionalism and the idea of an indivisible community ruled by politico-religious elders.

The interpretation of the African traditional community as presided over by just elders has been extended to reinterpret the type of political régime which Africans need. The state, some theorists argue, does not need to implement the "bourgeois" values of civil and political freedoms; it can directly take over the traditional consensus[21] and use it in modernizing a new society in which social and economic equality is the most important goal. In traditional society, the elders made the decisions for the tribe, clan, or kin-group through a process of "palaver," or discussion until a consensus was hammered out. It has been suggested therefore that the natural form for modern African governments may be the "palaver state" in which formal opposition is unnecessary.[22] Thus the formal structure of parliament and official opposition which the British set up in African colonies eroded very quickly because it was, in this view, antithetical to the much more intrinsically communitarian and moral basis of African society.

It is not clear, however, that the above interpretation of consensual African society is empirically correct. Even within communal groups, there were status divisions which could result in conflicts of interests—between elders and young men, males and females, freemen and slaves. African empires rose and fell, and conquered tribes were subject to their conquerors. The integration of African society into the world economy meant that there arose new forms of social stratification based on wealth. Moreover, some of the "integrative" religious customs of traditional societies, such as ritual deaths and the killing of twins,[23] would constitute supreme violations of human rights as they are defined in the twentieth-century context.

Thus there is no real evidence that injustice did not exist in traditional African society. There is merely the knowledge that principles of justice evolve over time. Calls to hearken to ancient moralities may in fact mask the interests which the retention of such moralities would serve. The South African scholar Archie Mafeje has argued that the ideology of the tribal leader has been used to mask exploitation: "There is a real difference between the man who, on behalf of his tribe, strives to maintain its traditional integrity and autonomy, and the man who invokes tribal ideology in order to maintain a power position, not in the tribal area, but in the modern capital city, and whose ultimate aim is to undermine and exploit the supposed tribesmen."[24]

Appeals to traditionalism can mask the desire to exploit, as Mafeje suggests. But they can also reflect exasperation with the incapacity of Western legal and political forms to deal with the many structural problems facing new African nation-states. It is to these structural problems that we now turn.

STRUCTURAL IMPEDIMENTS TO HUMAN RIGHTS POLICIES

Poverty

No discussion of human rights policy in Africa can ignore the existence of poverty whose alleviation is one of the prime prerequisites for "positive" human rights. Yet such alleviation implies a radical redistribution of wealth and a radical reorganization of the means of production in a manner which may be directly antithetical to civil and political freedoms. In the Western world, civil and political rights expanded slowly throughout modern history along with the expansion of wealth; but African statesmen are attempting to expand both their "positive" rights of social wealth and their "negative" civil and political rights[25] simultaneously. These two blocks of rights may be in conflict.

The most obvious example of the implicit conflict between positive and negative human rights is the question of property. In the post-1960 period, the international arena has seen more and more moves by Third World governments to nationalize the private property of individuals or corporations, often foreign, in the name of the social and economic betterment of their peoples. The Universal Declaration of Human Rights did not deal with the question of personal versus national property, but the two international covenants based on the declaration (on Civil and Political Rights, and on Economic, Social and Cultural Rights) explicitly do so. Both contain the provision that "the right of peoples to self-determination shall . . . include *permanent sovereignty over their natural wealth and resources.* In no case may a people be deprived of its own means of subsistence on the grounds of any rights that may be claimed by other States."[26] This clause pertaining to the right of self-determination, first proposed (but not accepted) in 1948, was one which directly affected the African colonies. It was proposed as a universal human right by the independent Third World nations and opposed by the so-called administering colonial powers, especially Britain and France, on the grounds that it was "a group or territorial right . . . of an entirely different character from . . . individual rights."[27] The United States, many of whose corporate citizens own substantial properties abroad, including ones in Africa, refused to ratify the 1954 Covenant on Civil and Political Rights because of the inclusion of this clause.[28]

The issue of foreign property-owners versus the rights of nation-states in Africa has generally been negotiated in a manner satisfactory to the national governments. However, the issue of the nation-state versus the property owner who is a citizen has been less easily resolved. Most Westerners know of the expulsion of over fifty thousand Asians, including citizens, from Uganda in 1972–73, in violation of article 15 of the Universal Declaration that "everyone has the right to a nationality" and article 13, that "everyone has the right to leave any country, including his own, and *to return to his country*" (my italics). Idi Amin's justification for the expulsion was that Asian traders controlled the economy which should be turned over to African Ugandans. Less well known is the expulsion of some 100,000 "aliens" from Ghana in 1970. Some of these "aliens" were Ghanaian citizens of Lebanese descent, while the vast majority were black Africans from other parts of West Africa. In this case, even those born in Ghana were not considered citizens unless their fathers had also been born there. Although the argument for expulsion was that Ghanaians should control their own economy, the expulsion of "non-Ghanaians" did not result in increased prosperity,[29] that is, in the increase of positive socio-economic rights which might have offset the abuses of the civil and political rights of the expellees.

A second example of the conflict between the civil and political rights of the individual and the right of the nation-state to control its natural resources in the interests of more socio-economic benefit for all is the Tanzanian "villagization" programme, introduced in 1968 to bring together previously scattered cultivators into villages where they could collaborate in the cultivation of land and the use of agricultural equipment. Originally voluntary, the programme was declared compulsory in 1973, thus violating article 13 of the Universal Declaration, which declares in part that "everyone has the right to freedom of movement and residence within the borders of each State." Many ordinary individuals in Tanzania, owing in some cases merely to bureaucratic intransigence, have been obliged to move against their will.[30]

The right to move of educated Africans

has recently been the subject of much debate. If, as article 13 of the declaration stipulates, "everyone has the right to leave any country, including his own," does this right apply to an individual in whom his government may have invested considerable national resources in home or overseas training? Or do clauses referring to the rights of all peoples to "permanent sovereignty over their natural wealth and resources" include sovereignty over individual citizens who have highly expensive skills? Many people who are sent to developed countries for training do not return, thus, from the point of view of their original homeland, wasting the investment of educational funds. On the international level, this problem is now being attacked through the discussion of a "brain drain tax," to be paid either directly by the individual or by the country which benefits from his immigration.[31] Presumably the tax would compensate the original country for the loss of its investment (if in fact such a loss were incurred[32]), while guaranteeing the individual's right to leave his country.

All these examples have dealt with violations of civil and political freedoms of the individual on the grounds that such violations would further the collective rights of the peoples concerned by contributing to redistribution of wealth (expulsion of minorities) or the increase of the national product (villagization, constraints on movement of the educated). There is another body of thought which argues that the violation of either positive or negative human rights is always untenable and that the two sets of rights must progress *in tandem;* that the participation of free and equal citizens in policy decisions is an important part of economic growth and wealth redistribution. This philosophy has emerged mainly in Latin America, where one of its chief exponents is Paulo Freire.[33]

Freire has argued that sycophantic imitation of Western models of economic growth should be replaced by local decisions on socio-economic investments, decisions which can only be made by an educated citizenry operating in an environment of free and uninhibited discussion. He maintains that if adults are taught literacy by focussing on politically relevant vocabulary, then they will quickly be able to participate in national political life. Such participation would not only allow civil and political rights of freedom of speech, but would also result in the evolution of less costly means of implementing "positive" human rights. Development funds would be better spent as prestige projects gave way to local needs for intermediate technology. Under this system, use could also be made of indigenous forms of social security, such as the Nigerian *esusu* (savings) societies,[34] rather than planning administratively costly and economically unfeasible national welfare systems.

To advocate the free participation of an educated citizenry in planning decisions is to suggest, however, open criticism of bureaucracy and government. Such criticism might result in the undermining of newly formed African nation-states, with possible detrimental consequences for all citizens.

Building the nation-state

Aside from the general poverty of independent sub-Saharan African states, there are other structural reasons for their denial of civil and political human rights. A state can only afford to grant its citizenry the right of criticism once it is secure. The new states of Africa are not yet nations; they are still engaged in the process of nation-building. In many of these countries, individual citizens have very tenuous loyalty to the state; there is not yet a sense that the persons who occupy positions of authority have a right to do so or that the state structure is a legitimate organ of coercion or lawmaking.

The original boundaries of independent English-speaking African states were largely administrative. Up to the time of decolonization, individual Africans simply saw themselves as members of particular ethnic groups who happened to live in a territory which the British occupiers designated X. Overnight, X became a country whose new masters had new tasks to fulfil, requiring much more interference in the day-to-day life of its citizens; yet, at the last minute, the British had also granted new political rights such as suffrage. The result was conflict between citizens and state, and in their confusion the new citizens looked to traditional symbols of their identity, such as ethnicity, religion, or language, which they could use against the state.

The "ideology of 'tribalism' "[35] has often been used to mask the similarity of ethnic conflict in Africa to the ethnic and national conflicts which shook Europe during its own period of nation-building. Ethnic problems are characteristic of new nation-states. In Africa, some ethnic groups are split between two or more states, as are the Ewe between eastern Ghana and Togo. In the mid-1970s the military government of Ghana took repressive measures against the Ewe to prevent what it perceived as irredentist threats. In Nigeria, the problem is that three very large ethnic groups, the Ibo, the Hausa, and the Yoruba, and many smaller ones were brought together into a new politico-administrative entity. The situation was exacerbated because the Ibo had been the most highly educated ethnic group and had spread over all parts of Nigeria, where they held positions of power in the bureaucracy and in business, as well as a disproportionate number of places in the limited educational facilities. The result was the 1966–69 civil war, in which Biafra, the Ibo state, attempted but failed to secede.

The Nigerian civil war resembled conflicts in Europe in the period of state formation in the sixteenth to eighteenth centuries and in the United States in the nineteenth. Eighty-five years after its formation, the United States had a civil war which enforced the ultimate domination of the North over the South. In Nigeria, the civil war erupted a scant six years after independence. When the federalist forces of Nigeria defeated the Biafrans, they did so partly because the alternative would have been the end of Nigeria. The United Nations does not guarantee the rights of minority groups to secede from nation-states; rather it specifies that though minority rights should be protected, nevertheless, "minorities must be loyal to the State of which they are nationals."[36]

Both in Africa and in Europe the myth of national unity has always been backed by the force and power of the state; indeed, a common definition of the state is as the institution which has a legitimate monopoly of coercion. In Africa, the coercive powers of the state have not yet been consolidated to the point at which secessionist movements can be controlled. Thus the rights of persons to freedom of speech or the press, if they intend to use these rights to proclaim religious, ethnic, or linguistic particularisms, are perceived as a threat to the unity of the state structure as a whole.

A specific example of the prohibition of religious freedom in defiance of guarantees in the Universal Declaration (article 18) has been the persecution of Jehovah's Witnesses in Malawi from 1967 to 1977. For religious reasons, Jehovah's Witnesses refuse to join political groups, including in this case the ruling Malawi Congress party. As a result, children have been refused school places, women have been raped, and in 1972 there was a pogrom of between fifty and several hundred members. About 21,000 people have been shuffled about between Malawi, Zambia, and Mozambique (which also demanded the Jehovah's Witnesses' political allegiance).[37] In 1977 Malawi had an amnesty for political prisoners, including the Witnesses.

Such political persecution of a dissident religious group is not surprising when one considers the religious history of the absolutist states of Europe during the early modern period, when the people took the religion of the king, and the kings established their legitimacy by declaring their divine right to rule. It was not until the state had established itself by both coercive and judicial means that the religion of the people became irrelevant; legitimacy was based on new means and God's sanction on the king was no longer necessary. In Africa, in states which are still unstable, one religious group's refusal to give political allegiance could be interpreted as a potential secessionist threat which might influence other persons for other reasons, for example ethnicity, also to withdraw their loyalty. When a good deal of propagandistic effort goes into convincing individuals that they are citizens of a new nation-state, to which they owe loyalty in return for the provision of goods and services such as schools, the refusal to swear allegiance is a threat.

Religious, linguistic, and ethnic particularisms in the sub-Saharan African context all constitute a threat for the same reason: the state has not yet established its legitimacy. In such a context, some political scientists[38] argue that the democratic rights of universal suffrage within an electoral system of party politics, as guaranteed by article 21 of the Universal Declaration, could be detrimental to the long-term survival of the state. If too many people are permitted to form too many political parties, the business of institution-building will be delayed. Moreover, an elected leader, who can be toppled at any time, will never have the authority to force through necessary reforms. In such situations, Seymour Martin Lipset suggests a "charismatic" leader might be more beneficial to the developing nation-state than an elected one. He compares Kwame Nkrumah of Ghana to George Washington. Both were charismatic leaders of their new states, and the enormous respect in which both men were held carried their nations through the early years of political schism. But unlike Washington, who eventually turned over the government to party politics, Nkrumah began to imprison his opposition and did not create the conditions for his own democratic succession.[39] Weber argues that charisma cannot last long on its own; it must be transformed into rational-legal forms of government or become stagnant or repressive.[40] Thus only in the short run, in this view, can Africa afford not to be democratic; as early as possible, plans must be made for the progressive introduction of democratic politics.

Nevertheless there is a very fine line between denial of civil and political rights for the good of the nation-state and denial of those rights for the good of the élite, ethnic group, or social class which happens to control the state at a particular time. Murder and rape of Jehovah's Witnesses is still murder and rape, regardless of justification. Positions of power are occupied by people who are usually tempted to act for their own personal or group ends. In the next section, we turn to élite violations of human rights in sub-Saharan Africa.

HUMAN RIGHTS AND ELITE PRIVILEGES

A common perception of African politicians is that they are corrupt. Those who argue that corruption causes the violations of human rights in Africa regard it as symptomatic of a set of *values* held by African leaders which is not conducive to civil and political liberties. Talcott Parsons maintains that in the transition from "traditional" to "modern" society people adopt new values. Universal norms of behaviour begin to take precedence over particular obligations and interests. Achievement takes precedence over ascription; what a person does and how he accomplishes it is more important than the status with which he was born.[41] A corollary of the principles of universality and achievement is meritocracy, the principle that the best trained and most qualified have the most important, well-remunerated positions in society. A further corollary is the separation of the individual from the position he occupies, so that, for example, the politician or bureaucrat separates his finances from the state's.

In the African context, it is argued that the politicians and bureaucrats have not yet absorbed these universalist, achievement-oriented norms; rather they still make decisions according to particularist family or clan ties and are more likely to appoint their relatives to a government position than to seek out the best qualified candidates. This does not imply dishonesty among African leaders, simply that, "poised as they are between the inherited public morality of the western nation-state and the disappearing public morality of the tribe, they are subject to very considerable cross-pressures."[42] A cabinet minister may wish to appoint his civil servants according to Western ideals of merit, but if he does not reserve some places for his family, his kin-group will find him morally reprehensible.[43]

Traditional norms of particularistic, ascriptive behaviour can, however, also be used as a cover for gross violations of principles of both modern and traditional morality by incumbents in governmental or bureaucratic roles. Public funds may be diverted to private businesses, or conspicuously wasted on ceremonial or trips to Europe designed to enhance an individual's prestige. The corrupt individual who ignores his duties to his kin-group may find himself reproved for violating both modern precepts against the personal use of public funds and traditional precepts regarding the sharing of wealth. The leader is then ousted from his position not so much because he was corrupt, in the Western sense of the term, but because he used his power and wealth for individual, not group, benefit.

However, to reduce the problem of corruption to individual "values" is to oversimplify the African context. Corruption is a consequence, not a cause, of socio-economic problems in underdeveloped countries. It is partly a consequence of those values which impel a man to look to the interests of his kin and tribe above all else, but it is also a consequence of a form of social organization in which social security is largely a function of the support of one's kin-groups. Furthermore, corruption is a consequence of economic insecurity in a society which is subject to extreme pressures from the world capitalist market place. Indeed one may even argue that corruption is functional in Third World societies in that it oils the bureaucratic wheels, cutting down on red tape.[44] Nevertheless, whatever its possible causes or benefits, corruption still implies that universal norms of administration and justice give way to particularist actions. Yet universalism is the basis of the *Universal* Declaration of Human Rights.

Elite corruption in Africa may seem less aberrant if the élite is regarded as the upper layer of a stratified society. All known societies are stratified: the problem in analysing Africa is to unwind the traditional systems of stratification from the modern. Tribal societies were stratified by age and sex; in addition, African empires were further stratified into nobility, freemen, and slaves. There were also further distinctions between tribal members and strangers.

Nowadays, however, there are also social strata in Africa which, like their counterparts in the Western world, are differentiated primarily according to degrees of wealth and income. It is not surprising that after five centuries of incorporation into the capitalist world economy, Africans should regard wealth as a basis for prestige, status, and power.

Those who have the wealth attempt to guarantee it and their access to more of it by taking over the reins of political power. In Kenya, for example, the family of the late Jomo Kenyatta is reputed to have acquired a considerable fortune under his rule. The wealthy in Africa constitute a stratum which is conscious of its own interests. Any decision, therefore, as to whether or not to allow civil or political liberties has to be weighed against how such liberties might affect this stratum's retention of its position of economic power. While the wealthy constitute a stratum, they have not yet clearly coalesced into a class which owns and controls the means of production. Their domination of the economy, hence their means of acquiring wealth, is contingent upon their control of the polity.

The problem is particularly exacerbated by the continued importance of overseas trading, banking, and industrial firms in African economies. Economic power is in the hands of foreigners; the African élite can share part of this power by controlling the relationship of the foreigners to the newly formed state. Personal wealth can be acquired by demanding bribes from foreign firms, or by ensuring that local suppliers are hired or local distributors given the right monopolies. As long as the wealthy stratum of Africans is dependent upon foreign business, then it cannot coalesce as an economically dominant class; but it is only when it coalesces as a class that it will be able to afford to let go of the reins of government and allow the independent formation of governmental, bureaucratic, and judicial institutions along the lines of universal, democratic precepts.

During the decline of totalitarianism in Europe, emerging independent foci of authority, such as trade unions, churches, and universities, acted as limits upon the absolute power of the state.[45] In Africa, such middle-level organizations, which can mediate between the individual and the state, are not yet institutionalized. The individual is no longer part of a small-scale traditional society where, *qua* individual, he can nevertheless act as a political man and where human rights are guaranteed to him by a moral consensus. But in the larger political arena, the state is still dominated by a developing ruling stratum which will use all possible means to hang on to its precarious power. Independent state institutions such as a universalistic bureaucracy or an independent judiciary threaten the interests of the ruling class in a way that they do not do in the West, where the ruling class has firm control of the economy. Mediating institutions in Africa such as trade unions or voluntary organizations have neither the membership, the organizational skill, nor the independence to act as "countervailing powers" to the state. Thus the political structure necessary to protect human rights on a day-to-day basis is not yet in existence: until it is, the ruling élites will continue to abuse human rights in their own interests.

I have stressed the development of social classes stratified by criteria of wealth because most of English-speaking sub-Saharan Africa has free-enterprise economies. However, abuses of political or civil liberties can also occur in socialist economies dominated by party-bureaucratic élites. Bureaucrats will try to amass privilege just as a capitalist will attempt to amass wealth.[46] The process of personification of the ruling class in the bureaucracy can be identified in Tanzania. Despite Nyerere's attempts to prevent bureaucrats from acquiring huge salaries or using their positions to facilitate the acquisition of wealth in the private sector, it would seem that a new bureaucratic class is forming which is unwilling to allow any challenges to its rule.[47]

Nyerere cannot stem the imperatives of power. Human rights in Africa, like human rights in the Western world, are continually threatened by the interests of the ruling class.

Conclusion

One cannot conclude this discussion optimistically. Unfortunately from the point of view of those who have a strong commitment to the ideals both of socio-economic justice and of civil and political freedom, human rights are an historically based phenomenon. Rights cannot be successfully legislated if the social and economic conditions are not opportune. The state of relative freedom in which most of the population of Western Europe and North America lives has been the result of some seven or eight centuries of political, economic, and philosophic evolution. Even within this evolution, as the Nazis have reminded us, it is possible for forces within Western society to generate massive abolitions of freedom.

In Africa, economic and social conditions are not conducive to human rights. Nevertheless, there is no excuse for some of the abuses of power which occur. Western liberals are caught in a bind; their sympathetic understanding of the conditions which cause the lack of freedom in Africa today is combined with their sympathy for the victims of political oppression. There are no systemic solutions; we do not yet know of any society which completely guarantees human rights. Socialism, while seemingly more capable of generating socio-economic equality than Western liberal capitalism, does not guarantee individual human rights. Western liberalism, while permitting civil and political freedoms, often does little to remedy socio-economic inequality. Philosophies of free and democratic local participation in political and economic decision-making sound attractive, but there is no evidence that such participation can work on the scale of the nation-state.

Such pessimism is balanced only by the hope that if those who do not know their history are condemned to repeat it, then perhaps those who do know their history can shape a better future.

NOTES

1. For discussions of human nature and human need, see Barrington Moore, Jr., *Injustice: The Social Bases of Obedience and Revolt* (White Plains, NY, 1978, and Abraham H. Maslow, "Psychological Data and Human Values" in Frank Lindenfeld, ed., *Radical Perspectives on Social Problems* (London 1968); also Terence des Pres, *The Survivor: An Anatomy of Life in the Death Camps* (New York 1976).

2. United Nations, Universal Declaration of Human Rights, General Assembly resolution 217 (III), part A, 10 December 1948 (hereafter Universal Declaration).

3. James Frederick Green, *The United Nations and Human Rights* (Washington 1956), pp. 38–39.

4. Warren Weinstein, "Africa's Approach to Human Rights at the United Nations," *Issue*, VI (winter 1976), 14; Laurie S. Wiseberg, "Human Rights in Africa: Toward a Definition of the Problems of a Double Standard," *Issue*, VI (winter 1976), 7.

5. Weinstein, "Africa's Approach," p. 16.

6. Wiseberg, "Human Rights," p. 4; Weinstein, "Africa's Approach," p. 18; Wiseberg, "Human Rights," p. 5.

7. For this perspective, see, for example, Rupert Emerson, "The Fate of Human Rights in the Third World," *World Politics*, XXVII (January 1975), 211.

8. Green, *The United Nations*, p. 56.

9. Kenneth Kaunda, *Zambia Shall be Free* (London 1962), p. 65.

10. Roger T. Thomas, "Forced Labour in British West Africa," *Journal of African History*, XIV (1973).

11. Kenneth Kaunda, *A Humanist in Africa* (London 1966), pp. 24–25.

12. Julius Nyerere, "Quand des africains oppriment des africains," *Jeune Afrique*, 8 October 1969, p. 6; quoted in Benyamin Neuberger, "The Western Nation-State in African Perceptions of Nation-Building," *Asian and African Studies* (Jerusalem), XI (1976), 255.

13. Wiseberg, "Human Rights," p. 4.

14. Personal communication.

15. Claude Ake, "The Congruence of Political Economies and Ideologies in Africa," in Peter C. W. Gutkind and Immanuel Wallerstein, eds., *The Political Economy of Contemporary Africa* (Beverly Hills 1976), pp. 203–4.

16. See, for example, Frantz Fanon, *Black Skins, White Masks* (New York 1967), and Hussein Abdilahi Bulhan, "Reactive Identification and the Formation of an African Intelligentsia," *International Social Science Journal*, XXIX (1977).

17. Suzanne Miers and Igor Kopytoff, "Introduction," in Miers and Kopytoff, eds., *Slavery in Africa* (Madison 1977), p. 17. For a criticism of their position, see Frederick Cooper, "The Problem of Slavery in African Studies," *Journal of African History*, XX (1979).

18. Max Weber, *The Protestant Ethic and the Spirit of Capitalism* (New York 1958).

19. J. N. D. Anderson, *Islamic Law in the Modern World* (New York 1959), p. 4.

20. J. N. D. Anderson and N. J. Coulson, "Modernization: Islamic Law," in Michael Brett, ed., *Northern Africa: Islam and Modernization* (London 1973), p. 73.

21. See, for example, P. F. Nursey-Bray, "The Polis, the African Traditional Community and African Natural Law," in Ali A. Mazrui and Hasu H. Patel, eds., *Africa in World Affairs: The Next Thirty Years* (New York 1973), p. 33.

22. Eddison Jonas Mudadirwa Zvogbo, "The Abuse of Executive Prerogative: A Purposive Difference between Detention in Black Africa and Detention in White Racist Africa," *Issue*, VI (winter 1976), 38.

23. All Africa Council of Churches, "Factors Responsible for the Violation of Human Rights in Africa," *Issue*, VI (winter 1976), 44.

24. Archie Mafeje, "The Ideology of 'Tribalism,'" *Journal of Modern African Studies*, IX (August 1971), 258. Cynthia H. Enloe, however, notes that ethnicity or "tribalism" can also be a rallying point for opposition to state élites: "Ethnicity, Bureaucracy and State-Building in Africa and Latin America," *Ethnic and Racial Studies*, I (1978).

25. Wiseberg, "Human Rights," p. 6.

26. Draft Covenant on Civil and Political Rights, and Draft Covenant on Economic, Social and Cultural Rights, United Nations Economic and Social Council, Eighteenth Session, Official Records, supplement no. 7, pp. 62–72, both reprinted in Green, *The United Nations*, pp. 179–94. Italics added.

27. Green, *The United Nations*, p. 48.

28. *Ibid.*, p. 67, fn 58.

29. Margaret Peil, "The Expulsion of West African Aliens," *Journal of Modern African Studies*, IX (August 1971).

30. P. L. Raikes, "Ujamaa and Rural Socialism," *Review of African Political Economy*, no. 3 (May–October 1975), 49–50.

31. Jagdish N. Bhagwati and Martin Partington, eds., *Taxing the Brain Drain I: A Proposal* (Amsterdam 1976), especially Frank C. Newman, "The Brain Drain Tax and International Human Rights Law," p. 193.

32. Harry G. Johnson, "Some Economic Aspects of the Brain Drain," *Issue*, IX (winter 1979).

33. Paulo Freire, *Pedagogy of the Oppressed*

(New York 1971).

34. Victor Gerdes, "Precursors of Modern Social Security in Indigenous African Institutions," *Journal of Modern African Studies*, xiii (June 1975), 211.

35. Mafeje, "The Ideology of 'Tribalism.'"

36. Covenant on Civil and Political Rights, article 25; United Nations Sub-Commission on Prevention of Discrimination and Protection of Minorities, Report of the Fourth Session, e/cn4/641 (25 October 1951), p. 43, cited in Green, *The United Nations*, p. 94.

37. Amnesty International Briefing, *Malawi* (August 1976), pp. 8–9.

38. Samuel P. Huntington, "Political Development and Political Decay," in Claude E. Welch, Jr., ed., *Political Modernization* (Belmont 1967), p. 254, quoted in Robert S. Jordan and John P. Renninger, "The New Environment of Nation-Building," *Journal of Modern African Studies*, xiii (June 1975), 201.

39. Seymour Martin Lipset, *The First New Nation* (Garden City, NY, 1967), pp. 20, 41.

40. Max Weber, *From Max Weber*, edited and translated by H. H. Gerth and C. Wright Mills (New York 1946), pp. 248, 253.

41. Talcott Parsons, *The Social System* (New York 1951), pp. 102ff.

42. Colin Leys, "What is the Problem about Corruption?" *Journal of Modern African Studies*, iii (August 1965), 226.

43. Ronald Wraith and Edgar Simpkins, "Nepotism and Bribery in West Africa," in Arnold J. Heidenheimer, ed., *Political Corruption: Readings in Comparative Analysis* (New York 1970), p. 336.

44. J. S. Nye, "Corruption and Political Development: A Cost-Benefit Analysis," *American Political Science Review*, lxi (June 1967), 420.

45. Max Beloff, *The Age of Absolutism, 1660–1815* (New York 1962), pp. 172–73.

46. Robert Michels, *Political Parties* (1st ed. 1915; New York 1959), p. 390.

47. Issa G. Shivji, *Class Struggles in Tanzania* (London 1976), part 3.

Parties, Coups, and Authoritarian Rule: Patterns of Political Change in Tropical Africa

Ruth Berins Collier

Cross-national research has devoted considerable attention to the conditions under which democracy emerges and persists.[1] Yet there are relatively few democracies in the world, and the other half of that question, concerning the conditions under which other kinds of regimes emerge and persist, has rarely been treated directly in cross-national analysis. Rather, this issue has been dealt with only in a negative way, in terms of the emergence of "nondemocratic" regimes under the "opposite" conditions. There has been little effort to break down what is generally a residual nondemocratic category or to specify the conditions under which different types of nondemocratic regimes appear.

For example, one of the more intriguing findings of this tradition of research concerns the relationship between the failure or success of the attempt to introduce democracy and the characteristics of the party system at the time when democracy is introduced (Pride, 1970). For those attempts that fail, however, there has been little or no analysis of the impact of different types of party systems on the way in which these democratic institutions are dismantled or of the different types of authoritarian rule that are set up in their place. This study will explore these issues regarding the emergence of authoritarian rule in tropical Africa.

The new states of tropical Africa provide an interesting setting for such a study.

These 26 countries went through a period of "tutelary" democracy in the decade and a half following World War II,[2] during a period of decolonization in which Western democratic institutions were introduced. After independence, however, these democratic institutions were dismantled. Democratic regimes were not maintained, but quite the opposite: the regimes moved increasingly in an authoritarian direction. There followed a period of institutional jockeying and regime experimentation which provides a useful laboratory for exploring the conditions under which different types of authoritarian regimes emerge. This study will explore the varied experiences of African countries with the introduction of democratic institutions and the different patterns of change through which they moved to establish distinct types of authoritarian rule in the postindependence period.

The framework employed in this study is derived from the work of Linz. According to Linz (1972: 27), authoritarian regimes commonly arise to control mass participation and to prevent the political expression of social cleavages that can easily emerge in a democracy. In Africa, these issues arose as a consequence of the introduction of democratic institutions in the preindependence period. The introduction of competitive party politics had the effect of politicizing ethnic and regional cleavages, since there was a widespread tendency for these cleavages to coincide with party cleavages (Emerson, 1960: 353–354; Zolberg, 1966: 21–22; Anderson et al., 1974: 68). Party competition thus became an important channel for the political expression (or political

From *Comparative Political Studies*, vol. 11, no. 1 (April 1978), pp. 62–88. Copyright © 1978 by Sage Publications, Inc. Reprinted by permission of Sage Publications, Inc.

stimulation) of societal cleavages. The introduction of Western democratic institutions also brought a new type of mass political participation on the national level, as universal suffrage was introduced in the space of relatively few years and the electorate was mobilized as part of the nationalist drive for independence. Following the emphasis of Linz, party dominance and level of voting in national elections are used as independent variables in this analysis.

Linz's framework for analyzing different types of authoritarian regimes once they emerge involves, in part, an extension of this concern with issues of popular mobilization and mass participation. He suggests that one of the major dimensions in terms of which subtypes of authoritarian rule can be distinguished is the degree and type of popular mobilization, and that controlled and noncompetitive elections are one important indicator at which one should look.

> The opportunity for popular participation, even if controlled, channeled, manipulated, and under co-opted leadership, makes such regimes different. . . . The flow and ebb of single parties . . . [deserves] special attention in the study of such regimes. The same is true for plebiscites, referenda, partial elections, etc. which should be studied as indicators of government policy rather than as free elections. Rates of registration, participation, void or blank votes, in this case are more interesting than the choices expressed and often reflect the attitudes toward the regime in addition to the intention of the rulers [Linz, 1972: 31].

Following this emphasis, the present analysis will devote particular attention to the way in which party systems and electoral systems were transformed or eliminated in the postindependence period as a starting point for distinguishing subtypes of authoritarian rule in Africa.

The goal of this study is thus to analyze the emergence in tropical Africa of distinct subtypes of authoritarian rule as an outcome of the different experiences the countries had with the introduction of democratic institutions in the period of decolonization. It is argued that African countries, starting with different preindependence experiences with mass political

participation and party dominance during the period in which democratic institutions were introduced, followed different sequences of events in dismantling these institutions and in setting up different subtypes of authoritarian rule in the first decade and a half of independence. The analysis focuses on the relationship between preindependence electoral participation and party dominance, and their effect on type of one-party regime formation, military coups, and postindependence regimes. The findings of the study are summarized through the presentation of five modal patterns of political change in tropical Africa.

SIMILARITIES AND DIFFERENCES IN THE STUDY OF AFRICAN POLITICS

At the same time that this analysis addresses certain broad issues concerning the emergence of authoritarian regimes, it is also relevant to a more specific issue in recent research on African politics: the tendency to place what may be an excessive emphasis on the similarities among the authoritarian patterns of national political change being followed by African countries. There has been a tendency to view the predominant as the universal and to overlook or minimize the significance of differences among countries. While this approach has provided some valuable insights into certain major political transformations that have occurred in Africa, it may tend to "overhomogenize" African politics (Bienen, 1970: 110). In methodological terms, it leads to the neglect of one of the most important means of gaining insights into political change: the systematic analysis of differences among countries.[3]

The emphasis on the similarity of developmental patterns throughout Africa has emerged primarily since these countries achieved political independence around 1960. In the first years of the independence period, the one-party regime came to be seen by many American and European analysts as the predominant form of government that was emerging virtually everywhere in Africa (for a discussion of this preoccupation with one-party regimes see Coleman and Rosberg, 1964: 4; Zolberg, 1966: 2–3). This generalization was later superseded by the conclusion that virtually no country was immune to the "rash" of military interventions that began to occur on the continent around 1965.[4]

Implicitly, at least, it was assumed that there was a single pattern that all but a few stray countries were following. The countries that were not yet following this pattern would presumedly do so shortly. To the extent that these predominant patterns were perceived as emerging in virtually all African countries, it appeared to be irrelevant to look for different patterns of national regime evolution.

At least two explanations for this tendency to emphasize similarities among countries may be identified. The first is a theoretical perspective that may be called the "constraints on development" thesis. This thesis identifies in African—or more generally Third World—countries common characteristics which account for a similar evolution of national political regimes. It suggests that because of the similar cultural, multiethnic, and historical context of African countries and the particular characteristics imposed by late-comer status, by economic and political dependency, and by the ever-growing gap between developmental aspirations and actual accomplishments, there are few options open to many countries on the continent (examples of this literature are: Lofchie, 1971; Wallerstein, 1971; Zolberg, 1968a, 1968b; O'Connell, 1967; Feit, 1968; Amin, 1973; Harris, 1975). It thus becomes reasonable to expect similar developmental patterns among African countries.

Though the constraints thesis raises an important issue, it can be carried too far. For instance, the argument about the external dependency can be carried to the point of economic determinism that leads to the neglect of important political differences among countries. Cardoso (1977), one of the most prominent analysts of the problem of external dependency, has insisted on the importance of the distinction between the broad type of economic system that exists in any country (e.g., dependent capitalism) and the particular type of political regime that may serve to maintain that economic system. He argues that any particular type of economic system may coexist with and be maintained by a variety of different types of regime, representing important differences in the political order that evolves in each country.

A second reason for the tendency to deemphasize differences may be a reaction to an earlier tradition of research on African politics that stressed the importance of different types of colonial rule and the different kinds of parties which gained control of the newly independent governments (Hodgkin, 1957; Wallerstein, 1961; Schachter [Morgenthau], 1961; and Coleman and Rosberg, 1964). The distinctions made in this literature have now been largely discredited.

The concern with type of colonial rule has become less widespread, probably for two erroneous reasons. First, following the initial period in which the differing philosophies and goals of direct and indirect rule were emphasized by a number of scholars, field researchers quickly discovered that indirect rule was not always applied in British Africa and that in French Africa it was often found necessary to work through traditional chiefs. Indeed, after 1917, this increasingly became official French policy (Alexandre, 1970). That the differences are not what they appear to be in theory or that they are not as great as expected, however, does not mean that they do not exist or are not important. Second, after the granting of independence, research began to focus on other, more immediate developments in Africa, such as one-party regime formation and military coups, and it appeared that these subsequent developments were occurring in ex-British and ex-French Africa alike. Thus, type of colonial rule dropped out of the analysis of African politics, and colonial legacy, to the extent that it still received attention, was often assumed to be roughly similar for all African countries regardless of former ruler.

The recent failure to distinguish among types of parties in Africa represents, in part, an overreaction to Zolberg's and Bienen's important revisionist interpretations of African party states. Bienen (1967), analyzing TANU in Tanzania, and Zolberg (1966), analyzing the five West African countries that were widely considered to have the strongest "mass" parties, demonstrated that these parties did not in fact have many of the characteristics that the current models attributed to them and that the contrast between these "mass," "mobilizing," or "revolutionary-centralizing" parties and other "patron," "elite," or "pragmatic-pluralist" parties had been greatly overstated. Zolberg further argued that the party-states that emerged in those five West African countries after independence had to be understood as weak regimes with a limited scope of authority.

Rather than use these findings to refine earlier distinctions, the major scholarly reaction to these analyses was to abandon distinctions. Because it had been shown that the strongest parties were most usefully described as weak, subsequent analyses assumed that all parties in Africa were weak and, therefore, there was little or no difference among them. All regimes were viewed as being equally vulnerable to military intervention. Distinctions were blurred and it was emphasized that the postindependence regimes were more similar than different: they were essentially weak, had emerged from relatively similar colonial situations, and were under similar political, economic, and social constraints.

These trends in African political research are unfortunate. Zolberg's major points are well taken: first, in order to understand the postindependence regimes in the party-states of West Africa, it is indeed useful to understand those parties as relatively weak rather than as strong, well organized, highly articulated, mobilizational parties eliciting overwhelming popular support. Second, and this follows from the first point, the differences between these parties and the others are not as great as had been supposed. The mass/patron, mass/elite, and revolutionary-centralizing/pragmatic-pluralist distinctions did not provide accurate descriptions and did exaggerate the differences between the types of parties. What is incorrect, however, is the implicit inference in subsequent writing on Africa that there are no distinctions to be made.

The thesis of this article is that though the earlier distinctions regarding colonial rule and political parties were misleading, some distinctions can be made. Differences in the experience with colonial rule and in the types of party systems and patterns of electoral participation that appeared in the preindependence period have led to different patterns of political change in African countries and to the emergence of distinct subtypes of authoritarian rule in the postindependence period.[5]

PARTY DOMINANCE AND ELECTORAL PARTICIPATION

Linz's framework points to the politicization of cleavages and the overall level of mass participation as two important factors in the emergence of authoritarian regimes in democratic settings. In the context of the transfer of democracy to colonial Africa, two of the most important manifestations of these factors are found in the issues of party dominance and party competition and in the dramatic increase in mass electoral participation. The following analysis focuses on the relationship between these two phenomena and their impact on postindependence regime outcomes.

If one considers all 26 countries, there is no relationship between electoral participation and the ability of a single party to achieve dominance over its competitors ($r = .00$).[6] Within colonial subgroups, however, a different picture emerges. Among the British colonies, the relationship is negative ($r = -.49$). Among the French colonies, by contrast, the relationship is positive. Though there is only a modest positive bivariate correlation between these two variables ($r = .20$), an examination of the scatterplot for this relationship reveals that the relationship is curvilinear and that there is an empty quadrant: there are no countries with a low level of dominance that had a high level of voting.[7] If one calculates a Q statistic on the basis of a dichotomized form of the data, there is thus a perfect positive association ($Q = 1.0$). The introduction of socioeconomic control variables does not substantially alter this finding.[8]

Three hypotheses concerning the linkages between voting turnout and party dominance are available in the literature that may help to interpret these opposite relationships in the British and French colonies. The first hypothesis posits a negative relationship in which voting affects dominance: higher levels of voting have a fragmenting influence which makes party dominance more difficult to achieve. According to the two other hypotheses, the causation goes in the other direction, from dominance to voting. The second hypothesis posits a positive relationship in which the presence of a dominant party may stimulate a bandwagon effect and/or a certain kind of dominant party may actively mobilize the vote in an effort to broaden its support. In a preindependence context, dominant parties may have found it advantageous to mobilize the vote in order to press for nationalist demands and to consolidate their power, even at the risk of increasing demand-making in other areas. The third hypothesis posits a negative relationship in which a lower level of dominance, i.e., a higher level of party competition, results in greater voting turnout. This corresponds to the pattern reported in the United States, where it has been suggested turnout is greater in close elections and was therefore relatively low in the traditionally one-party dominant South. This negative relationship between party dominance and voting turnout may be due both to the perception of voters that their vote is potentially more important in a close contest and to the competitive tactics of party leaders who, facing a close election, make a greater effort to mobilize the vote.

Among the French colonies, the relationship between turnout and dominance is positive, and only the second hypothesis posits a positive relationship: voting was greater where there was a more dominant party that attracted or mobilized the vote. More specifically, in light of the curvilinear relationship noted above, it would appear that a high level of dominance may have been a necessary, though not a sufficient, condition for a high level of voting among the French colonies.

Among the British colonies, the relationship between dominance and turnout is negative, corresponding to the other two hypotheses. An examination of variations across constituencies within colonies suggests that it is the third hypothesis which applies to British Africa: higher levels of party competition produced higher levels of turnout. The two colonies which were lowest on voting turnout were as low as they were because one party was so dominant that there were many uncontested constituencies where no voting took place. This relationship between party dominance and turnout, however, is not limited to the effect of voting in the extreme case of uncontested constituencies, but rather it is more continuous. In Ghana, for instance, it has been observed that turnout was low in certain areas because the CPP was dominant and the electoral outcome was not in question (Austin, 1966: 340). At the other end of the spectrum, it has been suggested that in Nigeria turnout was higher in given constituencies because of the high level of competition (Post, 1964: 351–354).

For British Africa there is an additional explanation of the variation in electoral turnout: colonial policy with regard to the rate and timing of the introduction of elections. Where elections were introduced later and where fewer preindependence elections were held, electoral participation was lower, as subsequent elections provided an additional opportunity for the parties to develop an organization, penetrate further into the countryside, and mobilize more people. For British Africa the correlations of electoral participation with number of preindependence elections and with the number of preindependence elections with universal suffrage are .48 and .89 respectively. The rate and timing of the introduction of elections does not explain any of the variance in turnout among the French colonies since French colonial policy was the same in all colonies.

It would thus seem that in French Africa, greater participation was at least in part the result of mobilization by an already dominant party, whereas in British Africa greater participation tended to result from colonial electoral policy and higher levels of party competition. For the French colonies, greater electoral participation was, as will be shown later, a consolidating, supportive factor for an already dominant party, whereas for British Africa greater electoral participation was not the result of the strategy of the dominant party and was not within the control of that party.[9]

PATTERNS OF ONE-PARTY REGIME FORMATION

The distinct patterns of party dominance and electoral participation that emerged in the period of decolonization meant that African leaders had different political resources and faced different political problems as their countries became independent. These differences led to different choices regarding mobilization and control in the new nations. The result has been distinctive sequences of political change in the decade and a half following independence.

The first important consequence of these preindependence processes was for the party system—specifically for whether or not a one-party regime was formed and how it was formed.[10] Some analyses of African politics have simply considered whether or not a one-party regime was formed. It is important, however, to consider the different ways in which one-party regimes have been instituted.[11] In some cases, they have been established by a broadly popular party with little opposition. In others, they have been formed in a situation of substantially less power and popular support. Within the African context, we may consider three patterns of one-party regime formation. One-party regimes have been formed by the total electoral success of a leading party, by the merger of parties, and by coercion—by the banning or repression of opposition parties. In addition, there are some cases in which one-party regimes were never formed. These four categories may be seen as representing an ordinal scale of the degree to which a one-party regime was formed as a "legitimate" consequence of the results of elections, with the final category reflecting the absence of one-party regime formation.

The type of one-party regime formation that occurred in each country depended in part on the degree of party dominance that emerged in the preindependence period, with the more dominant parties being more likely to establish a one-party regime by more "legitimate" means, according to the norms of the electoral system during the period of decolonization (rho = .59). While this relationship is hardly surprising, it has not received explicit attention in analysis of postindependence politics in Africa.

Within this overall relationship, however, the countries which formed one-party regimes by coercion cannot be distinguished in terms of degree of party dominance from those which never formed one-party regimes. Rather, the differences between these two groups of countries appear to result primarily from a difference in former colonial ruler. In the ex-French colonies, the leading parties tended to proceed relatively quickly to establish their final dominance either by overtly banning opposition parties or by effectively prohibiting them from contesting elections. Multiparty regimes were not retained in any of the ex-French African countries (see Table 1).

By contrast, among the seven ex-British

Table 1. Type of One-Party Regime Formation by Colonial Grouping

	Election	Merger	Coercion	One-Party Regime Not Formed
French	3	3	8	0
British	2	0	4	3
Belgian	1	0	0	2
TOTAL	6	3	12	5

N = 26

African countries which had not established a one-party regime by election or merger, there was much greater hesitancy to ban the opposition and a greater tendency to retain a multiparty regime for longer. In five of these countries, multiparty elections continued to be held after independence, though in two of them one-party regimes were eventually formed, six and eight years later respectively, by banning the opposition.[12] This greater hesitancy can also be seen in the fact that the remaining two ex-British colonies which formed a one-party regime by coercion, though they did not continue to hold multiparty elections, also waited a substantial interval after independence—seven years—before doing so. This pattern contrasts markedly with the ex-French colonies that did not form a one-party regime by election or merger. Nearly all of these countries had moved to form a one-party regime by coercion within a year or two of independence. It may be noted that the three ex-Belgian African countries likewise did not ban the opposition as a means of initially establishing a one-party regime.

This finding gives new credence to the earlier argument that once had greater currency, that the norms of democracy were somewhat more firmly rooted in British Africa than in French Africa.[13] Post has suggested that in contrast to the British,

the French left behind them an institutional pattern which put far less emphasis on the formal balancing of interests through such devices as bicameral legislatures, entrenched positions for chiefs, and official oppositions. Their legacy was rather one of greatly centralized decision-making and administration, and of the supremacy of the executive over all other branches of government [Post, 1968: 193].

Furthermore, the ex-British colonies had in their former colonial ruler a model of great continuity in competitive electoral politics. For the ex-French colonies, by contrast, the model provided by the metropole involved a far more uneven history of competitive elections (Zolberg, 1964: 104–105). Finally, the French Communist Party was linked to the dominant parties in most of the French colonies, so that the one-party ideologies and practice of European Communism may have been more readily diffused to French Africa.

In addition to the effect of preindependence party dominance, there was an independent effect of electoral participation on type of one-party regime formation. The impact of voting turnout is quite different for the British and French colonies, being negative for the former and positive for the latter. It would thus seem that higher levels of voting aided one-party regime formation by legitimate means among the French colonies, while it hindered it among the British colonies.[14]

This difference reflects the different causes of turnout in the two colonial groupings. Among the French colonies, greater participation occurred where there was greater party dominance and seemed to be the result of the mobilization of the electorate by these parties. It served as a source of support for those parties which had already achieved a high level of dominance, enabling them to form a one-party regime by election or merger. Among the British colonies, greater voter turnout was not the result of the strategy of a dominant party to demonstrate more support and thereby unequivocally eliminate its opponents. Rather, it was the result of colonial policy concerning the evolution and transfer of electoral arrangements to the colonies and also a result of party competition. As such, it was not within the control of the dominant party. Thus, while greater turnout aided the formation of one-party regimes by election or merger among the French colonies, this was far from the case among the British colonies.

POSTINDEPENDENCE REGIMES

The type of one-party regime formation that occurred around the time of independence had important consequences for the kinds of regimes that have emerged in the first decade and a half of independence in Africa. First of all, it had important implications for the pattern of military intervention[15] (see Table 2). Where a one-party regime was formed by election or merger,

Table 2. Coups by Type of One-Party Regime Formation as of 1975

Type of One-Party Regime Formation	Coup	
	No	Yes
Election or Merger	7	2
Coercion	2	10
Not Formed	1	4
		N = 26

these regimes were based on parties that had fared well under the competitive elections introduced during the period of decolonization. Furthermore, this method of achieving one-party status was more or less within the rules of the political game then being played. Consequently, these regimes had relatively little opposition and greater legitimacy. They have generally not been susceptible to military overthrow, but rather have experienced substantial political continuity in the decade and a half since independence.

Where one-party regimes were established by coercive means or where multiparty systems continued to exist, no party had fared as well under the competitive elections in the period of decolonization. In these cases, the attempt to form a one-party regime involved the elimination of rivals who were viable power contenders. The more coercive methods of forming a one-party regime were rarely successful, and instead of producing a more unified political system, they tended to intensify rivalries and increase opposition. Almost all of these regimes have been overthrown in military coups. Attempts to retain multiparty regimes likewise tended to fail. In fact, one of the direct and immediate causes for military coups in those countries which retained multiparty regimes was the unworkability of elections. In most cases, the outcomes of these elections were disputed. In the power struggle which followed, no acceptable solution could be reached, and the military intervened.

In addition to whether or not there were coups, certain other differences among postindependence regimes may be noted. It was argued above that it is reasonable to characterize most countries in contempo-rary Africa as having relatively weak authoritarian regimes. Within this framework, however, distinct subtypes of authoritarian regimes may be identified.

For Linz (1972, 1975), one of the most important aspects of an authoritarian regime is its limited political pluralism. In order to limit pluralism, authoritarian regimes pursue different policies toward political mobilization. Thus, he argues, differing patterns of political mobilization, including plebiscites, referenda, and controlled elections, are a significant dimension to consider in the analysis of subtypes of authoritarian rule.

Though virtually all African countries have undergone "departicipation" (Kasfir, 1976) through the elimination of competitive, multiparty elections since independence, the ways in which elections have been transformed have varied considerably. In the countries in which one-party regimes have persisted, electoral mobilization has been limited and controlled through the mechanism of the one-party election. In the case of the ex-French African colonies with one-party systems, these transformed elections have taken the form of plebiscites. In the ex-British colonies with one-party systems, they have taken the form of one-party competitive elections. Among the countries that have had coups, the policy of military governments has increasingly been to control electoral mobilization by eliminating elections. Preliminary evidence suggests that these alternative approaches to transforming elections imply somewhat different distributions of power, different roles of the party, different degrees or types of popular participation, and different bases for the legitimacy of the regime.

Plebiscitary One-Party Regimes

In the case of the contemporary one-party regimes of ex-French Africa, the elections are plebiscites quite strictly speaking. No opposition is permitted and the voter can vote only for or against official candidates. However, though there is no doubt about the outcome of these elections, the few available commentaries on them suggest that the governments in these countries take them seriously (Zolberg, 1964: 271–272; *Africa Contemporary Record*, 1970–71: B253). The extensive campaign and election coverage in the media also attests to this. It appears that these governments make a major effort to use elections to mobilize popular support, spread party and government propaganda, and manipulate symbols of legitimacy. The elections thus become a ritualistic occasion for the symbolic ratification of government policy and candidates. Official returns for these elections report exceptionally high levels of affirmative voting and turnout: the reported level of affirmative voting is typically either 99.9% or 100%, and turnout ranges between 88.9% and 99.9% of the total number of voters registered. What is important in official returns is not their accuracy, but the fact that they point to the importance of the election as a symbol or myth of the legitimacy of the government. Even allowing for substantial overreporting in the official figures, it appears that sizable numbers of people are mobilized in a ritual act of voting on election day.

These governments, then, are based on parties that were dominant and mobilizing in the preindependence period, when they mobilized high levels of voter turnout in order to eliminate completely the opposition and form a one-party regime electorally. They continue in the postindependence period to pursue a relatively vigorous policy of electoral mobilization in order to generate support and legitimacy for the regime. This plebiscitary alternative is characterized by the mobilization of a large proportion of the relevant population into the passive role of approving official candidates. Citizens do not mobilize, they *are mobilized*. This mobilization is thus primarily oriented around elite interests. Furthermore, mobilization is infrequent, coming at four- or five-year intervals, and other kinds of participation are not encouraged. Rather, levels of membership and participation in political and para-political organizations are low. This kind of situation has been called "low subject mobilization," in which "[c]itizens are mobilized on a temporary basis to ratify the decisions of the authoritarian elite and to demonstrate support for the regime. Much of the time, however, the regime does not encourage participation. As a result, the level of political participation is low" (Purcell, 1973: 30). The generally low level of participation, even in those countries where electoral mobilization is considerable, can be seen in the nature of the party. Linz has characterized the authoritarian party in terms that sound familiar to analysts of parties in Africa.

> First, and foremost, the authoritarian party is not a well organized ideological organization which monopolizes all access to power. . . . A considerable part of the elite has no connection with the party and does not identify with it. Party membership creates few, if any, duties. Ideological indoctrination is often minimal, the conformity and loyalty required may be slight. . . . The party is often ideologically and socially heterogeneous. Far from branching out into many functional organizations, in an effort to control the state apparatus and penetrate other spheres of life . . . it is a skeleton organization of second-rate bureaucrats [Linz, 1964: 314].

Nevertheless, the distinctive thing about these regimes is that they do engage in a periodic and apparently extensive mobilization of the masses through which they attempt to ratify, in the show of mass support, the regime, its office-holders, and its policies.

Competitive One-Party Regimes

A different pattern of electoral mobilization has appeared in the one-party states of ex-British Africa. Three types of competitive one-party elections have emerged in these countries: in one case there is a competitive primary within the party; in another case the party selects more than one official candidate to stand in the election; and in the final case there is competition within the party both in the primary and in the election. In these situations, electoral choice is not eliminated but is restricted to candidates within the single party who are running on the overall platform and program of the party.

Reported levels of electoral participation are considerably lower, ranging from about 43% to 73% of registered voters. This would appear to reflect in part a lower level of concern with mobilizing the electorate and also the absence of a felt need on the part of the government to give the appearance of massive participation by inflating the figures. In addition to a difference in degree, the type of mobilization in one-party competitive regimes is different from that in plebiscitary regimes. In these cases, what might be called modified subject mobilization has some "participant" qualities (to use Almond and Verba's terminology), in that the citizen does have some limited influence in leadership selection and the threat of non-reelection is a real one (Almond and Verba, 1963: 214). In Tanzania, 45% of the former Members of Parliament who ran in the 1965 elections lost their seats by vote of the electorate, as compared to only 7% in the 1972 elections for U.S. House of Representatives. The one-party competitive regimes thus involve a somewhat different distribution of power from the plebiscitary regimes. This can be seen in available analyses of these elections, which indicate that there is only limited use of campaigns to build support for the national government and its policies and much more of an orientation toward local issues and patronage politics (Hyden and Leys, 1972; Hill, 1974). Compared to the plebiscitary regimes, then, one-party competitive regimes involve less support manipulation and greater participant influence. Legitimacy in these regimes derives more from popular choice, however limited or controlled it may be, than it does from the ritual of mass ratification.

Military Regimes

The final type of authoritarian regime in Africa is the military regime. Military regimes actually represent quite a wide range of styles of rule, from very personalistic, such as Idi Amin's Uganda, to quite bureaucratic, such as Acheampong's Ghana

(Decalo, 1976: 240–254). In comparison with the two types of one-party rule, however, they have certain characteristics in common which set them off as a group. These regimes are dominated by coalitions of bureaucrats and army officers, and the usual pattern is for all parties to be banned, though a single official party is sometimes established. Though there have been some cases in which the military has held either competitive or controlled elections, the more general policy of the military has been to stay in power and to rule without holding elections. An interesting exception to this is Zaire where General Mobutu set up and legalized a single party, which he controls and which he apparently would like to use to move toward a more plebiscitary pattern of rule. In the more general pattern, however, military regimes do not make any use of the controlled or manipulated electoral mobilization present in the other two types of authoritarian rule. The decline in popular participation therefore is the greatest in these cases, since there are no electoral channels and often no party left at all. Finally, there is a difference in the basis of legitimacy of a military regime, since there is no use of elections of either type to provide the basis for apparent support, ratification, or representation. As a result, military regimes must put greater reliance on force as well as on the popularity of their policies in order to maintain themselves in power.

The findings of the above analysis may be summarized as follows. In those countries with leading parties which fared particularly well in the multiparty competitive elections introduced in the period of decolonization, these parties managed to eliminate the opposition and form one-party regimes in the course of these elections—either through complete electoral victory or through the merger of a weaker party into a clearly dominant one. Two different kinds of one-party regimes were formed, however, and this difference appeared to result from differences in former colonial ruler as well as differences in degree to which the parties mobilized the population electorally. In the first kind, primarily found in ex-French Africa, all electoral competition was eliminated, and plebiscitary regimes based on continued support mobilization were established. In the second, primarily found in ex-British Africa, electoral competition was retained within the framework of a one-party system. In those countries where the major party had not fared as well in the multiparty elections of the preindependence period, the final result has been military rule, though it is possible to distinguish alternative intermediate steps. In the ex-French African colonies, coercive means were used to establish a one-party regime; whereas in the ex-British and ex-Belgian colonies, a multiparty regime was initially retained. Neither of these subpatterns produced a viable solution to the problem of a lack of consolidation of power, however; and the regimes tended to be overthrown and military regimes ultimately established.

MODAL PATTERNS OF POLITICAL CHANGE

In the foregoing analysis, it was argued that three initial, interrelated conditions have had important effects on postindependence politics in tropical Africa: the degree of party dominance and the level of electoral participation which emerged in the preindependence period, and colonial ruler. In order to summarize these effects, it is convenient to dichotomize preindependence party dominance and electoral participation in order to assign countries to high and low categories on these variables.[16] Since there is a positive curvilinear relationship between these two variables among the French colonies, the cases of ex-French Africa fall predominantly in the low dominance/low participation, high dominance/low participation, and high dominance/high participation cells of the resulting fourfold table. Since the correlation is negative for British Africa, those cases fall predominantly in the low dominance/high participation and the high dominance/low participation cells. As a result, five different sets of initial conditions can be distinguished.

On the basis of these five subgroups, five modal patterns of change in Africa from the period of decolonization through the

first decade and a half of independence may be identified, involving distinct sequences in the relationship among preindependence electoral patterns, the type of one-party regime formation, and postindependence political patterns. These patterns are summarized in Figure 1. It must be emphasized that these patterns are derived from the analysis presented above. They thus summarize probabilistic relationships, and it is obviously not the case that all the countries come out "correctly" at each step in the pattern. Some follow the pattern perfectly and may be considered to be representative countries which exemplify the pattern. Others follow a sequence perfectly except for one deviation, whereas a few others either switch from one pattern to another or cannot be described in terms of these patterns.

Pattern I includes those ex-French African countries in which dominant parties in the preindependence period mobilized the population to build sufficient electoral support to enable the party either to eliminate opposition parties through total electoral victory or to absorb the opposition through mergers. One-party regimes in these countries were thus formed well before independence. After independence, this policy of support mobilization has been continued in the plebiscitary regimes that have been established. Though this analysis is concerned with the politics of the first decade and a half of independence, it might be mentioned that more recently, one country seems to be in a process of modifying the plebiscitary regime. In 1976, Senegal allowed the formation of two additional official parties: one to the political right and one to the political left of the ruling party which occupies the political center. The first national election in which these parties will be allowed to participate is scheduled for 1978.

Pattern II represents an intermediate sequence for ex-French Africa. The major party in each country achieved a high level of dominance on the dichotomized variable, but in fact party dominance was lower than for the parties in Pattern I (with the exception of Guinea, which like the cases in Pattern II also had low participation—Guinea might alternatively be charac-

Figure 1: Modal Patterns of Political Change in Africa, 1945 to 1975

	Pre-Independence Electoral Patterns		Transformation of Party System Around Independence	Post-Independence Outcome
	1	2	3	4
Pattern I: French Africa Ivory Coast Mauritania Senegal Guinea (2)[a]	High Party Dominance →	High Electoral Participation →	One-Party Regime by Election or Merger →	One-Party Plebiscitary Regime
Pattern II: French Africa CAE Niger Upper Volta Mali (3)	High Party Dominance →	Low Electoral Participation →	One-Party Regime by Banning → Plebiscitary → One-Party Regime	Military Coup: "Stable" Rule, Relative Regime Continuity
Pattern III: French Africa[b] Benin Ghana Togo Chad (4) Congo (2) Gabon (2, 4)	Low Party Dominance →	Low Electoral Participation →	One-Party Regime by Ratification Election →	Military Coup: Regime Experimentation, Greater Instability
Pattern IV: British Africa Tanzania Zambia Kenya (1) Malawi (4)	High Party Dominance →	Low Electoral Participation →	One-Party Regime Formed →	One-Party Competitive Regime
Pattern V: British/Belgian Africa Sierra Leone Nigeria Zaire Burundi (1) Gambia (4) Uganda (3)	Low Party Dominance →	High Electoral Participation →	Multi-Party, Competitive Elections Continued →	Military Coup: Regime Experimentation, Greater Instability

Independence

a. The numbers in parentheses refer to the steps in the sequence at which the country deviates from the indicated pattern.
b. One country in ex-British Africa, Ghana, also follows this pattern.

41

terized as having switched from Pattern II to I). These parties did not mobilize the vote and attract additional support with which they could establish one-party regimes by election or merger. Instead, like the Pattern III countries, they did so by coercion. The tactic adopted was the simple banning of the opposition parties, either before or within a couple of months of independence. When it was time for the next scheduled election, an attempt was made to set up a plebiscitary regime similar to those in the countries that followed Pattern I. These plebiscitary regimes remained in power for varying lengths of time, but eventually all have been overthrown by the military, again like the Pattern III countries. Nevertheless, the first decade and a half of independence was a period of relative "stability" as these military governments were still in power as of 1976. Throughout the postindependence period, therefore, these countries have had only two heads of state—one civilian and one military.

The countries in Pattern III are primarily the former French colonies which had low levels of party dominance and generally low levels of participation. None of these countries had one-party regimes at the time of independence, but all moved to form one through coercion within the next few years. The tactic employed differed somewhat from that employed by the Pattern II countries. In all cases some form of "ratification" election was used to establish a one-party regime. These elections took three forms: either one-party or one-list elections; competitive elections involving list voting in which the whole country was redefined as a single constituency, thus assuring the total victory of the dominant party; or, in the case of Ghana, the one non-French African country in this pattern, a referendum on the issue of the formation of a one-party regime. This attempt to legitimate the formation of a one-party regime through an election was generally not successful, and in all cases except Chad, the military ousted the government within a year or two. With the exception of the 1960 coup in Zaire, the first coups in tropical Africa are to be found among these countries. Unlike the case of Pattern II

countries, however, the military leaders in these countries have not established stable or continuous rule. Rather, postindependence history has been one of greater regime experimentation and instability. In general, the first military intervention, which came relatively early, was followed by the installation of a new civilian government, only to be followed by a second coup and usually the establishment of longer-term military rule. These changes have been accompanied on the whole by a higher incidence of unsuccessful coup attempts than is the case for Pattern II countries. Benin is the extreme example of this pattern, with 6 coups from 1963 to 1972 and a variety of different civilian arrangements alternating with military governments, producing 5 different constitutions and 10 different presidents in the decade and a half after independence (Decalo, 1976: 39). The deviations from this general pattern occurred in Gabon and Chad. In Gabon, the French intervened after the first coup and restored the ousted civilian government to power. The government has managed to retain power and set up a plebiscitary regime. In Chad the first coup did not follow the initial formation of a one-party regime, but came 13 years later, though the intervening years were a period of rebellion and civil war which might be traced to the formation of a one-party regime and the banning of the Muslim PNA (Morrison et al., 1972: 209; *Africa Research Bulletin*, 1975: 3594).

Before moving on to the ex-British and ex-Belgian colonies, it should be mentioned that the one ex-French African country which has not been mentioned, Cameroun, does not fit any single pattern of political change. Starting out at independence with low dominance and low participation (Pattern III), it has switched into the first pattern in that it formed a one-party regime by merger and has continued to have a plebiscitary pattern.

Pattern IV includes the ex-British African colonies that had a significant European settler population. Because of this special factor, the introduction of elections and the extension of the suffrage was generally delayed by the British government in order to protect the European settler interests. Furthermore, there was a tendency in these colonies for party differences to coincide with racial cleavages, so that there was, compared with other colonies in Africa, relatively little competition among Black African parties, the more general pattern being a dominant African party opposing a party representing European settlers. Electoral participation remained relatively low, first because there were fewer elections in these "late" decolonizers and hence fewer opportunities for the dominant party to build an extensive organization and mobilize the vote, and second because with relatively little intra-African party competition, a high proportion of constituencies were not contested and, following the British practice, no voting took place in such constituencies. (It might be added that this practice stands in sharp contrast to the French tradition, and indeed in French Africa turnout was often greater in uncontested constituencies.) By independence, the special arrangements for the representation of European settlers had been dropped and the dominant African parties moved to establish a one-party regime.

Whereas among the ex-French African countries there is an important difference between those which formed a one-party regime by coercion and those which did so by noncoercive, more legitimate means, among the ex-British African countries the major difference is between those which formed a one-party regime by any means and those which did not. In Tanzania and Malawi, a one-party regime was formed by the electoral victory of the respective parties which had no effective African opposition at all. In Zambia, an attempt was made over eight years of multiparty politics to eliminate the opposition in elections, but as this goal continued to elude party leaders, a one-party regime was finally established by banning the opposition. In Kenya, a one-party regime was initially formed by the merger of the second largest party into the most dominant, and a one-party regime existed for a year and a half before a splinter group established an opposition party. Three years later that party was banned. All of these countries are presently one-party competitive regimes, with the exception of Malawi, which continues

to follow the British practice of simply declaring the electoral victory of the sole candidate in uncontested constituencies throughout the country.

Pattern V includes the countries of nonsettler British Africa as well as two former Belgian colonies, Burundi and Zaire. These countries had low party dominance in the period before independence, and as a result of party competition, electoral participation was relatively high. Though Zaire and Nigeria had low turnout compared to the other countries in this group, this difference is in good measure due to the fact that universal suffrage was not introduced in these countries before independence, as it was elsewhere in Africa.[17] Zaire had only manhood suffrage, but nonetheless came within three percentage points of the cut-off point—a very high rate of participation among those eligible to vote. In Nigeria there was only manhood suffrage in the North, which has about half the total population. If it were not for this restricted franchise, the rate of participation would obviously have been considerably greater. In all of these countries, multiparty regimes were initially retained in the postindependence period and competitive elections were held. In each case, however, the election became a focus for intense political conflict, resulting in military takeovers. The two major deviations from this pattern are Gambia and Uganda. Gambia, the smallest country among the 26 considered here and one which lacks an army, has never had a military coup. It continues to have the only multiparty regime in tropical Africa. In Uganda, multiparty elections were never held in the postindependence period. Rather, the opposition was banned and an attempt was underway to switch into the pattern of one-party competitive regimes being followed by Uganda's neighbors. The military coup of Idi Amin interrupted this process, however. Like the countries in Pattern III, the postindependence history of these countries has generally been marked by greater regime change and experimentation.

CONCLUSION

This study has viewed the emergence of different types of authoritarian regimes in tropical Africa as outcomes of different patterns of political change rooted in the experience each country had with the introduction of competitive party politics. Specifically, it was found that the two independent factors suggested by Linz, the political expression of societal cleavages and mass participation, along with colonial legacy, had an impact on the emergence of different subtypes of postindependence authoritarian rule. Party dominance, an important aspect of the political expression of societal cleavages, had a strong effect on the types of postindependence rule which emerged. Continuous civilian rule has occurred only in those countries where the major party emerged as overwhelmingly dominant during the period of competitive party politics. Where party dominance was low, the civilian regimes did not endure either in the countries where a multiparty regime was retained, or where there was an attempt to create a single-party regime by coercion. In these countries the military has intervened.

Preindependence electoral participation, an important aspect of mass political participation, also had an impact on the type of postindependence regime, though the effect of this participation depended on its cause. Where greater participation was the result of mobilization by a dominant party, it took the form of support mobilization. The regimes in these countries have continued to mobilize electoral support in the postindependence period through one-party plebiscitary elections, which have thus become part of the legitimacy formula for maintaining authoritarian rule. Where greater electoral participation was the result of competition among parties, it had a "destabilizing" effect, inhibiting the consolidation of power by a single party and the creation of a one-party regime by more legitimate means. The result in these countries has been military intervention.

Though the thesis that African politics is heavily constrained in a way that sharply limits options and choices may in substantial measure be correct, this analysis has thus shown that at the level of national regime different patterns of political change have been followed in Africa. In this connection four points may be reiterated. The first is that colonial legacy has had an impact on patterns of political change in Africa and that this legacy was different for the French and British colonies. The neglect of former colonial ruler as an explanatory variable in much recent literature may have gone too far.

Second, one-party regime formation has not been a universal or uniform process in Africa, as was implied or anticipated in one phase of writing on African politics. Those countries where one-party regimes were not formed represent an identifiable subgroup which is distinctive in terms of colonial ruler and preindependence patterns of party dominance and electoral participation. Furthermore, one-party regime formation has occurred in a variety of different ways, reflecting differences in legitimacy and in the degree of dominance of the leading party. These differences have been important for the types of regimes which one can now observe in Africa.

Third, military coups have similarly not—at least to date—been a universal occurrence in Africa, as has likewise been implied or anticipated in a subsequent phase of writing on African politics. Even if those countries which so far have not had coups have them in the future, it will still be the case that some countries will have fewer coups or will at least have been more resistant to military intervention for longer periods. Again, the incidence of coups is not random but follows a fairly regular and predictable pattern.

Fourth, the strongest parties in Africa may indeed have been weak and may still be weak—relative to their on-paper organization, their intended level of activity as set out in ideological statements, other strong parties elsewhere in the world, and the "model" of organization which they may have adopted or which social scientists may have applied to them. Nevertheless, there have been differences among African parties and some parties have indeed been strong relative to other African parties.

These differences have had important consequences for the political patterns which have emerged.

In conclusion, I would like to raise two sets of speculative questions about the way in which the sequence of events described in this paper could be extended to include both additional "background" variables and additional consequences of the patterns that have been identified. With regard to the origins of these patterns, it is evident that the groups of countries identified with the five patterns of political change—patterns which were derived by grouping countries in terms of their scores on three variables—correspond closely to geographical zones within colonial groupings. The first pattern includes those ex-French African countries along the upper Guinea coast, the coast of the western "hump" of Africa. The second includes noncoastal ex-French Africa, with the exception of Chad. The third includes those countries of ex-French Africa, as well as Ghana, which lie along the Gulf Coast. The fourth includes ex-British east and central Africa; while the fifth includes ex-British west and ex-Belgian Africa.

In the terms of Przeworski and Teune (1970), one may ask what variables can be substituted for these geographic and colonial terms? What further explanatory factors do these groupings suggest? One possibility is diffusion among neighbors, especially within the colonial subgroups, and also, of course, simultaneous diffusion from metropole to a number of colonies.[18] In addition, there may be other distinct factors associated with these geographical groupings that act as internal causes for each country within the group. For instance, geographical grouping corresponds to the historical conditions of European penetration. In the coastal countries, particularly of West Africa, penetration was early, relatively great, and very uneven, producing a coastal-interior split with respect to many aspects of westernization (urbanization, religion, education, economy). The interior countries, on the other hand, had less European penetration, are very poor with limited possibilities for economic development, and are generally sparsely settled with much of the land often desert. Though Pattern IV countries are all in east or central Africa, it is clear that for this geographical definition we can more accurately substitute other variables and define the grouping, as we have above, as including colonies with settler politics. Though this analytical definition is more accurate than the geographical definition, which would also have included Uganda, the use of the geographical definition helps account for the diffusion, aborted by the Amin coup, of a one-party competitive system to Uganda. Pattern V corresponds least well to a geographic definition and may more accurately be described as the areas of nonsettler politics and indirect colonial rule.

This discussion is obviously preliminary. Work needs to be done to understand what prior conditions these geographical and colonial groupings really correspond to and to disentangle the logic or mechanisms which relate such prior conditions to the political patterns that have been described.[19]

Finally, what, if any, effects will these different patterns of political change and these different regime types have on future developments in Africa? There are, of course, important similarities among African countries, and the differences noted in the postindependence period may be eroded over a longer time span. There is another possibility, however. In his broadly comparative analysis, Pride (1970) suggests that patterns of party dominance, party penetration, and societal cleavages in the early period of modernization combine to have abiding effects on the evolution of national regimes. The present study suggests that so far this seems to be the case for Africa as well, and it will be interesting to see how the differences identified evolve over time.

It would also be interesting to explore the impact of differences in regime on policy outcomes such as the successful pursuit of development strategies. This topic has not yet been carefully analyzed by scholars concerned with Africa. Though it does not appear that one kind of regime tends to be either more radical or more conservative than another, the capacity of different governments to pursue development goals successfully (whether more capitalist or more socialist) may depend in part on the type of regime involved. It would be interesting to explore the different kinds of organizational, symbolic, and coercive resources that military regimes and the two types of one-party regimes bring to the task of building and executing long-term development policies. Evidence from Latin America, where the interplay between regime characteristics and policy performance has been more extensively studied, points to the particular importance of certain resources that may be available to African one-party regimes: the continuity of political institutions that may be provided even by an organizationally weak one-party system; the use of symbolic resources that may play a critical role in contexts in which payoffs based on material resources are in short supply; and the possibly greater political flexibility and cooptive capacity of party structures, as opposed to administrative structures directed by military elites, in responding to opposition and crisis (Kaufman, 1976; O'Donnell, 1975; Davis, 1976; Stevens, 1974). It may be the case for Africa as well that there is an important relationship between the differing structural characteristics and political resources of these regimes and their effectiveness in important areas of public policy. Such a relationship is suggested in the African setting by Schumacher's (1975: 226) analysis of Senegal, which points to the importance of the symbolic, ceremonial, and legitimating role of the party in Senegalese political life, as well as to the somewhat different distribution of power and the influence on policy that results from the presence of the party.

Apart from the question of effectiveness, the Latin American experience also suggests that the existence of different regimes may lead countries that have relatively similar economic development strategies to pursue them with quite different human costs. For instance, contemporary Mexico is pursuing economic policies that reflect a type of class domination in many ways similar to that found in Brazil, Chile, Uruguay, and Argentina. Yet Mexico has avoided the type of harshly repressive military regime that has clearly facilitated the pursuit of these policies in the other four countries. This may have occurred because of the existence of a highly developed, incorporating, integrative party in Mexico. This relationship between regime type and differences in human costs suggests another line of inquiry that could usefully be pursued within the African setting.

NOTES

1. See, for instance, Lipset (1959); Cutright (1963); Neubauer (1967); Pride (1970); Dahl (1971); and Flanigan and Fogelman (1971).
2. The countries included in the analysis are the former colonies and trust territories of France, Belgium, and Great Britain that are located south of the Sahara and north of the Zambezi.
3. It should be noted that these problems are not present in the growing cross-national literature on African politics, which is explicitly oriented around the examination of differences among countries. See, for instance, Morrison and Stevenson (1972), Duvall and Welfling (1973), Welfling (1973), and Hakes (1973).
4. This idea is explicit or implicit in many studies of military intervention in Africa. See, for example, Decalo (1976), First (1972), Lee (1969), Lemarchand (1972), Welch (1970), and Zolberg (1968a).
5. In its substantive focus, this study may be viewed as an extension of Zolberg's (1966) analysis of five West African countries. The difference lies in the fact that Zolberg's analysis sought to provide insight regarding one type of regime in Africa, the party-state, the present analysis seeks to explore the emergence of *different* types of regimes.
6. Except for social and economic background variables that were taken from Morrison et al. (1972), the data employed in this analysis were gathered by the author from a wide variety of monographic and periodical sources. A composite measure of party dominance was used which was based on ten variables: percent of the vote for the leading party in the last preindependence election; number of parties with legislative representation at independence; percent of legislative seats won by leading party in the last preindependence election and the percent held at independence; legislative fractionalization following last preindependence election and at independence; pattern of dominance of leading party over the preindependence period (low

throughout the period, higher but declining, increasing throughout to fairly high level, high throughout); and three variables derived from Hodgkin (1961); number of important parties in preindependence period; number of important opposition parties; and number of parties in ruling coalition at independence. Factor analysis was used as a data reduction technique to derive a single indicator from these ten component variables.

Electoral participation is operationalized as the percent of the population voting in the last national election before independence, except in Sierra Leone where the "independence" election in fact followed independence. In Sierra Leone, the last preindependence election was held four years before independence under a restricted franchise, whereas the comparable elections used for other countries were held not more than one or two years prior to independence, and almost all on the basis of universal suffrage. The first election with universal suffrage in Sierra Leone was in fact set up under colonial rule, but did not actually take place until a year after independence, and it is that election which was used for calculating electoral participation.

A word might be added about the reliability of the data used in this analysis. Many of the variables involve event data and present few problems because of the nature of the events. Scoring the occurrence of successful coups, how a one-party regime is formed, or whether an election is competitive, poses few of the problems encountered in determining the incidence of other types of events such as strikes, riots, and political arrests. The data on the distribution of seats in preindependence legislatures were more difficult to find. For this I have relied heavily on Welfling (1971), as well as on the standard political histories of each country, African news periodicals, and international yearbooks. The indicator of electoral participation as a percentage of population may pose somewhat greater problems because of issues regarding both parts of this ratio. In some countries there may have been some inflation of voting figures, though I have generally employed figures that have been used, and thereby implicitly treated as reliable, by country specialists. The population data is drawn from Morrison et al. (1972).

7. In Figure 1 in the final section of this article, two French colonies are represented as having low dominance and high participation. The discrepancy results from the fact that the above relationship is based on a dichotomous form of the variables which divides the cases at the middle of the range for French Africa, whereas the dichotomy used below divides the cases at the mean value for all 26 countries.

8. In light of the small case base within these subgroups, partial correlations based on the introduction of even one control variable must, of course, be treated with caution. It might be noted, however, that the introduction of indicators of socioeconomic modernization as controls does not alter the relationship between participation and dominance among the British colonies, while in a few instances it tends to strengthen it among the French colonies.

9. These interpretations are based on an examination of the monographic literature on African politics. For a more extended discussion of these relationships and the causes of the differences in the patterns between French and British Africa, see Collier (1974).

10. For present purposes, a one-party regime will be defined as involving cases in which only one party holds seats in the national legislature.

11. Bienen (1970) and Finer (1967) have both suggested that the concept of one-party regime should be broken down and that distinctions should be made among them. However, to my knowledge, no systematic analysis of different types of one-party regimes has been undertaken, except for the distinctions made by Huntington (1970), which continue to group virtually all the African single-party regimes within the same category. Even Finer, in the analysis which follows his criticism of a blanket single-party concept, analyzes all one-party regimes on the African continent as a single group without making distinctions among them. His analysis is particularly important for recent purposes because he finds that one-party states and multiparty states are equally likely to experience military intervention, an assertion about which more will be said below.

12. It may be noted that in one of these countries, Kenya, a short-lived one-party regime had been formed by merger five years earlier.

13. See Zolberg (1966: 78–79) for a similar argument made with reference to the party-states of West Africa.

14. A computer program that permitted calculating partial coefficients for rho, thus making it possible to control this relationship for party dominance, was unfortunately not conveniently available. However, the analysis was redone with a product-moment correlation substituted for the original rho (the values are similar). It was found that in a three-variable path analysis, the polarity of the relationship remained unchanged and its strength was likewise relatively stable.

15. Welfling (1973) also reported a finding which related coups to a party variable. Though her party variable, institutionalization, is very different from mine, it clearly does rank African countries in a similar way. Hence, though the two studies employ different analytic frame-

works and seek to explain different things, they do tap the same underlying relationship between characteristics of the party system and military coups.

16. The decision was initially made to dichotomize these two variables at the mean of the distribution of all 26 states. In both cases, however, the mean did not represent a natural break point in the distribution. As a result, the break point used was that nearest the mean which would divide the cases at a natural break. In fact, the break point used for electoral participation changed only one case, while that used for party dominance changed only two cases, in comparison with the results obtained when dichotomizing at the mean.

17. The only other country (aside from Sierra Leone—see note 6) which did not have universal suffrage before independence was Tanzania, but this fact does not distort the low score on participation for that country. In the first election with universal suffrage, turnout in Tanzania did not even approach the 23% cut-off point.

18. This corresponds to the distinction between "contagious" and "constant source" diffusion discussed in Coleman (1964; ch. 17).

19. The sorting out of these factors obviously goes far beyond the mere introduction of social and economic modernization variables as controls, which has already been done in this analysis. It might involve, rather, some further elaboration of the suggestive groupings of countries according to differences in the nature of European penetration, economic domination, and integration into the world capitalist system proposed by Samir Amin (1972).

REFERENCES

Alexandre, P. (1970) "Chiefs, commandants and clerks: their relationship from conquest to decolonisation in French West Africa," in M. Crowder and O. Ikime (eds.) West African Chiefs. New York: Africana Publishing.

Almond, G. A. and S. Verba (1963) The Civic Culture. Princeton: Princeton Univ. Press.

Amin, S. (1973) Neo-colonialism in West Africa. Harmondsworth, England: Penguin.

—— (1972) "Underdevelopment and dependence in Black Africa: origins and contemporary forms." J. of Modern African Studies 10: 503–524.

Anderson, C. W., F. R. Von Der Mehden, and C. Young (1974) Issues of Political Development. Englewood Cliffs, NJ: Prentice-Hall.

Austin, D. (1966) Politics in Ghana, 1946–1960. London: Oxford Univ. Press.

Bienen, H. (1970) "One-party systems in Africa," pp. 99–127 in S. Huntington and C. Moore (eds.) Authoritarian Politics in Modern Society. New York: Basic Books.

—— (1967) Tanzania: Party Transformation and Economic Development. Princeton: Princeton Univ. Press.

Cardoso, F. H. (1977) "On the characterization of authoritarian regimes in Latin America." Prepared for the Working Group on the State and Public Policy of the Joint Committee on Latin American Studies (SSRC/ACLS).

Coleman, J. S. (1964) Introduction to Mathematical Sociology. London: Free Press.

Coleman, J. S. and C. G. Rosberg, Jr. [eds.] (1964) Political Parties and National Integration in Tropical Africa. Los Angeles: Univ. of California Press.

Collier, R. B. (1974) "Electoral politics and authoritarian rule: institutional transfer and political change in tropical Africa." Ph.D. dissertation, University of Chicago.

Cutwright, P. (1963) "National political development: measurement and analysis." Amer. Soc. Rev. 28 (April): 253–264.

Dahl, R. A. (1971) Polyarchy: Participation and Opposition. New Haven: Yale Univ. Press.

Davis, C. L. (1976) "The mobilization of public support for an authoritarian regime: the case of the lower class in Mexico City." Amer. J. of Pol. Sci. 20 (November): 653–670.

Decalo, S. (1976) Coups and Army Rule in Africa: Studies in Military Style. New Haven: Yale Univ. Press.

Duvall, R. and M. Welfling (1973) "Determinants of political institutionalization in Black Africa: a quasi-experimental analysis." Comparative Pol. Studies 5 (January).

Emerson, R. (1960) From Empire to Nation. Boston: Beacon Press.

Feit, E. (1968) "Military coups and political development: some lessons from Ghana and Nigeria." World Politics 20 (January): 179–193.

Finer, S. E. (1967) "The one-party regimes in Africa: reconsiderations." Government and Opposition 2 (July–October).

First, R. (1972) Power in Africa. Middlesex, England: Penguin Books.

Flanigan, W. and E. Fogelman (1971) "Patterns of democratic development: an historical comparative analysis," in J. V. Gillespie and B. A. Nesvold (eds.) Macro-Quantitative Analysis. Beverly Hills: Sage Publications.

Hakes, H. E. (1973) "Weak parliaments and military coups in Africa: a study in regime instability." Sage Professional Papers in the Social Sciences (No. 90–004). Beverly Hills and London: Sage Publications.

Harris, R. (1974) "The political economy of Africa: underdevelopment or revolution," pp. 1–47 in Richard Harris (ed.) The Political Economy of Africa. New York: Schenkman.

Hill, F. (1974) "Elections in the local context,"

pp. 205–229 in the Election Study Committee University of Dar es Salaam, Socialism and Participation: Tanzania's 1970 National Elections. Dar es Salaam: Tanzania Publishing House.

Hodgkin, T. (1961) African Political Parties. Middlesex, England: Penguin Books.

——— (1957) Nationalism in Colonial Africa. New York: New York Univ. Press.

Huntington, S. P. (1970) "Social and institutional dynamics of one-party systems," pp. 3–47 in S. P. Huntington and C. H. Moore (eds.) Authoritarian Politics in Modern Society. New York: Basic Books.

Hyden, G. and C. Leys (1972) "Elections and politics in single-party systems: the case of Kenya and Tanzania." British J. of Pol. Sci. 2: 389–420.

Kasfir, N. (1976) The Shrinking Political Arena. Berkeley: Univ. of California Press.

Kaufman, R. R. (1977) "Mexico and Latin American authoritarianism," in J. L. Reyna and R. Weinert (eds.) Authoritarianism in Mexico. Philadelphia: Institute for the Study of Human Issues.

Lee, J. M. (1969) African Armies and Civil Order. New York: Praeger.

Lemarchand, R. (1972) "Civilian-military relations in former Belgian Africa: the military as a contextual elite." Paper delivered at the Annual Meeting of the American Political Science Association.

Linz, J. (1975) "Totalitarian and authoritarian regimes," pp. 175–241 in F. Greenstein and N. Polsby (eds.) The Handbook of Political Science, Vol. 3: Macropolitical Theory. Reading, MA: Addison-Wesley.

——— (1972) "Notes toward a typology of authoritarian regimes." Paper delivered at the annual meeting of the American Political Science Association, Washington, D.C.

——— (1964) "An authoritarian regime: Spain," in E. Allardt and Y. Littunen (eds.) Transactions of the Westermarck Society, Vol. X, Cleavages, Ideologies, and Party Systems. Helsinki: Academic Bookstore.

Lipset, S. M. (1959) "Some social requisites of democracy." Amer. Pol. Sci. Rev. 53 (March): 69–105.

Lofchie, M. F. (1971) "Political constraints on African development," pp. 9–18 in Michael F. Lofchie (ed.) The State of the Nations. Berkeley: Univ. of California Press.

McKnown, R. (1975) "Domestic correlates of military intervention in Africa." J. of Pol. and Military Sociology (Fall).

Morrison, D. G., R. C. Mitchell, J. N. Paden, and H. M. Stevenson (1972) Black Africa: A Comparative Handbook. New York: Free Press.

Morrison, D. G. and H. M. Stevenson (1972)

"Integration and instability: patterns of African political development." Amer. Pol. Sci. Rev. 66 (September): 902–927.

Neubauer, D. E. (1967) "Some conditions of democracy." Amer. Pol. Sci. Rev. 61 (December): 1002–1009.

O'Connell, J. (1967) "The inevitability of instability." J. of Modern African Studies 5: 181–191.

O'Donnell, G. (1975) "Reflexiones sobre las tendencias generales de cambio en el estado burocratico-autoritario." Documento CEDES/ G. E. CLASCO/ No. 1. Buenos Aires: Centro de Estudio de Estado y Sociedad.

Post, K. (1968) The New States of West Africa. Baltimore: Penguin Books.

——— (1964) The Nigerian Federal Election of 1959. London: Oxford Univ. Press.

Pride, R. A. (1970) "Origins of democracy: a cross-national study of mobilization, party systems, and democratic stability." Sage Professional Papers in Comparative Politics (No. 01-012) Beverly Hills and London: Sage Publications.

Przeworski, A. and H. Teune (1970) The Logic and Comparative Social Inquiry. New York: John Wiley.

Purcell, S. K. (1973) "Decision-making in an authoritarian regime: theoretical implications from a Mexican case study." World Politics 26 (October): 28–54.

Schachter [Morgenthau], R. (1961) "Single-party systems in West Africa." Amer. Pol. Sci. Rev. 55 (June).

Schumacher, E. J. (1975) Politics, Bureaucracy and Rural Development in Senegal. Berkeley: Univ. of California Press.

Stevens, E. P. (1974) "Mexico's PRI: the institutionalization of corporatism." Paper delivered at the annual meeting of the American Political Science Association. Chicago.

Wallerstein, I. (1971) "The range of choice: constraints on policies of governments in contemporary African independent states," pp. 19–33 in Michael F. Lofchie (ed.) The State of the Nations. Berkeley: Univ. of California Press.

——— (1961) Africa: The Politics of Independence. New York: Vintage Books.

Welch, C. E., Jr. [ed.] (1970) Soldier & State in Africa: a Comparative Analysis of Military Intervention and Political Change. Evanston: Northwestern Univ. Press.

Welfling, M. B. (1973) "Political institutionalization: comparative analyses of African party systems." Sage Professional Papers in Comparative Politics (No. 01-041) Beverly Hills and London: Sage Publications.

——— (1971) "Political institutionalization: the development of a concept and its empirical application to African party systems." Ph.D. dissertation, Northwestern University.

Zolberg, A. (1969) "Military rule and political development in tropical Africa: a preliminary report," in J. Van Doorn (ed.) Military Profession and Military Regimes. The Hague: Mouton.

——— (1968a) "Military intervention in the new states of tropical Africa: elements of comparative analysis," in H. Bienen (ed.) The Military Intervenes. New York: Russell Sage.

——— (1968b) "The structure of political conflict in the new states of tropical Africa." Amer. Pol. Sci. Rev. 62 (March): 70–87.

——— (1966) Creating Political Order: the Party-States of West Africa. Chicago: Rand McNally.

——— (1964) One-Party Government in the Ivory Coast. Princeton: Princeton Univ. Press.

Unit II

POLITICAL PARTICIPATION

Few aspects of African politics appear to have changed as much over the past two decades as the way African citizens in the aggregate participate in the political process. In large measure this change is the result of the decline of political parties as agencies of mobilization and the increase in the number of military regimes that displace civilian governments and minimize or control all forms of political participation. This change is also attributable to the changing purposes and goals of agencies of mobilization. Preindependence political parties focused on reform, then nationalist activities, and ultimately on independence; they organized the expanding electorates in accordance with these varying but primarily political goals. In the postindependence period—long after the independence elections determined which party would govern—political parties shifted much of their efforts toward shaping social and economic goals; sometimes this might have been in the pursuit of the free-enterprise system, as with the Parti Démocratique de Côte d'Ivoire (PDCI) in the Ivory Coast, or promotion of socialist principles, as by the *Chama cha Mapinduzi* (Party of the Revolution) (formerly TANU, the Tanganyika African National Union) in Tanzania. Their greatest successes, however, were achieved mainly in the early stages of the independence period and in the political rather than socioeconomic realm.

During the 1960s observers regarded African political parties as the most pervasive political organizations in African states, successfully "articulating" and "aggregating" interests and political demands, and channeling them into the institutions of government in the expectation (or hope!) that these demands would be converted by officials into the desired policy outcomes. Indeed, African political parties appeared to be more vital and popular than the formal structures of government. Organized and administered by Africans during the colonial era, they enjoyed longer histories of African control than the new formal structures of independence, and the average citizens were more familiar with their operations. Moreover, they were the conspicuous instruments of successful independence movements and were led by popular political figures who negotiated the transition from colonialism to independence. Consequently, there was a high level of public confidence in the capacity of political parties to transform rising expectations into realities. It was widely believed that these parties were not only fully representative of all their constituencies, but that the leaders

51

would continue to maintain the enthusiastic loyalty of the party's mass following.

There were, of course, other entities, such as trade unions, ethnic associations, and agricultural cooperatives, that participated in the mobilization process, but they were supplementary agencies during the nationalist period, not major ones, and they lacked the vitality and excitement, as well as the sheer numbers, that the parties could rally. While they were important as sources of significant support, they were primarily functional groups designed to serve specific economic or social purposes. To the extent that they represented or supported specific socioeconomic interests they were absorbed into the dominant political parties of the day. In any case, extraparty organizations rarely survived as independent centers of power in Africa because these systems are not sufficiently developed or stable to manage the consequences that flow from autonomous political behavior, especially if they have the appearance or potential for opposition. More recently, in some African states, voluntary or functional organizations that contribute to socioeconomic growth and do not appear to be a threat to the political stability of the state, or to the status quo, have emerged as significant political units, and in the future these may become important agencies of mobilization.

The early studies of African political parties during the colonial period were generally descriptive classifications of party organizations. In the 1950s investigators, such as Thomas Hodgkin, inquired how African parties differed among themselves in such matters as structure, membership, leadership, and goals.[1] Somewhat later, during the floodtide of the nationalist period—especially just before and immediately after independence—scholars shifted their attention to the dynamics of party formation and growth; it was in studies such as David E. Apter's *Gold Coast in Transition* (Princeton, 1955) that Max Weber's concept of "charismatic leadership" was first explored as an analytical tool for explaining political behavior.

Eventually, Africanists turned to studying the effects that particular types of parties and party systems have on their respective political communities. Early in the postindependence period almost all of the new African states were either one-party systems, or at least systems in which a single party dominated. Africanists directed much of their energies during this time to assessing the policy results that flow from systems with such minimal opposition. The questions asked most frequently were whether single-party or one-party dominant systems could be truly democratic, and whether they could mobilize political resources and modernize their societies more or less successfully. In due course many African states, especially those with strong personal leadership, began to recognize the hazards of limiting demand inputs and moved toward remedying the defects of one-party systems.

In time both observers and African politicians began to recognize that the effectiveness of political parties in Africa had been exaggerated. They were not as representative as they initially appeared, ethnicity and factionalism detracted from their unity, and their structures minimized the quality of their performance. With the passing of the first decade of independence, many political parties became mired in unresolved economic difficulties, individual incompetence or corruption, and paranoid reactions to nascent opposition. During the 1970s some writers concluded that the character of an African state's party system provided little or no explanation for the character of political, economic, or social change in that society.[2] It became more apparent that the reality of political control lay with state bureaucracies that were emerging as the most salient institutions within the typical African political system. Indeed, some political scientists began to refer to the African no-party state, wherein the bureaucracy controlled the distribution of political "rewards" without either reference or accountability to any other groups in society.

The debate over the nature of the party system in Africa resembles the efforts of the four blind men who attempted to describe an elephant. The varying analyses are products of different philosophical points of view and reflections on different points in time. In 1977 Irving Leonard Markovitz attributed the decline in African party systems in part to *"the loss of revolutionary momentum after the achievement of independence."*[3] On the other hand, in 1984 Ali Mazrui and Michael Tidy took notice of more recent developments in states such as Senegal, where multiparty systems were being restored, often for electoral purposes, and they took an optimistic view that this was a healthy trend toward increased and responsible participation.[4] A review of elections and party behavior since the beginning of the 1980s indicates a rejuvenation of party systems, suggesting that some form of popular participation may again become a significant part of the African political process as leaders and citizens seek more dynamic and representative ways to shape government policies.[5] This trend also reflects the awareness of Africa's founding fathers that the effectiveness of personalistic rule will decline with their passing. Thus they move to minimize the weaknesses inherent in depending on the mystique and charisma of one man by attempting to institutionalize the functions that political parties ordinarily serve.

Nevertheless, some African political leaders of one-party systems could not escape the consequences of their failure to preserve representative parties and to be accountable to their electorate. Their critics faulted them for political elitism, corruption, mismanagement, and apparent inability to cope with the pressing needs of economic development. But the critics could not replace the leaders because the political system ceased to allow for peaceful change or meaningful mass participation. Ultimately, these systems were overloaded with "demands," weakened by a decline in "supports," and dependent on coercion to make the structures function; consequently, many fell victim to the military forces on whom they depended. While the rash of military coups d'état in the late 1960s and early 1970s were surprising to many observers, in retrospect they were predictable outcomes of irresponsible political behavior.

Military regimes, however, did not quickly restore the democratic institutions or mass participation introduced at the time of independence; indeed, for many years, mass participation was eclipsed both as empirical reality and academic subject matter. By the early 1980s Crawford Young, a longtime observer and analyst of the African political scene, concluded that popular participation "has not been highly valued in most African states in the independent era, except in the ritualistic sense of mass turnouts for plebiscitary elections or presidential rallies."[6] At the same time, military regimes also encountered the same kinds of socioeconomic difficulties as their predecessor civilian regimes. Dependent on civilian administrators, many of whom were untrained to cope with political and economic issues, and cognizant that some form of political participation was essential to stability, military leaders either restored civilian rule through elections, as in Nigeria and Ghana, or civilianized military rule, as in Zaire. It was a case of learning that it is hard to live with widespread political participation, and also hard to live without it.

The articles we offer here to illustrate aspects of political participation are commentaries on African military hierarchies, alternative forms of participation, and the importance of popular participation for economic development in African societies. Samuel Decalo's article is a classical contribution to the extensive debate about the causes and effects of military governments; he finds that military cliques intervene more often for "over-riding preoccupation with personal and corporate aggrandizement" than for reasons related to modernization and socioeconomic change. Naomi Chazan's analysis of recent trends in popular participation speculates on the extent to which informal associational groups, such as ethnic or ascriptive ones, have been politicized and thereby transformed into pressure groups, which in turn revitalize political participation in African political systems. It remains to be seen whether these modernized forms of traditional pressures will have effects similar to the earlier forms of political participation that Samuel Huntington argued would result in "political decay." We conclude with Fred Hayward's rather different perspective, in which he argues the importance of political participation for the purpose of economic development. Although he says that mass participation is not a substitute for development, he focuses on the stimulating effect that participation can have on a nation's economic developmental efforts.

NOTES

1. Thomas Hodgkin, *African Political Parties* (London: Penguin Books, 1961).

2. See, for example, Roberta E. McKown and Robert E. Kauffman, "Party System as a Comparative Analytic Concept in African Politics," *Comparative Politics* 61, no. 1 (October 1973), 47–72.

3. Irving Leonard Markovitz, *Power and Class in Africa* (Englewood Cliffs, N.J.: Prentice-Hall, 1977), p. 299. Author's emphasis.

4. Ali A. Mazrui and Michael Tidy, *Nationalism and New States in Africa* (London: Heinemann, 1984), p. 291.

5. See, for example, Naomi Chazan, "African Voters at the Polls: A Re-examination of the Role of Elections in African Politics," *Journal of Commonwealth and Comparative Politics* 17, no. 2 (July 1979), 136–58.

6. Crawford Young, *Ideology and Development in Africa* (New Haven: Yale University Press, 1982), p. 319.

The New Politics of Participation in Tropical Africa

Naomi Chazan

Africa appears to be in the midst of a participation explosion. Since 1978, four countries—Upper Volta, Mali, Ghana, and Nigeria—have returned to civilian rule by electoral means. Niger is currently contemplating a similar transition. A number of states, notably Kenya and Somalia, have held elections in which key political personnel were changed through the ballot box.[1] In the fall of 1980, the Ivory Coast held the first competitive elections since independence. A few heretofore staunch single-party regimes have publicly considered prolonging bans on opposition politics. Senegal formally opted for a three-party system in 1976, and multiparty elections were held in the spring of 1978. More recently, Liberia entertained the possibility of permitting the Progressive Alliance of Liberia (PAL) to register as a political party.[2] When the activities of this new party were curtailed, the military intervened to overthrow the True Wing leadership, which had held sway in that country for over 100 years. In the past year, four governments were ousted (in Uganda, Equatorial Guinea, Chad, and the Central African Republic), in no small measure as a result of strong civilian resistance to the dictatorial and nonrepresentative regimes of Idi Amin, Francisco Macias Nguema, Felix Malloum, and Jean-Bedel Bokassa. And finally, in Zimbabwe the final withdrawal of colonial rule was effected through the ballot box. In short, to the untrained eye, the picture of African politics as nonparticipatory and closed to popular involvement is currently undergoing a significant change.

Is it, however, correct to assume that political participation was absent in the past decade and a half? Must one agree with Nelson Kasfir's generalization that "in most cases in post-independence Africa . . . the elimination of participatory structures has been so thorough"?[3] In what ways do current participatory politics differ from past endeavors? Is this participation more effective? For whom and why? The answers to these questions require a more systematic reappraisal of the nature of political participation in black Africa.

The purpose of this article is to look more closely at the units, bases, structures, aims, scope, and types of activity, and the impact of political participation in Africa during the past two decades in order to isolate those specific forms of participation operative in military regimes and one-party states. An effort will then be made to examine the reasons for the present resurgence of what appears to be open participatory politics in many parts of the continent.

This study contends that two distinct types of political participation have been apparent in postindependence Africa: formal and nonformal participation. While the possibility of engaging in formal participatory politics has varied drastically from country to country and from time to time, it is possible to demonstrate significant and steady increments in nonformal participatory efforts in recent years. The relationship between the two kinds of participation vacillates according to circumstances, but in general it may be suggested that the aims, scope, intensity, and impact of nonformal participation are augmented

From *Comparative Politics*, vol. 14, no. 2 (January 1982), 169–89. Copyright © 1982 by The City University of New York. By permission of the journal and the author.

as opportunities for legitimate political action decline. Moreover, an attempt will be made to show that, contrary to what seems superficially to be true, the political effects of informal participation are often much more direct than those of formal participatory mechanisms. Therefore, the present shift to formally sanctioned participatory politics may be seen both as an acknowledgement of participatory pressures and in no small measure as another means of political control by the state. Recent events, then, may best be viewed more as a multifaceted culmination of a variety of persistent participatory activities rather than merely as an indicator of an ephemeral liberalization of the political arena. The new trends in African politics are thus a reflection of the growing recognition of the centrality of voluntary group political participation in African political life.

FORMAL AND NONFORMAL PARTICIPATION

Within a few years of decolonization African states were in the throes of a noticeable process of what has been termed departicipation, or the decline of popular involvement in politics. The term *political participation* has itself been defined in different ways by a variety of observers. Some have used political participation to mean political acts.[4] Others have utilized "the term in a general sense to mean action which is directed at influencing (controlling, changing, supporting or sharing in) policy making and/or execution in a political structure."[5]

In this definition, the intent, and not the act itself, is viewed as the key to political participation. But other definitions abound. One key analyst of participation in Africa has stated that "to become involved in politics is to participate."[6] And two students of Nigerian politics have stated categorically that "many Nigerians took no part in politics at any level. Even though they might be 'mobilized' in Deutschian term on other scores, they did not even make the minimal participatory gesture of voting in an election."[7] For them, the political act,

especially of voting, constitutes the ultimate sign of political participation. Within the framework of this analysis, political participation will be used to encompass those political structures and actions whose purpose is to influence, or facilitate the influencing of, political decisions through the involvement of citizens in the political process.[8]

In these terms, it did seem appropriate to suggest that there was a lessening of the degree and extent of participation in the first few years after independence in Africa. Political opposition in many instances was curtailed and formal opposition parties disbanded. Single-party systems tried to develop political machines but in many instances deteriorated into weak instruments for curbing popular opinion. "An examination of political parties, the best-studied feature of the African scene, reveals such a wide gap between the organizational model from which the leaders derived their inspiration and their capacity to implement such schemes that the very use by observers of the word *party* to characterize such structures involves a dangerous reification."[9] What little political participation existed, so it seemed (with a few well-worn exceptions like Tanzania, Botswana, and The Gambia), was limited to ceremonial and symbolic acts geared to propping up weak and corrupt regimes. With the advent of the armed forces on the political scene in many African states, even these unspontaneous political gestures appeared to cease. The minimal opportunity for political involvement of the populace was, we are told, almost totally curtailed by this time.

Indeed, by the mid-1970s the process of departicipation was considered to be so complete that the relationship between participation and political development was viewed as being in need of drastic reassessment. The by then traditional view that participation is conducive to political development was assailed on all fronts.[10] The most systematic and measured counterthesis was presented by Samuel Huntington, who contended that the development of institutional capacity preceded political participation in the process of political development and that high rates of participation may severely threaten the fragile institutions of new states.[11] His position has since been echoed by key Africanists.[12] These arguments, though interesting in themselves, are not especially significant in this context: they are presented here merely as an indication of the high level of consensus that existed on the fact of departicipation.

The departicipation that did permeate African politics, however, was of a specific type. It consisted of a lack of formal voluntary participation in central government decisions and of an absence of appropriate channels for popular influence on regime policy. To label such formal impediments departicipation in the all-encompassing sense of the word is problematic on at least two grounds. On a superficial level, it confuses voluntary political participation with political participation in general. In many instances, during the years since African independence, manipulated political participation has continued to exist.[13] But second, and much more fundamental, the stress on the unavailability of formal participatory mechanisms tends to obscure the vital participatory processes that blossomed in the nonformal sector.

The propensity to ignore these usually subnational participatory patterns is an outcome of four key factors. First, most observers tend to correlate voting and elections with participatory politics without examining the amount of involvement and influence related to these acts. In Africa, as well as elsewhere, other modes and structures of participation are often more conducive to involving people in affecting their political environment. Second, many onlookers simply assumed that preparticipatory frameworks of the colonial period had coalesced in the dynamics of participation that had marked African politics during decolonization.[14] It was, however, unreasonable to presume that previous participatory trends would disappear entirely. Third, during the first decade of African independence, relatively few local political studies were carried out, and there was little opportunity to assess political dynamics beyond the center. This paucity was somewhat rectified in the early 1970s, and as a result, the notion of departicipation

underwent serious revision—if not in formal politics, at least in the informal system. And finally, small groups often but loosely connected to political affairs have only gradually undergone a process of politicization. It has taken a number of years for this pattern to evolve and for its main features to become discernible.

Nonformal participatory structures in Africa have continuously provided frameworks for interaction and community activity. Two main categories of structures are identifiable. The first consists of voluntary organizations of an interest-group type. A morass of such associations exists, ranging from trade unions to women's organizations, professional associations, associations of chiefs, youth and student groups, literary societies, religious societies, self-help groups, rotating credit associations, the military, sports clubs, and the like. These structures have in common the voluntary nature of their membership, specific common interests uniting their adherents, their fairly democratic nature of decision making, and the rotation of their leadership.[15] Voluntary organizations of the interest-group kind are generally located in or around urban centers (although they may be found in rural areas as well) and tend to have an ethnically cross-cutting composition. In this sense, these organizations are horizontally based associations linking people around specific interests or potential benefits.

The second type of association is ascriptive, or primary, in essence.[16] It includes ethnic associations, traditional political units,[17] kinship associations, *associations des originaires* in Francophone Africa, local improvement associations, and regional or home-town groupings. These groups have in common an ascriptive or delimited geographic definition of membership, an adherence to patterns of authority established by traditional or revised custom, a commitment to a primordial tie—be it ethnic, cultural, or geographic—and some perception of a commonality of goals and interests. Participation in these associations, and acceptance of their dictates, is nevertheless carried out on a voluntary basis, although membership is restricted by ascriptive means. Because of their localized nature, voluntary associations of the primary type are usually more homogenous ethnically than their interest-group counterparts. They are constructed on a vertical, solidarity basis.

These two main forms of association have in common a number of key characteristics. First, the base of political and social activity is clearly defined as the group (and not the individual).[18] Second, the type of activity promoted in these settings is usually of a voluntary, as opposed to manipulated, participatory kind.[19] And third, despite the multiplicity of such organizations, they all tend to be limited in their geographic scope. When extremely large organizations do exist, as in the case of some religious groups, practical decentralization appears to be the norm. These groups can hence best be understood as subnational or local in nature. As such, they differ markedly in scope from the admittedly state-wide focus of formal participation structures. The unit of analysis and of action of informal political structures varies, therefore, from that common in the formal sector.

The fundamental features of nonformal contexts of political participation in Africa are an outgrowth of traditional forms of political association. The group bases of African politics have been emphasized since the precolonial period. So too have the voluntary nature of these activities and the difficulties involved in manipulating group activities from above. The political culture of voluntarism and group action is hence deeply embedded in African tradition.[20]

In the colonial period, the dual form of these associations began to take shape. In part this phenomenon may be viewed as a continuation of existing social structures. In part it was an outgrowth of the new opportunities for mobility presented by the introduction of Western education and new modes of economic production. And, in part, the proliferation of voluntary associations during colonial times may be related to the constrictions placed on formal political activity by the colonial authorities.[21] At the time, primary organizations and voluntary groups proliferated on the social landscape and constituted prepolitical frameworks from which nationalist leaders came and upon which political support was drawn.[22] When formal party activity was launched, many of these early organizations became the cornerstones of party structures. During the phase of intense party activity, the political aspects of both interest-group and primary voluntary organization activity were incorporated in many instances into the party frameworks.

But though the contribution of voluntary organizations of both sorts to anticolonial activity has been recognized and well documented, the extent of their expansion since independence has not always been so carefully noted. The range of groups in any given political context today varies widely. In Ghana, literally hundreds of separate associations of these kinds have been recorded in the past five years alone.[23] Nigeria, too, has witnessed a plethora of voluntary groupings under military rule.[24] A steep rise in the formation of these groups has been traced in the Ivory Coast, and similar indications exist for Zaire, Zambia, Kenya, and Senegal.[25] Although the range and extent of this kind of organization has yet to be fully uncovered, it would not be an exaggeration to suggest that voluntary associations are by now a distinct type of participatory structure on the African political scene. This phenomenon includes not only bona fide voluntary associations of an interest or primary kind but also, within each category, a wide spectrum of specific types vacillating from street gangs to full-fledged urban guerrilla movements and from family networks to archaic movements with pseudoreligious overtones.[26] When taken together, voluntary groups can account for many fundamental (material and other) needs of the population. This may help to account for the fact that individuals tend to belong to a variety of voluntary groups of both the primary- and interest-group type.[27]

No less significant than the increase in the volume of informal organizations in recent years is the gradual transformation of their functions. From voluntary organizations concerned primarily with specific interests, local communal concerns, or both, these groups have become increasingly politicized over time. This transition can be traced through an analysis of the forms of activity of these associations.

The first consists of activities of the groups vis-à-vis their supporters. Voluntary associations are specifically concerned with catering to the needs of their members. Needs in this context may be defined broadly. However, ability to dispense goods and services is a decided asset. Horizontal associations engage actively in fund raising and make concerted efforts to provide welfare services for members. Class and ethnic associations are the initiators of self-improvement schemes and also engage in welfare activities. The strength of these associative networks grows in direct relationship to the resources they control and distribute.[28] One of the main reasons for the upsurge in the acceptance of traditional authorities in West Africa during the past decade has been that, on a comparative basis, in many instances they control a major proportion of nongovernmental resources.[29] By addressing themselves to the tangible needs of their members, voluntary organizations are in a position to respond to demands in a much more direct fashion than formal bodies.

This capability is further enhanced by the second form of activity of voluntary associations: that related to internal organizational participation. Voluntary associations provide small-scale settings for meaningful political participation in a context frequently devoid of possibilities for popular political action on the state level. Leadership of groups of this sort relies on popular legitimation. Succession to office is legal, and clear-cut mechanisms do exist for the transfer of power. In the various horizontal associations, constitutional guidelines provide for orderly changes in administration. Thus, such diverse associations as student groups, women's organizations, and self-help groups hold regular elections for the major offices in the association.[30] Traditional leadership and kinship positions are filled according to long-accepted rules, which in many instances provide for some popular participation. In both types of organization, turnovers in top leadership positions are a norm. These reciprocal relations between leaders and members have important implications for decision-making processes. At this level, decision making is consultative, at times collective, and real political activity takes place. It is sufficient to have attended a meeting of a chief-in-council in Ghana or of a women's association in Nigeria to appreciate the degree of substantive interchange that exists in these groups. In a very real sense, the nonformal sector provides frameworks in which people not only are involved, but also can influence decisions.

The most noticeable shift in organizational activities has occurred, however, in a third sphere: that connected to actions taken at the societal level (specifically at the governmental level) to further the position and claims of their particular membership. Leaders of voluntary organizations are expected to reflect specific constituencies and represent them. They have, therefore, increasingly taken on the role of purveyors of measurable public opinion. On a countrywide basis, voluntary organizations can and do present demands and attempt to influence decisions on matters of concern to them.

The purpose of these activities may be threefold. First, attempts may be made to influence specific policy decisions by making carefully delineated suggestions.[31] Such demands or reactions may vary from specific requests for feeder roads or freshwater wells to general proposals to improve the economy or combat inflation. Second, efforts may be made to affect the composition of the political leadership. For example, in June 1977, the Association of Recognized Professional Bodies in Ghana published a newsletter in which it called for a change of regime. "Fellow Ghanaians, you will remember that [at] a meeting held on 23 June 1977, the Association of Recognized Professional Bodies passed a Resolution in which it called upon the government of the Supreme Military Council to resign and hand over to a Presidential Commission because the Government has shown by various acts and omissions that it had become increasingly incompetent to govern this country."[32] And third, in more extreme cases, the aim of these activities may be to induce a fundamental, revolutionary change in the political system. This was most in evidence in the activities of student groups and trade unions in Ethiopia prior to the 1974 revolution but has also been apparent in other countries as well.[33]

Whatever the precise aims of these activities, their target has moved squarely to the political center. The political activities of voluntary organizations do take place within the state framework and attempt to influence state decisions. The type of pressures they exert is of a group, rather than an individual, nature. Because they rely on, depend on, and attempt to affect, national policies, their subnational standing is highlighted. The group strength that they control stems to a large extent from their success in achieving declared goals— in many cases, from their ability to extract concessions from the center. This ability depends, to no small degree, on the fact that the minimal societal task fulfilled by all interest and primary groups is one of monitoring the activities of the political center. Such an activity requires both constant scrutiny of events and the development of innovative means of information collection and communication. Along with high rates of utilization of the press and especially the radio, sophisticated informal networks for information exchange have been established.[34] In short, the image of the uninformed public in Africa that has been nurtured in the past bears little resemblance to the widely distributed political communication systems that actually exist in many African states.[35]

The increase in the scale of these activities has been accompanied, too, by a growing intensity of activity. The manner in which demands are forwarded may range from contacting individuals in power to lobbying or making overt petitions to government. In particular situations, when no responses to requests are forthcoming, violence may erupt at the instigation of the leadership of these associations. Ranging from strikes and demonstrations to incidents of mass violence, this form of societal activity of voluntary organizations has usually been utilized as a last resort when other options have been expended.[36] It is interesting to note that violent methods have been used by a variety of horizontal and vertical groups, including those of students, women, ethnic groups, trade unions, and various professional and parapolitical societies, both within and outside the boundaries of the state. The degree of violence tends to vary in relationship to the existence of mediating networks in the polity. Where such mediation exists, more legal types of activity appear to be the norm. In instances in which mediatory mechanisms have broken down, violent types of activities may occur.[37]

Thus, perceptible movement towards more focused, specifically political, variegated activities at once broader in scale, greater in volume, and higher in intensity has marked nonformal organizational functions since independence. The three forms of activity of informal groups are interconnected. The ability to provide for members' needs is related to bargaining power, which depends on internal support. Each type of activity includes different forms of participation, with the type of involvement in national politics mostly informal. On the internal level, participation remains meaningful, and the direct benefits of this participation are measurable.[38] It would seem, then, that the political functions of the nonformal sector can best be understood as providing sustenance on an immediate basis, and as bargaining, protesting, and resisting at the national level.

The rapid politicization of the informal associational arena since independence has transformed what were heretofore voluntary or interest organizations into veritable pressure groups. It is not that in the past individuals and groups abstained from exerting pressure, formally and informally, directly and indirectly, upon African governments, but that the incidence of continuous political involvement of these groups is on the rise, and that it often takes on the characteristics of direct confrontation with incumbent regimes.

The reasons underlying these participatory processes are sadly underresearched, and at this juncture it is possible to point to some preliminary explanations for the societal and internal participation of the nonformal sector in African politics. First, the increase in informal political participation can be attributed to governmental policies. The curtailment of participation in the formal sector, unless buttressed by the exercise of considerable effective force—a rarity on the African scene—tends to enhance the participatory value of structures of the voluntary type. In many cases, such groupings act as a substitute for party structures simply because no structural alternatives exist. Second, politicization may occur under these conditions also as a reaction to specific socioeconomic policies or processes. In instances where some resources are available, concerted pressure by groups may influence distribution patterns; where such resources are scarce, the intervention of groups is necessary to supply basic services. In recent years, the stimulus for this politicization may be the failure of governments to fulfill promises of socioeconomic development. "Great contrasts in political and socioeconomic opportunities for individuals and groups amidst a general condition of scarcity may stimulate new forms of political action."[39] The phenomenon may also be related to historical processes, and especially to the continuation and redefinition of notions of self-determination carried over from the period of decolonization.[40]

On a more fundamental structural level, the politicization of informal groups appears to be linked to the evolution of the new state structures. On the one hand, the focus on the government as the object of activity and pressure may be viewed as an acknowledgement of the resource functions and associated capabilities attached to the state mechanism. On the other hand, the development of autonomous, multifunctional nonformal groupings may be seen as an initial indication of the fragility and even breakdown of state operations. In both cases, the voluntary group format for political participation is utilized because of its familiarity, past utility, and general efficacy.

Although the explanations for the politicization of nonformal groups are still extremely rudimentary, it does seem that the type of regime and the level or pace of socioeconomic development are less significant than variables in policy, norms, and structures.[41] Moreover, the process of internal politicization appears to be a double-edged tool that may be used to react to certain measures or conditions or to assist in the adaptation to official lacunae in these spheres. In either eventuality, the voluntary, group-based form that these adjustments take closely relates to entrenched political culture modes prevalent throughout many parts of the continent.

Whether nonformal political action is of a protest or constructive type, there is little question that involvement in politics at the center is informal and indirect and that no hard evidence can be presented of inclusion in decision-making processes. Nevertheless, the weight of these actions in real terms cannot be underestimated. Unlike party political action, most informal political activity is instrumental rather than symbolic, effective as opposed to ineffective; and its outcomes are in some ways also beneficial.[42] These results are equivalent in the two broad types of responses to informal pressures: governments may accede to demands and hence produce immediately palpable results,[43] or they may reject or ignore demands and run the risk of creating the civic unrest that may eventually topple the entire regime. In these two instances, the time span in which effects are measured varies markedly. But in both cases the common denominator is some sense of political efficacy.[44] The type of outcome is dictated by government response. If requests are denied out of hand and not backed by extremely strong repressive measures (as in the case of Idi Amin's Uganda), what were heretofore diffuse and sporadic pressures from the nonformal sector undergo a process of entrenchment and consolidation that leads to widespread political discontent. The example of Ghana under Achaempong provides an archetype of this dynamic. Zaire in the latter part of the 1970s is another. In these and other instances, what is clear is that the impact of informal political participation on the political system tends to be much more direct than indirect.

The reasons for this either immediate or long-range influence of the informal polity are complex, although several major explanations may be proffered. First, in states where direct access to governmental organs is barred, few moderating structures, such as political parties, exist. In such a political environment, demands raised at the local level are transferred almost directly to the top. In places that have developed strong mediatory devices, these demands can be answered selectively and with despatch. In such cases, immediate benefits may be received. Kenya has developed such a patronage network in recent years.[45] So too have Senegal, the Ivory Coast, and to a certain extent Ghana and Nigeria.[46] In other countries, in which mediatory institutions are inherently weak or ineffective, the groundwork is laid for more fundamental political unrest. Such was the situation in Uganda and Chad at the close of the last decade. A second reason for the close impact of such actions is related to the nature of demands created in conditions of modernization. Although it was assumed by some observers that heightened participation would lead to an increase in demands, it now seems more likely that participation does not foster demands but rather that demands exist and participatory structures provide channels for their expression. Economic malaise, socioeconomic expectations, political wants—all are related to basic developmental conditions.[47] Since demands persist and find no outlet in formal institutions that may moderate them, when raised through nonformal networks they tend to take on more extreme overtones. The confrontation established in such a context yields direct political outcomes despite the specific decisions rendered in reponse to informal political actions. A third possible cause for this direct impact of informal structures may be found in the degree of autonomy of state leaders from either horizontal or solidarity groupings. Low autonomy of leaders points to high levels of interaction with existing groups and hence to a tendency to capitulate to persistent pressures. High autonomy of the national leaders stresses their isolation from political currents and provides a suitable background for generalized political unrest.[48] In cases of extremely high or extremely low autonomy, the center's leaders are thus particularly exposed to informal pressures. Finally, the independence of the non formal network from formal governmental institutions allows it to react more quickly to policy decisions and government actions. The lack of institutional brakes therefore makes the relationship between the formal and the informal polity much more direct.

The taxonomy of nonformal participation structures, aims, activities, forms of actions, functions, and impact has sought to underline the vibrancy and import of elaborate nongovernmental political mechanisms operative in contexts in which formal participatory channels either no longer exist or have been bereft of content. The informal participatory network that has developed and thrived in many African states during the second decade of independence sheds a different light on assessments of the nature and quality of participation in African politics. Although political involvement through these means is at best informal and indirect, the political influence of such efforts may be said to be both instrumental and direct.

The Formalization of Nonformal Participation

In view of these comments on nonformal participation, the manner and the meaning of recent moves to reintroduce formal participatory measures must be reviewed again. Virtually every African state, by the mid-1970s, was under immense participatory pressures from the informal sector. Reactions of regimes to these activities usually occurred in two stages. In the first phase, attempts were made to gain control over key voluntary structures. These efforts were concentrated on unifying and consolidating under government control trade unions, farmers, organizations, women's groups, and youth and student associations and on circumscribing other groups.[49] In some cases, governments tried to initiate the creation of regime-run voluntary associations. The establishment of "Operation Feed Yourself" in Ghana in 1973 is just one example of such measures,[50] although many other instances may be listed. In virtually all these cases, these rather weak governmental actions, at times interesting in themselves, could not stem the tide of demands emanating from informal groups. Hence the move to the second stage, in which the issue of the need to adjust the formal structures of participation was confronted more directly.

By the mid-1970s a number of key military regimes had announced their intention of returning their countries to civilian rule. The first proclamation was made by General Murtala Mohammed in early October 1975,[51] who appended a timetable to this declaration. The Nigerian example was then followed by Upper Volta, and, in July 1977, in a situation of economic chaos, Acheampong announced in a dawn broadcast that Ghana, too, was planning an orderly transition to civilian rule.[52] Mali followed suit a year later. At approximately the same time, Senegal instituted constitutional changes for a return to multiparty politics. In short, a process of opening up heretofore nonparticipatory systems had been launched.

Many reasons for these moves have been raised. Some have suggested that economic difficulties presaged the need for a regime change. Others have claimed that military withdrawal may be related to the corporate interests of the army, or to the disappearance of those conditions that led to the initial intervention.[53] But even if these factors could help to account for some cases of military overtures in the direction of civilian political control, these explanations do not contend with the fundamental issue of legitimacy, which confronted both civilian and military regimes in postindependence Africa. Faced with the common dilemma of demands for, and incidences of, increased participation, these authoritarian regimes, whether of a military or civilian character, had to consider ways of dealing with the problem. It is possible to distinguish three main reactions to the legitimacy crisis, each involving recognition of the question through adjustments in the formal machinery of participation.

The first reaction, by Senegal, the Ivory Coast, Upper Volta, Mali, Ghana under Acheampong (the Union Government concept), and earlier on by Zaire and Togo, consists of utilizing existing calls for participation to increase control of the popula-

tion by the state. This has involved, in the case of military regimes, the conscious civilianization of the military.[54] In civilian-run states a gesture towards multiparty politics has been made. Whatever the precise form through which formal participation is expanded, the key consideration remains the utilization of seemingly participatory devices to enhance governmental power. As a result, some kinds of elections have signaled the beginning of the new phase. In Senegal, the ideological division into three parties brought what were heretofore opposition elements into the formal system without affording political freedom to truly threatening groups.[55] In Zaire, Togo, or Mali, care was taken to curb participatory claims that deviated from the wishes of the regime. In short, while formal political participation is now sanctioned, the limitations placed on such activities are such that freely competitive participatory politics cannot be carried out. The first type of reaction to the crisis of legitimacy has been, consequently, to use participation in order to avoid the more negative repercussions of nonformal politics and to maneuver instrumental politics into more symbolic channels. The move to manipulate participation does not necessarily bring about the demise of voluntary participatory structures, which may continue to coexist with new forms. If recognition of this coexistence is manifest, then future conflict in the society may be reduced.[56] If, on the other hand, the explicit purpose of the control strategy is to displace informal structures, conflict between manipulated and voluntary participatory networks, as in Zaire, Togo, and Upper Volta, may ensue. These center-initiated changes in informal structures do, nevertheless, constitute a not insignificant change in what, up to recently, had been monolithic, closed systems.[57]

A second strategy to deal with pressures for participation has been to attempt overtly to repress them. Uganda under Amin, the Central African Republic during Emperor Bokassa's rule, Liberia in the final days of the Tolbert government, and Ghana in its last six months under Acheampong provide examples of this approach. The regime decision to withdraw from the legitimacy debate implies a willingness to apply force to curtail nonformal participation. The effectiveness of such a policy therefore rests on the repressive efficiency of the particular regime. In most instances, the structures of African governments are either too fragile to implement such measures or incapable of doing so because participatory political values have been integrated into the political culture. Such was the case in Ghana and Liberia, where the unsuccessful implementation of force resulted in heightened nonformal political action and consequently in the creation of a situation of political anomie. In both these instances, the instruments of force—the military—intervened to topple the regimes in question.

When repressive measures are successful in stemming the tide of nonformal political activity, as in Equatorial Guinea, the Central African Republic, and Uganda, such participation ceases within the boundaries of the state, and oppositions regroup in exile.[58] In these cases either court cabals, external intervention, or a combination of both are necessary to oust these coercive regimes.

The results of either effective or ineffective coercive methods to deal with the problem of legitimacy attest to the long-range counterproductiveness for the initiating regime of such a policy. Indeed, while the application of the use of force may bring about a temporary participation vacuum, it has been extremely difficult to sustain such a situation for a prolonged period because force cannot usually act as an ultimate substitute for legitimation.[59] In fact, the manner in which legitimacy problems are handled in this method tends to raise the value of the notion of participation in general. As the aftermath of the fall of Africa's dictators affirms, the result is the development of political participation as a means for power accumulation by different, already highly politicized segments of society. The function of the yet qualitatively undetermined political setting in the first postoverthrow stage is to allow for active participation often centered on the manipulation of force, and usually resting on existing social cleavages, in the for-

mulation of the nature of future government institutions.

The third reaction differs from the previous two extremes. Both in Nigeria and in Ghana under Akuffo, incumbent administrations have acknowledged demands for more participation and gone about creating the machinery for an orderly transfer of power to duly elected popular representatives. The emphasis is placed, in these cases, first on constitutional questions to safeguard fundamental rights and to devise appropriate institutions, and then on party organization and electoral procedures.[60] The change of government is effected through elections. In both these cases, the military withdrew from the political arena according to plan, leaving behind a multiparty competitive and participatory system. In this type of reaction, participation is viewed both symbolically and instrumentally. Participatory organs have the function not only of aggregating, but also of moderating and directing political demands. At least in the first posttransfer stage, then, some norm for legalized popular political interaction based on the merger of nonformal and formal structures is laid down.

The three types of responses to pressures for participation in Africa apparent in recent years differ in their approach to the problem of legitimacy and in their understanding of the nature of participation. In the first type of reaction, participation is to be controlled and steered toward more symbolic modes. In the second type of reaction, demands are ignored and participation provides the overt justification (but not the mechanism) for removing unwanted regimes. In the third response, incumbent regimes acquiesce to the need for legitimacy and promote orderly frameworks and procedures for popular participation.[61] The amount of actual political change that takes place therefore also varies. In the first case, there is a remarkable degree of political continuity; in the second, there is a clear break with past regimes; and in the third, new governments are created but accommodation with previous regimes is evident. The extent of administration change is related to who makes the decision to open up formal political participation. When the decision comes from the government, some degree of continuity is assured. When pressures from below force the demise of a ruling group, a departure from the past seems almost inevitable. In the long run, though, stability hinges on the extent to which nonformal structures are accommodated within the formal system: when some adjustments are made in this regard, stability is possible; when nonformal networks are displaced or repressed, stability is threatened.

Despite the differences in the functions of participation and the manner in which participation is introduced into the formal political arena, all three responses have in common an acknowledgement of the fact that governments cannot remain in power indefinitely unless the question of popular participation in the political system is tackled directly. The absence of outlets for participation creates a vacuum in the structures of political communication that, if not backed by sheer terrorism, gives rise to nonformal participatory organs that constitute a more direct threat to the legitimacy of the regime. The solution to these processes is found first in the creation of frameworks for participation that, while they may differ in the degree of political freedom they permit, all rely on the state level as the basic unit for action.

In the nonrepressive solutions, the structure of participation, the political party, is also similar. In most instances, the utilization of the political party gives undue advantage to the government-backed party or to previously outlawed parties that reform with alacrity when the ban on formal activity is lifted. The result is that formal participation takes place in structures that are familiar from the period of decolonization and early independence. In Ghana, this has meant the re-creation of the old Convention People's party (CPP), the People's party (PP), and even the United Gold Coast Convention.[62] In Nigeria, in spite of vigorous attempts to avoid the resurgence of factional politics, the two surviving leaders of political parties at independence, Azikiwe and Awolowo, were prominent among the main contenders for the presidency. In the Central African Republic, the former president, David Dacko, was able to fill quickly the void resulting from the demise of Bokassa. Former parties maintain an organizational base that can be easily revived when the opportunity to do so is given. As a result, especially when key leaders are still active, these revived old parties have a head start over newly formed groups that lack the internal cohesion of older agglomerations. The uneasy stigma of overpredictability attached to party activity in these new conditions is problematic on two counts: it does not augur well for vibrant participatory politics, and it does not relate directly to some groups in the nonformal sector, which continue to subsist and operate even in the new participatory setting.[63] These problems are particularly magnified in instances when military regimes create their own parties and undergo a process of civilianization.

Not only are the units and structures attached to the nonrepressive responses similar; so too are their forms of activity. The notion of participation through the formal mechanism of elections is well entrenched in the new regimes. The utilization of the ballot box, although natural and superficially democratic, is nevertheless problematic. Unlike nonformal politics, elections are a time-bound and spaced-out type of activity that essentially act as a brake on constant participation. The suspicion attached by many Africans to the ballot box was highlighted by the high proportion of active abstentions in recent elections. Abstentions here are a sign not of indifference, but rather of distaste for the choices presented and the means available for affecting decisions.[64] The type of activity, then, that is utilized as the mark of participation holds forth many more obstacles for direct influence than those of the nonformal sphere.

The actual impacts of the various new forms of participation now being implemented do, however, differ. In those instances in which participation is utilized as a way of popular control, the influence of participatory mechanisms is curtailed almost a priori. In Upper Volta during the civilian interregnum, or in Mali, or Zaire—even in Senegal—the result is the creation of a single-party dominant system with varying degrees of participation. This type of system fosters continued activity in the nonformal sector, which may be attenuated periodically by incorporating problematic elements into the ruling party.[65] In the opposite case, where oppressive regimes were removed, participation per se becomes a justification for virtually any kind of political action. In Uganda in particular, but also in the Central African Republic, the aftermath of the demise of the previous leadership has severely weakened governmental institutions and permitted such heavy competition and, in fact, conflict through the almost total politicization of the nonformal sector that the immediate prognosis for a modicum of political order is not particularly promising. In between these two extremes of institutionalization through symbolic participation and participation as a substitute for institutionalization lies the third possible outcome: that which attempts to use participation and institutionalization as mutually reinforcing and complementary elements in political development.[66] The vision of participation is a constructive one that rests on the creation of a multiparty competitive system backed by central institutions that are continuously bolstered by constant, albeit indirect, participation. Although this mode of participation has not been particularly stable in Africa in the past, the fact that it is being revived today after a hiatus of close to fifteen years is indicative of the importance attached to linking participation and institutionalization in a meaningful manner.[67] The successful implementation of such formal participatory devices precludes political pressures from the nonformal sphere and relegates such activities to the articulation of specific interests of a basically nonpolitical nature.

By no means of a uniform order, the formal participatory measures now being taken in different African states vary considerably in their approach to the concept of participation, in the manner in which such participation is effected, and in the consequent relationship of formal and non-formal structures in the new arrangement. The outcomes of these different approaches are qualitatively distinct, and each approach has built-in difficulties related not only to problems of institutionalization but also to questions of the nature of continued nonformal political action. Despite these variations, the new politics of participation, because of its formal involvement and indirect impact, differs substantially from nonformal patterns apparent in recent years. "The opportunity for popular participation, even if controlled, channeled, manipulated and under coopted leadership, makes such regimes different."[68] The range in the extent of control and participation, in attitudes and results, has been sketched briefly in order to highlight some basic elements of the emerging political dynamic in African states.

Conclusion

This analysis has focused on the examination of recent trends in patterns of political participation in Africa. An attempt was made to show that group-based, voluntary political participation has been an integral part of African politics for many years. This type of participation has been conducted in both formal and nonformal frameworks. During the first decade of African independence, nonformal frameworks became increasingly politicized, and their political impact grew. In the past few years, crises of legitimacy emanating from the growth of nonformal politics have forced incumbent regimes to seek methods of co-opting participatory pressures to further regime goals. From here the distinctive features attached to each type of participation in the past became apparent: nonformal participation has permitted only indirect group involvement, but because it is of an autonomous nature its effects on politics have been more immediately palpable. On the other hand, formal participation has usually allowed direct, individual involvement. However, because it is within the domain of the political system and therefore dependent upon its rules and regulations, its impact on public decisions has ultimately been more indirect than its non-formal counterpart. These distinctions are by no means inviolable, and they may vary depending upon the relationship between formal and nonformal political frameworks in any given setting. Formal structures may repress, displace, coexist, or merge with nonformal ones. In each instance, the implications for conflict regulation differ. The key point remains that of the centrality of voluntary, group-based participation in African political behavior. The current transition to formal participation, be it as a means of controlling popular pressures, as a consequence of the successful application of such pressures, or as an acknowledgement of their existence, should be viewed as an effort to reformulate relationships between the formal and nonformal sectors. In this light, these attempts constitute a departure from previous patterns current in African politics.

The precise significance of this new dynamic remains clouded. The fact that innovative processes have been set in motion is important in itself. But whether the weaknesses inherent in early formal participatory mechanisms can be overcome and new forms and norms of participation can be established is still open to question. What does emerge in this analysis is the vitality of political participation in contemporary African politics. The ability of the new politics of participation to balance formal and nonformal pressures and to link participation meaningfully with the processes of institutionalization may permit the closer alignment of the political and social spheres in African countries.[69] Such a coming together may yet presage a positive break with the familiar spiral of weak authoritarian regimes and military governments that has come to characterize the code of African politics.

NOTES

The author would like to acknowledge the assistance of the Harry S. Truman Research Institute of the Hebrew University of Jerusalem for the facilities that made research for this paper possible.

1. For a more detailed discussion see N. Chazan, "African Voters at the Polls: A Re-examination of the Role of Elections in African Politics," The Journal of Commonwealth and Comparative Politics 17, 2 (July 1979): 136–158.

2. See West Africa, no. 3255 (3 December 1979): 2219. The new party planned to call itself the Progressive People's Party.

3. Nelson Kasfir, "Departicipation and Political Development in Black African Politics," Studies in Comparative International Development 9, 3 (Fall 1974): 8.

4. Lester W. Milbraith, Political Participation (Chicago: Rand McNally, 1965), p. 13 and elsewhere. More recently this association has been made by Samuel P. Huntington and Joan M. Nelson, No Easy Choice: Political Participation in Developing Countries (Cambridge: Harvard University Press, 1976), p. 4.

5. Fred M. Hayward, "Political Participation and its Role in Development: Some Observations Drawn from the African Context," The Journal of Developing Areas 7, 4 (July 1973): 594.

6. Kasfir, "Departicipation and Political Development," p. 4.

7. K.W.J. Post and Michael Vickers, Structure and Conflict in Nigeria, 1960–1966 (London: Heinemann, 1973), p. 48.

8. In this definition there is some deviation from acceptable theory in that intent is seen as an integral part of participation and that politics may refer to levels other than the state. See Huntington and Nelson, No Easy Choice, p. 6; and Sidney Verba, Norman H. Nie, and Jae-on Kim, Participation and Political Equality (London: Cambridge University Press, 1978), pp. 46–48 and passim.

9. Aristide Zolberg, "The Structure of Political Conflict in the New States of Tropical Africa," American Political Science Review 62, 1 (1967): p. 72.

10. Upholders of this view include Myron Weiner, "Political Participation: Crises of the Political Process," in Crises and Sequences in Political Development, ed. Leonard Binder (Princeton: Princeton University Press, 1976) and Stein Rokkan et al., Citizens, Elections, Parties: Approaches to the Comparative Study of the Process of Development (New York: D. McKay, 1970).

11. Samuel Huntington, Political Order in Changing Societies (New Haven: Yale University Press, 1968).

12. Nelson Kasfir, Getting People Out of Politics: Ethnicity and Participation in Africa with a Case Study of Uganda (Berkeley: University of California Press, 1975).

13. Argument on this question abounds. Huntington and Nelson, No Easy Choice, pp. 7–10, question the exclusion of mobilized participation as propounded by Weiner, "Political Participation," p. 164 and by Norman H. Nie and Sidney Verba, "Political Participation," in Handbook of Political Science, ed. Fred Greenstein and

Nelson Polsby (Reading: Addison-Wesley, 1975), vol. III, p. 2.

14. Richard L. Sklar, *Nigerian Political Parties* (Princeton: Princeton University Press, 1963), pp. 503–504, stresses this point for Nigeria. Although Karl Deutsch and others have pointed to the centrality of voluntary organizations as pre-participatory networks, they did not delve into their structure after the establishment of formal participatory organs.

15. Kenneth Little, *West African Urbanization: A Study of Voluntary Associations in Social Change* (Cambridge: Cambridge University Press, 1967).

16. Margaret Peil, *Nigerian Politics: The People's View* (London: Cassel, 1976), p. 162.

17. These should be distinguished carefully from associations of chiefs, which are interest groups in the previously mentioned sense.

18. The significance of group-based political participation is highlighted in Verba et al., *Participation and Political Equality*, p. 18 and passim.

19. This distinction is preferred over the autonomous versus mobilized dichotomy drawn by Huntington and Nelson, *No Easy Choice*, p. 7.

20. Most recently this point was forcefully made by Adda Bozeman, *Conflict in Africa* (Princeton: Princeton University Press, 1976).

21. For good descriptions of voluntary associations in the colonial period see I. Wallerstein, "Voluntary Associations," in *Political Parties and National Integration in Tropical Africa*, ed. James Coleman and Carl Rosberg (Berkeley: University of California Press, 1965); I. Wallerstein, *The Road to Independence: Ghana and the Ivory Coast* (The Hague: Mouton, 1964); Yaw Twumasi, "Prelude to the Rise of Mass Nationalism in Ghana, 1920–49: Nationalist and Voluntary Associations," *Ghana Social Science Journal* 3, 1 (May 1976): 35–46; and Thomas Hodgkin, *Nationalism in Colonial Africa* (New York: New York University Press, 1957).

22. Wallerstein, "Voluntary Association," details the political functions of these groups, and also their traditional, transitional, and modern nature.

23. Robert Vineberg, "The 1979 Elections in Ghana" (mimeo) (Jersualem: Harry S. Truman Research Institute, 1979), presents the most extensive list.

24. Peil, *Nigerian Politics*, pp. 162–168, describes these groups with great perspicacity. Also see Verba et al., *Participation and Political Equality*, p. 101.

25. Unfortunately there is not even one volume on pressure groups in Africa. But cumulative evidence does exist. See Michael Cohen, *Urban Policy and Political Conflict in Africa: A Study of the Ivory Coast* (Chicago: University of Chicago Press, 1974) and Claude Salem, "Pluralism in the Ivory Coast: Political Attitudes and Socialization of School-Leavers in a One-Party State," Ph.D. Dissertation, Department of Political Science, University of California, Los Angeles, 1974. A fair amount of work has been done on students. See John Hanna, ed., *Students and Politics in Africa* (New York, 1975).

26. For a fictionalized version of street gangs see Cameroun Duodu, *The Gab Boys* (London: Fontemu Books, 1969). On archaic movements: John R. McLane, "Archaic Movements and Revolution in South Vietnam," in *National Liberation: Revolutions in the Third World*, ed. Norman Miller and Roderick Aya (New York: Free Press, 1971), pp. 68–101.

27. The idea of multiple membership is highlighted in Peil, *Nigerian Politics*.

28. The dynamics of these exchanges are detailed in N. Chazan, "The Political System and the Informal Polity: Patterns of Elite Formation and Leadership Recruitment in Ghana and Nigeria," Harry S. Truman Institute *Occasional Paper*, Jerusalem; 1980.

29. Peter Osei Kwame, "The Future of Chiefs in Ghana," *West Africa* 26 June and 3 July 1978. Also Peil, *Nigerian Politics*, p. 154; Opeyemi Ola, "Traditional Political Systems in a Modernizing Nigeria," *Presence Africaine*, no. 96 (1975): 641–692.

30. The growing literature on women's associations provides a useful case study. See Kenneth Little, *African Women in the Towns* (London: Cambridge University Press, 1973).

31. Donald Rothchild, "Comparative Public Demand and Expectation Patterns: The Ghana Experience," *African Studies Review* 22, 1 (April 1979): 127–148.

32. Association of Recognized Professional Bodies, *News Bulletin* 1, 1 (1977): 1 (mimeo).

33. M. Ottaway, "Social Classes and Corporate Interests in the Ethiopian Revolution," *Journal of Modern African Studies* 14, 3 (1976): 469–486. This is also apparent in Zaire: G. Muhumi, "Mobutu and the Class Struggle in Zaire," *Review of African Political Economy* 5 (1976).

34. In the Ivory Coast, this is called Radio Treichville. Other forms of "bush telegraph" have been established elsewhere.

35. Fred M. Hayward, "A Reassessment of Conventional Wisdom about the Informed Public: National Political Information in Ghana," *American Political Science Review* 70, 2 (1976): 433–451. This position has since been echoed by many.

36. Peil documents violence in Nigeria, *Nigerian Politics*, pp. 168–178. Huntington and Nelson, *No Easy Choice*, p. 13, also see violence as a form of participation. The typology of Verba and Kim, *Participation and Political Equality*, is insufficiently developed to account for the many types of nonformal activity outlined herein.

37. Ibid., pp. 53–55 discuss patronage networks and participation.
38. This thesis is elaborated in Hayward, "Political Participation."
39. Cohen, *Urban Policy and Political Conflict*, p. 3.
40. See Dov Ronen, *The Quest for Self-Determination* (New Haven: Yale University Press, 1979).
41. This stands in contrast to thrust of Huntington and Nelson, *No Easy Choice*, p. 43 and elsewhere. There appears to be no direct correlation between levels of modernization and intensity of nonformal participation.
42. See Murray Edelman, *Politics as Symbolic Action* (Chicago: Markham Press, 1971).
43. Concessions of this sort on a small scale are discussed in Michael Cohen, *Urban Policy and Political Conflict*.
44. Peil, *Nigerian Politics*, pp. 139–155. This point is also stressed in N. Chazan, "Political Culture and Socialization to Politics: A Ghanaian Case," *Review of Politics* 40, 1 (1978): 3–31.
45. Mordechai Tomarkin, "The Roots of Political Stability in Kenya," *African Affairs* 77, 308 (July 1978): 297–321.
46. Rene Lemarchand, "Political Exchange, Clientilism and Development in Tropical Africa," *Cultures et Développement* 4, 3 (1972): 483–517. Also highlighted in Robert Price, "Politics and Culture in Contemporary Ghana: The Big-Man Small-Boy Syndrome," *Journal of African Studies* 1, 2 (1974): 173–204.
47. See Fred M. Hayward, "Perceptions of Well-Being in Ghana: 1970 and 1975," *African Studies Review* 22, 1 (April 1979): 109–126. Also see his "Political Participation."
48. This point is developed in N. Chazan, "The Africanization of Political Change: Some Aspects of the Dynamics of Political Cultures in Ghana and Nigeria," *African Studies Review* 21, 2 (September 1978): 15–38.
49. Nkrumah's attempts in this direction are notable. His efforts in the youth sphere are documented in N. Chazan, "The Manipulation of Youth Politics in Ghana and the Ivory Coast," *Genève-Afrique* 15, 2 (1976): 38–63.
50. See I.K. Acheampong, "Towards a Brighter Future" (Accra: Information Services Department, 1973), p. 10.
51. *Le Monde*, 4 October 1975.
52. *West Africa*, no. 3131 (11 July 1977), p. 1394. The return to civilian rule in Upper Volta lasted only until the military coup of November 1980.
53. Claude Welch, "Cincinnatus in Africa: The Possibility of Military Withdrawal from Politics," in *The State of the Nations*, ed. Michael Lofchie (Berkeley: University of California Press, 1971), pp. 215–237.
54. Claude Welch, "The Dilemmas of Military Withdrawal from Politics: Some Considerations from Tropical Africa," *African Studies Review* 18, 1 (1974): 213–228.
55. Rita O'Brien, *The Political Economy of Underdevelopment: Dependence In Senegal* (New York: Sage, 1980). Donald Cruise O'Brien, "Multi-Party Politics in Senegal," paper presented at Institute of Commonwealth Studies, 2 February 1976 (mimeo), esp. p. 3.
56. The role of interest groups as mitigators of conflict is highlighted in Cohen, *Urban Policy and Political Conflict*, pp. 208–228.
57. See Ruth Berins Collier's excellent analysis: "Parties, Coups, and Authoritarian Rule: Patterns of Political Change in Tropical Africa," *Comparative Political Studies* 11, 1 (April 1978): 62–93.
58. The first twenty years of independence in Guinea under Sekou-Touré may provide another example.
59. The introduction of force to maintain power increases the probability of the exercise of countervailing force. See Zolberg, "The Structure of Political Conflict."
60. For a summary of literature see Michael Afolabi, *Nigeria in Transition 1978–1979: An Annotated Bibliography* (Zaria: Department of Library Science, Ahmadu Bello University, 1980). For Ghana, Vineberg, "The 1979 Elections in Ghana," describes this process in detail. Elements of the procedures are also discussed in Ian Campbell, "Military Withdrawal Debate in Nigeria: The Prelude to the 1975 Coup," *West African Journal of Sociology and Political Science* 1, 3 (1978): 316–337.
61. L.O. Dare, "Nigerian Military Government and the Quest for Legitimacy, January 1966–July 1975," *Nigerian Journal of Economic and Social Studies* 18, 2 (1977), pp. 32–54. Also see Henry Bienen, "Military Rule and Political Process: Nigerian Examples," *Comparative Politics* 10, 2 (1978): 206–225.
62. See Dennis Austin, *Politics in Ghana, 1946–1960* (London: Oxford University Press, 1964), for a discussion of early parties, and Dennis Austin and Robin Luckham, eds., *Politicians and Soldiers in Ghana* (London: Frank Cass, 1976), for their revival in the 1969 elections.
63. This point stressed by Vineberg, "The 1979 Elections in Ghana."
64. N. Chazan and N. LeVine, "Politics in a 'Non-Political' System: The March 30, 1978 Referendum in Ghana," *African Studies Review* 22, 1 (April 1979): 177–205.
65. See Henry Bienen, *Kenya: The Politics of Participation and Control* (Princeton: Princeton University Press, 1974).
66. My thanks to Richard L. Sklar for his clarification of this and other points developed in this paper.

67. Both Kasfir, in "Departicipation and Political Development," and Hayward, in "Political Participation," stress this point.

68. J. Linz, "Notes Towards a Typology of Authoritarian Regimes," paper presented at the American Political Studies Association, Washington, D.C. (1972), p. 31, as quoted in Collier, "Parties, Coups, and Authoritarian Rule," pp. 63–64.

69. John Dunn, "Politics in Asunafo," in Austin and Luckham, *Politicians and Soldiers in Ghana*.

Praetorianism, Corporate Grievances, and Idiosyncratic Factors in African Military Hierarchies

Samuel Decalo

In the past several years there has been a proliferation of studies on coups d'état in Africa and the political role of African military structures. Armies have been analyzed in terms of their social and ethnic composition, training, ideology, and socializing influences. Intense debate has focused on the reasons for their intervention in the political arena. Simple and complex typologies of civil-military relations and of military coups have been constructed; both hard and soft statistical data has been marshalled and subjected to factor and regression analysis, in order to validate general or middle-range theories of military intervention. And the officer corps' performance once in power has been examined in order to generate insights into its propensity to serve as a modernizing or development agent.

With over one-third of the continent ruled at any particular moment by military elements or by military-civil coalitions, the previously fashionable discourse on the merits of unipartyism, mass vis-à-vis elite parties, pan-Africanism and African socialism in all its varieties has largely petered out, clearing the ground for the handful of qualitatively superior in-depth empirical case studies. This may also be the case with the current intense interest in African military hierarchies, for much of the contemporary outpouring takes place

From *Journal of African Studies*, vol. 2, no. 2 (Summer 1975), 247–73, by permission of the journal, a publication of the Helen Dwight Reid Educational Foundation.

within a theoretical vacuum filled with mutually contradictory hypotheses, neither tested operationally nor based on solid empirical data. Military intervention is practically always defined a priori as a dependent variable, the focus shifting to the more easily analyzable systemic parameters for the "detection" of the particular catalysts that evoked the intrusion in the political realm. This has inevitably resulted in a gross reification of African armies, and an uncritical acceptance of formal organization theory as the explanatory framework for military behavior, and of military-stated motives for their interventions—all faults associated with the previous era's uncritical examination of the party-states in West Africa. Of equal importance has been the general neglect of the idiosyncratic factor, the "personal element," which plays such an important role in syncretic and unstructured societies, and which is of paramount importance for an understanding of military upheavals.

The purpose of this article is to shift attention away from the discipline's fixation upon the systemic weaknesses of African states or the alleged organizational features of African armies as reasons for coups, to the internal dynamics of African military hierarchies, their officers cliques and the corporate and personalist ambitions therein. It is essentially within this domain that the core motivations for military upheavals reside, with the fragmented societal power context merely allowing, even encouraging, their unfettered expression.[1]

MILITARY INTERVENTIONS: MOTIVES AND RATIONALIZATIONS

There are essentially two schools of thought regarding the causes of military takeovers in developing nations and in Africa in particular. The first tends to stress societal and structural weaknesses—the institutional fragility, systemic weaknesses and low levels of political culture of new states—which act as a sort of magnet, pulling the armed forces into the power and legitimacy vacuum. Typical of this approach is the work of Samuel Huntington, who argues that "the most important causes of military intervention in politics are not military but political and reflect not the social and organizational characteristics of the military establishment but the political and institutional structure of society."[2] The second interpretation of military coups, which Huntington also at one time adopted,[3] relies on formal organization theory in attibuting to African military hierarchies certain characteristics of professionalism, nationalism, cohesion and austerity which impel them to move into the political arena and rescue the state from the grip of corrupt and self-seeking political elites.

In a sense both conceptualizations are really two sides of the same coin and when the analytic gunsights are trained at a *specific* coup situation, the distinctions between the approaches tend to become blurred. There is hence a general consensus among most scholars about a broad syndrome of destabilizing strains and stresses in African societies that provoke the armed forces to overthrow the civilian regime in power. Military intervention in the political realm is viewed as a function of chronic systemic disequilibrium and alleged professional characteristics of armies, the precise dimensions of which as well as its specific ingredients and "boiling point" may differ from country to country.[4]

The disequilibrium may be primarily economic in nature.[5] The army may feel compelled to intervene in order to implement unpopular austerity policies that political elites have been unable or unwilling to undertake, or to correct politically or ideologically inspired fiscal imbalances that have led the economy to the brink of collapse. Instability may also be the highly disruptive consequence of overly ambitious social mobilization drives that unleash social demands and civic unrest as populations are torn from traditional moorings.[6] Politicization of ethnic cleavages and intra-elite strife in governmental structures may result in political and administrative paralysis that attracts the mediating efforts of armed forces.[7] Corruption, nepotism, governmental inefficiency and tribal favoritism may also tip the legitimacy pendulum away from discredited civilian elites to allegedly apolitical and untainted military hierarchies that are trusted to provide competent national leadership.[8] Moreover, viewed as corporate structures armies may lash out at regimes that attempt to politicize them, tamper with established lines of command or threaten otherwise the military's corporate autonomy.[9] And recently civil-military tensions have been conceptually linked to the burgeoning field of the social psychology of political violence, although no Africanist has fully pursued this line of analysis.[10]

A wide variety of other factors that allegedly draw armed forces into the political scene can be culled from the extensive literature that has developed in this field.[11] Yet the basic contention that coups occur as a result of systemic deficiencies as professional armies move in to prevent further aggravation in socioeconomic and political conditions grossly lacks in explanatory value or utility, much as it might be appealing to many to romanticize the "man on horseback" (or command car) as the heroic savior of nations from rapacious politicians. Such explanations are usually based upon highly contentious and inapplicable theoretical assumptions about African armies, or generalizations transferred from other geographical areas, and inadequate empirical examination of data to the contrary. Their core analytic flaw is the confusion of the very real and existing systemic tensions in African states which are, however, the universal backdrop of all political life in the continent, with other factors, lodged in the internal dynamics of the officer corps and which are often the prime reasons for a military upheaval. It is both too simplistic as well as empirically erroneous to relegate coups in Africa to the status of a dependent variable, a function of political weaknesses and structural fragility of African states and failings of African civilian elites.

On the theoretical level the positive image of African militaries that underlies idealizations of motives for military coups is implicitly or explicitly anchored in formal organization theory that is largely inapplicable to Africa. Briefly stated, African armies and officer corps are seen as acquiring certain specific characteristics consequent to the corporate requirements of their skills and their training in staff colleges abroad. They are molded into cohesive, nontribal, disciplined and national units; as a result of their command of sophisticated weaponry and their membership in a complex hierarchical structure, African armies are viewed as the most modern, Westernized and efficient organizations in their societies and the repositories of bureaucratic and managerial skills. In like manner they internalize in metropolitan academies the values of noninterference in political matters and the supremacy of civilian over military authority. Allegiance to the latter values is severely tested upon their return home by the spectacle of corruption, mismanagement of resources and intra-elite strife, and is finally shattered as the austere, nationalist and apolitical officer corps can no longer tolerate the crass abuses of power and intervene to correct the imbalances and create a new political order.

The body of empirical evidence weighs heavily, however, to the contrary. African armies are rarely cohesive, nontribal, westernized or even complex organizational structures. Near-hierarchical command charts camouflage very intense fissiparous cleavages in the armed forces, an extension of wider societal chasms shared by most African states. Differential recruitment and promotion patterns cause endemic tensions which reinforce other lines of division based on rank, age, tribe and education. And these have barely been papered over by flimsy and brief training programs that metropolitan countries set up in the last few years of colonial rule. Many of the current top officers were rapidly promoted from the ranks or the officer hierarchy at independence in the drive to achieve Africanization of army commands. Their relative youth and spotty formal education, coupled with the limited number of senior positions in Africa's minuscule armies, has created grave promotion bottlenecks for junior officers anxious to imitate the meteoric rise of the preceding generation of officers.

Personal animosities and ambitions have also been rife in the officer corps. And whatever fragile organizational unity African armies may have originally possessed has usually been rapidly eroded by the politicization of their internal cleavages after independence and the sharpening of the internal personal jealousies and power struggles. Indeed, many African armies bear little resemblance to the modern complex organizational model, being more a coterie of distinct armed camps owing primary clientelist allegiance to a handful of mutually competitive officers of different ranks and seething with a variety of corporate, ethnic and personal gripes.[12] One direct corollary of this is that when the military assumes political power it frequently is not able to provide a more efficient, nationally oriented and stable administration, not only consequent to the immensity of the systemic loads it assumes, but also as a result of its internal multifractured cleavages and competitions. In instances where the latter are especially intense, military regimes may devote considerably more time and more effort in consolidating and warding off alternate challenges to their authority than in providing the country with purposeful leadership.[13]

Studies of civil-military relations in Africa have also practically always yielded to the temptation to accept officially declared reasons for military takeovers as valid, especially since the toppled civilian regime has only obviously been manifesting the weaknesses for which it has been attacked. Consequently, other covert motivations for army coups have not been detected or given sufficient weight. Motives are rarely simple, and proper assessment of their relative weight or importance in a particular coup situation may be extremely difficult.

Still, detailed empirical analysis and field-work can reveal a variety of factors of much greater significance for an understanding of a military upheaval than the essentially static assumptions that clutter the literature.

Widespread government corruption is a case in point: this has been the most commonly cited complaint of army leaders moving against their civilian counterparts in political office. Yet as Dennis Austin has remarked, the charge of corruption is usually used ex post facto to justify intervention by military forces that are often neither truly aggravated by it nor that untainted themselves.[14] The Ugandan army was probably more ridden with corruption *before* the 1971 coup than the regime they replaced, though government corruption was one of the prominent reasons cited for the assault on Milton Obote. In the Central African Republic the most widespread complaint of junior officers and the rank and file was not so much governmental corruption (though again, this was one of the official reasons for the coup) as its unequal spread, which allowed the "politicians" to corral the best mistresses in Bangui.[15]

Neither was corruption in Modibo Keita's administration the true reason for Lieutenant Moussa Traore's coup. And as Fisher has pointed out, corruption was one of a successive list of official justifications for the second 1967 coup in Sierra Leone which suggested the military itself was not sure what the official excuse for intervention should be. For the upheaval in that country was largely a result of major internal tensions within the officer corps exacerbated during Brigadier Lansana's tenure as chief of staff.[16]

Even in cases of seemingly non-controversial "umpire" coups—where the army appears to be drawn reluctantly to mediate betwen civilian cliques or to preside over a shift of power from one group to another—motives may be murkier and more convoluted than they appear at first sight. A good example of this comes from Dahomey, a country that has suffered six coups since independence. In 1965 General Soglo intervened in the harsh clash between President Apithy and Vice President Ahomadegbe, each one of whom had mobilized his ethnic clientelist support in the adminstration and in the urban centers leading to extreme tension in the country and complete governmental paralysis. While Soglo's intervention has been regarded as an "arbitrator" coup, the background was somewhat more complicated to warrant such a designation. For within the tangled web of the dual power gambit that provided the background for the coup existed another basic factor which throws more light on Soglo's motives: the personal element of the situation. In this specific instance the personal element refers to a long history of friction between Soglo and Ahomadegbe (though both were Fron from Abomey), the latter's close links with Soglo's immediate subordinate Colonel Aho, which were exploited when he tried to get the army on his side on the eve of the coup, and Ahomadegbe's public humiliation of Soglo the day before the coup.[17]

Neither inter-ethnic tension in the south, which was slowly abating, nor the governmental deadlock, which had been resolved with Ahomadegbe's victory in the party over Apithy, nor the poor performance of the regime, and indeed all regimes in Dahomey since independence, can fully account for the 1965 coup without taking into consideration the personal element. In a very real sense Soglo's intervention can be seen to have stemmed (at least to an equal extent) from his own anger and hurt pride within a political context that allowed them unfettered expression in the form of a coup, one of several options, which could not but gain acclaim in two of Dahomey's three ethnic regions. Moreover, many of the army's high- and middle-level officers were not averse to a military takeover for reasons of personal self-aggrandizement. The 1967 coup that toppled General Soglo was also not so much consequent on the nepotism, vacillation and corruption of his own regime, but on the impatience of the more junior elements in the army about their own professional advancement.[18]

In like manner the 1965 coup in the Central African Republic occurred *within* the context, and not as a *result* of a harsh budgetary crisis, crass corruption of the entire political hierarchy and overt attempts to displace the wearied and disenchanted President David Dacko. The most important cause of the coup was the personal ambitions of Colonel Bokassa, the chief of staff, who had already manifested his inclinations on a number of previous occasions, including when he had unilaterally taken over the War Ministry cabinet portfolio. Dacko's attempt to balance off the army against the police was not so much a juggling of corporate interests as an unsuccessful effort to ward off the personal ambitions of both Bokassa and Izamo, the chief of police who lost out.[19]

The idiosyncratic or personal element in army coups in Africa is possibly most clearly visible in General Idi Amin's takeover in Uganda in 1971. The various failings of civilian leadership in that country—enumerated by Amin in his eighteen-point justification for the coup[20]—do not go far in explaining the military upheaval, or its timing. These problems had afflicted Uganda even prior to independence. Inter-ethnic strife and cleavages, in particular, always acute, were being continuously denounced by President Obote, and the depressed economy appeared to be on the verge of an upward swing. Government corruption, moveover, had not been the sole preserve of the civilian regime; the military (including Amin personally) partook in it to an even larger degree and with greater alacrity.

More cogent reasons for the coup were Amin's personal fears and ambitions, combined with a deep malaise in the army, which had been in a state of convulsion even prior to the short-lived 1964 mutiny. Amin was correct in believing in his imminent removal from his position as commander of the army; indeed, hours before the coup President Obote called from the Singapore Commonwealth Meeting to have him arrested.[21] Already in October 1970 Amin's powers had been curtailed when two other command positions parallel to his own were created. He was, moreover, involved in the death of at least one top officer prior to the coup and the recent attorney general's report noted both misuse and embezzlement of defense funds.[22] Finally, the Obote-Amin tacit alliance of the mid-1960s had recently fallen apart, and

the latter's contempt for many of Obote's ideological pronouncements and his intense aggravation over the large numbers of Acholi and Langi troops and officers in the army were well known in Kampala. All these considerations form an overwhelming motive for a personal power grab which had little to do with the failings of civilian rule in Uganda. Neither can the coup be seen as "class action" by the military against civilian authority, an eruption of corporate grievances, as one observer has recently argued.[23] Rather, the 1971 coup was a classical example of a personal takeover triggered by Amin's own fears and ambitions. The background context of widespread civic malaise and a fissiparous fratricidal army rife with corporate and personal grievances only facilitated the coup, assured it a measure of support and helps to explain the intensity and brutality with which personal and ethnic scores were settled following the takeover.

Personality differences, competing power ambitions and corporate grievances also played a role in both the 1966 and 1972 coups in Ghana. In the first instance Colonel Kotoka, one of the architects of the coup, was known not to get along under General Barwah and (like several other officers in the army) was doubtful about his professional advancement under the new commander. Strong corporate gripes were also widespread throughout the officer corps, including resentment at the "political" promotions (Colonel Hassan) and retirements (Generals Otu and Ankrah), cutbacks in amenities and services for the armed forces, rumors regarding the possible dispatch of the army to fight in Rhodesia, attempts to indoctrinate it with Nkrumahist philosophy and the direct corporate threat to the army's professional autonomy and self-image lodged in the increasingly powerful, better equipped and more trusted units of the President's Own Guard.[24] The timing of the coup is directly linked with the aggravation of these resentments, for the numerous failures and the corruption of the Nkrumah regime had been quite manifest as far back as 1961. The existence of scores of other valid complaints against Nkrumah's abuse of power and the fact that the army did not move against civilian authority until their personal and corporate interests appeared overwhelmingly threatened. This only underscores Ruth First's observation that when the military stages a coup d'état, "whatever its declarations of noble interest, [it] generally acts for Army reasons."[25] Though they may be predominant, secondary or merely coincide with civic unrest, personal and corporate motives are invariably present in coup situations and cannot be ignored.

Important corporate and personal grievances against both the Busia government and the senior hierarchy of the Ghanaian army precipitated the second coup in 1972. Indeed, many of the complaints voiced by Colonel Acheampong against the Busia civilian regime that succeeded Ghana's first experience with military rule were quite reminiscent of the 1966 justifications: cutbacks in defense spending, officers' salaries and fringe benefits, and discrimination in favor of those officers that had helped him come to power. Underlying this was a powerful resentment at the way in which Acheampong and many other officers had been totally bypassed in the promotion scramble that developed after the 1966 coup and which seemed to have virtually frozen their chances for rapid professional advancement in the near future.[26]

Nor can the 1967 overthrow of President Grunitzky in Togo be viewed solely in terms of the collapse of the alliance with his northern Vice President Antoine Meatchi and the general weaknesses of Grunitzky's government. Possibly more than anywhere else the coup in Togo was a direct result of the threat to Colonel Eyadema's position. Viewed against the background of the November 1966 Ewe demonstrations against Grunitzky in Lomé, and the nonavailability of alternate and viable northern civilian leadership, Eyadema's choices as the de facto strong man of Togo were extremely limited. The option of a southern-dominated government was foreclosed in light of Ewe pledges that the arrest and trial of the chief of staff for the murder of former President Sylvannus Olympio in 1963 would be their first act once in power. Whatever the disadvantages of thrusting the army into the

center of the political arena at that time (though there was significant demand for such a course of action in the officer corps), Eyadema could not evade the fact that just as there was no possibility of setting up a civilian Kabre government, neither could he allow the Ewe leadership to assume power.[27]

Personal power ambitions have also been an integral part of the long and turbulent history of civil-military relations and military rule in Congo (Brazzaville). Indeed, Major Marien Ngouabi's coup that overthrew Massemba-Debat and all attempted coups since are better viewed as personal attempts to seize power by different clientelist armed segments of the army within a textbook example of a praetorian system—with the Left-Right ideological tug-of-war and the country's ethnic cleavages merely complicating rather than explaining the sequence of power grabs in that country.[28]

Hence quite apart from the theoretical misconceptions and idealizations of African armed forces as cohesive, disciplined and dedicated national armies, detailed examination of motivations for coups frequently reveals a highly idiosyncratic factor which is usually glossed over in the discipline. The main weakness of attempts to explain military interventions by pinpointing major areas of systemic stress is *in not placing sufficient weight on the personal motives of ambitious or discontented officers* who have a much greater freedom and scope of action within the context of fragmented, unstructured and inherently unstable political systems. If armies intervene because of the endemic failings of civilian regimes, as it has been argued, then cross-national analysis would reveal key clusters of variables that are highly correlated with military intervention. Dimensions might be developed to adequately differentiate between relatively stable civilian regimes and countries that have experienced military coups. For the underlying assumption is that political systems that suffer continuous takeovers by their armed forces, as Congo (Brazzaville), Dahomey, and Sierra Leone, have more acute ethnic, socioeconomic and intra-elite cleavages than countries that have not had similar takeovers, such as Chad and Kenya.

Such a hypothesis does not hold up to empirical examination, since, as has already been demonstrated, many of the motives for coups in Africa have not been directly linked with systemic failings of civilian regimes. Cross-national multivariate analysis has also been unable to account for the relative frequency of the military's role-expansion activities in some political systems as opposed to others. Reducing the analytical distinction between the two groups of countries to the degree and intensity of internal weaknesses and failings of each state poses, moreover, some very thorny problems of quantification. Yet quite apart from the difficulties in correctly measuring and comparing relative levels of governmental efficiency, corruption, ethnic cleavages and intra-elite strife, such analytical pretensions verge on being tautological. It can be taken as axiomatic that most African states are afflicted with the whole range of systemic problems consequent to their fledgling economies, complex ethnic configurations, clientelist politics and harsh inter-elite competition for the few high-level positions and plums of office.[29] Similarly, most civilian regimes have had occasion to tamper with the internal hierarchies of their armed forces and to curb military budgets. As Zolberg has pointed out, "it is impossible to specify as a class countries where coups have occurred from others which have so far been spared."[30] And increasingly sophisticated attempts by scholars employing factor analysis on scores of societal and military variables (including both hard and soft data) continue to reveal statistically insignificant correlations with military intervention.[31] Needless to say, such links between what are essentially structural characteristics of political systems and cross-national incidence of military takeovers will *not* appear if some of the key variables in a coup—the idiosyncratic element, or personal ambitions of military officers—are not taken into consideration. On the other hand, a proper assessment of the relative importance of the behavioral dynamics of the key leaders in any specific civil-military crisis can be of considerable assistance in evaluations of the performance and policies espoused by the military once it assumes

power. Knowledge of the true motives of military officers in overthrowing civilian regimes can afford us deeper insights into the kinds of policies they are likely to follow once in office.

THE MILITARY AS RULERS: MYTH AND REALITY

Students of the Third World have all along had two conflicting images of military rule. The first, largely derived from the experience of Latin America, is one of incompetent, corrupt and reactionary administration, committed to the socioeconomic status quo.[32] The second, of more recent vintage, viewed military regimes as benevolent and progressive administrations committed to rapid transformation of their societies and the purge of the former corrupt practices of civilian autocracies.

Military regimes in Africa have usually been seen through the latter prism, as examples of "the most efficient type organization for combining maximum rates of modernization with maximum levels of stability and control."[33] At the same time, the army's lack of developmental ideologies and its hierarchical conception of authority and political rule have been recognized as limiting somewhat the effectiveness of military administration.

Since the mid-1960s when such idealized images of African military rule first emerged, the academic pendulum has shifted only marginally in the opposite direction. Yet much of the debate about the alleged modernizing propensities of African military regimes has taken place within an empirical vacuum hindered by the nonavailability or noncomparability of data on military performance in office and clouded by the kinds of erroneous underlying assumption about the motives that brought the army to power that have been noted previously. Hence while there is a growing awareness among Africanists that military rule *does not* necessarily lead to policies of socioeconomic change suggested by the accepted theoretical frameworks, the discrepancy between theory and reality has tended to be explained away in terms of the enormity of the systemic loads assumed by military regimes.[34]

While it is certainly true that by the very nature of their size and lack of certain skills the minuscule armies of Africa would of necessity have great difficulties when in power in reordering their countries' priorities and initiating socioeconomic change, this should not obfuscate the core fact that the conceptual models of African armies as dedicated, nationalist and cohesive hierarchies committed to change, is simply not valid. To better understand the rise to power of military regimes pledged to a "New Deal" which is neither achieved nor usually attempted, it is necessary first to examine the true motives for the coup and the internal dynamics of the military hierarchies. Such a comparative and empirical analysis suggests that the officer corps be viewed as essentially a coterie of competing personalist elite cliques, primarily concerned with corporate and individual interests, in a societal context of acute scarcity and intense competition of other elites (politicians, civil servants, unionists, students) for the same very limited societal rewards and benefits. Whether or not these military cliques (which often establish clientelist relations with their subordinates) are committed to modernization and socioeconomic change—and most appear on the whole not much different in their orientations from the civilian regimes they replace[35]—is largely of secondary importance in light of their prime characteristic: overriding preoccupation with personal and corporate aggrandizement. Only from the aforementioned conceptual viewpoint can one better accommodate the empirical reality of allegedly dedicated military regimes that promote personal and corporate interests which disregard the socioeconomic limitations of their states. Moreover, with such a new conceptual approach one can better understand the frequent fragmentation of army discipline once a coup succeeds; a fragmentation that is only *indirectly* and *secondarily* along ethnic, class or ideological lines and which is primarily consequent to the eruption of competing personal ambitions (previously contained under the army's hierarchical umbrella) once a particular clique of officers is seen as having seized supreme civil as well as military power.

One of the main charges made against toppled civilian regimes has been that they stultified economic growth through inappropriate policies and corrupt practices. Conversely, the most universal pledge made by new military juntas is that of honest and efficient administration leading to economic development. Yet weak unicrop economies in traditional societies are usually more affected by considerations totally extraneous to the issue of whether a civilian or military clique is in power, while the "new" policies that the military regimes initiate are administered on the local level by the very same civil service, often apathetic or corrupt, that served the preceding civilian government. The expansion of the economies of a few countries under military rule—usually cited as attesting to the abilities of the junta to spur economic recovery—cannot be traced to any specific domestic or external policies espoused by military administrations. Intervening external variables need to be assessed—something which has not been done rigorously—before any correlations may be established between military rule and economic development. The sharp rise in world cocoa and diamond prices, for example, merely coincided with the advent of the military regimes of General Ankrah, Eyadema and Bokassa in Ghana, Togo and the Central African Republic. The "economic pick-up" in these countries at that time was therefore really related to the upward fluctuation of world commodity prices. Likewise, another aspect of the Togolese economic "success story" under General Eyadema (expanding phosphate exports and German nostalgia for, and financial largesse, to their former Musterkolonie) was laid long before the military came to power in 1967.[36] Had President Grunitzky managed to hold on to power for one more year, he might have been credited for the economic upturn. And Zaire's economic potentials would have been exploited no matter the regime in power—a start was made under Moise Tshombe—as long as it could assure social tranquility.

Public and private aid and investments,

the sine qua non of any modest program of economic development, are usually attracted to Africa more by economic potentials, expectations of profits and political stability than by the mere existence of military cliques in power. Indeed, in several instances the emergence of military regimes has completely dried up the minute trickle of foreign investment or assistance that reaches Africa, as in the case of Amin in Uganda (though some alternate aid was secured from the Arab world), Micombero in Burundi, Acheampong in Ghana and Kouandete and Kerekou in Dahomey. Both Busia's civilian government and the military regimes of Andrah and Acheampong had extreme difficulties in attracting foreign funds or developing Ghana's economy. Paradoxically, world cocoa prices are once again going up after their decline during the Busia administration, a situation that is being exploited by Acheampong. Neither President Dacko, favorably regarded by Paris, nor General Bokassa, who has been kept at arm's length, have had much success in developing the Central African Republic's untapped diamond and timber resources, or in interesting any but shady financial consortiums in the country's tourist and economic potentials. Nigeria's current economic boom, based as it is largely on increased oil exports, can hardly be attributed to its military regime, just as the Voltaic army's competent and dedicated administration of their country's wobbly economy and finances had not resulted in greater world confidence or domestic transformation of Upper Volta's nonexistent economic potentialities. Neither has much changed in the Malian economy since Modibo Keita was toppled, while in Dahomey it was under the Zinsou and Maga administrations (1970–72), and not under the variety of military juntas, that a measure of economic development was noticeable.

The army's frequent inability to spur economic development while it is in power is further buttressed by Eric Nordlinger's aggregate data analysis that suggests that if economic development proceeds it is often in spite and not because of the military regime in power.[37] Increases in military budgets and salaries quite frequently wipe out any marginal increments in economic productivity that might result from the partial and temporary streamlining of administrative procedures that occasionally accompanies the entry of the army in the political sphere. Only in economies that are naturally buoyant and have potentials for internal and self-sustaining expansion—and there are very few of these in Africa—will economic development proceed under military auspices. Yet even here, this is not because of any specific magic formulas the military men may have provided. Examples of Attaturk-style socioeconomic transformations of new nations are extremely rare.

Nor is there much evidence in the military regimes of tropical Africa, beyond pious declarations, of any sincere desire to bring about fundamental social change or a rearrayal in the structure of power within African states. This is true cross-nationally, whether one analyzes the policies of the so-called radical military juntas such as in Congo (Brazzaville), conservative military regimes such as the Ankrah or Bokassa administrations in Ghana and the Central African Republic, or "populist" military autocracies as under Amin in Uganda.[38] As one observer of the African scene recently noted, "The coup as a method of change that changes little has become endemic to Africa's politics."[39] And in the vast majority of cases a change in political style, a redistribution of political and economic power among elites (with the army assuring itself of the lion's share) and the satisfaction of personal and corporate gripes of the dominant officer clique are more often than not the most significant outcomes of military rule.[40]

The change in political style has usually included a return to apolitical rule characteristic of colonial administration. Stronger corporate and personal links are established with the police and the civil service, the new vital control and administrative arms of military regimes in which only a handful of officers are expendable for the staffing of political offices. With the imposition of a nonintegrative grid of administration, social mobilization and national integration policies are deemphasized as overly costly and potentially disruptive;

eroded traditional authority is retrenched; and a loose consensus of traditional and modern elites is pursued as the key to stability.[41] Where traditional values and personal idiosyncracies favor it, an "Imperial" style of personal rule may emerge, as in Uganda and the Central African Republic.

If corruption was widespread in the preceding civilian government, commissions of inquiry may be set up, but the purge will be largely illusory and limited, the army consciously avoiding the implication of too many civil servants, its own personnel or its allies in the coup. All too often the political elite, whose venality has been cited as a core reason for the intervention, will be treated with a magnanimity that meshes poorly with the impassioned accusations leveled against them previously. In the 1963 coup in Dahomey, for example, General Soglo did not contemplate even at the outset the detention of President Maga and some of his more corrupt ministers, nor was Chabi Mama, the powerful power-broker behind Maga, arrested until he had started to foment opposition to the new government in his northern fiefdom.[42] And while the young putschists of 1967 did initiate a purge of some of the more corrupt officers involved in Soglo's 1965 administration, this was more in the nature of a settling of personal scores consequent on an internal rearrayal of power within the military.

In Ghana General Ankrah's widely heralded sweeping inquiries into corruption during the Nkrumah era left intact the bulk of the civil service and the army and hardly touched the police, one of the most corrupt structures in the country. The same is true of investigations in Sierra Leone, Mali, Nigeria and the Central African Republic following their coups. In Upper Volta former President Maurice Yameogo was brought to trial for embezzlement (as was the case with Maga in Dahomey) only after strong pressure from Ouagadougou's trade unionists and junior officers in General Lamizana's army. Ironically, Central African Republic's former President Dacko (not particularly corrupt by Bangui standards) has not been, nor is he likely to be, brought to trial in light of the damaging things he might reveal in public about the military clique currently in power.[43]

Within military regimes corruption tends to seep in if it is not already present, as if to epitomize that greed and avarice know no distinction between soldier and civilian. Contrary to the pseudotheoretical literature about its austerity and puritan tastes, the officer corps does not differ too markedly in its bourgeois tastes from other elites, traditional cultural values not usually placing a high premium on ascetic lifestyles. There can be a few saints, apparently, in conditions of acute economic scarcity, especially in cultural social security systems where the rise to eminence of one individual triggers off his obligations to provide for the welfare of an entire kinship group.[44]

Though exceptions exist (Upper Volta is a good example), military regimes have not tended to be significantly freer of instances of corruption or nepotism than the civilian governments they replaced because of these practices. Police corruption continued unabated in Ghana during the Ankrah military regime, and it was common knowledge in Accra that many officers had financially profited from the coup. General Ankrah himself had to resign from the army when it was discovered that he had been soliciting funds in anticipation of his civilian presidential candidacy. Actually Ankrah had been involved in several shady deals even before he assumed power in 1966. And in 1970 former Chief of Staff Brigadier Kattah was placed on trial on a five-year-old charge of theft. General Amin's involvement in the 1964–65 Congolese ivory and gold affair were only minor precedents for his extravaganzas following the coup that toppled his former ally, Obote, while the army as a whole only grew more brazenly open in its extortionist practices with the wild promotions of several of Amin's self-seeking cronies to high officer rank. General Bokassa's imperial mannerisms in Bangui include treating state coffers as his own personal preserve,[45] and the same process is visible in Zaire since General Mobutu took over power, though in this case the treasury can better afford these presidential splurges.

The more modest commercial activities of Major Adewui and a few of his army colleagues in Togo, petty corruption (and occasional grand larceny) in the Nigerian armed forces[46] and the almost routine participation of Dahomean, Togolese, Ghanaian and Nigerian border patrol officers in smuggling activities across their states' borders are only additional examples of the pervasiveness of a non-Spartan ethic in African armed forces. At official border-crossing points in Nigeria, as in several other states, payment of a "gift" is virtually a precondition for entry, and military patrols in the interior exact similar "tolls" on commerce and other traffic. Fully one-third of Togo's exports, especially of coffee and cocoa, comes from across the Ghanaian border. And if Togo's imports of cigarettes, liquor, watches and soap are taken at face value, the country's per capita consumption of these items is the highest in Africa: actually as much as fifty percent of these imports are destined for immediate "re-export" across the porous Togo-Ghana frontier with the active connivance of military officers on both sides.

Military juntas have been as prone to favor certain ethnic groups once they come to power as the civilian regimes they replace. In Congo (Brazzaville) the rise to power of Major Marien Ngouabi resulted in a concerted attempt to pack the police and promote in the army Mbochi and other northern elements. Every time a northern group percolates to power as a consequence of an upheaval in Dahomey, it has tried to purge the army's senior Fon and Yoruba officers while in Togo the overwhelmingly Kabre and Moba army has pushed northern elements into high-level political and administrative positions. In both Burundi and Uganda large-scale massacres and "disappearances" accompanied the shift of power from one group of officers to another, and these brutal purges have been extended in both countries to eliminate broad sections of the opposing ethnic group's intellectuals and educated personnel.

In the rearrayal of political and economic power that accompanies the overthrow of civilian authority the military, police and civil service are the net gainers, the masses in the countryside and development plans the prime losers. African armies, and their officer corps in particular, are very small, and except for Burundi and Uganda are not prone to use excessive force or terror to remain in power. The stability of military regimes is therefore contingent upon a close cooperation with the civil service, much as civilian regimes have discovered in the past. Since civil service salaries already consume fifty-five to eighty percent of government budgets, the satisfaction of the sharpened corporate interests of the army, police and civil service can be achieved only through reductions in expenditures in the countryside.

Nowhere has this been more visible than in Ghana's experience under both the 1966 Ankrah and 1972 Acheampong military administrations, the former having been regarded abroad as an example of progressive, enlightened and self-sacrificing military rule. Yet an analysis of the budgetary allocations under Ankrah reveals a somewhat different picture. Despite the austerity policies deemed necessary to pull Ghana from the economic mire bequeathed it by Nkrumah, army allocations went up by an annual twenty-two percent, the police and civil service similarly received salary adjustments and increases while social services in the countryside drastically declined by twenty-eight and seventy-eight percent.[47] Whatever the failings of the Busia successor government may have been, Colonel Acheampong's 1972 intervention was very much an "officers' amenities coup," at least in terms of the motives at its inception. For the overthrow of Busia was unaccompanied by any attempt to camouflage the new military clique's desire to redress both personal and military grievances. High on the official list of reasons for the coup were Busia's tinkering with the defense budget, the removal of many of the army's (and civil service) fringe benefits, and the erosion of the purchasing power of military salaries through the draconian devaluation of the cedi.[48] On a more personal level, Acheampong and the officers on his National Redemption Council had been bypassed in the promotion and patronage scramble that resulted after Ankrah's 1966 coup, and they were eager to redress the balance and settle personal scores. Once again as in Ankrah's time there were cuts in social and infrastructure-building allocations, increases in defense expenditures and a major scaling down of Busia's austerity measures on the civil service and military officials. Since the economic picture was equally bleak, this was achieved in part by renunciation of several of Nkrumah's international debts and a unilateral postponement of the repayment of the rest.

The same bias in favor of army, police and civil service salaries and fringe benefits can be observed in practically every military regime in Africa. Indeed, this should not be surprising for it is a most cardinal and elementary fact that whenever an elite group (civil or military) acquires power, its own corporate interests tend to be satisfied and protected above all. In Congo (Brazzaville) pay measures of twenty to forty percent were announced for the army and civil service following the Ngouabi coup. Libya's mercurial Colonel Qaddafi assured his control over the army and the urban elements by doubling army salaries—probably the highest in the world—increasing civil service wages and decreeing a thirty percent cut in all rents.[49] And in Uganda widespread military corruption and embezzlement of funds coupled with unchecked allocations to the armed forces had practically led the country to financial bankruptcy until it was temporarily bailed out with Libyan and Saudi Arabian funds.[50]

Occasionally, of course, acute financial pressures or empty state coffers preclude such a course of action. A classical example is the experience of Upper Volta. There General Lamizana's natural inclination after the coup led him to abolish most of President Yameogo's austerity cuts that had sparked the massive unionist demonstrations preceding the latter's fall. Yet the very same cuts coupled with other austerity measures were reimposed upon the civil service as the army grew to realize the precariousness of the economy; when the unions tried to repeat their previous show of force many of their rights were curtailed.

Even here, however, the Voltaic officer corps—more conscientious in office than their counterparts elsewhere in Africa—exempted their own salaries from the austerity measures. And in Dahomey, where the financial picture was only slightly less bleak, the 1965 Soglo regime maintained and even increased the squeeze on civil service salaries inherited from the civilian regime even as it declared customs exemptions for officers wishing to import private vehicles. It was essentially left up to President Zinsou to enact the even more draconian measures necessary for a budgetary equilibrium, and his efforts, which caused considerable unrest in the urban areas, were cut short by Colonel Kouandete's 1970 coup. Hence there is actually little empirical validity to contentions that African military regimes even aim at radical socioeconomic change, reduce corruption or spur economic development. In essence, despite the differences noted above, the officers' conduct in office is not significantly different from that of their civilian predecessors, except that with control of the purse strings they tend to find greater justifications for increased "defense" allocations and personal ameliorations. One may also recollect that the withdrawal of the military from the Ghanaian political scene in 1969 was accompanied by "gratuities" given them by the state.

Likewise military administrations rarely aim at political development, the exceptions of Nigeria (still to be substantiated), Ghana (Ankrah's regime) and Upper Volta notwithstanding. Insofar as political development is defined in terms of political institutionalization, that is, the development and legitimation over time of stable complex political structures and procedures with a degree of sub-system autonomy,[51] most military regimes can be regarded as dysfunctional to the development of a stable political order. Indeed, a pattern of political coups in any specific country, such as Dahomey, Congo (Brazzaville), Sierra Leone and Ghana, only attests to political decay and the development of the praetorian syndrome.[52] African officers have usually had both an intense contempt for the political process and an even more intense desire to keep themselves in power; hence rarely have they been inclined to begin building a new political order. While most military juntas have integrated civilians into their decision-making structures, set up civil-military consultative organs and established general policy guidelines or operational procedures for bureaucracies, few have considered either a return to civilian rule or the setting up of viable political structures.

The occasional creation under military auspices of national "political" parties attests, however, that the army is aware of its quasi-isolation from the bulk of the population and the legitimation that might accrue to them through such structures. On the other hand, fearful that any such "liberalization" may snowball into a demand by their own parties that the military junta step down from power, the political organs created to date have either been paper structures or very tightly controlled by the military. Hence Zaire's Mouvement National Révolutionnaire (MNP), Congo (Brazzaville)'s Parti Congolais du Travail (PCT), Burundi's Union et Progrès National (UPRONA), and the Central African Republic's Mouvement pour l'Evolution Sociale de l'Afrique Noire (MESAN) cannot be considered as even modest attempts at political institutionalization. Togo's Rassemblement du Peuple Togolais (RPT) may still turn out to be a deviant example.[53] Still, just the creation of such largely hollow structures with their limited possibilities of upward mobility and political patronage has somewhat consolidated military rule, especially in Togo and Zaire.

Nor have military regimes proven to be more nationalistic than their civilian counterparts, as current theoretical frameworks would have them be. The acute poverty of most of these countries and the relative nonexistence of easily exploitable natural resources practically forces them to remain tied to the aid and budgetary subsidy apron strings of the metropolitan countries and the West, creating a neocolonial relationship. This of necessity precludes a great deal of nationalistic maneuverability for most African governments, civilian and military alike. While some military juntas may adopt radical international or domestic postures, these rarely tend to affect their relationships with the metropolitan country, nor does it usually imply anything beyond the adoption of empty slogans, manifestation of convictions and expectations, perhaps, but devoid of immediate practical import.

Congo (Brazzaville) illustrates this point to the ultimate degree. There the Ngouabi military regime has acquired most of the outward trappings and symbols of a Marxist state: a red flag, a revolutionary anthem, a nonenforced decree on the wearing of Chinese-style tunics[54] and talk of a "cultural revolution," state industries and the nationalization of service sectors and a few marginal and flagging enterprises, a "vanguard" party, Marxist-Leninist jargon, extensive relations with other "progressive" states and sharp internal periodic power struggles whose ideological justifications resemble the Left-Right struggles in early Stalinist Russia. Yet all this has not prevented the regime from anxiously and jealously reinforcing its ties with France, encouraging French public and *private* investments and adopting a non-nationalist yielding posture with respect to French expatriate interests in the country.[55]

Even military regimes in control of more developed economies have not tended to adopt radical nationalist policies. Robert Price has demonstrated the degree to which several top Ghanaian officers had internalized British and Western values regarding noninterference in the private sector of the economy and reliance upon the West for the development of Ghana. Such an orientation on the part of the Ankrah regime led to the strongly pro-West foreign and domestic policies of Ghana that at times tended to actively discriminate against indigenous entrepreneurs and in favor of foreign interests.[56] (Though there was also undoubtedly a reaction to the reverse posture of the Nkrumah government that had just been toppled.)

The Nigerian and Zaire military regimes have also, in different degrees and on only partly justifiable economic grounds, adopted non-nationalist postures regarding their national resources and foreign policies, though this is certainly less true for Zaire than for Nigeria. Even General Amin's quasi-nationalist and extremely popular policies (that is, expulsion of Uganda's Asian minorities, appropriation of British and other expatriate commercial and plantation enterprises, rejection of British and Israeli military assistance) are less consequent on his nationalist credentials than an outcome of a wide variety of factors including personal idiosyncracies and Amin's urgent need to popularize himself with the masses.[57] Moreover, with these unilateral decrees Amin has been able to annul international debts ($30 million to Israel alone),[58] cajole alternate financial aid, and expropriate without compensation vast plantations, commercial enterprises and choice urban sites, all vitally needed to replenish state coffers drained by financial anarchy and increased military spending and corruption since the 1971 takeover.

Finally, stability—the ultimate justification for military rule—is not a necessary outcome of the replacement of bickering and plotting civilian leaders by a military junta, though here the record is somewhat more mixed. Sources of opposition to military rule have rarely emerged from the masses in the countryside, remarkably quiescent and in reality not often affected by the policies of civilian or military regimes. Nor has opposition usually stemmed from modern or traditional elites that have usually been "bought off" in manners that have already been noted, though the occasional eruption of union or student demonstrations is not uncommon. Rather, military hierarchies often carry within them the seeds of their own destruction or instability. Military regimes have been rocked by internal power struggles, factionalism, decay of cohesion and discipline, personal power gambits and successful and attempted counter-coups, as in Dahomey, Congo (Brazzaville), Sierra Leone, Uganda and Mali, though their intensity and frequency have at times been low or moderate, as in Ghana, Nigeria, Somalia, and Zaire. Only in three states has military rule been relatively free of such tensions: Upper Volta, Togo and the Central African Republic. Since the stability of the military in office is a function of the nonexistence or resolution of competing personal ambitions in the army and the satisfaction of factional corporate interests, even a cursory examination of the internal dynamics of the military forces in these three countries underscores that the prerequisites for stability have been met. This has certainly been the case, for different reasons, in Togo and Upper Volta, where internal military cleavages have been less intense. In the Central African Republic's minuscule army the few alternate contenders for the politico-military throne have either been eliminated (Colonel Banza) or strategically dispersed to remote outposts. Such manipulations are not easily executed everywhere and, coupled with more significant internal personalist power formations, account for either the immobility of military juntas, as in Dahomey, Mali and Sierra Leone, or their acute susceptibility to internal power grabs and instability, as in Dahomey and Congo (Brazzaville).

Hence a comparative analysis of the features and characteristics of army rule in sub-Saharan Africa confirms the statistical correlations slowly being established by several scholars and validates the negative image of military elites in office. The specific army faction that initiates the coup, and the officer corps in general, is neither more cohesive, nationalist, progressive or free from desires for self-promotion than the civilian clique being toppled. While there is no reason to doubt the sincerity and good intentions of some military leaders (especially in the earlier phase of coups), their motives for intervention have always been complex and included personal considerations and ambitions which acquired a leitmotif of their own in light of the fragility of the political order. Consequently, existing and endemic systemic problems have been exaggerated by military cliques seizing power, and personal motives for intervention have been camouflaged. Once in power military leaders have not been able to resolve the socioeconomic and political issues facing them if only because many are linked to external factors outside the control of any African elite, others are either intractable or not amenable to easy solutions, and still others require social and fiscal policies contrary to the inclinations of the army or incompatible with prerequisites of stable military rule. A proper understanding of military coups and military regimes in Africa must take cognizance of all these factors.

NOTES

1. For a more thorough development of this theme see Samuel Decalo, *Coups and Army Rule in Africa* (New Haven, Conn., 1976).
2. Huntington, *Political Order in Changing Societies* (New Haven, Conn., 1968), p. 194. See also Samuel Finer, *The Man on Horseback: The Role of the Military in Politics* (London, 1962).
3. Huntington, *The Soldier and the State* (New York, 1964). See also Morris Janowitz, *The Military in the Political Development of New Nations* (Chicago, 1964); John J. Johnson, ed., *The Role of the Military in Underdeveloped Countries* (Princeton, 1962).
4. The fullest tabulation of structural deficiencies underlying instability in Africa is contained in Aristide Zolberg, "Military Intervention in the New States of Africa," in *The Military Intervenes*, ed. Henry Bienen (New York, 1968); and Claude E. Welch, "Soldier and State in Africa," *Journal of Modern African Studies* 5, no. 3 (November 1967): 305–22.
5. "In every country, the issues which best account for the ease of military access to power relate to economic circumstances and their social consequences" (Dorothy Nelkin, "The Economic and Social Setting of Military Take-overs in Africa," *Journal of Asian and African Studies* 2, nos. 3–4 [July and October 1967]: 231).
6. Samuel Huntington, "Political Development and Political Decay," *World Politics* 17, no. 3 (April 1965); James O'Connell, "The Inevitability of Instability," *Journal of Modern African Studies* 5, no. 2 (September 1967): 181–91.
7. "The Army coup d'état is plainly a short-circuit of power conflicts in a situation where arms do the deciding" (Ruth First, *Power in Africa* [New York, 1970], p. lx).
8. Fred Riggs, "Bureaucrats and Political Development: A Paradoxical View," in *Bureaucracy and Political Development*, ed. Joseph LaPalombara (Princeton, 1963).
9. This interpretation is familiar to students of Latin America, but is a rather recent one in African studies. See Claude E. Welch, "The Roots and Implications of Military Intervention," in *Soldier and State in Africa: A Comparative Analysis of Military Intervention and Political Change*, ed. Welch (Evanston, Ill., 1970), pp. 34–35; and Henry Bienen, "The Background to Contemporary Studies of Militaries and Modernization," in *The Military and Modernization*, ed. Bienen (Chicago, 1971), p. 4.

10. For the general approach see Ted Gurr, "Psychological Factors in Civil Violence," *World Politics* 20, no. 2 (January 1968); James Davies, "Toward a Theory of Revolution," *American Sociological Review* 27, no. 1 (February 1962); Betty A. Nesvold, "Scalogram Analysis of Political Violence," *Comparative Political Studies* 2, no. 2 (July 1969): 172–94; Ivo K. and Rosalind L. Feierabend, "Aggressive Behavior within Politics, 1948–1962: A Cross-National Study," *Journal of Conflict Resolution* 10, no. 3 (September 1966): 249–71.
11. See for example Uma O. Eleazu, "The Role of the Army in African Politics: A Reconsideration of Existing Theories and Practices," *Journal of Developing Areas* 7, no. 2 (January 1973): 265–86. For an excellent review of some of the conceptual confusion in the literature see Robert E. Dowse, "The Military and Political Development," in *Politics and Change in Developing Nations*, ed. Colin Leys (Cambridge, 1969).
12. "Where a society's impersonal legal guarantees of physical security, status and wealth are relatively weak or non-existent, individuals often seek personal substitutes by attaching themselves to 'big men' capable of providing protection and even advancement." This general observation is also valid on a subsystem level. See Richard Sandbrook, "Patrons, Clients and Factions: New Dimensions of Conflict Analysis in Africa," *Canadian Journal of Political Science* 5, no. 1 (March 1972): 109.
13. This has certainly been true of many military regimes, but particularly those of Mali, Dahomey, Congo (Brazzaville), and Sierra Leone.
14. Austin, "The Underlying Problem of the Army Coup d'Etat in Africa," *Optima* 16, no. 2 (June 1966): 65–72.
15. J. M. Lee, *African Armies and Civil Order* (New York, 1969), p. 100.
16. Humphrey J. Fisher, "Elections and Coups in Sierra Leone 1967," *Journal of Modern African Studies* 7, no. 4 (December 1969).
17. See Maurice A. Glélé, *Naissance d'un Etat Noir* (Paris, 1969).
18. Samuel Decalo, "The Politics of Instability in Dahomey," *Geneva-Africa* 7, no. 2 (1968): 5–32.
19. Pierre Kalck, *Central African Republic: A Failure in De-Colonisation*, trans. Barbara Thomson (London, 1971).
20. Uganda, *Birth of the Second Republic*, Entebbe, 1971.
21. Judith Listowel, *Amin* (Dublin, 1973), pp. 69–71.
22. Ibid.
23. Michael Lofchie, "The Uganda Coup: Class Action by the Military," *Journal of Modern African Studies* 10, no. 1 (May 1972): 19–35.
24. See Jon Kraus, "Arms and Politics in Ghana," in *Soldier and State in Africa*, ed. Welch;

Robert M. Price, "Military Officers and Political Leadership: The Ghanaian Case," *Comparative Politics* 3, no. 3 (April 1971): 361–79; and idem, "A Theoretical Approach to Military Rule in New States: Reference-Group Theory and the Ghanaian Case," *World Politics* 23, no. 3 (April 1971): 399–430.

25. First, *Power in Africa*, p. 20.

26. See Valerie Plave Bennett's two articles, "The Military under the Busia Government," *West Africa*, no. 2854 (25 February 1972) and "The Nonpoliticians Take Over," *Africa Report* 17, no. 4 (April 1972); and *New York Times*, 17 and 22 January 1972.

27. Samuel Decalo, "The Politics of Military Rule in Togo," *Geneva-Africa* 12, no. 12 (January 1973).

28. For an excellent critique of the relevance of the terms "Left" and "Right" in African politics, see Immanuel Wallerstein, "Left and Right in Africa," *Journal of Modern African Studies* 9, no. 1 (May 1971). See also Arthur H. House, "Congo (Brazzaville): Revolution or Rhetoric?" *Africa Report* 16, no. 4 (April 1971).

29. Aristide Zolberg, *Creating Political Order: The Party-States of West Africa* (Chicago, 1966).

30. Aristide Zolberg, "Military Intervention in the New States of Tropical Africa," in *The Military Intervenes*, ed. Bienen, p. 71.

31. See for example Roberta Koplin Mapp, "Domestic Correlates of Military Intervention in African Politics" (Paper presented at a meeting of the Canadian Political Science Association, Winnipeg, Manitoba, Canada, 1970); Donald G. Morrison and H. M. Stevenson, "Political Instability in Independent Black Africa: More Dimensions of Conflict Behavior within Nations," and Louis Terrell, "Societal Stress, Political Instability and Levels of Military Effort," both in *Journal of Conflict Resolution* 15, no. 3 (September 1971).

32. Lucian W. Pye, "Armies in the Process of Political Modernization," in *Military in Underdeveloped Countries*, ed. Johnson, pp. 69–70. See also Pye's *Aspects of Political Development* (Boston, 1969), p. 182 inter alia.

33. Marion J. Levy, *Modernization and the Structure of Societies* (Princeton, 1966) 2: 603.

34. As in Claude Welch's works, especially *Soldier and State in Africa*.

35. Though some research which is not conclusive indicates that the military cliques may indeed be more conservative.

36. See the analysis of Togo's economy in Samir Amin, *L'Afrique de l'Ouest Bloquée. L'économie politique de la colonisation 1880–1970* (Paris, 1971), pp. 125–34, 148–49. On the other hand Eyadema's decision to drastically cut taxes on imports and exports swiftly led to a greater propensity of Lomé's market women and smugglers on the Togo-Ghana route, which greatly stabilized his regime.

37. Nordlinger, "Soldiers in Mufti: The Impact of Military Rule upon Economic and Social Change in the Non-Western States," *American Political Science Review* 64, no. 4 (December 1970): 1131–48.

38. See Decalo, *Coups and Army Rule in Africa*.

39. First, *Power in Africa*, p. 22.

40. See also Anton Bebler, "Military Rule in Africa" (Ph.D. diss., University of Pennsylvania, 1971); and his *Military Rule in Africa* (New York, 1973).

41. Edward Feit, "Military Coups and Political Development," *World Politics* 21, no. 2 (January 1969); and idem, "The Rule of the Iron Surgeons: Military Government in Spain and Ghana," *Comparative Politics* 1, no. 4 (July 1969).

42. Decalo, "Politics of Instability in Dahomey," pp. 18–19.

43. From interviews in Bangui, June 1972.

44. See Stanislav Andreski, *The African Predicament: A Study in the Pathology of Modernization* (New York, 1968), especially chap. 7, "Kleptocracy or Corruption as a System of Government."

45. The dispatch of a mission to search for his illegitimate daughter, the pomp of the wedding of the "two Martines," the distribution of diamonds at diplomatic receptions, the airfield built in his home village (only forty-five miles from Bangui), etc.

46. Such as the embezzlement of ten percent of the navy's budget in 1966 by three officers.

47. See for example Price, "Military Officers and Political Leadership," p. 471.

48. Bennett, "Military under the Busia Government"; and idem, "Nonpoliticians Take Over"; Dennis Austin, "The Army and Politics in Ghana," *West Africa*, no. 2858 (24 March 1972); *Times* (London), 22 January 1972.

49. *New York Times*, 4 June 1970.

50. Government borrowing from the Bank of Uganda went up from 103 million shillings at the time of the coup to one billion shillings by the end of 1971.

51. Huntington, "Political Development and Political Decay."

52. See David C. Rapoport, "A Comparative Theory of Military and Political Types," in *Changing Patterns of Military Politics*, ed. Samuel Huntington (New York, 1962); Amos Perlmutter, "The Praetorian State and the Praetorian Army," *Comparative Politics* 1, no. 3 (April 1969); and Claude E. Welch, "Praetorianism in Commonwealth West Africa," *Journal of Modern African Stuidies* 10, no. 2 (July 1972).

53. Decalo, "The Politics of Military Rule in Togo."

54. Enacted largely in order to subsidize the

Chinese-built and government-owned textile factory.

55. See Wallerstein, "Left and Right in Africa"; and House, "Congo (Brazzaville): Revolution or Rhetoric?"

56. Price, "Military Officers and Political Leadership."

57. Intellectually inferior to many of his colleagues and from one of Uganda's smaller and lesser developed tribes (Kakwa), Amin has instituted "policies" that are really a combination of earthy shrewdness and emotional outbursts.

58. *New York Times*, 12 January 1973.

Political Participation and Its Role in Development: Some Observations Drawn from the African Context

Fred M. Hayward

Political participation has come to be seen as both a panacea and a curse for development. It is argued that mass participation promotes a sense of efficacy, understanding, and responsibility without which development is difficult if not impossible.[1] Others conclude that it raises expectations, creates disorder, results in popular cynicism, and leads to instability which is detrimental if not fatal to development.[2] In either case, the impact of participation on development, or the conditions for development, is felt to be strong. In societies where mass participation is both an important value and a major part of the political process, its desirability under "proper" conditions of freedom, competition, and authority (or its detrimental potential where these conditions cannot be met) has been a major factor in both the descriptive and prescriptive writing of our time.

The experiences with political participation in Africa over the last ten years have generally been unsuccessful—despite the assessments of scholars and commentators on the independence and postindependence periods who felt that African states were alive with highly mobilized, dedicated, broadly participatory political organizations. There is little evidence (except perhaps in Tanzania) that this enthusiasm, organization, and participation has been employed in development. What seems to have occurred is the demise of mass par-

ticipation, the rise of oligarchies, widespread suppression, and little development. This has led some to conclude that the reported mass participation did not exist at all, that Apter, Morgenthau, Hodgkin, et al. were either misled or carried away by the romanticism of the moment; or perhaps the participation they saw was of a different kind—one not transferable to development. In any case, there is a growing feeling that its past champions were wrong, that one should not look to participation to foster development, but rather focus on political structures which can provide stability, order, and strong institutions.

Scholars, such as Aristide Zolberg, writing later are critical of the emphasis placed on mass parties and political participation by earlier writers. Zolberg suggests that the parties were structurally weak and their power and influence were actually limited.[3]

To be sure, not all observers of the independence and postindependence periods found highly mobilized masses or extensive mass participation. In countries like Sierra Leone which benefited from the nationalist struggles elsewhere and experienced close cooperation between local leadership and the colonial administration, there was little mass political activity. Writing about his research in Sierra Leone in 1959–61, Martin Kilson notes that the new elite and the colonial administration had common interests in a calm transfer of power.[4] These interests excluded extensive mass participation. My research in Sierra Leone indicates that it was not until the

From *Journal of Developing Areas*, vol. VII, no. 4 (July 1973), 591–612, by permission of the journal and Western Illinois University, 1973. Abridged by the editors.

furor over the one-party state and the 1967 elections that political conflicts between elites and over elite values led to mass mobilization and participation.[5]

What happened to the promise of mass participation and mobilization for African development? Were Apter and others too romantic in their projections? Why, for example, did political parties seem to slow down after their initial burst of effort? Did political leaders fail to capitalize on mass mobilization (where it existed) because of the underlying weakness of political structures, as Zolberg argues,[6] or was mass participation itself the problem, as Huntington and others of the "antimobilization school" have suggested?[7] Did the rapid mobilization and expansion of participation in the preindependence period create conditions of instability and decay which made it difficult if not impossible for postindependent political organizations to work with the masses and to establish highly institutionalized government structures? If this is the case, what are the prospects for political participation in Africa? Can participation be used to foster political development?

I wish to suggest that the emphasis on stability and strong institutionalized political authority is fraught with its own dangers, that the skeptics and critics of mass participation are only partly right (and often for reasons other than their own), that the "causal" link between participation and disorder is a doubtful one, and that in the context of most existing African governments, further institutionalization is neither desirable nor likely to lead to stability. I also argue that part of the confusion about the role of participation in development stems from a tendency to equate participation with democracy which results in turn from a general uncertainty about the meaning of participation. Finally, I suggest that there are some statements about participation and development which should free us from the present morass, that serious mass participation has failed in Africa largely because it runs counter to the aims of most dominant elites, and that mass participation has therefore been little, if at all, tried.

POLITICAL PARTICIPATION AND DEVELOPMENT DEFINED

Before delving into substantive questions about participation and development in Africa, it is important to specify how these terms are to be used here. Many of the problems found in works on political participation are due to the confusion resulting from ambiguous or undefined terminology.[8] Relationships between phenomena cannot adequately be determined unless the phenomena can be identified clearly in such a way as to be empirically verified. Although the literature on participation is not devoid of definitions, they are often too ambiguous to be of much help.

The study of political participation suffers from another serious problem—participation is frequently approached within a democratic framework, and sometimes even equated with democracy. Because most of the research has been done in the United States and Western Europe, assumptions about competition, opposition, freedom, civil liberties, and so on become part of the baggage of participation. While one might choose to define participation in such a way, this is seldom done; rather, these notions unintentionally become part of the assumptions and values affecting the analysis. It seems more useful to define and use the term participation in ways that are distinct from democratic notions. It is possible to conceive, for example, of participation at high levels in both competitive and noncompetitive political systems and, likewise, at low levels in systems with and without civil liberties.

In considering political participation, I will use the term in a general sense to mean action which is directed at influencing (controlling, changing, supporting, or sharing in) policy making and/or execution in a political structure. It may be as overt as running for office or service on a planning board. It can include voting, attending political meetings, petitioning political leaders, and taking part in a works project. The key distinction is that the actions are *intended* to influence policy making or implementation from the point of view of the participant. These actions may, in fact, have no influence either from the observer's point of view or from the actor's (the difference in point of observation may be very important). If one votes because the cost of not voting is too high, rather than because one wants to influence politics, then such voting is not an act of political participation. While the question of intent is difficult to measure empirically on a large scale, it is important to remember that actions normally associated with political participation in the United States (such as voting) may not represent participation in other contexts. Thus the question of intent is important, and in most cases it can be adequately judged without extensive surveys or intensive interviews. It is also important to note that actions not intended to have political impact may be viewed by others as political participation.

Development is defined in terms of the agricultural and industrial output of a nation. The level of development can be measured by the per capita level of productivity. It should be noted that development is defined in *economic* and not *political* terms, though many writers include political criteria in their definitions.[9] I exclude what is often called political development or the political components of development for two reasons. First, including political elements in the definition of development runs the risk of guaranteeing a strong relationship between participation and development *by definition*. It is conceivable that a political system which is highly participatory and/or has a highly differentiated, complex political structure may have a low level of economic growth and development. Second, and more importantly, so little is known about development that it seems more efficacious to restrict the concept so that relationships which affect it can be identified. There are no doubt many routes to development, some requiring strong active direction from the national government and other political structures, mass participation, and so on, while others may preclude (or not require) extensive political activity. These conditions are partly determined by the availability of natural resources and capital and by the status of the technical base. It seems likely that in

the African context most states will need strong government action in the economic sector and a substantial degree of public participation in development, but it is important to deal with the political aspects of development as independent variables—not as intrinsic characteristics which become "important" by definition.

THE RECORD OF POLITICAL PARTICIPATION IN AFRICA

Without going into detail, it is useful to look at political participation in Africa in a simplified fashion. Prior to the invasion and occupation of Africa, starting in the late 1800s, political participation was carried out primarily within clans, tribes, kingdoms, and a few large-scale empires. The nature of participation varied from structures which were highly authoritarian with extremely limited participation to those which were highly participatory.

The colonial conquest and occupation, which lasted generally until the late 1950s and early 1960s, shifted the locus of power and therefore the nature of participation. The colonial authorities fostered, to a large degree successfully, the reorienting or redirecting of political allegiances and eventually political participation toward a new and arbitrarily constructed territorial entity. In the early 1900s there were a few urban centers in West Africa where limited popular participation was permitted, as in the towns known as the four communes of Senegal and among the Creoles of Freetown, Sierra Leone. In rural areas political participation was restricted to traditional ruling authorities (or those so designated or regarded by the colonial power). In some instances these elites included western educated Africans. Mass participation was not significant in most areas until after World War II, thus when it came, it was with unexpected force and consequences which were often undesired by the colonial administration and/or the "cooperating" indigenous elite.

With the end of World War II it became clear that the colonial era could not continue indefinitely. Participation was heightened by constitutional reforms and by the expansion of the franchise during the 1940s and 1950s. Part of the appeal of the new political organizations of the colonial period was their ability to transcend traditional and ethnic boundaries. In most cases, traditional societies were unable to expand either their activity or the authority of their political structure to compete successfully on a national scale.[10] Almost without exception, indigenous organizations lacked a valid claim to hegemony, or even a theoretical bond to foster it, within the European-formed territorial entities.[11] Attempts to create such a bond were met with strong opposition from other traditional societies within the colony. Furthermore, traditional political structures were closely bound up with particularistic religious, social, kinship, and historical ties which were often at odds with those of their neighbors. In attempting to overcome the divisive character of particularistic attachments, the new organizations tended to be narrowly political in focus, formally open in their recruitment of members, and national in stance if not always in outlook.[12] One consequence of this change was to open up a whole new area of participation, initially to those with education or ties to traditional leadership, later to almost anyone who wished to identify with it.

It was primarily by demonstrating success as leaders, ability to recruit a mass following, and capacity to utilize rules defining legitimacy in the colonial context that aspirants to national leadership could hope to participate in ruling. Mass support was important also for those who wished to assert the illegitimacy of the colonial regime. With rare exceptions (most notably Algeria) revolution against colonial authority was neither regarded as a realistic option nor was it felt to be necessary by political organizations, although mass demonstrations were powerful tools for convincing reluctant administrators.

For the colonial administration postwar participation became important as a continuing symbol of its own legitimacy, as well as its responsiveness and long-term commitment to popular government. Where possible, this participation was utilized to bolster and to facilitate colonial policy. If necessary, it would be restricted as part of the "great experiment" in teaching democracy.

The most striking effect of participation on mass attitudes during the period prior to the 1960s (when most African states gained their independence) was the creation of an awareness of the new national entity and some general understanding of its functions.[13] This awareness, weak though it was, included some common orientations about government, some common political knowledge, and some conscious sharing of institutions among previously autonomous or semi-autonomous societies. The reorientation of political activity around a new "national" political structure, coupled with the failure of traditional political organizations and the growth of new organizations, fostered efforts at political education.

New organizations crosscutting traditional units of organization required explanations. To some extent these were provided in the usual ways—family loyalty, patron-client relationships, ethnic-cultural ties, deference to traditional leaders—but it soon became clear that something beyond the normal pattern was required. Competition for support often cut across the usual loyalties to patron, chief, or clan. Furthermore, voting, campaigning, and mass meetings introduced new rules and techniques which had to be explained and followed if participation was to have the desired results. For example, during election campaigns in Sierra Leone, major parties spent more than half of their time explaining the system of national government, how to cast a ballot, and political practices defined as corrupt. During elections in 1967 Siaka Stevens, later president, talked about the nature of government and stressed that the voter should not let the chief tell him how to vote.

Now the white man went away and we have independence. That means we get to pick the government. The first government was picked by white men. Now we pick the government. The white government was bad, bad, bad. We were afraid of the District Commissioners and the officials. Now the government is our own. Thus we get to pick it. So the government before now and the government now are different. The first one we were afraid of. But now we pick it so we are not afraid of it. Now you are not a slave to anyone. So the government now is our government. If you don't act, don't complain about the government.

Now the Paramount Chiefs have power too. When the white man left, he left two keys. He gave one to the Paramount Chief and one to the country. Now if you have your box with money in it and you have two keys, you keep one key, you give one key to your wife. You don't give two keys to your wife. (laughter). So here there is one key to the chief and you keep one key. If you let the chief tell you what to do, you have given him two keys.[14]

The leaders of political parties had learned from sad experience what happened when loyal supporters failed to vote or to vote properly, or became so enthusiastic that they did things which invalidated the results for their candidate.

Much of the writing about the independence period paints a picture of extensive mobilization. We are shown a rising crescendo of participation encompassing the masses in expanding waves. In speaking of Ghana, Dennis Austin notes that the stunning victory of the Convention Peoples Party was somewhat of a mystery even to its organizers. "Its appeal to the 'Common Man' and for 'Self-Government Now' ran like a flame through the Colony and Ashanti chiefdoms and branches were formed in many instances without the knowledge of the national headquarters."[15] It was assumed that the flame kindled for national independence would continue to light the way for political and economic development. When it did not, many observers, scholars, and politicians came to feel that the culprit was mass participation itself. Others argued that mass organizations collapsed because they lacked an adequate structural foundation.

It is Zolberg who most cogently criticizes the "optimist's" view of mass participation. He suggests that early observers saw party activity at its height, bringing together varied interests which were not really held together by the party structure, but by common interests of the moment. There was mass mobilization but no organizational base strong enough to sustain and direct it.[16] Authority was shared with traditional structures and other organizations. The party, even in one-party states, did not have a monopoly of authority. In fact, he argued that the domain of the party-state was very limited.[17] Zolberg is correct when he points to the weakness of the structure of most political organizations, but in his attempt to right the errors of the optimists and steer a path between them and the pessimists, he runs the risk of understating the impact and importance of the political and structural changes which occurred during the colonial and early postcolonial periods.

The mass participation of the 1950s and 1960s was not conjured out of thin air, but rather was built on the changes, alliances, discontents, and reorientations which had occurred previously. The fact that people could be mobilized for the nationalist effort as they were in Ghana, Nigeria, Kenya, and elsewhere was not accidental. That men in leadership positions chose (on the whole) not to build on this potential base after independence is less a comment on organizational frailty than on leadership values. While it is true that Kwame Nkrumah and other national leaders complained periodically about the lack of organizational structure and party discipline, others in leadership positions desired decentralized organization and benefited from the loose structure of political organizations. The coalition character of most political organizations gave leaders of each faction an independent power base and made them important to the national leaders for what they could deliver. Any attempt to "rationalize" the structure would weaken their positions. One has only to look at Senegalese politics to see this process played out to the fullest extent. Parties broke up or factions separated, and their leaders proceeded to negotiate with other actual or potential power holders to form new coalitions. When one group felt it was doing badly the whole process would start over again. An excellent example of this was the long history of negotiations between the Parti du Regroupement Africain-Sénégal (PRA-Sénégal) and the governing Union Progressiste Sénégalaise (UPS) almost from the moment of the formation of the former from factions of the UPS and other groups. In the end there was a merger, with the division of government and party posts and guarantees for the autonomy of individual power bases among the last stumbling blocks to be overcome.[18]

While this early period did represent, as Zolberg says, the "initial spurt" prior to the decline of mass participation in most of Africa, the decline is equally a function of the disinterest of national leadership and the cyclical nature of politics. We expect this cyclical character of political participation in Europe and the United States—the highs generally coinciding with elections. There is no reason why its existence should surprise us in Africa. If one looked at the Republican or Democratic parties in 1972, one would find an entirely different animal than in 1973. The nationalist or independence period in Africa generally coincided with high levels of participation and often national elections. Since then most leaders have been slow to call elections. Elections when called are often noncompetitive—in fact if not in intent. That the Sierra Leone elections of 1967 were competitive is not a tribute to the governing Sierra Leone Peoples party (SLPP), but to the organizational ability of the opposition All Peoples Congress and the desire of the masses to express their hostility to SLPP policies and leadership. Given the general reluctance of governing elites to foster participation and the limited number of opportunities for participation, it is not surprising that Zolberg and others have seen a decline in mass political participation. Mass participation did exist for brief periods, but few leaders capitalized on it. In trying to ascertain why, let us turn to arguments of the antimobilization school.

Put most simply, the argument is that rapid mobilization and growth in participation undermine political institutions and lead to instability and political decay.[19] Since modernization or development require strong institutions, participation and mobilization should therefore be slowed or limited to allow for institutionalization.[20] Political participation and mobilization are seen to be destabilizing in Africa, Asia, and Latin America because they raise expectations beyond what people would otherwise expect of government. Changes in expectations, if not properly channeled, can lead to actions which will inhibit the effective operation of government. In short, the failures of national institutions in Africa can be traced to the legacy of rapid mobilization and mass participation—a legacy of instability and political decay. Specifically, rapid increases in participation in the 1940s and 1950s led to competition among groups for participant support; during this competition promises were made which led people to expect things of government they would otherwise not have expected; when these expectations generally could not be (or were not) met, instability resulted and development was thereby hindered or prevented.[21]

Several important questions should be asked at this point. What effect does participation have on expectations? Does the process of mobilization create unrealistic demands and expectations? Are there influences other than participation which lead people to expect things which they would not otherwise expect of government?

There is one sense in which political participation very clearly *changes* expectations. Where political participation serves to foster identity or recognition of the national government in the place of other structures, it changes and usually raises expectations by introducing new notions about the political system. The extreme effect of this shift is easily seen in the results of my survey of five rural Ghanaian villages in 1970. Respondents were asked who they felt should be responsible for local projects such as wells and local roads.[22] The results are striking in that in every case more than 50 percent of the villagers felt that the national government should be responsible. Not one person felt that the villagers themselves were responsible. When asked why the national government should be responsible for these local projects, respondents replied most frequently that it was simply responsible for these kinds of things, or secondly that the national government had the power and the resources to do them. Yet clearly, prior to the colonial period when these villages were largely autonomous, these same projects had been carried out by the villagers—or occasionally by laborers employed by the chief.

During the last dramatic days of the colonial period, amid the euphoria of coming independence or the struggle to attain it, promises were made which could not be fulfilled and the expectations of leaders and followers were unrealistically high. These factors plus the novelty and excitement of self-government and the interest engendered by participation (the festive air, the feelings of accomplishment, the heightened sense of identity) undoubtedly raised expectations to unrealistic levels. With the departure of the French in Algeria, for example, housing was occupied by people who thought it was theirs for the taking, and it was years before the government could collect rents on some of this "nationalized" property. In Sierra Leone many thought that the head tax would disappear, in Ghana that the cutting out of diseased cocoa trees would cease, in Kenya that land would be available for everyone. These expectations were not to be realized. This period of heightened expectations was short, however, and the novelty and romanticism soon passed. Once experienced it was not likely to be repeated, although the fallout from these experiences was an important ingredient in mass political education. Except for this brief moment (and partly because of it) expectations have been generally modest and realistic.[23]

It is often suggested that competition raises expectations and causes instability. For example, Sir Albert Margai, former prime minister of Sierra Leone, argued that competition pitted brother against brother, resulted in lying for political gain, and caused many people to be taken advantage of and misled. Referring to the activities of the opposition All Peoples Congress (APC), he stated:

> When you go to the Provinces, to some of the villages, you will find that the opposition is trying everywhere to divide the people. By a campaign of lies, they have put the people against the Chiefs and the Chiefs against the people. What benefit do we get from such disunity? When it comes to development and the people select a project, and A.P.C. comes and turns their minds from it by false propaganda. And so the country suffers.[24]

What effect does political competition have on expectations of participants? With almost every political organization making promises and simultaneously calling into question the promises of others, do the people come to expect new or unusual things of government? Although the survey data are not extensive, in 1970 72 percent of the Ghanaian respondents agreed with the statement, "There is practically no connection between what a politician says and what he will do once he gets elected." Their responses to related items were consistent with this example.[25] My work in Sierra Leone during the 1967 elections tends to confirm this view of politicians' behavior once in office. It would seem then that, in general, promises made in the name of political organizations do not significantly raise expectations of government action. To varying degrees they already expect government to build schools, provide or improve roads, and develop water systems. These expectations are a function of the activity of colonial and postindependence governments—not a consequence of political participation.

There is one sense, however, in which expectations are sometimes raised by competition—that is, the hope that these projects will be brought to *our* area sooner if X is in control rather than Y. Despite the general skepticism about unusual promises since the early excitement and romanticism of the independence period, now coupled with widespread cynicism about politicians, when people in one area feel relatively deprived compared to other areas, promises of redress are much more likely to be believed.[26] Promises to correct distributive deprivation will be more important in the future than general promises of well being, but such expectations are in line with a visible reality in some other area and are therefore reasonable. Furthermore, promises are not now the major factor in adherence to political organizations. Identification with a political organization is based on multiple loyalties to clan, ethnic group, patron, region, and faction; individual issues and related promises play only a part.[27]

Even where political participation affects mass attitudes to the extent that it creates unwarranted expectations and fosters discontent or instability, is it the major influence or are there other factors? Clearly there are other operative factors which suggest that the problem of raised expectations will occur without mass participation. The distinction that some people in a society are "better off" than others is virtually universal, and individuals are quick to recognize the ability of other people to do things which they themselves cannot do or to do them in ways which seem to be easier or better.[28] People may not always be correct, however, in their perception of the reasons for an "advantage." In Sierra Leone the Chinese set up demonstration farms to show what could be done through intensive farming methods in growing vegetables. Farmers were brought in to observe the methods in the hope that they would use them to improve their own yield, but little came of the effort. Rather, the typical response was, "Yes, the Chinese sure can grow vegetables."[29]

I suggest that contact with technological innovations is the major influence on raising men's expectations and as such is often subversive to the existing order. This contact may be facilitated by participation and by promises, but in the main it comes through other means—experience with government officials and extension workers, formal education, watching those with technical competence in action, working in technical concerns or with those possessing such skills, and so on.

In short, rising expectations are influenced primarily by factors over which both the governments and political organizations have little control. Rising expectations are a consequence of direct and indirect exposure to modernized societies, education, news media, radio, the very development projects governments institute, and a wide range of other experiences. To try to limit or dampen participation and mobilization, as some have suggested, will not get at the problem.[30] Furthermore, where expectations have been increased, it does not follow that governments can lower them as easily as they were raised.

This is not to suggest that governments have no influence on expectations. They can clearly limit or decrease by marginal increments the level of expectations by sustained isolation from the international community (as Burma has done), or by limiting speculation about rewards and change. Governments can also marginally raise expectations through overly ambitious programs or irresponsible promises. It seems likely that states with open economies and high levels of tourism, foreign developments, readily available consumer goods, and foreign films experience expectations higher than those without them.[31] What is being suggested then is that the ability of governments to affect expectations upward or downward is limited and of an incremental nature, that the major factors raising expectations cannot be eliminated by governments, and that extensive efforts to do so are misdirected. Policies aimed at preventing rising expectations are thus doomed to failure, and would be more usefully directed at trying to meet the social, political, and economic needs represented and expressed by these expectations.

Another argument of critics of mass participation is that the masses are politically inexperienced and are thus likely to make irresponsible decisions which will lead to political instability. It is largely true that a substantial portion of the populace in Africa does not understand the operation of the national political system. On the other hand, these same people tend to be informed about politics and to have a relatively accurate conception about who is aiding them and who is taking advantage of them. In *A Man of The People*, Chinua Achebe makes this point.

> Some political commentators have said that it was the supreme cynicism of these transactions that inflamed the people and brought down the Government. That is sheer poppycock. The people themselves, as we have seen, had become even more cynical than their leaders and were apathetic into the bargain. "Let them eat," was the people's opinion, "after all when white men used to do all the eating did we commit suicide?" Of course not. And where is the all-powerful white man today? He came, he ate and he went. But we are still around. The important thing then is to stay alive; if you do you will outlive your present annoyance. The great thing, as the old people have told us, is reminiscence;

and only those who survive can have it. Besides, if you survive, who knows? It may be your turn to eat tomorrow. Your son may bring home your share.[32]

Inexperience becomes a serious problem when the populace generally does not know its rights or how to gain redress or protect itself from official abuses even when effective procedures exist.

Two aspects of the inexperience argument are suspect, despite its basis in fact. First, most of the criticism comes from government political leaders who find their positions threatened by growing discontent, and it is usually used as an excuse to suppress opposition and to limit or neutralize participation. Second, these leaders take few if any steps to improve citizen competence once they have voiced their criticism. Very few African political parties function systematically as vehicles for political education and redress. The attempt of President Julius Nyerere in Tanzania to utilize TANU in this positive way is one of the most obvious exceptions; Ghana's Center for Civic Education, which made serious efforts to explain the operation of government and citizens' rights and responsibilities until it was abolished after the 1972 coup, is another.[33] Despite the suspect nature of much of the criticism leveled at the inexperience of the masses, however, the consequences of inexperience remain.

These consequences are not the major reason for the failures of mass participation in Africa; rather the responsibility for failure rests more properly with the political elites—the same elites who control and benefit from highly centralized, nonparticipative regimes favored by many. Huntington argues that mass participation and rapid mobilization should be deemphasized and limited if political and economic development are to occur.[34] Huntington values order and stability above other conditions. He defines public interest as the interests of those governing, not as the will of the people. Public interest is "whatever strengthens governmental institutions." It "is the interest of public institutions. It is something created and brought into existence by the institutionalization of government organizations."[35]

There seems to be no place for ideology or values other than order. Legitimacy is defined by those who have power, as is the public good. The quality of life seems to be unimportant, rather life should be predictable. While Huntington's emphasis on the institutionalization of authority is important, his overwhelming concern for order leads him to overlook the values embodied in the institutions. Order and stability have long been excuses for suppression, mediocrity, and inaction. And whose institutions are to be strengthened? Those of the former colonial power? Those of a particular traditional society—the Ashanti, the Kikuyu, the Mende? Those of a privileged elite? Will the institutionalization of most existing political structures in Africa lead to development? A good guess is that it would continue the reign of ruling elites, increase the growing economic chasm between the elite and the masses, and maintain the endemic pace of failure in national development.

Major issues during the nationalist period focused on the question of governing personnel rather than on governing procedures—who should govern rather than how should the system be governed. By the post–World War II period it was increasingly clear to major participants (colonial and indigenous) that independence was forthcoming. While local political organizations differed markedly on how the system should be governed and for whose benefit, it seemed clear that pressing these issues would risk delaying independence. Thus, with rare exceptions, the ideals and rules for participation were not seriously challenged. Men competed for leadership positions and offices because they felt that he who had power at independence would control the state thereafter; changing or fundamentally transforming the political system could wait.

When the question of national leadership was settled (or at least set aside between elections), mass participation became secondary to leadership recruitment, coalition formation, and other elite activities. A majority of "mass" organizations turned out to have limited contact with and interest in the masses except on special occasions. Many other organizations (military, trade union, student) which seek to speak for the nation had even less contact. Leaders participated in organizations without much concern for or reference to the bulk of their "supporters." The masses might benefit from the "grace" of being a part of a particular leader's organization and thus gain some material and symbolic rewards. But they were only "needed" and sought after in the few weeks of an election campaign or when a show of strength was desired. One sees this again and again in tracing political activity over a period of years. In Ghana, in Sierra Leone, and in Senegal during the relatively long periods when political competition was possible, political activity directed to the masses was limited almost exclusively to election periods. The consequences of this periodic interest are reflected in the response of a Ghanaian villager to the prohibition of taking bribes from candidates during the 1969 election campaign. He asked, "Why shouldn't I take money from the candidate when he comes to ask for my vote? I am poor and probably will never see him again except perhaps if another election comes along."[36]

As long as the major national political issues revolved around the question of who was to govern—the colonial administration, some indigenous group or groups, or both—mass participation served primarily to inculcate positive orientation toward the indigenously operated national political apparatus. When the focus shifted to the question of how the system ought to be changed or structured, the role of participation came to be seen in a different light. As divisions and factions grew, leaders tried to use supporters to buttress their positions, but those in power responded by limiting or suppressing both opponents and their supporters. Many opposition leaders were bought off, imprisoned, killed, or exiled; others had difficulty in publicly expressing their views. In the course of all this, mass participation came to be meaningless, and the needs and the potential talents of the masses were generally forgotten.

The focus on institutions therefore misses the mark. In most of Africa the new elite now has adequate institutions for its own benefit. The status quo does not require their expansion or alteration. Instability occurs when it is recognized that these institutions are designed to perpetuate privileged positions. While Huntington is correct when he suggests that political systems which have legitimized and institutionalized their political structures are likely to be stable, most African regimes have had and will continue to have trouble in legitimizing the values they represent. If they could create myths and symbols which justified highly privileged and exclusive positions for themselves, they might maintain stability. While it is theoretically possible to institutionalize a system patently disadvantageous to the populace, to do so is unlikely on a grand and lasting basis (although there are historical precedents for it). Attempts to institutionalize privileged positions are much more likely to create instability—and here, the antimobilizationist is correct. Under a privileged governing elite, any move toward popular participation (even if intended to be nominal rather than real) is likely to become the Achilles' heel of the regime.

Finally, if Huntington is saying anything more than that he makes a value choice for order rather than mass participation, he needs to show a positive relationship between stability and development. It may well be, as Rustow suggests for democracy, that instability is a necessary cost of development for many nations.[37] If this is the case, continued stability may only forestall development. The problem of instability in Africa will therefore not be solved by greater institutionalization, but rather by restructuring value systems to insure that all benefit. One way to promote this is through mass participation in the political process, which means real, not controlled or guided, participation—and that is the crux of the problem given the privileged position of political elites in most of Africa.

THE RELATIONSHIP OF POLITICAL PARTICIPATION TO DEVELOPMENT

Is there a role for mass participation in development? If there is, why has mass participation been so difficult to mobilize for these efforts? There has been, quite rightly, an extensive and often heated debate about the degree and nature of political participation that should be an integral part of development planning. This debate has focused on questions of competitiveness, competence, efficiency, right, expediency, necessity, and a variety of other factors. I do not propose to add to that debate here; rather I would like to comment on the kinds of public responses that are essential to the success of different types of development projects.

Development programs can be categorized on the basis of the amount and extent of compliance required of the populace, that is, how much are individuals asked to do and how many people are asked to do it.[38] Some projects, such as an industrial facility built on open land and externally financed, require very little compliance. On the other hand, a project to raise the yield of a major crop will require changes in methods by a large segment of the population. One implication of this is that rural development will be the real test for most African governments; taxing civil servants, collecting customs duties, and starting industries are no tests at all by comparison.

Where individuals are affected by development projects their response becomes very important. Governments can try to inform them about the benefits of such projects; can pay, compensate, or bribe them to support such efforts; or can use force to compel compliance. Each method has a variety of long- and short-run costs and the methods are not entirely interchangeable. As the number of people affected increases, the costs of both financial compensation and the use of force grow much more rapidly than those designed to gain compliance voluntarily. Clearly, if the people decide that a project is a good idea (either through participation in policy making or discussion of the problem) or are informed about it in a way that engenders support, the costs are lower and the likelihood of success greater. Given the past experiences of broken promises and failure, and the resultant growing cynicism, this is not easily done.

Mass participation will only have significant results if the participants view it as real, as having a genuine impact on planning and implementation. The problem for most of Africa is that real participation has not been given much of a chance. It was confined almost exclusively to the nationalist period and then, after a brief moment of political effectiveness, was relegated to insignificance. Thus it was not surprising that, despite the claims that the CPP in Ghana was a mass party of dedicated, loyal, highly motivated people, Nkrumah's overthrow was greeted by general rejoicing rather than outrage.

In thinking about the relationship between participation and development, first, it is useful to differentiate participation which is regarded as effective by the participant from that which is not. One problem with many studies of participation is the tendency to assume that most participation is effective. Milbrath distinguishes active and passive participation, including under the active category instrumental and expressive participation. Each of these he divides into categories of inputs to and outtakes from the system. Among the inputs are party activity, political argument, voting, contributing money, keeping informed, and allegiance.[39] Although his classification is from the point of view of the actor, it implicitly assumes effectiveness.

Now we know that in Africa, voting, party activity, political argument, and so on are often ineffective actions and are so recognized by large numbers of participants. Furthermore, some of these actions are not viewed as having a potential impact and are therefore not participation at all in terms of our earlier definition. There seems, therefore, to be a significant qualitative difference between what is regarded as participation by observers and what is deemed to be participation by the actors, and this difference is vital to the viability and success of government projects. If participation and relative deprivation are dealt with similarly—from the point of view of the actor—much can be learned. For example, observers might argue that most Africans suffer relative deprivation in comparison with most Englishmen and with their own political elite; however, this deprivation becomes politically important only when it is so recognized by large numbers of people within the political system. In assessing participation, then, it is important to check for definitional consistency—to be sure that actions labelled as participation in a particular case are truly that, given the implications of the actions in that society. In terms of my definition, this would exclude actions *not* directed at influencing policy making and/or implementation, which might eliminate items such as voting in certain societies.

Second, it is useful to distinguish participation regarded as instrumental from that deemed to be symbolic.[40] One may wish to do this from either the point of view of the actor or analyst, or from both, depending on the aims of the research. Instrumental participation is that which is regarded as having direct consequences for making or implementing policy, for example, in building a road or in allocating funds for a dam. Symbolic participation is regarded as having an indirect or intangible impact on policy making or implementation; it is action directed at influencing government in ways that do not seem to have clear policy outcomes. Such actions are exemplified in demonstrations of support, as for Nasser after the Six-Day War. Egyptians probably viewed their actions as expressions of personal support for Nasser and his efforts on behalf of Egypt, rather than as actions calculated to produce specific policy results. While such demonstrations might have instrumental outcomes, such as preventing Nasser's removal from office or his resignation, these possible consequences are not clearly related to the actions.

Finally, it is instructive to examine the outcome of participation. Is it in fact effective (or deemed so by participants), or is it not effective? For example, the backyard iron furnaces of the Great Leap Forward in China generated tremendous instrumental participation, yet the furnaces turned out to be largely ineffective in terms of increasing iron output and a good deal of cynicism resulted from this effort. Such failures, if repeated, could have tremendously negative effects upon future development efforts. In this case, since the failure was in large part collective, it did not seriously

inhibit new development efforts at the mass level. This is probably part of the explanation for the limited outcry in China after the failure of the Great Leap Forward or in Cuba after the failure of the ten-million-ton sugar harvest. Where participation is effective, as with human investment during the immediate postindependence period in Guinea, the payoff is substantial.[41]

In Africa a large part of the political action which we regard as political participation in the United States and Europe is not functionally equivalent. Political participation, where it occurs, is often symbolic and ceremonial with little if any instrumental content for the participants. One of the favorite rituals regarded as mass participation by the elites is the mass meeting. The organizers go out days in advance and ask chiefs, local notables, government officials, and religious leaders to set up a meeting for the head of state or other important officials. Bands are hired and dancers and drummers are obtained. The day arrives, loudspeakers are set up, the band begins long before the arrival of the expected guests, messengers summon the people, and the chiefs and notables, dressed in their best, await their leaders. The people gather—in most cases not to hear the speeches, not because of love for the political elite or the national government, but out of curiosity and for the enjoyment of a festive occasion. For most of them this aspect of national politics is recreation, not political participation. Ayi Kwei Armah describes this sentiment wonderfully in *The Beautiful Ones Are Not Yet Born.*

> It is not true at all that when men are desperate they will raise their arms and welcome just anybody who comes talking of their salvation. If it had been so, we would have been following the first men who came offering words and hidden plans to heal our souls. But we did not run out eager to follow anyone. In our boredom, we went out to the open public places to see what it was people were talking about, whether it was a thing we could go to with our hopes, or just another passing show like so many we had seen and so many we are seeing now. How long will Africa be cursed with its leaders? There were men dying from the loss of hope, and others were finding gaudy ways to enjoy power they

did not have. We were ready here for big and beautiful things, but what we had was our own black men hugging new paunches scrambling to ask the white man to welcome them onto our backs. These men who were to lead us out of our despair, they came like men already grown fat and cynical with the eating of centuries of power they had never struggled for, old before they had even been born into power, and ready only for the grave.[42]

No doubt the politicians go back to the capital pleased with the response to their remarks, thinking that they have a strong following. The organizer too is happy, for the crowd was good, the people enjoyed the music, dancing, and drumming, and the leader was happy. And if you asked him, he would tell you that the people listened, understood, and liked what they heard. If you asked the people—you might get quite a different story.

There are, of course, exceptions—Julius Nyerere, Siaka Stevens in 1966–67, Amilcar Cabral, Gamal Abdul Nasser, and a handful of others. These men have had a tremendous effect on the masses. Again, Armah describes the difference beautifully.

The new man must have begun to speak only moments before we arrived at Asaman-sudo, because his voice was still low. He was not making any attempt to shout, and the quietness of his sound compelled us all to listen more attentively.
. . . "Can we ourselves think of nothing that needs to be done? Why idle then. . . ?" Words about eyes needing to be opened and the world to be looked at. "Then we can think. . . . Then we will act." There was power in the voice that time, a power quickly retracted, and replaced by the low, calm voice. . . .
I stood there staring like a believer at the man, and when he stopped I was ashamed and looking around to see if anybody had been watching me. They were all listening. The one up there was rather helpless-looking, with a slight, famished body. So from where had he got this strength that enabled him to speak with such confidence to us, and we waiting patiently for more to come? Here was something more potent than mere words. These dipped inside the listener, making him go with the one who spoke.
". . . in the end, we are our own enslavers first. Only we can free ourselves. Today,

when we say it, it is a promise, not yet a fact. . . . Freedom! . . ." The whole crowd shouted. I shouted, and this time I was not ashamed.[43]

Nyerere is trying to channel this trust into participation for development, although he has had only limited success. He has had to contend with an elite which is loathe to give up its privileges, resources are limited, and few in the top leadership positions are as committed and active as he is in this effort.[44] Stevens has been plagued by problems with the military and has thus neglected both the masses and those in his party who place their personal interest before that of the populace. Amilcar Cabral was working, until his death in 1973, to build a political organization dependent on the masses, while at the same time fighting a war of liberation.[45] Nasser failed in his efforts to create parties of real mass participation, in part because he was not willing to give up enough power to them, in part because no clear tasks were set for the parties.

Participation of this sort—participation which is designed to be instrumental—is seldom tried, even less often does it result in effective policy making or implementation. This is because of failures at various leadership levels or, more often, because it is not allowed to be effective. Those in power feel that they have too much at stake to delegate or share their authority, even where failure to do so often means no policy or program. In short, most participation in Africa is only theoretically expected to influence policy and is usually not even symbolically effective. When it is effective in fact, the payoff for development should be substantial whether the systems are competitive, semicompetitive, or noncompetitive.

Yet instrumental participation is an important value which can significantly affect both development and stability, for it gives the masses an opportunity to understand the complexity of development problems, the limits on available resources, and the costs of alternative ways of utilizing resources. Giving people more control over their lives reverses the usual assumption of the elitists, those who favor only elite competition and who assume that the masses are unable to make serious choices in their own interest and that such choices therefore must be left to, or screened by, an enlightened leadership. Political elites in Africa (and in much of the rest of the world) have demonstrated little capacity for working in the interest of the masses. It seems that real mass participation could better that record. Instrumental participation, in the sense of the classical Athenian ideal, also makes a contribution to building a practical and responsible citizenry. It is important as a check on centralized bureaucracies which tend to operate in their own interests if not scrutinized, and it is likely to subject the distributive consequences of development policy to public evaluation. Such participation and evaluation can be expected to make the decisions more acceptable than if left to an elite (even though the elite might come up with the same policy). Finally, instrumental participation can provide an antidote for the cynicism engendered by the present pretense of participation which makes real participation that much harder to achieve in the future.

While political participation which is effective will not solve the problems of development, it should create an understanding and a commitment to policies or projects which increase the chances of success and greatly reduce the costs of failure. Except for a few experiments, as in Tanzania and in the PAIGC-liberated area of Guinea Bissau, it has been only briefly and sporadically tried. Given the limited resources of most African nations, the number of failures and setbacks in the quest of development will be legion. Where the failures are popular failures they are more likely to be borne collectively rather than to be blamed on an unknown bureaucrat or politician. Participation is not a substitute for achievement. It can, however, provide a greater margin for failure, lower the level of cynicism, and raise the threshold of despair high enough and long enough to allow for concerted development efforts.

NOTES

1. These views are well expressed by Douglas Ashford, *Morocco-Tunisia: Politics and Planning* (Syracuse, N.Y.: Syracuse University Press, 1965); David E. Apter, *Politics of Modernization* (Chicago: University of Chicago Press, 1965), and Apter, *Gold Coast in Transition* (Princeton, N.J.: Princeton University Press, 1955); Thomas Hodgkin, *African Political Parties* (London: Penguin Books, 1961); Ruth Schachter Morgenthau, "Single-Party Systems in West Africa," *American Political Science Review* 55 (June 1961); and *The Role of Popular Participation in Development: Report on a Conference on the Implementation of Title IV*, M.I.T. Report no. 17 (Cambridge, Mass.: M.I.T. Press, 1969).
2. Most articulately expressed by Samuel P. Huntington, "Political Development and Political Decay," in *Political Modernization*, ed. Claude E. Welch, Jr. (Belmont, Calif.: Wadsworth, 1967). Also, see this argument in modified form in Myron Weiner, *The Politics of Scarcity* (Chicago: University of Chicago Press, 1962), esp. chap. 9. Weiner is primarily concerned with what governments can do to lessen the gap between resources and demands and in dealing with irresponsible demands.
3. Aristide Zolberg, *Creating Political Order: The Party-States of West Africa* (Chicago: Rand McNally, 1966), esp. chaps. 4–5.
4. *Political Change in a West African State: A Study of the Modernization Process in Sierra Leone* (Cambridge, Mass.: Harvard University Press, 1966), pp. 284–86.
5. Fred M. Hayward, "Predominantly Politically Oriented Organizations in Sierra Leone and Senegal" (Ph.D. diss., Princeton University, 1968).
6. Zolberg, *Creating Political Order*, p. 34.
7. A wide variety of literature fits this category. Huntington, "Political Development and Political Decay," is perhaps most explicit about the dangers of rapid mobilization and participation and the need to limit participation at least initially, but there are many others who share an antimass participation bias. Part of this literature grew out of the Fascist period, which seemed to indicate that the masses were too accessible to an elite which used them for destructive ends; see William Kornhauser,*The Politics of Mass Society* (Glencoe, Ill.: Free Press, 1959). Others, such as Bernard R. Berelson, Paul Lazarsfeld, and William N. McPhee, *Voting: A Study of Opinion Formation in a Presidential Campaign* (Chicago: University of Chicago Press, 1954), esp. pp. 314–15, 321, stress the stabilizing value of the uncommitted and the indifferent—a stability fostered in part by nonparticipation of those marginally interested in the political process. A modified

form of the antimobilization school found in much of the pluralist writing argues that mass participation is (or ought to be) filtered through groups, elites, and competition between groups, thus improving the quality of decisions and insuring that issues of the moment do not lead to instability.

8. To cite but one example, even in Lester W. Milbrath, *Political Participation* (Chicago: Rand McNally, 1965), I could find no definition of participation, despite his declaration that "participation must be defined" on page 5. His typologies do give some idea of what he (and others) has in mind, and the term "political acts" seems to be used interchangeably with "political participation" (p. 13). Although such usage is not too helpful, it is possible to guess what he means by political participation (although it has multiple meanings), since Milbrath, unlike many writers, tries to be precise about political participation.

9. Economists are not agreed about how one measures either economic development or human and capital investment in infrastructure, and no claims to having solved these problems are made here; rather my concern is with being able to make general statements about the direction and level of economic growth. Cyril E. Black, in his *The Dynamics of Modernization* (New York: Harper and Row, 1966), p. 7, is one who argues that a "holistic definition is better suited to the complexity and interrelatedness of all aspects of the process."

10. Exceptions include the Mourides of Senegal and the Kabaka of Buganda in Uganda. See D. B. Cruise O'Brien, *The Mourides of Senegal* (Oxford: Clarendon Press, 1971), and David E. Apter, *The Political Kingdom in Uganda* (Princeton, N.J.: Princeton University Press, 1961).

11. Islam in North Africa and the notion of Arab unity are two such theoretical bonds which can promote mobilization.

12. Open membership did not preclude identification with a particular ethnic group or the somewhat exclusive allocation of leadership positions; Nigeria provides a number of such examples.

13. This knowledge was not universally profound, but my data from rural Ghana in 1970 compares favorably with U.S. data. Six Ghanaian towns and villages were surveyed, five in rural areas and one in a clearly defined suburb of a city. Four of the rural villages had populations ranging between 1,000 and 2,000, one had approximately 250 people. The urban suburb had about 1,000 inhabitants (the city itself about 40,000). The villages were all primarily agricultural, relatively stable communities. Each was 10–30 miles from a large city. None of them, however, was situated on a major road. The respondents in the urban sample were mainly involved in technical, business, professional, and labor occupations. The samples in each case were randomly selected and comprised approximately 8 percent of the population over 18 years of age. After numbering each household in the sample area, two individuals were selected on the basis of a table of random numbers to be interviewed. The total sample was 378. The communities in this exploratory research were not selected randomly; each was chosen because it had special characteristics which would reflect a maximum variation of representative responses.

In the four rural villages surveyed in northern, southern, and central Ghana, 90 percent of the respondents could name the prime minister at independence, 85 percent knew the current prime minister, and 76 percent knew his party. Forty-seven percent knew who their representative was and 23 percent could name one or more ministers in the government. While these figures were gathered more than ten years after the "nationalist period," with the exception of the north, they were probably nearly as high at independence—and in some cases probably higher. For comparable U.S. data, see Hazel Gaudet Erskine, "The Polls: The Informed Public," *Public Opinion Quarterly* 27 (Spring 1963): 133–41.

14. Siaka P. Stevens, speech given in Kabala, Sierra Leone, 5 March 1967, translated from Krio by the author.

15. Dennis Austin, *Politics in Ghana* (London: Oxford University Press, 1964), p. 114.

16. Zolberg, *Creating Political Order*, p. 34.

17. Ibid.

18. Interviews with Assane Seck and Abdoulaye Ly, Dakar, Senegal, 1966–67. See also Francois Zuccarelli, "L'Union Progressiste Sénégalaise" (Thèse de Doctorate en Droit, University of Dakar, draft of 1967).

19. Especially Huntington, "Political Development and Political Decay," pp. 207–8.

20. Ibid., pp. 233–37.

21. It should be noted that those making this argument are generally thinking about participation in systems which are or have been open to at least some political competition.

22. The question was: "Who should be responsible for local roads, village water, schools, and so on—the chief, the villagers, local councils, the government?"

23. See Philip Foster, *Education and Social Change in Ghana* (London: Routledge and Kegan Paul, 1965), chap. 8, on the surprisingly realistic and moderate expectations of Ghanaian secondary school pupils.

24. Albert Margai, "The Honourable Prime Minister's Address on the Introduction of a Democratic One-Party State in Sierra Leone" mimeographed by the Ministry of Information (Speech delivered at the Queen Elizabeth II Playing Field, 28 January 1966), pp. 7–8.

25. Although not a national sample, the oc-

cupational distribution of the six communities coincided closely with that for Ghana as a whole as reported in the 1960 census. The findings of the 1970 Ghana sample are reported in much more extensive detail in Hayward, "Political Expectations in Rural Ghana," *Rural Africana* (Fall 1972).

26. An average of 62 percent of the Ghanaians sampled in 1970 responded cynically to the following statements: (1) There is practically no connection between what a politician says and what he will do once he gets elected. (2) To me, most politicians don't seem to really mean what they say. (3) Most politicians are looking out for themselves above all else. (4) Most politicians can be trusted to do what they think is best for the country. The statements are from Herbert McClosky, "Consensus and Ideology in American Politics," *American Political Science Review* 58 (June 1964): 361–84. One should bear in mind that this cynicism was probably higher than it would have been prior to the turmoil and disillusionment which typified Ghanaian politics in the mid-1960s.

27. For example, see the discussions on party recruitment in W. J. M. Mackenzie and Kenneth Robinson, *Five Elections in Africa* (Oxford: Clarendon Press, 1960), pp. 976–85. My work on political organizations in Ghana, Senegal, and Sierra Leone also emphasizes the limited role of issues as a basis for adherence to or support for political organizations.

28. Levy suggests that "if there is contact, some set of members of that society will always attempt to take up some of those structures even if those structures are not forced upon them. They will do it for the following reasons: (1) There is no society whose members are in general unaware of material factors. (2) There is no society whose members fail to distinguish between being relatively better off and relatively worse off materially. (3) There is no society whose members in general do not prefer to be better off than worse off materially." See Marion J. Levy, Jr., *Modernization and the Structure of Societies*, 2 vols. (Princeton, N.J.: Princeton University Press, 1966), 1:125.

29. Even more striking, but atypical, are the cargo cults and some of the other religious cults. It was clear that something was done by the strangers which gave them special power; if it could be emulated, then advantages of that technology would flow to the indigenous society. For an excellent description of cargo cults, see Peter Worsley, *The Trumpet Shall Sound* (New York: Schocken Books, 1968).

30. For example, see Huntington, "Political Development and Political Decay," pp. 233–35.

31. It would be interesting to determine if such states also manifest improved government performance, system outputs, and satisfaction of expectations.

32. (New York: Doubleday, 1967), p. 136.

33. See Fred M. Hayward, "Ghana Experiments with Civic Education," *Africa Report* 16 (May 1971): 24–27.

34. "Political Development and Political Decay."

35. Samuel P. Huntington, *Political Order in Changing Societies* (New Haven, Conn.: Yale University Press, 1968), p. 25.

36. Interview in Ghana, 1969.

37. Dankwart A. Rustow, "Transition to Democracy: Toward a Dynamic Model," *Comparative Politics* 2 (April 1970): 361–62.

38. Deane E. Neubauer and Lawrence D. Kastner, "The Study of Compliance Maintenance as a Strategy for Comparative Research," *World Politics* 21 (July 1969): 629–40, make some interesting suggestions for examining compliance.

39. Milbrath, *Political Participation*, p. 14.

40. For an instructive and insightful discussion of symbolic and instrumental political action, see Murray Edelman, *The Symbolic Uses of Power* (Urbana: University of Illinois Press, 1964), and his *Politics as Symbolic Action* (Chicago: Markham Press, 1971).

41. The initial enthusiasm in Guinea soon waned, however, as voluntary labor efforts were diverted from projects which had instrumental outcomes for the participants, such as roads and schools, to other projects such as party headquarters and mosques. I am indebted to Ken Post for calling this to my attention.

42. (Boston: Houghton Mifflin, 1968), p. 94.

43. Ibid., pp. 100–101.

44. For a useful case study which demonstrates the limited impact of the party and its many difficulties, see Joel Samoff, "Politics, Politicians and Party: Moshi, Tanzania, 1968–69" (Ph.D. diss., University of Wisconsin, 1971). See also Henry Bienen, *Tanzania: Party Transformation and Economic Development* (Princeton, N.J.: Princeton University Press, 1967).

45. Amilcar Cabral, *Revolution in Guinea: An African People's Struggle* (London: Stage 1, 1969). As with most revolutionary situations a degree of cohesiveness is created by the conditions of war. The costs of nonparticipation are often great in terms of lives, suffering, and prolonged agony. The enemy alone usually promotes a common bond around which participation can be based. The ultimate test, however, is whether real participation continues after the revolution, or whether it collapses amid struggles over leadership and disagreement on values. Algeria was a prime example of the latter difficulties.

Unit III

STRUCTURES AND PROCESSES OF GOVERNMENT

Until the period of self-government in the 1950s, governmental institutions in Africa were essentially adjuncts of the colonial administration, and Africans held few, if any, positions of influence within them. On the local level, Africans participated in the regulation of community affairs, as in the Native Authorities within the former British colonies; their powers were limited, however, and clearly distinguished from colonywide policy-making. On the national level Africans were frequently admitted to legislative bodies, but on the whole these institutions were primarily advisory to the executive rather than true partners in policy-making, and the Africans' role in any case was minimal. As Barry Munslow has pointed out, "Colonial rule was by no means a preparation for post-independence democratic government. It was extremely hierarchal, at best paternalistic and at worst authoritarian."[1]

All this began to change shortly after the end of World War II. As nationalist activities quickened in the early 1950s, Africans increasingly achieved status as elected members of legislative councils and as appointed members of executive councils. In the pursuit of independence Africans used legislatures as forums to publicize their grievances and their aims. The opportunities to advise and to oppose provided valuable experiences for African leaders, but less in the formulation of substantive policies than in the areas of political organization and procedural tactics. During the usually brief period of self-government before independence, Africans did enter fully into policy-making, but the institutions themselves continued to be oriented toward models fashioned by the colonizers. Not until the postindependence period were Africans finally free to shape their governmental structures in terms of their own political outlooks.

In the two decades since the early 1960s, when most African states achieved their independence, their major goal has been to establish and nurture the kind of legitimacy that promotes public acceptance of government decisions and peaceful maintenance of law and order. On the whole, this legitimacy—where it exists—can be observed operating on the national scene in a number of ways. One looks, for example, for voluntary public compliance with the law rather than mere allegiance to the nation's current leader; peaceful executive succession (as in Kenya upon the death of President Kenyatta); enforcement of the law without the need for a persistent dependence on coercion (as in the Central African Republic under Bokassa); ability to alter public policies gradually rather than suffer drastic and radical upheaval after long periods of stagnation; and in general capacity to manage conflicts, such as those arising out of ethnic competition, and avoid civil war (as occurred in Angola). On occasion, legitimacy is also tested by a state's ability to survive threats to its very existence (as with Nigeria and the Western Sahara) or even to come into existence in the first place, as is the case presently with Namibia.

The particular difficulty of this search for legitimacy on the part of African states turns on the character of the historical roots of their regimes. Nearly all of the new political systems were not congruent with either the precolonial or colonial systems and were thus planted in shallow ground. Most have not had sufficient time or experience to penetrate deep layers of tradition, factionalized ethnic loyalties, or outdated forms of education or economic modes of behavior. It is important to note that while few countries in the world have begun their existence with such careful official arrangements for the transfer of power and legitimation of the new system, many of these preindependence arrangements proved to be more symbolic than real and more procedural than substantive. Although the constitutional conferences, preindependence elections, ritualistic investitures, and independence celebrations were necessary conditions for establishing the legal aura of legitimacy, only the passage of time and the development of a tradition of compliance with law could provide the final sanctions essential to legitimacy. Yet despite challenges to the initial institutions of independence—the rash of military coups d'état and the erratic paths of single-party states—modern African political systems have proved to be resilient structures. After a period in office, not a few African military governors have returned power to civilian rulers, and even "life" presidents have sought electoral confirmation of their regimes. The search for legitimacy is as enduring as the quest for political effectiveness. But, as Ali A. Mazrui has noted: "The cement is still wet, the bricks are still new. The African state has not taken [final] shape yet—either for better or worse."[2]

Although constitutions and the various symbols of sovereignty are essential to the legitimation process, they are of limited and only legalistic value unless governments are capable of making effective use of power and converting it into durable and acceptable political "outputs." Samuel Decalo closely examines this point from the perspective of the African military in his article elsewhere in this collection. Africans no less than Americans are pragmatists, judging institutions mainly by the results they produce. In Africa the most important institution is the executive, and it is to this office that Africans primarily attribute the successes and failures of government policies.

African executives share many of the characteristics of presidents and prime ministers in other parts of the world. They have wider powers over foreign than over domestic affairs; they tend to dominate their legislatures; they are expected to formulate and administer economic policy; and usually they must at some point and in some manner account to the general public for the content of their administration. Yet, unlike their counterparts in many countries, African executives operate within a political context, in David Apter's terminology, of low information levels and few effective structures of accountability. Many of these executives have tried to prevent, or at least hinder, the rise of powerful and organized groups as a way of minimizing the public criticism of elite behavior that is so familiar in the policy-making process of all Western democracies. As a result, these African leaders are frequently "on their own" politically, because by prohibiting independent centers of power, they also minimize the quality and number of credible sources of support and "feedback" that might otherwise reinforce their regimes and leaven their official judgments. Under such circumstances moments of executive succession can thus herald dramatic swings in policy.

The power of African executives reflected in constitutions, institutions, and practices is the product of numerous forces. In the colonial era, legislative activism and initiative were not notable characteristics, and when African leaders moved into executive positions during the transitional stage of internal self-government, their followers readily supported them and contributed to the pattern of concentrated power in the executive. But anthropological evidence indicates that traditional political systems themselves rarely differentiated between political, social, and economic powers, or between executive, legislative, and judicial authority. Thus while African legislators may look to some form of separated powers, the general public is often indifferent to politicians who claim that executives are usurping their legislative prerogatives or infringing on the independence of the judiciary.

It is important to remember, however, that the concept of "limited power" is a uniquely Western idea, evolved out of centuries of practice, philosophical exchange, and political experience. Africans do not share this experience, nor for that matter the cultural and historical context that provided the reasons for limited government. Indeed, the authority of the colonial government in no way suggested that power ought to be limited. Even in Western societies the distinctions between differentiated structures are increasingly blurred by the need for rapid and carefully planned responses to human problems that are the product of the complexities of modern life. In much the same way, African leaders recognize the need for extensive executive powers because of the enormity of the development and modernization tasks to which they are committed. In the light of these purposes, African leaders are generally less concerned with limiting power than with using it effectively for their purposes. The result has been a persistent, even dramatic, increase in the role of bureaucratic structures and a parallel lessening in the importance of representative institutions that were inherited at the time of independence.

Given the extent of their powers, most African executives do not, or often cannot, utilize their positions as effectively as they might. Factors such as low literacy rates, inexperienced and uncertain bureaucrats, and inadequate or inefficient channels of communication result in faulty public perceptions of what government agents need or what government can actually achieve. In consequence, initial efforts at economic planning suffer from capriciousness and inefficiency, have minimal effectiveness, and produce public bewilderment or discontent.[3] In many instances corruption and appeals to narrow self-interest have been necessary to secure the support of participants in the political process.

But executive dominance, bureaucratic inefficiency, and corruption have in many cases weakened public support; indeed, the leaders of most of the military coups in Africa have justified their interventions in terms of the need to remedy precisely these deficiencies, although Samuel Decalo casts some doubt on the veracity of these claims. Even so, military leaders in time must establish the authority of *their* regimes, for the coercion of the military, no less than the inefficiency or corruption of civil administrations, is an inadequate foundation, in the end, on which to build a stable government. It is interesting to note that almost all leaders of coups in Africa have initiated their administrations with promises of a new constitution, new elections, and a speedy return to civilian rule. The search for legitimacy may be difficult, but its purposes are not forgotten even in moments of great national crisis.

The first selection in this unit is Richard Sklar's perceptive and instructional analysis of five types of democratic states in Africa—"liberal," "guided," "social," "participatory," and "consociational." He examines their strengths and weaknesses and concludes that Africa needs yet another type of democracy, "developmental democracy," which could respond to "problems of economic underdevelopment, social stagnation, and political drift."

The second selection is by Lanciné Sylla, who provides a résumé of Max Weber's classic analysis of legitimacy, and carefully and succinctly applies the theory to practice in an historical overview of several patterns of succession in Africa. These include routinization of charismatic leaders, succession marked by violent change such as a coup d'état, and democratization of the process by arranging the transfer of power prior to the departure of the charismatic leader. Students should find examples of each of these patterns and test, for themselves, the circumstances under which each is likely to occur.[4] Finally, William N. Brownsberger's article deals with the problem of corruption. He has designed a theoretical framework that catalogs causes of corruption and analyzes the costs and benefits; he then applies this theory to Nigeria and examines the extent to which factors such as custom, pressures, the political environment, and ethnicity cause corruption. He concludes "that in the long run the development of a vital, differentiated private economy, with a broader, better, more patriotic élite, will reduce corruption."

NOTES

1. Barry Munslow, "Why Has the Westminster Model Failed in Africa?" *Parliamentary Affairs* 36, no. 2 (Spring 1983), 224.

2. Ali A. Mazrui, "Political Engineering in Africa," *International Social Science Journal* 30, no. 2 (1983), 293.

3. For an illustration of this kind of critique see: David B. Jones, "State Structures in New Nations: the Case of Primary Agricultural Marketing in Africa," *Journal of Modern African Studies* 20, no. 4 (December 1982), 553–69.

4. A currently successful illustration of this mode of executive behavior is Senegal, where Leopold Senghor resigned in 1981 to allow his prime minister, Abdou Diouf, to succeed him in a peaceful process which was later reinforced by the 1983 elections. An example of failure to arrange a peaceful succession occurred in Guinea; a military coup followed President Sèkou Touré's death in 1984, despite his earlier efforts to liberalize the country's political and economic structures.

Democracy in Africa

Richard L. Sklar

I am often asked to explain what possessed me, a white American political scientist, to undertake African studies. Usually, I reflect upon my state of mind in the mid-1950s and mention the allure of a new horizon for democracy, limned by the doctrine of self-determination for subject peoples. Even then, however, realists warned that democracy in Africa, as in Asia, would bleed and die on the altars of national consolidation and social reconstruction.[1] But democracy dies hard. Its vital force is the accountability of rulers to their subjects. Democracy stirs and wakens from the deepest slumber whenever the principle of accountability is asserted by members of a community or conceded by those who rule. Democracy cannot be destroyed by a coup d'etat; it will survive every legal assault upon political liberty. The true executioner of democracy has neither sword nor scepter, but a baneful idea. Ironically, the deadly agent is an idea about freedom.

In Africa today, freedom from want is a universal goal. Millions of lives are blighted by the effects of poverty, unemployment, malnutrition, untended illness, and inadequate education. In all countries, political leaders dedicate themselves to the cause of economic and social development. Most leaders also claim to respect the principle of accountability to the people. However, the imperatives of development are far more demanding than the claims of democracy. Appalled by the human condition and waste of resources in Africa and other nonindustrial regions, many intellectuals proclaim the validity of an antidemocratic idea, to which the term "developmental dictatorship" is aptly applied.

According to A. James Gregor (1979), the principles of developmental dictatorship were first formulated by Italian Marxists during the course of intense theoretical debates before the outbreak of World War One. Eventually, they came to understand that orthodox Marxism was not relevant to the social realities of their underdeveloped country. Left to itself, they reasoned, the feeble Italian bourgeoisie, fettered by its dependence upon foreign capitalists, would not create an industrial society. Fatefully, they forsook the ideal of proletarian internationalism and embraced statist nationalism in order to mobilize all talents and resources for a program of forced and rapid industrialization. With heretical abandon, they entrusted responsibility for the direction of events to an "audacious minority" or "vanguard elite" (Gregor, 1979: 87). Faced with a similar predicament in the 1920s, the post-capitalist regime in Moscow adopted a similar nationalist and statist strategy. Ever since, national struggles to overcome economic backwardness in many parts of the world have been intensified if not actually led by proponents of developmental dictatorship.

The hardships of developmental dictatorship are well known: liberty is suppressed; labor is regimented and exploited; freedom of movement is curtailed; personal choice is severely restricted. From his pre-revolutionary vantage point, Karl Marx advised his readers to anticipate painful transitions, or "birth pangs," during the creation of new social orders. "The country that is more developed industrially only shows, to the less developed, the image of its own future" (Marx, 1967: 8-10). Must we, now, believe that Africa, rid of external rule but bowed-down in social and economic agony, with burgeoning populations and a dearth of jobs, should or will resort en masse and in extremis to developmental

From *African Studies Review*, vol. 26, no. 3/4 (September–December 1983), 11–24, by permission of the journal and the author.

dictatorship? Shall we avert our eyes from an unforeseen alternative and disregard an abundance of evidence for the thesis that Africa today is a veritable workshop of democracy?

Democracy in Africa is as varied as the ever-changing forms of government in more than fifty sovereign states. Democracy in Africa is an experimental process in a new generation of countries.[2] We should study this process not only to learn about Africa, but also to refresh our knowledge about the meaning of democracy itself. As the African philosopher, Edward Wilmot Blyden, might have said, in our time, these experiments in democracy constitute "Africa's service to the world."[3]

For this assessment of democracy in Africa, I have distinguished four existing types at the level of national government and one other which has been proposed. The first type is liberal democracy, wherein the powers of government are limited by law and citizens enjoy freedom of association to compete for office in free elections at regular intervals. Numerous liberal democracies were bequeathed to Africa by the former colonial rulers; all but a few of them, however, were rudely swept away by military coups, political usurpations, and constitutional changes shortly after (or within a decade of) independence.[4] A few hardier breeds of liberal democracy have been planted and nurtured by African statesmen themselves.

At the present time, one person in five on the continent of Africa lives in a truly liberal democracy with genuine freedom of expression and freedom of political association. (Among black Africans the percentage is higher: one in four.) The citizens of liberal democracies include an estimated one hundred million Nigerians plus the citizens of five other states, namely, Botswana, The Gambia, Mauritius, Senegal, and Zimbabwe. However, the serious qualifications to which this observation is liable underscore the experimental and highly contingent nature of liberal democracy in Africa.

During the past two years, ventures in liberal democracy have been aborted by paternalistic military guardians in Upper Volta, (arguably) the Central African Republic, and Ghana. At present, liberal democracy lingers in Zimbabwe, but the political leaders of that country have expressed their strong preference for a democracy without party competition. Until the electoral victory of Mauritian socialists in June 1982, no national government in an independent African state had ever been transferred to an opposition by electoral means. Confirming the historic importance of this event, the Mauritian socialists have pledged to strengthen a constitutional guarantee of free elections at regular intervals. In The Gambia, liberal democracy nearly succumbed to an insurrection in July 1981. It has since been fortified by the establishment of a confederation with a protective sister-republic, Senegal. Since the retirement of President Léopold Sédar Senghor in January 1981, Senegal has emerged as a full-fledged liberal democracy. President Abdou Diouf leads a moderate socialist party which enjoys a commanding majority in the national assembly. The party is also a haven for conservative and parasitical interest groups. To rejuvenate this party for the urgent tasks of economic reconstruction, and to defuse a potentially revolutionary opposition, President Diouf has opened the door of legality to all political parties. Inevitably, the opposition parties sparkle, like the fragments of a Roman candle, in splendid sectarian isolation. Diouf's open air treatment of illiberal dissent is a milestone for democratic socialists in Africa.

Given the large number of sovereign entities in today's Africa, and the preponderance of illiberal governments, the crucial accounting for African liberal democracy must be rendered in populous Nigeria. Scholars have pondered and variously explained the remarkable resilience of constitutional liberty in Nigerian government. Without prejudice to the importance of other explanations, notably the influence of indigenous constitutional traditions, I am particularly impressed by the impact of federalism upon Nigerian political thought. While the number of states in Nigeria's federation has varied and remains contentious, federalism per se is an article of national faith, the virtually unquestioned premise of national unity. It is instructive to recall that federalism was a shared value for rival nationalists during the colonial era (Azikiwe, 1943; Awolowo, 1947; Coleman, 1958); it was the indispensable basis for Nigerian unity under military rule, when the threat of national disintegration loomed large. At present, nineteen states accommodate a richly textured and wondrously complex tapestry of democratic political life.

Truly federal governments are necessarily liberal governments, predicated on the division and restraint of power. In Nigeria, the rights of citizens and constituent states alike are protected by a staunchly independent judiciary. In fact, Nigeria is an exceptionally legalistic society; many political issues of great moment are finally resolved in the courts, for example, the outcome of the 1979 presidential election. Nor did the courts lose their vitality under military rule. Shorn, temporarily, of their formal constitutional independence, the judges still retained their authority in the states, where, in the words of a legal scholar, they performed "prodigious feats of courage" defending the rights of citizens (Achike, 1978: 184). Should constitutional government in Nigeria be suppressed once again, the potential for its early revival would be preserved by federalism, the legal profession, and the determined practice of judicial independence.

Despite its apparent vigor, liberal democracy in Nigeria is debilitated by the effects of economic anarchy and social distemper. A small minority of the population is conspicuously wealthy and privileged while the vast minority seethes with discontent. Keepers of the national conscience frequently deplore the plunder and waste of Nigeria's wealth by corrupt officials in collusion with unscrupulous businessmen.[5] Scholars discern the portents of revolutionary mass action, particularly in the northern states, where class conflict is pronounced (Diamond, 1982). Disillusioned intellectuals renounce democracy and urge the merits of developmental dictatorship in one form or another. Both the Leninist and the corporatist, or Brazilian, versions have their advocates. In Nigeria, as in Senegal, liberal democracy is democracy with tears and many reservations.

A second type of democracy in Africa accepts the principle that rulers should be accountable to their subjects but dispenses with the political method of multiparty electoral competition. I shall adopt the term guided democracy for this type of government by guardians of the public weal who insist upon political uniformity. Guided democracy is, to be sure, a form of developmental dictatorship; it is classified separately because the other forms of developmental dictatorship make little or no pretense of accountability to the people on the part of exalted persons or national saviors.

The late President Jomo Kenyatta of Kenya was one of a number of African presidents who have ruled beyond the reach of accountability. When he died, in 1978, the barons of Kenyan politics and society could not imagine, nor would they have tolerated, another episode of such highly personal rule. Kenya had become a de facto one-party state in 1969, when the sole opposition party was banned. Yet the one-party political process in that country has been highly competitive; the triumphal party itself has been described as a "confederation of arenas" where the bosses of rural factions "collide" and "collude" in their "perennial struggle" for power (Jackson and Rosberg, 1982: 103). Survey research on the electoral process tells of a well informed electorate which imposes the norm of accountability upon its representatives; for example, in 1979, 45 percent of the incumbent members of Parliament were defeated at the polls (Jackson and Rosberg, 1982: 111; Barkan, 1979: 83–84). When, in 1982, Kenya became a one-party state de jure, her commitment to guided rather than liberal democracy was decisively confirmed.

During the course of a purely formal parliamentary debate on the establishment of a one-party state, the Vice-President, Mr. Mwai Kibaki, explained that constitutional change was needed to preclude the election of persons who would favor experiments based upon Marxist theories. Such theories, he argued, have been disproved by the poor economic performances of communist systems (*The Weekly Review*, 1982: 5). This kind of reasoning, from a different ideological perspective, is used by the leaders of those authoritarian regimes which have socialist orientations to preclude the practical advocacy of capitalist ideas. In such cases, political monopolies are justified by persons who assert the moral necessity or scientific truth of an official doctrine, e.g., "Humanism" in Zambia, the "Third Universal Theory" in Libya, and Marxism-Leninism in several countries.

The touchstone of guided democracy is the existence and operation of a political mechanism which can be expected to ensure the accountability of rulers to the people. Various developmental dictatorships in Africa, both capitalist and socialist, do not pass muster as guided democracies because their leaders rule without regard to the principle of accountability. Those which do qualify as guided democracies include a variety of political forms and ideological orientations. Some, such as Guinea-Bissau, Tanzania, and (arguably) Zambia, have mass-mobilizing parties with open memberships. Others, including Congo People's Republic, Angola, and Mozambique, have created Leninist parties with doctrinal restrictions on membership and statutes on the required accountability of leaders. In these and other instances of one-party or, as in Libya, no-party rule, the degree of democracy varies with the intensity of passion for political accountability and its effective enforcement.

In socialist thought, the concept of democracy extends beyond the precept of accountability to the idea of social justice. From that perspective, democracy implies the effective pursuit of an egalitarian social order in addition to a government which is accountable to the people. For the principal instance of social democracy (my third type for this survey) in Africa I turn, necessarily, to Tanzania.

Ever since the famous Arusha Declaration of 1967, the Tanzanian Government has endeavored to minimize social inequality and to counteract various tendencies toward class division. In the commentaries of President Julius K. Nyerere, two aspects of the quest for social equality are strongly emphasized: first, the problem of privilege, or differentials in both personal consuming power and access to public services; second, the importance of popular participation in the decision-making processes of both political and economic organizations (Nyerere, 1977; Green, 1979: 19–45). On the first count, impressive achievements have been recorded in reducing income differentials and providing economic, educational, health, and other essential services to the public at large. Furthermore, the conversion of public trust into personal wealth has been checked by progressive taxation, lean salary scales for the administrators of public agencies, and the enforcement of a socialist code of conduct for leaders and officials.

On the second count, that of progress toward popular and democratic participation in government and economic decision-making, Tanzania's record is more difficult to assess. In 1967, the sole legal party accepted an historic challenge: to build socialism in an agrarian country without resort to coercive methods of collectivization. At the same time, every effort would be made to raise the standard of living and enhance the quality of life in peasant and working class communities. However, the vast majority of rural dwellers did not respond favorably to the party's call for collectivization on a voluntary basis. Finally, at the end of its patience, the government used compulsion to move and resettle millions of peasants from their dispersed homes and farms into clustered villages between 1974 and 1976. That process, known as "villagization," has made it possible for the government to reach the entire rural population with basic services. However, the related aim of socialist farming—the collectivization of production—was, at first, deemphasized and then virtually abandoned in the face of peasant resistance, a food crisis, and the critical views of potential donors, notably the World Bank, at a time of dire need for foreign aid.[6]

Suddenly, the socialist venture in Tanzania was awash in a sea of academic and intellectual doubt.[7] Could rural socialism be reconciled with an acceptable level of agricultural efficiency? Had the socialist venture been sabotaged by non- or pseudo-socialist officials and their class allies in concert with antisocialist foreign powers?

Those who seek honest answers to these hard questions and still believe in the viability of socialist policies in Tanzania have set great store by the party's avowed commitment to popular and democratic participation in economic and political life. They also view with concern the lack of evidence to show that workers and peasants participate effectively in the formulation and adoption of public policies. At the center of power, the ruling party itself sets a decisive example for all other institutions. In his empathetic assessment of party life, Cranford Pratt (1979: 211) finds an "oligarchic" and "profound bias against any opposition to the leadership."

If, as Nyerere (1977: 11) maintains, democratic particpation is a cornerstone of social equality, sincere socialists cannot disregard the inevitably repressive effects of legal barriers to freedom of association. Socialists of participative conviction cannot sidestep a pluralist question: Is democratic participation viable in a one-party state, where political competition is severely restricted by the virtual elimination of group rights to pursue self-determined political aims? This question, which reflects the liberal critique of guided democracy, has engaged the attention of intellectuals in several other African countries where the search for social democracy is less resolute than it has been in Tanzania. An illuminating example is the constitutional declaration of a "One-party Participatory Democracy" in Zambia. It signifies experimentation with a fourth, familiar but elusive, type of democracy, namely, participatory democracy.

The theory of participatory democracy is a product of the current era. It affirms the existence of a reciprocal relationship between democratic political institutions and participative social institutions, with particular emphasis upon the educative effects of democratic participation in the workplace.[8] In Zambia, the concept of participatory democracy was introduced as a national goal by President Kenneth D. Kaunda (1968: 20) in 1968. Subsequently, Kaunda (1971: 37) construed the concept to connote democratic participation in all spheres of life, so that "no single individual or group of individuals shall have a mo-nopoly of political, economic, social or military power." To his mind, the public interest suffers when politicians monopolize political power, or soldiers monopolize military power, or intellectuals and technocrats monopolize knowledge, or publishers and writers monopolize the power of the pen, or workers monopolize power through strikes, or chiefs monopolize the power of tradition (1971: 37). In the near future, he forecast (1970), participatory democracy would be practiced in all Zambian institutions, including the civil service and the army.

Objectively considered, however, the record of participatory democracy in Zambia has fallen far short of Kaunda's expectations. Careful studies (Bratton, 1980: 237–8; Ollawa, 1979; 415–18; Quick, 1977: 394, 399) attest to the very low levels of popular attachment to, or involvement in, participatory institutions in rural Zambia. The sole legal party has not become a truly popular institution. Membership in the party has dwindled to few than five percent of the population despite its availability to Zambians without restriction (Ollawa, 1979: 319, 395, 404–6; Scott, 1980: 155–6). A "commandist" and "paternalistic" style of administration at the local level (Bratton, 1980: 234; Ollawa, 1979: 324) is magnified at the national level by a domineering office of the president. As William Tordoff observes (1980: 25), "Ironically, no one emphasizes the virtues of participatory democracy more than the President himself, yet his own style of increasingly personalized decision-making renders its realization difficult." As in Tanzania, the party-state in Zambia abhors the very idea of political pluralism. Yet the Zambian government, unlike the Tanzanian, must contend with a formidable and resourceful labor movement; indeed, the Mineworkers Union of Zambia, 60,000 strong, has never accepted the hegemony of the party in the sphere of industrial relations. Its long-term struggle for autonomy from an imperious government lies at the very heart of conflict in Zambian politics.

Truly democratic participation is self-motivated and self-determined; it is not coerced. In Africa, participatory democracy implies a commitment to the self-motivated assertion of peasant and working class interests in political affairs. But the Zambian leadership has tried to induce popular participation into channels which would be controlled by a monopolistic political party. From a democratic standpoint, however, induced participation comes close to being a contradiction in terms; indeed it is a form of coercion. And it has been rejected by the Zambian workers and peasants.

In 1981, following a spate of wildcat strikes, four leaders of the labor movement, including the chairman and secretary-general of the Zambia Congress of Trade Unions, and an eventually successful aspirant for the presidency of the Mineworkers' Union, were detained for nearly three months on charges of plotting against the government. Announcing this action, Kaunda accused the labor leadership of capitalist deviations.[9] In 1982, Kaunda turned a corner in his personal ideology. Much to the amazement of Kaunda-watchers, most of whom were confident of his apparently unshakable commitment to nondoctrinaire "humanist" socialism, he decided that Zambia's official ideology should be Marxist (or "scientific") socialism. But this is not, after all, an arbitrary choice. Scientific socialism marks a strictly logical progression in ideology for a ruling group of socialist inclination which intends to control the working class. It also signifies the maturation of basic tendencies toward an undiluted developmental dictatorship in Zambia.[10]

As a result of Kaunda's ideological demarche, the beleaguered labor movement has acquired a powerful ally in its bid for autonomy, namely the interdenominational Christian Council of Zambia. Following his release from detention, Frederick Chiluba, chairman of the Congress of Trade Unions, is reported to have "made a point of going to church almost every day" (*Africa Confidential*, 1982: 2). As in Poland, the strugle for participatory democracy in Zambia has forged an alliance between two social institutions which are second to none other in popularity, namely the labor movement and the churches. Like his Polish counterpart, Lech Walesa, Chiluba stands for participatory democracy from without, rather than from within, the party.

In Zambia, as in Tanzania, the acid test for participatory democracy is the attitude of the national leadership toward self-assertion by the working class and the peasantry. Neither regime has passed that test; each has chosen to promote induced, rather than spontaneous, participation. It may be instructive to contrast these instances with the noteworthy practice of worker self-management in Algeria, inaugurated spontaneously by urban and rural workers at the end of the war for independence. For twenty years, this genuine expression of working class democracy has survived the rigors of interaction with an authoritarian government. The vitality and lasting effect of this participatory institution in Algeria is attributable to its spontaneous, as opposed to induced, genesis.[11] By contrast, a memorable episode of induced participatory democracy under revolutionary conditions in Guinea-Bissau, called by Amilcar Cabral "revolutionary democracy," appears to have faded in the postrevolutionary, one-party state (Chaliand, 1969; Davidson, 1969; Rudebeck, 1974, 1981).[12]

A fifth type of democracy has no legal guardian in Africa, but its adoption is often contemplated. Its name is consociational democracy, so christened by a Dutch political scientist, Arend Lijphart, and widely celebrated by like-minded scholars. This type of democracy is prescribed by its advocates as a long- or short-term solution to the problem of cultural, i.e., ethnic, racial, or religious, group conflict in deeply divided societies. In fact, it is a version of liberal democracy with the addition of special arrangements to protect the vital interests of cultural groups. In culturally plural societies, such as Switzerland, federalism and cantonal autonomy are exemplary consociational devices; the principle of proportionality for both political representation and the distribution of benefits is also important. In Nigeria, the constitutional requirement that political parties must reflect the federal character of the country in order to qualify for registration is one of several consociational devices which have been designed to prevent sectional domination. Consociational mechanisms and techniques are routinely used by the governments of plural societies. According to

Lijphart (1977), however, the hallmark of specifically consociational democracy, as a distinct type, is effective and voluntary political cooperation among the elites and truly representative leaders of the main cultural groups.[13]

In South Africa, the banner of consociationalism has been unfurled by legal opponents of the ruling National Party, principally the white Progressive Federal Party (Slabbert and Welsh, 1979)[14] and *Inkatha*, a Zulu-based mass organization, acting through a multiracial commission appointed by Gatsha Buthelezi, Chief Minister of Kwazulu, in 1980. Drawing upon the ideas of Professor Lijphart, who served as a member, the commission has proposed a consociational constitution for the Province of Natal as an example for the country as a whole. The key features of this proposal include universal adult suffrage, a legislative assembly elected by means of proportional representation in electoral districts, and an executive body chosen in accordance with consociational principles (Buthelezi Commission Report, 1982: I, Chap. 5). These recommendations have been rejected by the government. Meanwhile proposals for consociational democracy in South Africa have also been criticized by rigorously democratic thinkers. Heribert Adam, for one, notes that group identities and ethnic labels in South Africa have been imposed upon subject groups by the dominant group. "For example", he observes (1979: 288), "there are no enthusiastic Coloureds in the self-perceptions of those classified as Coloureds." Furthermore, a growing number of black liberation leaders are social revolutionaries with little or no interest in consociational compromising. Increasingly, the liberation struggle involves collective demands for "redistributive" or social and, in the workplace, participatory democracy (Adam, 1979: 290-302).[15]

In divided societies, like South Africa, where revolutionary action involves a large and increasing measure of class struggle, consociational democracy cannot fulfill its promise of stabilizing social satisfaction. Yet it would be mistaken to believe that the consociational idea of self-determination for self-regarding communities is counterrevolutionary per se. Insofar as subnational group rights command general respect, democratic movements which disregard consociational precepts do so at their peril. In Africa, the value of consociational democracy would be more clearly apparent in countries, such as the Democratic Republic of the Sudan, where the nature of cultural cleavage is less ambiguous than it is in the apartheid republic.[16] This type of democracy should not be underappreciated because of its current association with moderate reform in South Africa.

Democracy in Africa is widely approved but everywhere in doubt. Democratic dreams are the incandescent particles of current history which gleam brightly in the sunlight of liberation only to fade beneath the lengthening shadow of grim economic realities. This survey of types may help to sort some of the problems of democracy in Africa. Liberal democracy founders in a rising tide of tears and social despair. Reflecting on two recent setbacks for liberal democracy in West Africa, an acute observer offered this judgement: "it was only the appalling economic situations in Ghana and Upper Volta, and the impotence of the respective governments faced with this situation that led to the collapse of their parliamentary systems" (*West Africa*, 1982: 111).

Social democracy introduces a standard for the just distribution of wealth and material benefits; but its success and survival cannot be ensured by redistributive policies alone. In an age of social optimism, people will not settle for the redistribution of misery and poverty. Everything depends upon the timely creation of national wealth and wealth-producing assets by means of public and collective, rather than private, enterprise. In many African countries, however, statist economic policies, espoused in the name of socialism, have discouraged or prevented the release of creative, wealth-generating energies. In Guinea, for example, the regime outlawed all private markets in 1975; private trading was made a criminal offense. State agencies were supposed to fill the void, but they were riddled with corruption and proved to be hopelessly inefficient. Econoimic collapse and starvation were avoided only because the law was erratically enforced and eventually allowed to lapse.[17] In this and many other cases, statism has been mistaken for socialism.

For reasons that are, in the main, historical and contingent rather than theoretical or necessary, socialism has often been identified with statism by friends and foes alike. Increasingly that identification discredits socialism as a mode of development in the eyes of the world on the ground that statist strategies are plainly impractical and unrealistic apart from their troubling political aspects. In the past, a few countries, notably the Soviet Union and China, have constructed socialist economies with capital extracted from the countryside and appropriated by the state for purposes of investment and essential purchases abroad. That classic strategy is plainly unsuited to conditions in the agrarian countries of Africa for several reasons, among them rural resistance to collectivization, exponential population growth, the high cost of critical imports, and endemic problems of statist economic management. Furthermore, socialism is supposed to signify the democratization of economic life. Coercion is contrary to the spirit of socialism. Statism, the most general form of coercion, is the graveyard of socialism as well as democracy.

Participatory democracy is a logical response to the challenge of statism. Its appearance and reappearance in Africa should be a source of inspiration to democrats and, in particular, democratic socialists. However, the practice of participatory democracy cannot be regimented by the state without detriment to its integrity. Where participatory institutions have been created in factories and farms by self-motivated and self-directed workers, as in the case of Algeria, they countervail the power of the one-party state. By contrast, where participative decision-making is narrowly restricted and subject to close supervision by a party-state, as in Tanzania and Zambia, participatory democracy succumbs to the assault of guided democracy and developmental dictatorship.

Shall we conclude, with Gregor (1979: 327, 333), that developmental dictatorship is the wave of the future for Africa? The empirical support for that viewpoint is weak. Its sole rationale—the presumed power to produce rapid economic development—is scarcely tenable. Democracy is a far more popular alternative, but democracy must take up the challenge of development where dictatorship has failed. Africa needs a developmental democracy, a democracy without tears. Developmental democracy could represent a synthesis of all that has been learned from the many experiments with simpler types. It would probably be liberal and social, participatory and consociational all at once. From guided democracy it could inherit an appreciation for the function of leadership. The core of guided democracy could even be refined and transformed into preceptoral democracy, or leadership without political power.[18] In a complex, developmental democracy, intellectual guidance would operate by means of persuasion alone; its efficacy in Africa would be ensured by that immense respect for learning and scholarship which is a characteristic quality of modern African societies.

Developmental democracy does not imply a specific formulation of democratic principles based upon distinctive core values, such as political liberty for liberal democracy, social equality for social democracy, popular participation for participatory democracy, or group rights for consociational democracy. The content of developmental democracy would vary with the views of democratic theorists. One such theorist, the Canadian, C. B. Macpherson (1977: 44–76), introduced the term to designate a stage in the evolution of liberal democracy, marked by the emergence, in theory and practice, of equal opportunity for "individual self-development." This advance was promoted by the political doctrines of John Stuart Mill and his early twentieth-century successors. In our time, it is surely appropriate to broaden the meaning of developmental democracy so that it will accommodate the goals of social reconstruction in the nonindustrial countries. Developmental democracy today should, I believe, be enlarged to encompass the core values of social, participatory, and consociational democracy as well as the specifically liberal elements of limited government and individual self-development.

Broadly conceived, developmental democracy would evoke fresh and original responses to the problems of economic underdevelopment, social stagnation, and political drift. Original thought is the heart of the matter. Gregor has shown, convincingly, that the essential ideas of developmental dictatorship were formulated during the first decade of this century by revolutionary syndicalists in Italy. By the ninth decade these ideas have surely run their course. There is no good economic reason for Africans today to propitiate the European gods of developmental dictatorship.

From the early stirrings of modern African nationalism to the onset and consolidation of political independence, Africa has resisted foreign intellectual domination. In all but a few countries, African governments conduct their foreign relations on the basis of a deep and abiding commitment to the principle of nonalignment in world politics (Mazrui, 1977: 179–83, 280–83). African statecraft reflects a determination to formulate the challenges of international relations from a self-defined standpoint. In the social thought of twentieth-century Africa, intellectual self-reliance is a paramount theme; it spans the ideological spectrum as indicated by its prominence in the francophonic philosophy of Negritude, the Africanist tradition of Anton Lembede and his followers in South Africa (Gerhart, 1978), the "African" and democratic socialism of Nyerere, and the revolutionary socialism of Amilcar Cabral.[19] Students of social thought should recognize the quest for an intellectual synthesis and transcendence of capitalism and socialism in their classical and contemporary, or neoclassical, forms. In an essay entitled "The Emancipation of Democracy," W. E. B. Du Bois (1970: 65) assessed the contribution of black people in America to democracy thus:

It was the black man that raised a vision of democracy in America such as neither Americans nor Europeans conceived in the eighteenth century and such as they have not even accepted in the twentieth century; and yet a conception which every clear sighted man knows is true and inevitable.

Might this not be written of Africa's contribution to democracy in our time?[20]

Where shall we look for the signs of intellectual and political synthesis which would signify the emergence of a new democracy? Where have the forms of developmental democracy begun to take shape? Every national workshop bears inspection, for each, in its own way, contributes to the aggregate of democratic knowledge and practice. Consider Zimbabwe, where revolutionary socialists in power prepare to terminate a transitional period of liberal government in favor of a more restrictive, one-party political formula. Their long-term objective has been described in an official document (Government of the Republic of Zimbabwe, 1981: 19) as "a truly socialist, egalitarian and democratic society." Zimbabwean leaders and theorists will be challenged by the fact that there are no models for that kind of social construction on the face of this earth.

In pacesetting Zambia, where wage labor constitutes a comparatively large component of the total work force (more than one-third), the struggle for trade union autonomy is fundamental to the cause of developmental democracy. But for the democratic vitality of the labor movement, developmental dictatorship in the guise of "scientific socialism" could not be counteracted by other popular groups in Zambia. While clergymen, businessmen, intellectuals, and professional people are, in the main, opposed to the adoption of "scientific socialism" as an official doctrine, they could not resist it effectively without the firm support of democratic labor. In this matter of ideological choice, the principal restraining force on Zambia's political leadership is neither foreign capital nor the Zambian bourgeoisie; it is the Zambian labor movement.[21]

In the Sahelian nation of Niger, a military government has proclaimed the institution of a new political order, known as "the development society." Founded upon the twin pillars of traditional youth organizations and village-based agricultural cooperatives, the new system of government functions through a series of elected councils, culminating in a National Development Council, which has been directed to frame an "original" and "authentically Nigerian" constitution (*Africa Research Bulletin*, 1982: 6417A; *Africa News*, 1982: 9–11).

Here, too, the spirit of developmental democracy is abroad.

In neighboring Nigeria, the prospects for developmental democracy are enhanced by a federal system of government which provides a multiplicity of arenas for social and political experimentation. Federalism is also the essential foundation of Nigerian national unity. The relevance of that example to pan-African thought merits attention. Dictatorship may be the most formidable barrier to pan-African unity. Pan-African federalism would foster democracy at the expense of dictatorship in many countries. As a pan-African principle, federalism would also facilitate the exchange of democratic discoveries among African polities and thereby promote the growth of developmental democracy. Increasingly, African freedom would radiate African power.

Metaphorically speaking, most Africans today live under the dictatorship of material poverty. The poverty of dictatorship in Africa is equally apparent. It offends the renowned African tradition of community-wide participation in decision-making.[22] By contrast with dictatorship, democracy is a developing idea and an increasingly sophisticated form of political organization. The development of democracy in Africa has become a major determinant of its progress in the world.

NOTES

1. See the sensitive assessment by Emerson (1960: 272–92).

2. I am indebted to C. R. D. Halisi for this formulation.

3. The title of an address, delivered in 1880, in which Africa's contribution to world culture is judiciously assessed. See Blyden (1888).

4. On "post-independence political change," see Collier (1982: 95–117).

5. For a candid statement by the Secretary to the Government of the Federation, see Musa (1981); on the roots of corruption, see Ekeh (1975).

6. On the consequences of rural resistance to collectivization, see, among many fine analyses, Lofchie (1978); McHenry (1979); the essays by Barker, Boesen, and Mascarenhas in Mwansasu and Pratt (1979: 125–44); Ergas (1980); and Hyden (1980).

7. I have borrowed this phrase from Crawford Young's (1982: 11) piercing observation that Tanzania presents a "paradox of self-reliance awash in a sea of aid."

8. As Carole Pateman (1970: 43) observes, in her path-breaking exposition of participatory democracy, "most individuals spend a great deal of their lifetime at work and the business of the workplace provides an education in the management of collective affairs that is difficult to parallel elsewhere."

9. Statement by President Kenneth Kaunda, July 28, 1981. Embassy of the Republic of Zambia, Washington, D.C.

10. In formulating this interpretation of Kaunda's ideological shift, I have benefitted from the clarifying insights of C. R. D. Halisi.

11. For an informed, optimistic assessment of democratic participation in Algeria, see Nellis (1977; 1980).

12. Rudebeck (1981) is a pessimistic reappraisal.

13. The theory of consociational democracy has a partly African pedigree, namely, the classic analysis of West African politics by the Jamaican Nobel Laureate, Sir W. Arthur Lewis, Politics in West Africa (1965). See Lijphart (1977: 143–46, 177–81, 216–22).

14. Slabbert, a former professor of sociology, became parliamentary leader of the Progressive Federal Party in 1979.

15. Despite his cogent critique of consociational democracy for South Africa, Adam subsequently participated in the deliberations of the Buthelezi Commission and commended (1983: 140) consociational reform as "the only realistic alternative to escalating strife . . . an institutionalized truce instead of open warfare."

16. Surely, the intractable north-south conflict in the Sudan virtually cries out for a consociational solution. See Wai (1979).

17. For the climactic, violent sequel, see Young (1982: 173–73).

18. This differs from Lindblom's (1977: 52–62) concept of a "preceptoral system," which denotes the fusion of intellectual leadership and political power by dictatorial means.

19. Especially, "National Liberation and Culture," in Africa Information Service (1973: 39–56).

20. C. R. D. Halisi drew my attention to this parallel and stimulated my thoughts about the ideas in this paragraph.

21. I am indebted to C. Chipasha Luchembe, an historian of the labor movement in Zambia, for this interpretation.

22. See, for example, the Akan-based "paradigm of African society," especially its "theory of government" in Abraham (1962: 75–80).

REFERENCES

Abraham, W. E. 1962. *The Mind of Africa*. Chicago: University of Chicago Press.

Achike, Okay. 1978. *Groundwork of Military Law and Military Rule in Nigeria*. Enugu: Fourth Dimension Press.

Adam, Heribert. 1979. "Political Alternatives," pp. 286–302 in Heribert Adam and Hermann Giliomee, *Ethnic Power Mobilized: Can South Africa Change?* New Haven: Yale University Press.

———. 1983. "The Manipulation of Ethnicity: South Africa in Comparative Perspective," pp. 127–47 in Donald Rothchild and Victor A. Olorunsola (eds.), *State Versus Ethnic Claims: African Policy Dilemmas*. Boulder: Westview Press.

Africa Confidential. 1982. 23/10, 12 May.

Africa Information Service. (ed.) 1973. *Return to the Source: Selected Speeches of Amilcar Cabral* New York: Monthly Review Press.

Africa News. 1982. 28/24, 14 June.

Africa Research Bulletin. 1982. 19/4, 15 May.

Awolowo, Obafemi. 1947. *Path to Nigerian Freedom*. London: Faber.

Azikiwe, Nnamdi. 1943. *Political Blueprint of Nigeria*. Lagos: African Book Company, Ltd.

Barkan, Joel D. 1979. "Legislators, Elections, and Political Linkages," pp. 64–92 in Joel D. Barkan with John D. Okumu (eds.), *Politics and Public Policy in Kenya and Tanzania*. New York: Praeger Publishers.

Blyden, Edward Wilmot. 1888. *Christianity, Islam and the Negro Race*. Second Edition. London: Whitingham.

Bratton, Michael. 1980. "The Social Context of Political Penetration: Village and Ward Committees in Kasama District," pp. 213–39 in William Tordoff (ed.), *Administration in Zambia*. Manchester: Manchester University Press.

Buthelezi Commission Report. 1982. Vol. I. Durban: H and H Publishers.

Chaliand, Gérard. 1969. *Armed Struggle in Africa*. New York: Monthly Review Press.

Coleman, James S. 1958. *Nigeria: Background to Nationalism*. Berkeley: University of California Press.

Collier, Ruth Berins. 1982. *Regimes in Tropical Africa*. Berkeley: University of California Press.

Davidson, Basil. 1969. *The Liberation of Guiné*. Baltimore: Penguin Books.

Diamond, Larry. 1982. "Cleavage, Conflict and Anxiety in the Second Nigerian Republic," *Journal for Modern African Studies* 20/4: 629–68.

Du Bois, W. E. Burghardt. 1970. *The Gift of Black Folk*. New York: Washington Square Press.

Ekeh, Peter P. 1975. "Colonialism and the Two Publics in Africa: A Theoretical Statement," *Comparative Studies in Society and History* 17/1: 91–112.

Emerson, Rupert. 1960. *From Empire to Nation*. Cambridge, Mass.: Harvard University Press.

Ergas, Zaki. 1980. "Why Did the Ujamaa Village Policy Fail?—Towards a Global Analysis," *Journal of Modern African Studies* 18/3: 387–410.

Gerhart, Gail M. 1978. *Black Power in South Africa: The Evolution of an Ideology*. Berkeley: University of California Press.

Green, Reginald Herbold. 1979. "Tanzanian Political Economy Goals, Strategies, and Results, 1967–74: Notes Towards an Interim Assessment," pp. 19–45 in Bismarck U. Mwansasu and Cranford Pratt (eds.), *Toward Socialism in Tanzania*. Toronto: University of Toronto Press.

Gregor, A. James. 1979. *Italian Fascism and Developmental Dictatorship*. Princeton, N.J.: Princeton University Press.

Hyden, Goran. 1980. *Beyond Ujamaa in Tanzania*. Berkeley: University of California Press.

Jackson, Robert H. and Carl G. Rosberg. 1982. *Personal Rule in Black Africa*. Berkeley: University of California Press.

Johnson, R. W. 1978. "Guinea," pp. 36–65 in John Dunn (ed.), *West African States: Failure and Promise*. Cambridge: Cambridge University Press.

Kaunda, Kenneth D. 1968. *Zambia's Guideline for the Next Decade*. Lusaka.

———. 1970. *"Take up the Challenge . . ."*. Lusaka.

———. 1971. *A Path for the Future*. Lusaka.

Lewis, Sir W. Arthur. 1965. *Politics in West Africa*. London: Allen and Unwin.

Lijphart, Arend. 1977. *Democracy in Plural Societies*. New Haven: Yale University Press.

Lindblom, Charles E. 1977. *Politics and Markets*. New York: Basic Books.

Lofchie, Michael F. 1978. "Agrarian Crisis and Economic Liberalisation in Tanzania," *Journal of Modern African Studies* 16/3: 451–75.

Macpherson, C. B. 1977. *The Life and Times of Liberal Democracy*. Oxford: Oxford University Press.

Marx, Karl. 1967. *Capital, Vol. I*. New York: International Publishers. (Preface to the First German Edition, 1867).

Mazrui, Ali A. 1977. *Africa's International Relations*. London: Heineman.

McHenry, Dean E., Jr. 1979. *Tanzania's Ujamaa Villages*. Berkeley: University of California Institute of International Studies.

Musa, Shehu A. 1981. *National Discipline, National Commitment and Development*. Lagos: Federal Government Printer.

Mwansasu, Bismarck U., and Cranford Pratt (eds.). 1979. *Towards Socialism in Tanzania*. Toronto: University of Toronto Press.

Nellis, John R. 1977. "Socialist Management in

Algeria," *Journal of Modern African Studies* 15/4: 529–54.

———. 1980. "Algerian Socialism and its Critics," *Canadian Journal of Political Science* 13/3: 481–507.

Nyerere, Julius K. 1977. *The Arusha Declaration Ten Years After.* Dar es Salaam.

Ollawa, Patrick E. 1979. *Participatory Democracy in Zambia.* Illfracombe, Devon: Stockwell.

Pateman, Carole. 1970. *Participation and Democratic Theory.* Cambridge: Cambridge University Press.

Pratt, Cranford. 1979. "Tanzania's Transition to Socialism: Reflections of a Democratic Socialist," pp. 193–236 in Bismarck U. Mwansasu and Cranford Pratt (eds.), *Toward Socialism in Tanzania.* Toronto: University of Toronto Press.

Quick, Stephen A. 1977. "Bureaucracy and Rural Socialism in Zambia," *Journal of Modern African Studies* 15/3: 379–400.

Republic of Zimbabwe, Government of the. 1981. *Growth with Equity: An Economic Policy Statement.* Salisbury.

Rudebeck, Lars. 1974. *Guinea-Bissau.* Uppsala: The Scandinavian Institute of African Studies.

———. 1981. "Consequences of Decolonization Even Through Political Mobilization for Armed Struggle." Paper presented to a seminar on "Liberation and Development" at the Institute of Political History, University of Turku, Turku, Finland.

Scott, Ian. 1980. "Party and Administration Under the One-party State," pp. 139–61 in William Tordoff (ed.), *Administration in Zambia.* Manchester: Manchester University Press.

Slabbert, F. van Zyl and David Welsh. 1979. *South Africa's Options.* Cape Town: David Philip.

The Weekly Review. (Nairobi). 1982. 11 June.

Tordoff, William (ed.). 1980. *Administration in Zambia.* Manchester: Manchester University Press.

Wai, Dunstan M. 1979. "Revolution, Rhetoric, and Reality in the Sudan," *Journal of Modern African Studies* 17/1: 71–93.

West Africa. 1982. 3377, 26 April.

Young, Crawford. 1982. *Ideology and Development in Africa.* New Haven: Yale University Press.

Succession of the Charismatic Leader: The Gordian Knot of African Politics

Lanciné Sylla

The central problem of recent political development in Africa is one that has been familiar to sociologists since Max Weber: the succession of the charismatic leader. Change, whether violent (assassination, coup d'état, or civil war) or peaceful (the orderly transition of power, liberalization, democratization), has been guided by underlying forces whose concrete, often dramatic manifestations conceal their essential nature and real significance. How is power transferred in a given society? How is the succession to leadership determined (in practice as well as theory)? In the new African nations, which have experienced many political crises in the course of their development, there seems to be no generally accepted answer to these questions. Or at any rate, there seems to be no understanding of the fact that agreement as to how power should be transferred is the *sine qua non* of political stability and of society's peaceful development. Change, therefore, has often been chaotic and haphazard, and attempts at rational organization of the state have been erratic at best, usually coming in the wake of military coups or other crises of the sort that are all too familiar in most African countries. Indeed, it is because difficulties have been encountered in trying to organize the state rationally, and to establish a consensus concerning the transfer of power, that coups have become endemic, and that experiments with democracy and civilian rule have so often

proved disappointing. If the winds of democracy are blowing over Africa today, one reason may be that democracy provides a rational solution to the problem of succession. Liberalization of the regime in a sense forces a country to establish a rational system for transferring power. Thus, by beginning the liberalization process, the aging charismatic leader sets the stage for his own succession. From Bourguiba in Tunisia to Senghor in Senegal and Houphouet-Boigny in the Ivory Coast, democratization in one form or another has lately been laying the groundwork for new leadership by changing the balance of power among the various opposing political forces, forces that can no longer be controlled by what Weber calls the "routinization of charisma." Thus it is no exaggeration to say that the problem of succession is one that all African states must confront.

What solutions to this problem have been proposed? This is the question that I shall try to answer in this essay. I also want to look at the nature of power itself. Indeed, to speak of a "mode of succession" is really to speak of a "mode of legitimation of power," for any mode of succession necessarily corresponds to some mode of legitimation. In other words, no transfer of power is likely to succeed unless it is sanctioned by the prevailing form of authority. Thus the kinds of political crisis and conflict that we have been talking about until now may be described as "crises of legitimacy," to borrow Habermas's phrase. In short, the problem of finding successors for charismatic leaders in Africa is one aspect of a general crisis of political legitimacy that different countries have tried to resolve in different ways.

Reprinted from *Daedalus*, Journal of the American Academy of Arts and Sciences, Cambridge, MA, "Black Africa: A Generation After Independence," vol. 111, no. 2 (Spring 1982), 11–28, by permission of the journal. Translation by Arthur Goldhammer.

The point of the present essay, then, is to examine the foundations of political authority in Africa in the light of Max Weber's analysis of charismatic leadership. We shall be looking at the forms that charismatic power has taken in Africa, how they came into being, and how they operate. In short, we shall be studying the history of charismatic power in Africa and its influence on African political development in general. We shall also be looking at the problems that charismatic leadership poses for political development in Africa, and in particular, at the one central problem that overshadows all the rest, namely, the problem of continuity, or how to find a successor for a charismatic leader. Concrete examples will be given to illustrate the points being made, examples drawn from the experience of various African nations. Since an exhaustive analysis is impossible within the confines of an essay, I shall focus on typical cases that exemplify my general points.

Beyond irrational political behavior and other perverse consequences of charismatic authority, African societies must confront a more general problem: namely, how to organize their governments. In my view, without a rational organization of the state, no political development is possible. Here we touch not only on questions of sociological method and scientific outlook, but also, if I may say so, on matters of political faith. Let me make my own position clear: for better or for worse, every society must agree on a principle of political legitimacy. The rationalization of the state is a crucial prerequisite of all social development. It is in this connection that Weber's ideas about charisma and the rationalization of power turn out to be most relevant to the analysis of political systems in the developing countries. Because of the profound cultural changes that these countries are being forced to undergo in the course of development, it is more likely than not that they will give rise to charismatic leadership of one sort or another. Before turning to a detailed examination of the situation in Africa, therefore, I should like first to relate the topic of the present essay to Weber's general theory of charismatic authority.[1]

THE NATURE OF POWER IN AFRICA AND WEBER'S THEORY OF CHARISMA

For methodological reasons, it is convenient to digress a moment to explain the concepts we will be using and a little about the general theory they are part of. I start from Weber's analysis of "types of legitimacy," because the notion of charisma can really be understood only in relation to the two other types of authority that Weber defines. It will soon become apparent that all the African regimes that have come into being since 1960 have been based on authority of the charismatic type.

According to Weber, all power is based on legitimate authority. By "legitimate authority," he means an authority that invokes generally recognized principles to justify its exercise of power. There are three ways in which an authority may obtain legitimacy, or recognition of its right to govern. More precisely, Weber defines three pure forms of legitimate authority, three "ideal types" that exist nowhere in their pure state. By combining these three ideal types in various proportions, however, we can gain a clearer understanding of actual political regimes. The three ideal types defined by Weber are traditional authority, legal-rational authority, and charismatic authority.

Traditional authority is recognized as legitimate by virtue of tradition, custom, and veneration of previous generations. Typically, it is found in monarchical societies, ancient kingdoms, and traditional African tribes. Traditional authority depends in one sense on the force of habit. It is rooted in an ancestral past. The current leaders thus become the supreme guardians of tradition, the defenders of the age-old institutions that they control. Under this type of authority, laws and customs handed down from earlier generations are used to justify the current political structure. Thus the transmission of authority is characteristically hereditary in this type of regime. Status is normally inherited and is not due solely to an individual's personal merit.

Legal-rational authority derives from a coherent system of rules that are commonly submitted to the entire population for acceptance or rejection. Typical examples of such rules are the constitutions and legal systems of modern states. Modern administrative and bureaucratic structures are also typical of this form of authority. Institutions, laws, and constitutional order are the only source of legitimacy in a legal-rational system. The law is sovereign, not individuals or particular groups of individuals. The institutions created by constitutional laws take precedence over the individuals and groups who happen to hold power at any given moment. Those in authority derive their right to govern from the provisions of the constitution and laws currently in effect. The rules governing succession or alternation of power are also defined by the constitution. Modern democratic states are the most striking example of this kind of authority: in democratic systems, universal suffrage settles the question of how power is to be transferred.

Finally, charismatic authority, the focus of this essay, is based on an almost religious respect for, or faith in, a leader to whom exceptional qualities are attributed. These qualities may be thought to be of divine origin, as in the case of a religious prophet, or they may simply manifest extraordinary personal talents. According to Weber, this type of authority is characterized by "absolutely personal devotion and personal confidence in revelation, heroism, or other qualities of individual leadership. This is 'charismatic' domination, as exercised by the prophet or—in the field of politics—by the elected war lord, the plebiscitarian ruler, the great demagogue, or the political party leader."[2] It is the "personal grace"—the charisma—of the leader that is the prime mover of the political system. The charismatic leader is obeyed because of his charm, his prestige, his influence, his personal magnetism and power to sway crowds. Pomp and ceremony, mob passion, ritual, the cult of personality, deification and personalization of power—in short, all the symbolic and emotional components of politics—assume greater importance in this kind of regime than rational decision-making. As Weber says, "Men do not obey [the charismatic leader] by virtue of tradition or statute but because they believe in him."[3] This explains why all charismatic power is in essence revolutionary: breaking with custom, respecting no law, it rises against the established order and stands as the creator of a new order. Accordingly, charismatic rule is generally linked to a social movement that establishes a new order. A revolution led by a charismatic figure is one of the most effective ways of overthrowing regimes based on traditional or legal authority. But since charismatic power depends on the exceptional qualities of an individual, sooner or later its legitimacy will be called into question, most notably when it comes time to find a successor for the charismatic figure. Thus the great question of charismatic authority is succession. In effect, when the authority of a leader extends beyond the limits laid down by custom and law, the crucial question is how to make sure that authority will endure when the individual in whom extraordinary powers are vested is no longer on the scene.

In Weber's view, charismatic power is in essence ephemeral and transitory. It sets the stage either for a traditional form of authority, by establishing a new tradition, or for a legal-rational form of authority, by institutionalizing procedures for the transfer of power. Before either of these possibilities is realized, however, the charismatic leader or his successors may try to capitalize on the leader's legendary prestige in order to "routinize" his charisma, to use Weber's now celebrated term. Weber goes into considerable detail about the ways in which charisma may be routinized. Space does not allow us to recapitulate his account here in full detail. Let me say simply that the end result of routinization is the glorification of the period during which the new regime was founded. Either the aging charismatic leader himself or his successor (who benefits from the prestige accruing to his illustrious predecessor) attempts to prolong the period of charismatic rule by staging festivals, establishing public holidays, and creating new political rituals (involving outdoor speeches, meetings, ceremonial state visits, international conferences, and so forth, with a judicious admixture of ethnic color, stirring ideology, and appeals to ancestral roots). In Africa it is common for the leader to emphasize the symbolic, emotional, and utopian, rather than the rational, institutional, and practical, aspects of politics. Thus the consequences of the routinization of charisma, in the forms it has generally taken in Africa, have been unfortunate: these include economic and political inefficiency, the development of one-party rule, excessive personalization of power, authoritarianism, slowing of political development, coups d'état, and military dictatorships. In African politics, the coup d'état has come to be seen as an almost normal way of transferring power from a charismatic leader to others.

Weber's account of the development and routinization of charisma seems to fit African political realities fairly well. Before turning to the main topic of this essay, the succession of the charismatic leader, it will therefore be useful to take a brief look at what Weber has to say on these topics.[4]

All of the recently decolonized African nations have had to deal with problems created by charismatic power. Conditions favorable to the development of charismatic leadership were created in Africa first by colonization itself and later by the problems that developed not only after independence, but even more during the period of struggles that led to decolonization. The hope of a savior or a hero capable of putting an end to colonial domination, and the need for a great teacher to restore a shattered cultural identity and establish a new political order, created a situation that fairly demanded the emergence of a charismatic leader. Pushing the point somewhat, we might even say that the very anticipation of a savior, the expectation of a new political order, made the society itself charismatic, even before the advent of the charismatic personality. The masses were "starved for charisma," to use Erik Erikson's expression.[5] Thus the historic figure who leads the anticolonial forces and succeeds in winning his country's independence becomes the leader of a triumphant party and a national hero, the father of his country. He becomes the symbol of the long-awaited new order, and whether he likes it or not, the adulation of the masses makes the providential hero into a charismatic leader.

To recapitulate, then, the emergence of historic leaders in the fight for independence, the problems of modernization and economic development that all new nations must face, and the general mobilization of the populace in the face of these problems all contribute to the development of charismatic forms of power. Charismatic governments are, as we mentioned earlier, typically associated with social movements that create a new social order. Weber in fact emphasizes the connection between the emergence of charismatic leadership and situations involving a transition from a traditional to a modern type of society, situations in which the foundations of the traditional order are for one reason or another shaken. In short, charismatic governments are quite likely to emerge in societies that, like those in Africa, are undergoing profound cultural transformation.

Once a charismatic government is established, however, there are urgent tasks to be accomplished: power must be consolidated, political control established, governmental institutions created, and an administrative network extended to cover the full extent of the national territory. In trying to carry out these tasks, the new government immediately comes up against all of the problems associated with charismatic regimes, problems that in Africa are all the more acute owing to the lack of a legal tradition and to the reemergence of older forms of authority in the wake of decolonization. There is no doubt that in the postindependence period, political development throughout Africa has been hampered by problems inherent in charismatic forms of government. Indeed, the reemergence of older forms of legitimacy, coinciding with the period of consolidation of the newly established regimes, has created a general crisis of legitimacy on the continent.

This crisis of legitimacy sets the stage for a kind of political drama that is quite familiar in Africa. What we commonly see in this phase of legitimation and consolidation of new regimes is conflict between the different principles of legitimacy. In African nations today we find all three principles at work, and none outweighs the others sufficiently to insure the permanence of the system. The sources of instability inherent in each type of legitimacy reinforce one another, with the result that the political system is always potentially in crisis. The way in which power is transferred is of course a crucial feature of the general crisis situation. Political conflict in general revolves around the crisis of legitimacy, and the new nations must therefore find ways to resolve this crisis. The situation in Africa is one in which traditional authority has crumbled and yet no new authority (whether institutional or charismatic) is sufficiently established to take its place. This leads to social disintegration and to a breakdown of the political order, both old and new, with the result that the developing countries are beset with constant political conflict.

Indeed, I want to argue that, whenever a society experiences a conflict between different principles of legitimacy, it enters upon a long period of crisis marked by incessant struggle over the fundamental nature of the political system, struggle that brings social unrest in its wake. Society itself becomes "sick," or as Emile Durkheim would say, "anomic." As long as African societies fail to agree on a principle for the legitimation of power, they will continue to be subject to this kind of conflict and to permanent political instability in the form of civil war, subversion, conspiracy, governmental crisis, or coups d'état. Indeed, as was mentioned earlier, in the absence of any rules governing the transfer of power from a charismatic leader to his successors, the coup d'état has become almost an accepted way of making the transition. Before turning to a discussion of the specific ways in which this transition has been accomplished in Africa, it is worth pausing a moment to consider the theoretical connection between the crisis of legitimacy and the problem of succession in a charismatic regime.

When a political system must confront a crisis of succession, the entire population becomes subject to a sort of mass hysteria, particularly in charismatic regimes, where the people's only sense of political security and stability comes from their enthusiastic support for the charismatic leader. This hysteria, which grips masses and political leaders alike, is but the outward expression of the crisis of political legitimacy that is the inevitable consequence of the departure of a charismatic leader. All thought turns to the question of how best to assure the continuation of power once the leader is gone. Even though laws may exist that in theory spell out the way in which power is to be transferred, the mere existence of an appropriate body of law is not enough to ensure that its provisions will be accepted by the leader's "followers," whose relationship to him is more emotional than rational or legalistic. Where a long-standing legal-rational system exists, as in Western Europe, for example, the emergence of a charismatic leader seems purely circumstantial. There, charismatic authority will sooner or later give way to a traditional or institutional regime based on the existing legal tradition. But in newly established countries, like those of Africa, that lack any legal tradition of their own, the problem of succession is the Gordian knot of politics.

With the leader gone and everyone in the grip of political hysteria, the leader's aides and other political figures then try to discover or, by manipulating the masses, to fabricate a replacement, a new bearer of charisma, someone with characteristics similar to those of the departed leader. Sometimes the charismatic leader himself, while he is still in power, designates his own successor. The nomination of a prime minister or vice-president may alleviate the hysteria, but the central problem remains, for charisma cannot be taught or improvised. Alternatively, the leader may appoint himself president for life or crown himself emperor in an effort to establish a tradition in terms of which the hereditary transmission of his charisma can be justified. Or the masses may try to predict who the eventual successor will be by interpreting the ruler's statements, predilections, and desires, or by taking the temperature, so to speak, of the ruling class, whose members often compete for the succession in an atmosphere of general discord, not to say animosity and fierce rivalry. At the grassroots, these conflicts within the ruling class may translate into nothing more complicated than traditional tribal rivalries: since the ruler is a member of tribe A, someone is bound to argue that his successor must come from tribe B, C, or D. This kind of rotating leadership is familiar to ethnologists who have studied societies divided along generational lines. Dahomey (present-day Benin) experimented with a system in which co-presidents drawn from each of the country's three major ethnic groups were supposed to govern in turn, but the experiment proved unsuccessful.

Because of the difficulty of transferring power peacefully in charismatic regimes, recent years have seen a growing number of military coups in African states ruled by charismatic figures. Consequently, I should like to turn now to a discussion of present-day conditions in Africa, applying Weber's theoretical ideas to actual situations.

THE SUCCESSION OF CHARISMATIC LEADERS IN AFRICA: A HISTORICAL OVERVIEW

We now shift the ground of our discussion, moving from general sociological theory to empirical political science. It is therefore important to bear in mind that Weber's ideal types of authority are never found in the pure state. In most political systems we find all three types, mixed in varying proportions. In discussing any real polity, we must take account of both what kind of political system the founders intended to create and what form of authority actually predominates. In particular, the routinization of charisma does not always go according to the charismatic leader's plan. What actually takes place is a contest involving charismatic, institutional, and traditional forces, each seeking supremacy over the others. If the political system is to achieve stability, the contest must sooner or later result in the victory of either a traditional or a legal-rational structure. The charismatic element will not totally disappear, however, at least not in the current state of African politics. Rather, it will be absorbed into the other elements and thus outlive the original authority figure. In this power struggle, the political actors will try various strategies to achieve one of two possible goals: either they will seek to establish the charismatic system on a permanent footing, or they will try to change it to establish

either a traditional system or a more legal-rational form of government. No matter what mode of succession is chosen, the aim is always to resolve what we have been calling the crisis of legitimacy.

We are now ready to begin discussing concrete cases. But since there have been so many different kinds of attempts to resolve the problem of succession in Africa, for ease of understanding I will group the cases into three broad categories.

First of all, there have been efforts to perpetuate charismatic rule, with or without the historical leader's participation. These may be subsumed under the head of routinization of charisma. Second, there have been attempts to use violence to put an end to charismatic rule, usually in order to establish a legal-rational system. Here I am thinking of the efforts that have been made in some African states to normalize or democratize military dictatorships established subsequent to a coup d'état. Finally, in certain other states, the leader himself has initiated democratization by decreeing systematic rules for the transfer of power, thus paving the way for his own succession. Summarizing, then, we have the following three categories:

(1) Routinization of charisma
(2) Violent seizure of power, followed by transformation of political system
(3) Democratization initiated by the charismatic leader himself

Of course this typology, though useful for analytical purposes, does not do justice to the complexity of real political situations. There is in fact some overlap: a coup d'état may lead not only to democratization, but also to routinization of charisma; a charismatic leader may justify his power in traditional ways instead of moving toward more rational institutions and greater democracy; and finally, a crisis in an institutionalized form of government may be resolved by turning to a charismatic leader. Since an exhaustive treatment is beyond the scope of this essay, I repeat that only a few more or less typical cases will be considered here.

Routinization of Charisma

Quite dissimilar situations are grouped together under this head. To begin with, the charismatic leader himself may seek to perpetuate his reign. Or he and his aides, or both, may look for another charismatic personality. Or again, a general may be thrust into power in the wake of a coup d'état and be transformed by a society starved for charisma into a new charismatic head of state. The modality of change is immaterial; the important point is that in each case the result is routinization of charisma.

To look first at some extreme examples: a charismatic leader may appoint himself "president for life" or crown himself "emperor." This may be done in stages. For example, Macias Nguema, the former president of Equatorial Guinea, who wielded a personalized and deified form of power that can only be regarded as charismatic, appointed himself "president for life, major general of the army, chief educator of the nation, supreme scientist, master of traditional culture, and chairman of the *Parti Unique National des Travailleurs* [the One National Workers' Party], as well as the only miracle that Equatorial Guinea ever produced." Outlawing the Christian religion, he replaced it with his own personality cult: all prayers were required to begin with the words, "In the name of Father Macias, our savior and redeemer." Doubtless, this is an extreme example, and the dictatorship and tyranny that almost inevitably result from such excesses ultimately set the stage for a coup d'état, such as the one that toppled Macias and so many others like him. Still, the important point to be made here is that the institution of a life presidency has frequently been used in Africa as a way of routinizing charisma. And if Macias Nguema declared himself president for life in violation of the Guinean constitution, another dictator, General Bokassa, had the support of his party when he did the same thing in 1972. After winning power in the Central African Republic in 1965, Bokassa, then a colonel, proclaimed himself first general and then field marshal of his army. He then had his appointment as president for life approved by the members of the only party in the country, MESAN, in 1972. Finally, in December 1977 a special party congress declared him emperor of the Central African Republic. A new constitution inaugurated a constitutional monarchy, with the intention of making the succession hereditary. Of course, as everyone knows, this attempt to turn the Central African Republic into a traditional empire proved unsuccessful. Like Macias Nguema and Idi Amin Dada, who were also preparing to elevate themselves to the status of emperor, Bokassa was turned out by a military coup.[6]

If the routinization of charisma led to a return to a traditional type of regime in Equatorial Guinea, the Central African Republic, and Uganda, events took a different turn in Tunisia. there, Habib Bourguiba became president for life and succeeded in institutionalizing his charismatic authority. The "commander in chief and father of the Tunisian nation," Bourguiba gained independence for his country in 1956. Article 40 of the Tunisian constitution states clearly that "no person shall be elected President of the Republic for more than three consecutive terms." But Bourguiba, after having been elected three times, in 1959, 1964, and 1969, ran for office a fourth time and was once again elected. He resorted to the simple expedient of having the constitution amended by referendum to provide for his own election as president for life.

The case of Tunisia invites reflection, not so much on questions of power politics or legal niceties, but rather on the crucial role of elections in the routinization of charisma in Africa. Given the political realities prevailing in Africa today, a head of state need not declare himself president for life or stage an election to sanction his life tenure. It is common for the incumbent to garner 99.99 percent of the votes cast in many elections, so that a sitting president becomes in effect president for life, whether or not he officially assumes the title. Barring resignation or a military takeover, he is assured of a life term in office. Yet elections also have a cathartic function. They enable the head of state to mobilize his people and to reestablish contact with the masses. And they renew and reaffirm the legitimacy of the historic leader of the nation. Furthermore, since African states are generally ruled by one-party regimes, it is hardly to be expected that elections will sweep a rival party into power as in a pluralist democracy. Rather, they serve a ritual function, reinforcing the power of the charismatic leader. Pluralism is out of the question in any truly charismatic society, for the opposition would be doomed in advance to lose every election. Each electoral contest provides the leader's party with an opportunity to strengthen its hand. Since all good fortune is thought to flow from the divine grace (charisma) of the true historic leader, members of the opposition are likely to be viewed as traitors and enemies of the state.

Another strategy for perpetuating and reinforcing charismatic power is the threat of resignation, real or feigned. For instance, rumors of the leader's possible retirement may be circulated at the party convention in order to whip up political hysteria, with the result that the president is soon besieged with requests that he remain in power lest the nation fall into chaos. President Eyadema of Togo was three times persuaded to remain in office by his people and his party, despite his stated intention to resign. A similar scenario has been played out at party conventions in other countries, such as Cameroon and the Ivory Coast, where Ahidjo and Houphouet-Boigny were persuaded by their parties to remain in office rather than retire. In these one-party states, the role of the party congress is to strengthen the leader's position. Like elections, the resignation strategy enables the chief of state to test his popularity, bolster his legitimacy, and assure the continuity of his regime.

The death of the leader can also play a part in the routinization of charisma. Generally, either the leader handpicks his own successor before he dies or his staff makes the decision after his death. The man chosen will usually be another charismatic figure with qualities similar to those of his predecessor. If the staff makes the decision after the leader's death, there may be a power struggle over the leadership.

A case in point occurred with the sudden death of Angola's historic leader, Agostinho Neto, in September 1979. Neto had never considered designating a successor, but he did leave behind a well-oiled and highly disciplined political machine, the MPLA (Popular Movement for the Liberation of Angola), put together during the war for independence. To succeed him, the party chose the current president, Dos Santos, one of Neto's earliest supporters and the man to whom he ordinarily entrusted the reins of government when he was out of the country. He was confirmed as president by a special party congress.

In the Congo, a similar course was followed after the assassination of President Marien Ngouabi, but splits within the ruling party ultimately proved fatal to the man designated to serve as acting president, Yhombi Opango, the most senior and highest ranking officer in the country's army. Because of opposition to Opango within the Congolese Workers Party (PCT), the central committee was forced to consider three candidates: Opango, another officer, Colonel Sassou Nguesso, and a civilian member of the party central committee, Mr. Tchicaya. Opango received fifteen votes, Tchicaya fourteen, and Nguesso seven in the first round of balloting, but on the second round, contrary to all expectation, Nguesso was elected when Tchicaya withdrew in his favor.

The death of Kenyan president Jomo Kenyatta provoked a crisis that was resolved by a combination of political dealing in the party central committee and recourse to constitutional procedures. Eighty-five when he died, Kenyatta had had ample opportunity to prepare for his succession, but avoided doing so for fear of sowing bitter dissension in the ranks of his ruling party, the KANU (Kenya African National Union). As political leaders became increasingly impatient for a solution to the problem of succession, certain changes were made in the country's constitution. These proved insufficient, however, to quell the conflict that ensued upon Kenyatta's death. The constitution provided that a vice-president, appointed by the president, would become acting president for a period of ninety days, during which presidential elections were to be held. The candidates in this election were to be designated by the duly authorized political parties—in reality, therefore, by KANU, the only legal party in Kenya. The constitution further stipulated that if there was only one candidate, no election need be held; hence, if KANU chose to designate a single candidate, he automatically became president of Kenya. In the event, the party split into two factions. One favored the incumbent vice-president, Arap Moi. The other, which opposed him, organized an assassination plot that was to be put into effect on the day following Kenyatta's death. The plan was to murder Arap Moi in Nakuru, the residence of President Kenyatta. But when Kenyatta died in Mombassa rather than Nakuru, the plan was aborted. Events then followed one another in quick succession. The plot was dismantled, and Arap Moi was sworn in as acting president under the provisions of the constitution. He was then elected chairman of KANU and named as the only candidate for the presidency, making him automatically the head of state. The decision of the party was then bolstered by the usual charisma-enhancing ritual: rallies were held in support of the new president, resolutions of support were drafted, and elections by acclamation were held in various places around the country.

As these examples show, there is a potential for violence whenever a successor has to be chosen for a charismatic leader. It is to the examination of cases of violent change that we shall turn next.

Change by Force: From Charisma to Institutional Order

A coup d'état may do either of two things: help to routinize charisma or transform a charismatic regime into a legal-rational one. It is common in Africa for masses starved for charisma to invest with charismatic attributes a military leader who has successfully seized power. Typically, the officer is lifted out of obscurity and raised above the general run of mankind on a wave of popular frenzy stirred up by ritual, magic, music, dance, folklore, festivals, and mass demonstrations. Given that the conditions prevailing in some African countries today are not compatible with institutionalized politics, a temporary solution to the problem of transferring power has been found in the coup d'état. As Carl Schmitt has said, "He is sovereign who takes charge in extraordinary circum-

stances."[7] Now, a crisis of succession creates extraordinary circumstances on which the leader of a coup may capitalize. The cycle is endless: a charismatic regime enters upon a crisis, the crisis is resolved by a coup, the leader of the coup is invested with charisma, and the whole sequence begins all over again.

Striking instances of the transformation of a victorious general into a charismatic figure may be found in Togo, Zaïre, and Benin. In Togo, for example, a referendum held in November 1971 put the following question to a vote: "Do you want General Eyadema to become president of the republic and carry on with the mission entrusted to him by the People's Army?" The overwhelming answer was Yes. Since his 1967 coup, Eyadema has made repeated use of charisma-enhancing techniques of the sort discussed above. In particular, since the 1971 referendum he has often expressed his desire to withdraw from politics and return to the barracks. Now that the army's mission of preserving the unity of the nation is accomplished, presumably it is safe to turn power back over to a civilian government. But the Togolese, fearing a return to anarchy without Eyadema, have always prevailed upon him to remain in power.[8]

If some military dictatorships have served to perpetuate charismatic rule, others have moved deliberately toward the institution of democracy and a return to civilian government based on legal-rational authority. The military itself takes the initiative in drawing up a new constitution, authorizing political parties to resume their normal activities. The liberalization process begins with legislative and presidential elections, followed by a withdrawal of the army from politics. To be sure, not all such attempts have met with success. But Nigeria and Ghana, after several earlier failures, have recently established multiparty parliamentary regimes.[9]

The normalization process accentuates the legal and rational, rather than the traditional and charismatic, aspects of power. Charisma and tradition may still be influential, however, at lower levels of the political structure. Political parties may, for example, try to organize ethnic, linguistic, regional, or religious groups, or may try to capitalize on the charisma of a former national leader by borrowing his slogans, ideology, or program, while the national authorities may attempt to hinder the activity of parties organized along such lines in order to favor a more legal-rational mode of legitimation. The result is a contest between different kinds of legitimacy, in which the law can be used to set the rules. In such cases, the aim of reinstating normal forms of political activity is ultimately to achieve a political system based on legal-rational forms of authority.

In Nigeria, for example, the military government began liberalizing political life in September 1978 by lifting the ban on political parties that had been imposed by past military regimes over the previous twelve years. Political parties were required to register with a federal electoral commission prior to December 18, 1978. Parties quickly proliferated, and by the deadline, more than forty had registered. But the military authorities, determined to avoid past errors and to prevent a return to regional and tribal politics (which had taken such a toll on national unity), laid down strict rules to ensure that only truly national parties would survive and be able to participate in national elections. To be eligible to participate in the national campaign, a party had to prove to the electoral commission that it was represented in two thirds of Nigeria's nineteen states. Only five of the more than forty parties in the country were able to do so. In this way, Nigeria has been able to establish a form of liberal democracy that closely resembles the American system. Elections are held regularly, and the country's institutions are functioning normally. Pluralist democracy seems to have made an orderly transfer of power possible.

Ghana too has established a pluralist democracy under quite similar conditions. However, the winning party there has borrowed its slogans, program, and ideology from Ghana's former charismatic leader, Kwame Nkrumah, so that elements of charisma linger on. It is nevertheless correct to say that Ghana is firmly on the road to institutionalizing a democratic form of government. Ghanaians now turn to their constitution to resolve the problem of succession.

We have seen, then, that some military dictators have been able to democratize their regimes and thus lay the groundwork for institutionalized politics. The same thing has also been attempted—and achieved—by certain charismatic leaders. Charismatic authority has been successfully transformed into legal-rational authority. It is to the discussion of this kind of change that we turn next, in the third and final section of this essay.

Democratization of Charismatic Regimes

Presidents Senghor of Senegal, Houphouet-Boigny of the Ivory Coast, and Ahidjo of Cameroon are all charismatic leaders who have successfully transformed their regimes into democratic political systems. But before considering these examples, I shall first examine the case of Houari Boumedienne of Algeria, a case that falls midway between that of the military dictatorship that turns toward democracy, discussed in the previous section, and that of charismatic democratization, to be considered below.

After Algeria's historic national leader Mohammed Ben Bella unexpectedly suspended the constitution and assumed plenary powers, he was overthrown in a June 1965 coup led by General Houari Boumedienne, one of his earliest supporters. Boumedienne became president of both the Revolutionary Council and the state of Algeria, remaining in office until his death in December 1978. He had concentrated so much power in his own hands that, when he became incapacitated for a lengthy period prior to his death, the country was faced with almost insurmountable problems. Although the constitution he had given Algeria did provide for succession to the presidency in case of death or resignation, it did not cover the case of illness or incapacitation. Nor had Boumedienne appointed a vice-president or prime minister, even though the constitution provided for such appointments. The country's other political leaders were thus plunged into a state of deep anxiety when Boumedienne became ill. The Revolutionary Council, which had supplanted the political wing of the National Liberation Front (FLN), temporarily took power. But the president's illness precipitated a power struggle within the council. Hence it was impossible for Algeria to follow the route taken in Angola, the Congo, or Kenya, by having the council appoint one of its members to head the country and then convoke a congress of the ruling party to confirm him in office. When Boumedienne finally died, the situation was somewhat altered. The constitution provided that the president of the National Assembly should become acting president for a period of forty-five days, long enough to allow the ruling party to meet in special congress to designate a candidate for the presidency. But the acting president was prohibited from becoming a candidate himself. It was therefore necessary to look to the Revolutionary Council, of which all of Boumedienne's earliest supporters were members, to find a potential candidate. Boumedienne's opponents now ended their silence and began calling for the inauguration of total democracy, liberation of political prisoners, and immediate elections open to all comers. Meanwhile, the Revolutionary Council split into three factions. The main bone of contention was of course the procedure for designating candidates: Which official body was to be empowered to select the candidate or candidates for the presidency? The opposition parties were officially illegal. But the ruling party, the FLN, had been reduced to a caretaker role since Boumedienne's takeover in 1965. The Revolutionary Council had relieved the party's political wing of its functions pending the party's reorganization, scheduled for 1979. Finally, within the council, none of the three factions was strong enough to dominate. Two were almost equal in size, while the third, much smaller, favored following the constitution and calling a special party congress, even though the party had for many years played only a minimal role in government. In the words of this faction's leader, "A party congress is the only politically feasible and constitutionally lawful way of resolving the crisis of the moment." Meanwhile, the opposition wanted full democratization of the regime, and the army favored strict enforcement of the constitution: "The officers of the People's National Army declare their unshakable devotion to the Constitution, which they wish to see

strictly enforced, in order to carry the Revolution forward and preserve what it has already achieved."[10] In the end, a party congress was convoked to choose Boumedienne's successor.

In the forty-five days following Boumedienne's death, the constitution was strictly adhered to. The president of the National Assembly became acting president, and ordered that a special party congress be held. At the congress, the same factions that existed within the Revolutionary Council made their presence felt. To avoid a deadlock, it was suggested that a candidate be chosen who was not associated with any of the factions. Only one man was acceptable to all the interested groups: Chadly Bendjeddid, an uncommitted Boumedienne supporter. He was chosen to be the party's candidate, elected president on February 7, and sworn in on February 9. Thus, although Boumedienne did not handpick his own successor, he did establish the constitutional procedures that made the transfer of power possible.

Other African leaders have also tried to set procedures for the transfer of power while still in office. Some of these experiments were even more far-reaching than Boumedienne's constitution. In Senegal, for instance, President Senghor personally initiated a process of democratization that culminated in an orderly transfer of power that was without precedent on the African continent. Senghor had of course succeeded in building a one-party state around his own party, the UPS (Senegalese Progressive Unon), even though Senegal was a country with long-standing democratic and pluralist traditions. A 1971 constitutional amendment provided for the appointment of a prime minister, and Senghor named a young technocrat, Abdou Diouf, to the post. Further amendments in 1976 did away with the one-party system and reinstated a multiparty regime with at first three and later four legal parties. Even more important, the 1976 revision of the constitution stipulated that the prime minister automatically became president for the remainder of the current term if the president should die or resign.

The UPS, renamed the PS (Socialist Party), ran candidates in the February 1978 elections against the candidates of two other parties, the PDS (Senegalese Democratic Party) and the PAI (African Independence Party). Senghor's ruling party emerged from this election even stronger than it had been, since in this kind of situation, elections serve more as a ritual to enforce charisma than as a way of choosing leaders. The PS took eighty-three of the one hundred seats in parliament, the remainder going to the PDS. Later on, a fourth party was also legalized, but even this did not put an end to the clamor of "illegal" parties for a full multiparty regime. In the midst of this controversy, Senghor announced his retirement. Prime Minister Diouf was sworn in as president on January 1, 1981, before the Supreme Court. He immediately announced his intention to proceed toward a totally democratic regime and a full multiparty system. His term of office runs until 1983, at which time all parties will be free to compete for the presidency.

President Ahidjo of Cameroon is following a similar course. As his plan was originally conceived, succession was not as automatic as in Senegal. The president of the National Assembly was to become acting president for a period of fifty days if the presidency became vacant. This arrangement did not eliminate the danger of power struggles of the sort we have seen occurring elsewhere. Ahidjo's threats to retire revealed the seriousness of the problem of succession, and each party congress provided renewed evidence of the threat of a power struggle in case the president should die. As a result, Ahidjo took the second step of appointing a prime minister who would become acting president in case of the death, resignation, or incapacitation of the president. The choice of a permanent successor, however, was to be left up to the ruling party. At the 1975 congress of the party, held in Douala, Ahidjo stated that "the selection of a prime minister should not be thought of as the appointment of an heir apparent. God willing, I shall make that choice in conjunction with the party's central committee. It is up to the party to choose my successor and thus to allow our joint efforts to continue."[11] But even this measure could not allay the fears of Cameroon's political leaders or alleviate

the ongoing power struggle. Ahidjo therefore took a third and final step: in June 1979 the constitution was amended once again, this time putting the prime minister first in line to succeed the president. Just as in Senegal, if the president is incapacitated, resigns, or dies, the prime minister finishes out his term.

In all three cases we have looked at thus far—Algeria, Senegal, and Cameroon—the emphasis has been more on institutional arrangements and legal technicalities than on politics per se. Now, in a charismatic regime, politics is of course the heart of the matter, and as long as the political problems are not resolved, political leaders will continue to worry about the fate of the regime. This anxiety leads to constant tinkering with the provisions of the constitution in search of a viable political solution. This is what happened in the Ivory Coast, for example, where all of the various constitutional arrangements discussed above were tried out at one time or another, only to be rejected in the end as unworkable. Finally, at the September 1980 congress of the ruling party, the PDCI (Democratic Party of the Ivory Coast), President Houphouet-Boigny opted in favor of a "definitive" political solution. An earlier amendment to the constitution, adopted in 1975, had provided for the president of the National Assembly to complete the unfinished term of the chief of state, at which time national elections would be held. Speculation had been that, instead of this arrangement, a new amendment would provide for the appointment of a prime minister, who would then become the constitutionally designated successor to the president, but this rumor proved false. In Houphouet-Boigny's view, the only answer to the problem of succession was to democratize the regime. But by this he did not mean establishing a multiparty state, as in Senegal. Rather, he favored democratization of the PDCI, through reorganization of its internal structures and an injection of new blood. If the party hoped to survive, the president said, it would have to "abide by the fundamental rules of all true democracies. . . . Our people have come of age. We must decentralize political responsibilities in an orderly way and trust the people to choose their own representatives at every level of government." Thus the definitive solution of the problem of succession, according to the Ivory Coast's president, must rely on universal suffrage and not on mere institutional adjustments. When one reporter asked the president what he had done to prepare the way for his own succession, Houphouet-Boigny first compared himself to George Washington, who left office voluntarily, and then put the following question to his interlocutor: "Do you think Lenin realized that Stalin would succeed him? Or Stalin that his successor would be Khrushchev? For my own part, I place my trust in people. I am trying to put together a new government. The man who follows me will probably come out of this new cabinet."[12]

After his reelection as president, Houphouet-Boigny put these ideas into practice. He regained control of the ruling party from the political bosses who had allowed it to become rigid and unresponsive. The party was reorganized to allow for greater democracy and to inject fresh blood. Party secretaries were now popularly elected, and young technocrats worked shoulder to shoulder with old political infighters. Where once the party bosses had drawn up the only list of candidates in this one-party state, now elections were free and open. Anyone who wished to run might do so. Neither the party nor its leader, Houphouet-Boigny, would intervene on behalf of any candidate.

But this was not all. Not only would the revitalized party bring forth a new leader, but the people themselves would participate in naming him when the office of president became vacant. Now that the political solution to the problem of succession was in hand, the constitution had to be amended to facilitate its application. Accordingly, the following amendment was adopted: "The president of the republic shall choose a vice-president to be elected along with him. . . . If the office of president becomes vacant as a result of death, resignation, or total incapacitation duly determined by the Supreme Court upon petition of the government, the vice-president shall become, ipso jure, president of the republic for a period not to exceed the un-expired term of office of the previous president."

Thus the system adopted in the Ivory Coast is modeled on the American idea of a "ticket," pairing the president and the vice-president. As a political solution to the problem of succession, this bestows a two-fold legitimacy on the man who succeeds to the presidency: first, he benefits from the charismatic authority of his predecessor, who chose him for the job, and second, he obtains the legal-rational (institutional) sanction offered by popular election, coupled with constitutional due process. In this one-party state, these arrangements would appear to offer ample guarantees of continuity.

Since, however, no vice-president has yet been designated, is there not reason to fear a situation such as that which developed in Algeria after the death of Boumedienne? And how can a vice-president be elected now, when the president himself has just been elected for a five-year term that does not expire until 1985? A look at what happened when the National Assembly debated the proposed constitutional reforms will help to shed further light on the changes. When one deputy asked what would happen if the head of state were elected without a vice-president, and the need for a successor arose, the president of the National Assembly answered that "cases make law and not the other way around." He then evoked the case of President Nixon: when Nixon resigned, Vice-President Ford automatically became president, and he in turn named a vice-president who had not been elected. In other words, the president of the Ivory Coast is free to choose his own vice-president until the next presidential elections in 1985, at which time the president and vice-president must run together on a single ticket. Still, since no vice-president has yet been named, the fear remains that a situation may come to pass such as that which occurred in Algeria upon the death of President Boumedienne.[13] Is Houphouet-Boigny afraid that nominating a vice-president will precipitate a power struggle? Or is he simply waiting for a viable candidate to emerge from within his new government?

The problem of succession is not unique to African regimes. Any political system must constantly cope with problems arising from the fact that more than one kind of authority is found in any real polity. Different forms of authority are always found in unstable amalgams, and there is always conflict over which principle of legitimacy should dominate. The ultimate goal of any political system is to establish rules governing the transfer and use of power, no matter what form that power may take. The way power is transferred—the mode of succession—is thus an important attribute of any political system.

In today's world, where all national problems become international ones, a government whose mode of succession is securely established inspires confidence not only domestically, but also abroad. This is of great concern to African nations, whose developmental problems involve international as well as internal considerations. In the current geopolitical climate, it is more than ever imperative that states succeed in rationalizing their political behavior. I therefore believe that a rationally organized state is a prerequisite for all national development.

Development, though, involves rationalization not only of political behavior but also of the economic, technological, and cultural aspects of a social system, since each is intimately associated with all the others. Indeed, the types of authority that we have examined in this essay can never really be isolated from other aspects of social reality. Hence the economic, technological, and cultural environment should always be kept in mind when discussing political questions. In the developed countries, such political structures as the nation-state and multiparty parliamentary democracy became stable only after the development of specific forms of social stratification and economic and cultural change. It was only after the global social context had been modified that it became impossible for older charismatic and traditional forms of authority to survive (or at any rate to flourish as they once did).

What emerges, then, from the foregoing analysis is that the rationalization of power may take different forms in different societies. Rationalization cannot run its course, however, until the importance of charismatic and traditional forms of power has waned. In particular, democracy—that is, the broadening of popular participation in political institutions regardless of their type—also appears to contribute to political rationalization.

The approach I have taken in this essay derives from Max Weber. It is of course only one of many possible approaches to the study of political science. Still, I think it has been shown to be useful for understanding the problems of succession, democratization, and political rationalization in African societies, which in turn can help political scientists to gain a deeper understanding of political development generally.

NOTES

1. Weber's theory of charisma is used here only as a convenient instrument for the study of power in Africa. Since the theory has already proved abundantly fruitful in sociology and political science, it seems reasonable to employ it in the study of African societies. Still, it is essential to guard against confusing the nature of the European societies studied by Weber with the quite specific nature of African societies. Charisma, however, is a general concept, useful for the study of any society; Weber studied specifically European variants of charismatic authority, whereas we will be examining African instances of the same kind of power.

2. Max Weber, "Politics as a Vocation," in *From Max Weber*, edited by H. H. Gerth and C. Wright Mills (Oxford: Oxford University Press, 1946), p. 79.

3. Ibid.

4. Generally speaking, African heads of state acquire charismatic attributes through myth and symbol. One might go so far as to say that charisma is commonly attached to the office itself, and that any head of state automatically becomes a charismatic figure (whether the role suits his character or not). Dictators and tyrants are thus able to make use of their ex officio charisma, as it were, to establish their hold over the people bit by bit. Such leaders as Bokassa, Nguema, and Idi Amin fit this description. On this subject, see especially Jean Girard, *Genèse du pouvoir charismatique en basse Casamance (Sénégal)* (IFAN-DAKAR, 1969).

5. Erik Erikson, "The Leader as a Child," cited by Jean Lacouture, *Quatre hommes et leurs peuples, sur-pouvoir et sous-développement* (Paris: Seuil, 1969), p. 25.

6. Lanciné Sylla, *"Dictatures aux abois,"* afterword to *Flux et reflux des dictatures civiles et militaires en Afrique* (Paris: *Association Française de Science Politique,* 1981), colloquium on the end of dictatorships.

7. Carl Schmitt, *Politische Theologie—Vier Kapitel zur Lehre von Souveranität* (Munich-Leipzig: 1934), p. 11.

8. Lanciné Sylla, *Flux et reflux.*

9. Ibid.

10. *Demain l'Afrique* 18 (January 15, 1979).

11. Ibid., 30 (July 2, 1979): 23.

12. *Jeune Afrique* 148 (February 4, 1981): 30.

13. See the report on the National Assembly debate on constitutional reform in *Fraternité matin,* the Ivory Coast's major newspaper, for Thursday, November 27, 1980.

Development and Governmental Corruption—Materialism and Political Fragmentation in Nigeria

William N. Brownsberger

Some have tried to explain corruption in the Third World by reference to anachronistic traditions and to the special pressures on officials in developing countries. In this article, I argue that, at least in the case of Nigeria, the roots of corruption go deeper, to a materialism and a political fragmentation that are the products of a moment in development. After a schematic review of the relevant literature, I examine the causes of Nigerian corruption, and conclude with the suggestion that the future of good government depends on an expansion of the private economy.

GENERAL THEORY—REVIEW OF THE LITERATURE

Definitions of corruption invariably refer to a misapplication of public goods (broadly construed) to private ends.[1] But, since notions of what is public, what is held in trust for the people, vary across cultures, corruption is a relative concept. Suffice it to say that I am concerned here with misapplications of public goods—bribery, nepotism, political favouritism—in violation of the western legal and regulatory codes that have been inherited by many developing countries, along with western state structures, from their colonial governments.[2]

From *Journal of Modern African Studies*, vol. 21, no. 2 (1983), 215–33, by permission of the journal and its publisher, the Cambridge University Press.

Some Explanations of Corruption

In this section, I briefly catalogue the main factors which scholars have identified as causing corruption in developing countries, and review political patterns that encourage corruption. My purpose is heuristic—to collect ideas.

Customs, attitudes, and habits

Two related customs have often been seen as corrupt when they appear in a modern context: *gift-giving* as an expression of goodwill and respect towards partners and consensual leaders, and *tributes* (resembling interest or taxes) to authoritarian rulers, such as feudal lords or local emissaries of empires.[3]

Other authors have related corruption to various constellations of attitudes: greed or love of ostentation,[4] either in the culture at large, or only among an élite or a clique;[5] materialist religion where divine justice is purchased by offerings;[6] and lack of rational/scientific education, again either in the culture or among the government élite.[7]

In addition, there is evidence that many of the new élites have mismanaged their own careers and financial affairs—they may plan their assets poorly, or they may set unattainable career goals, the result in either case being special temptations to corruption.[8]

Pressures on officials

Obviously, poverty strengthens all temptations for public officials,[9] especially when, because of instability, they know their opportunities may vanish,[10] or where, because of high status, their kinsmen place expanded demands on them, or they feel compelled to maintain a high visible standard of living.[11] Also, where neither individuals nor organisations have accumulated funds for the legal support of their activities, politicians may feel forced to apply public goods to personal or sectional ends—by embezzling, taking bribes, or distributing resources (jobs and contracts) politically.[12]

Even where officials are not poor, individuals and organisations seeking benefits from the government may make them offers that are very difficult to refuse.[13] As state control of the economy expands, the private sector needs help from administrators and politicians more often.[14]

Forces which deter corruption are often weak in developing countries. There may be little threat of detection from audit controls,[15] or even from police operations.[16] Equally important for politicians, public opinion may sleep because the government controls the press or the population is illiterate.[17] Professional organisations may be non-existent or incapable of sanctioning their members.[18] Finally, corruption may be so widespread that it is actively disapproved by only a few.[19]

Political environments
Often in democratic societies, the wealthy are excluded from political power—as an unpopular class or ethnic minority,[20] as foreign,[21] or constitutionally, like George III.[22] To control government intervention in their pursuits, the politically excluded wealthy élite must use their economic power, either at the parliamentary stage, through campaign contributions and "gifts" to legislators, or at the enforcement stage, through bribes to administrators.[23]

More generally, where the channels of interest-group expression have not developed, corruption may be the only way to influence government decision-making.[24] In developed democracies, the public can affect policy; interest groups act in legislative and other public processes (e.g. administrative rule-making hearings) to influence the policies which dictate the decisions that affect their lives.

In a less-developed political system, the policy influence of interest groups is less effective in two ways: first, they are unorganised and may not even be aware of themselves as groups; second, even if they were organised to win policy victories, these might be rendered useless by the inadequacies of administrative machinery. Since they cannot affect decisions at the policy level, people who need public goods seek to influence enforcement and implementation, i.e. to corrupt officials.

Politicians may also initiate corruption in this environment: they may build political machines, via which public goods are distributed in return for votes. Where traditional loyalties have begun to break down, but where class/interest loyalties have not developed, as is often the case in the cities of developing countries, political entrepreneurs seeking to bind heterogeneous ethnics into parties may find patronage the most effective available adhesive.[25]

Notice the power of this analysis: it applies not only to articulated commercial interests (e.g. the importers of vehicles who instead of trying to liberalise import policy, corruptly secure licenses for themselves), but also to broad popular interests (e.g. the urban poor who, instead of pressing for welfare programmes and public housing, seek to provide for their families by corruptly obtaining employment, or even by selling their votes outright to political bosses).

Ethnicity
Often related to, but running deeper than, the underdevelopment of interest groups, is the dominance of ethnic loyalty in politics. Colonialists pacified warring groups and set up administrative regions bearing little relation to local loyalties. With independence and self-government, tribes who for centuries had dealt with each other only through war and commerce were forced to co-operate.

Given this history, it was to be expected that politicians in many developing countries would view their national governments as collections of resources and opportunities for self-dealing, and that patronage and corrupt exchange would be the cement used to bind together various ruling coalitions.[26]

Costs and Benefits of Corruption

Corruption may have advantages as well as disadvantages in society, and several authors have tried to identify these. Most of what follows in this section has been suggested by J. S. Nye, who has made the most comprehensive analysis to date.[27]

Economic dimensions

Corruption gives those with money more power, and makes governmental decision-making subject to market direction. Therefore, it may give politically excluded economic élites the freedom they need to develop the country[28]—this is one of the most popular arguments—or it may guarantee them the power they need to subjugate the peasants and workers. It may cut through red tape, or it may distort policies that would improve the quality and fairness of development over the long run. As a general matter, it may be that corruption in regulatory matters, which often tends to restore free market conditions,[29] is less damaging than corruption in the award of contracts, which often leads to shoddy public products.[30]

Political/governmental dimensions

As suggested above, corruption may facilitate the participation of excluded or unorganised élites in governmental decision-making, or may provide opposed ethnic groups with a *modus operandi* for their peaceful co-operation. On the other hand, corruption may lead to conflict by encouraging *quid pro quo* relationships in politics that cannot withstand zero-sum decisions (which inevitably arise).[31] And it may destroy the legitimacy of government in the eyes of forces with the power to destabilise it—especially the army.

The prevalence of corruption may provide an incentive for talented youths who need money to enter government service and thereafter improve the quality of the bureaucracy; or it may distract civil servants from the business of governing and discourage the best from joining the public service at all.[32] It may, by providing the political glue for a government, expand the power to govern,[33] or it may enfeeble the régime by weakening administration.

The bottom line

It is not possible to frame any general statement as to when corruption will be beneficial on balance. Nye probably came as close as one can to generality: he examined a full list of costs and benefits, and designed a matrix showing under what conditions corruption may be beneficial on balance. However, the likelihoods that he generates are too soft to be meaningful.[34] Moreover, the various pros and cons are incommensurate—for example, how does freedom for capitalists "trade off" against a reduction of governmental legitimacy in the eyes of the army?

In this brief review of the relevant literature, my purpose has been to gather conceptual tools to use in explaining corruption in Nigeria. I have not considered the empirical salience of any concepts—the general literature gives no such answers, for it cannot; social concepts have different salience in different social contexts.

CORRUPTION IN NIGERIA—CAUSES

There is reason to expect that good government in Nigeria will slowly replace the widespread corruption that has been characteristic of the first two decades of independence. I am optimistic, because I see Nigerian corruption as the product of a materialism and a political fragmentation which will pass in development, and I present below a collection of thoughts for discussion and verification by time and further research.

Three Kinds of Corruption and Their Salience

In this section, I shall define and discuss the salience of three kinds of corruption, each with different causes: (1) polite corruption; (2) nepotism (or parochial corruption); (3) alienated (or market) corruption.[35] The first two follow from traditional values, unlike the third which is now profound and pervasive in Nigeria.

Polite corruption

I shall first elaborate the notion that some corruption flows from traditional gift-giving, and then argue that this comprises only a small, benign portion of Nigerian corruption.

Let us begin with the image of the low-born but strong and determined young Okonkwo in Chinua Achebe's novel, *Things Fall Apart*, who goes to the "great man" of his Ibo village to ask a favour.[36] He seeks the loan of yam seeds to plant a first harvest of his own, and brings a cock, a pot of palm-wine, a kola nut, and an alligator pepper. Offering them he says "[Our father], I have brought you this little kola. As our people say, a man who pays respect to the great paves the way for his own greatness. I have come to pay you my respects and also to ask a favour."

In his autobiography, the well-known Nigerian politician, Obafemi Awolowo, remembers the visits of the British Administrative Officer or *Ajele* (as he was called) to the village of his childhood.[37] The *Ajele* would pitch his tent in the market place, and in the days before his arrival, the *Oba*, or local king, would have "caused a public proclamation to be made for firewood, yams, chickens, water and other necessaries to be provided in plenty in the market place for the use of the *Ajele*." Awolowo recalls that no able-bodied person, except the *Oba* and his chiefs, would go near the *Ajele* for fear of being pressed into service as a bearer on the next leg of his tour.

Okonkwo's gift-giving shades into tribute to the *Ajele* which shades into corruption of public officials. Some have *explained* corruption by reference to traditional gift-giving. Monday Ekpo, for example, reminds us that this occurs in the patron/client, big-man/small-boy context, and argues that the ethics of dependency relations, combined with ethnic loyalties, underlie much of Nigerian corruption.[38]

Certainly, some corruption, some misuse of government power for personal ends, *is* continuous with the receipt of traditional gifts. Some would label the *Ajele's* conduct in accepting gratuities from the villagers as corrupt. In any case there is little doubt that this form of "politeness" became prevalent under the Richards constitution which formally delegated local British power to the *Obas*,[39] because when they first took governmental office they continued to accept their traditional gratuities,

in violation of modern concepts of the duty of civil servants.[40]

Even where local "big men"—retaining their local legitimacy—enter local government service, it is wrong to place much reliance on traditional gift-giving as an explanation of corruption, because most *bribes* are simply not traditional. Except in parts of Northern Nigeria, traditional rulers held office only as long as they pleased their people. They were fatherly figures who reigned but did not rule.[41] They were chosen for good character and integrity, and they were responsible to the people.[42] Those who offended public opinion, were quickly deposed by "younger elements."[43]

Even in modern Nigerian towns, those who become "big men" retain their status by balanced generosity, and can be sanctioned by their beneficiaries.[44] A number of authors have pointed out that tribal associations are run honestly—that there is no generical inclination to delinquency in fiduciary office.[45] Others have emphasised that Africans do know the difference between a polite gratuity and a bribe.[46] In short, traditional Nigerian culture does recognise that the community leader has a duty to his people, and that this bars systematic exploitation of office.

There is a second reason why modern bribery may not be seen as cognate with traditional gift-giving. Most of the time, it takes place outside the context of a patron/client, big-man/small-boy relationship. The average man mistrusts and vaguely fears bureaucrats, even if they are black.[47] The affection and reverence with which Okonkwo approaches the "great man" of his village—he sits with the man's sons to drink the wine he offered—are utterly absent when a young woman seeking a scholarship offers herself to Okonkwo's grandson, the civil servant.[48] Ethically and historically, the poor man's bribe to the faceless power he will never meet again is completely distinct from his traditional gift to a patron. And when an official is bribed by a regular client, such as a contractor or importer, who is the "big man"?—the salaried civil servant or the entrepreneur?

In this section, I have elaborated by example the notion of traditional gift-giving, but have argued that Nigerian *community* leaders recognise a duty to their people which would prevent them from systematically exploiting their office. I have suggested further that the relationships of patronage and attitudes of reverence that characterise traditional gift-giving simply are not present in much of modern corruption. One last point deserves mention: in some parts of Nigeria, in the Hausa north, the chiefs in power at the time of the British arrival were corrupt exploiters—the delinquent agents of absentee Fulani rulers—who remained dishonest under British rule. *Their* taking may well be the historical antecedent of some corruption in the north, but theirs was the corruption of the despot, not the polite corruption of the patron.[49]

Nepotism

Clearly, traditional loyalties and responsibilities to family and tribe lead many public officials to divert jobs and contracts away from those who promise most to the public. Many authors have noted this phenomenon,[50] which needs only these comments: (1) It *is* possible to exaggerate the force of family duty in Nigeria—see, for example, the poor treatment, apparently standard, that Awolowo received at the hands of his extended family after his father died.[51] (2) Much corruption in Nigeria involves those who are unconnected by family or tribal loyalties to the official, or competing parties who all have the same degree of connectedness to him. This seems intuitively clear given the size and diversity of the country.[52] (3) Finally, not all intra-family corruption should be *explained* as nepotistic, since this suggests a (half-virtuous) loyalty to family. The young civil servant, risen alone from his community into the government, who helps his family and village friends, may be regarded as virtuous,[53] but the familial or tribal cabal that robs the public in concert is morally indistinguishable from the isolated grafter pocketing funds for himself; family duty does not demand or explain the latter behaviour.

High family loyalty underlies many acts which by western codes of conduct amount to corrupt patronage. The three comments made above all cut for the following limited point: nepotism explains only a fraction of the universe of corruption in Nigeria.

Alienated corruption

Above, I have argued that a probably large, but undetermined fraction of Nigerian corruption is simply an abuse of office unsoftened by traditional etiquette or love of family—the plain, selfish diversion of public goods to the highest bidder in violation of the western fiduciary norms that are not only embodied in Nigerian law but largely shared by traditional communities. This is the deep fascinating question: Why should this alienated corruption be more prevalent in Nigeria now, and during the last 20 or 30 years, than it has typically been in western democracies over the same period?

The first answer is superficial—really only a restatement of the problem: Nigerian public officials (and, perhaps, the developed society generally) are remarkably materialistic. It is worth reviewing the consensus on this point to firmly establish that the problem exists.

President Shagari: [W]hat worries me more than anything among our problems is that of moral decadence in our country. There is the problem of bribery, corruption, lack of dedication to duty, dishonesty and all such vices.[54]

General Obasanjo: The Nigerian society, in spite of all our efforts since 1975, is not sufficiently disciplined.[55]

Chief Awolowo: [S]ince independence, our governments have been a matter of a few holding the cow for the strongest and most cunning to milk. Under the circumstances, everybody runs over everybody to make good at the expense of others.[56]

Similar criticisms have been made by African scholars elsewhere. For example, in 1968 by Ernest Boateng of Ghana: "We must use every means in our power to wean people away from the notion that the most important thing in life is money and that the true end of politics is wealth."[57] The Organisation of African Unity went so far as to name a break with materialism as one of its goals for the year 2000.[58] Many other authors have identified unusual greed, pure and simple, as a cause of corruption in Africa.[59]

Understandings of materialism

Why does materialism seem to be so prevalent in Nigeria, especially in officialdom? Below, I offer three explanations. The first may be unsatisfactory, but the latter two are useful hypotheses about how the history of Nigerian development has created an unusually materialistic culture.

The Avalanche Effect. This argument says that Nigerian culture is *not* unusually materialistic; rather, a materialistic mode of administration has come into existence mainly through its own dynamics. Corruption, it is said, arose through traditional gift-giving and nepotism, and has since flourished because: (i) a climate of corruption had developed which legitimises such acts;[60] (ii) people fear that their competitors are corrupt, and so act likewise;[61] (iii) those in power commit corrupt acts to remain in power and to avoid exposure of their earlier actions; and (iv) having tasted "polite offerings," officials realise the potential to make money and are tempted on to ever greater corrupt acts.[62] Moreover, the audit and police controls are so weak, and the general confusion so great in the developing civil service, that nothing hampers the expansion of corruption in recent years.[63]

Clearly, all of these dynamics are real; they contribute to many individual cases of dishonesty, and make corruption hard to eradicate. As explanations of widespread practices, I find them unsatisfactory. First, *if,* as argued above, bribery and violation of the public trust are immoral for traditional Africans, and distinct from the acceptance of gifts, then the "avalanche" should have stayed on the mountain. The question is: What corrupting forces caused civil servants to go beyond internalised barriers and begin wholesale corruption? Second, the passion of local observers (suggested in the quotations above, on p. 000) must be a response to more than mere popular habit—it must be a reaction to perceived true materialism in officials.

Great Expectations. The argument here is that the dazzling status of the white man (and the successor black élite) burned into the populace a desire to appear and act as did their dominators, and this led the most successful to corrupt excesses. Certainly, to rural Nigerians—and at independence, 87 per cent of the population was rural[64]—and even to many city dwellers, the European was "superman."[65] The trappings of his total dominance—his clothes, his automobiles, his houses, his written words, and regal life—represented perfect success and nobility to most blacks.

Through education and, perhaps, entry into the civil service, a black man could approach the status of the white man. Awolowo tells of how his father urged him to study so that he could become a clerk, and of how men in their 40s entered the white man's schools so that they might participate in his administration.[66] When the anti-hero of Achebe's *No Longer at Ease,* a youth of 25, attains a minor civil service post, he is a great man whom his gathered tribesmen greet with dancing and cheers.[67]

But it was not enough to enter the civil service; one had to live like a white man, to drive an expensive car, and to go to night clubs in western clothes. Achebe's character, Obi, thinks again and again of the prestige costs of failing to appear fully a member of the élite. Two American scholars have written about the identification of status with the perquisites given to the British colonial administrators. Like Obi, the new Nigerian élite "*had* to have each and every advantage—particularly those which would be seen and touched—formerly identified with status, or they might well be seen by the masses as only secondary to the British."[68] In Achebe's novel, the expenses of Obi's lifestyle (combined with his obligations to family and tribe) bring him to indebtedness, driving him to forget his scruples. Perhaps tongue in cheek, Awolowo says of his brief stint as a money lender, "My main clients were civil servants who never seemed able to live within their means."[69] Other authors have pointed to the love of ostentation as a pressure to corruption.[70]

Passion to live the highest élite life could easily lead a bureaucrat into corruption—especially when coupled with a sense of entitlement born of hard work for a post, and of comparison with the British. P. C. Lloyd makes a related point: the great expectations raised by the examples of the white man and the successful blacks are unrealistic for the majority, and when people find themselves failing to meet their career and other goals by legitimate bureaucratic means (and losing self-esteem irrationally), they resort to bribery and patronage—great expectations push one to offer as well as to take bribes.[71]

I have suggested that a passion for, and sense of entitlement to, visible élite status is a major factor in the corruption of public officials in Nigeria, and have seen this concern as born of the vast status gap between the white colonialists (and their black successor élite) and the average poor rural Nigerian. A question worth asking is whether the love of ostentation had other antecedents in Nigerian culture before the white man. Perhaps, but even if some tribes were very status-conscious and ostentatious,[72] this history may be irrelevant. Only the most profoundly other-worldly culture could withstand total domination by aliens without beginning to thirst after their ways. Even Khomeini's Islam has flourished only after the vanquishment of an especially brutal western-style ruler; Britain's willingness to relinquish colonial rule deprived the Nigerians of an expiating victory, which would have delegitimised the ways of their former rulers.

Urban Élite Nihilism. There is evidence that *participation* in colonial rule, and the very process of economic development and urbanisation, both operated to weaken idealism in Nigerian officials, especially before the major move to independence began. The educated few who took office before the indigenisation of the civil service under British rule in the 1950s were to varying degrees "traitors"; they were participating in the domination of their people. Awolowo's circle branded those merely friendly with whites as "imperialist agents."[73] The division of loyalty in the hearts of these most successful black men cannot but have taken its toll on their self-esteem, and therefore on their capacity for selfless public service.

A similar if less profound conflict may have troubled civil servants who took office during the pre- and post-independence periods of indigenisation. They began to identify with their class, as against their people. They had struggled long and hard in the white man's schools, and they oc-

cupied offices that put them above their people and made them responsible to the Crown or to the almost equally alien independent national government. Especially if they had travelled, they had had experiences which they shared only with other members of their class; they lived away from home in a new urban world. Achebe's Obi, while continuing to meet family and tribal obligations, finds friends and confidants only among other educated civil servants; his encounters with his family and kinsmen are often painful and filled with differences in understanding. The shift to élite loyalty is perhaps deepened psychologically by the civil servant's needs to defend himself against a sense of the "parasitic potential" of his class.[74] This division of loyalty between parentage and class, like the division between Crown and country, also weakens the moral fibre of the civil servant.

Deeper and more pervasive than the division of loyalty is the cultural disorientation resulting from the transition from rural or urban life. In the teeming slums, the brothels, and hot night-spots of growing cities around the world, people lose their bearings and accede to desires that they would resist in the stable social frame of their rural homes. Cyprian Ekwensi's short story, "Lokotown," is about this urban disorientation: two railwaymen based in Lagos are both involved with a bad woman of the night who kills the engineer's baby son as she scuffles with his jealous wife, and distracts the fireman from his beautiful, wholesome girlfriend.[75]

Nigerians are moving to their cities—from independence in 1960 to 1980, the urban dwellers increased from 13 to 20 per cent of the total population.[76] My argument is that urbanisation destroys values; civil servants are often among the in-migrants, and must suffer the same "unmooring" as their townsmen who came as labourers (and they may suffer this more keenly, given their class separation from their former peers in the supportive tribal associations). Together with the conflict of élite identifications, this "unmooring" could be fatal to ideals of disinterested public service.

Political Environment and Corruption

In this section, I shall briefly discuss features of Nigerian politics that, especially during the years of democracy before the coups of 1966, may have contributed to corruption generally. Two relevant and often coexisting political situations have already been characterised: the underdevelopment of interest-group politics, and the dominance of sectional/ethnic allegiances over national loyalties. The first increases corruption because when people are not organised to affect important decisions at the policy stage, they have to adjust them at the enforcement level; the second likewise, because (i) during the formation of the national government, bargaining will dominate, and (ii) public employees, like ordinary citizens, will feel justified in getting what they can out of the regime.

Both of these situations obtained in the First Republic. In 1967, Lloyd commented on the non-consciousness of class among Africans generally.[77] Policy was not an issue in national election campaigns, but sectional loyalties were, as emphasised by Richard Harris when reporting the politicking during the 1965 elections:

> From the start of the campaign, it was clear that many of the politicians considered the essential issue to be simply whether the federal government would be dominated by the "South" or the "North"—or, as it was more often put, by the "Ibos" or the "Hausas."

The second ranking issue was whether the imprisoned opposition leader, Awolowo, would be released.[78] Another observer saw patronage bargaining as a key factor in securing cross-over voting in parliament during this period.[79] Given that the political parties were not initially mass based but "founded by nuclei of educated elite,"[80] patronage may have been very widespread as the new organisations tried to buy support at lower levels.

Causes of Corruption in Nigeria

In my discussion of the causes of Nigerian corruption, I have not talked about the pressures on officials, discussed earlier—poverty *per se*, insecurity, demands of family and party (for direct financial support), good opportunities for making money, lack of fear of detection. Clearly, all of these exist in Nigeria, and encourage corruption—but do they actually cause it? Although the vast majority of the inhabitants may have a low standard of living, civil servants have incomes that place them high above that level.[81] Why should they feel compelled or entitled to supplement their incomes extra-legally?

More generally, fiduciaries in different circumstances around the world resist similar pressures successfully. Why should Nigerian civil servants persist in helping themselves? I have argued that traditional community leaders recognise fiduciary duties, and that they are morally predisposed to execute public responsibilities honestly. Moral men are not pure maximisers that behave corruptly as soon as the net discounted payoff exceeds zero. It is necessary to look beyond pressures and opportunities to inner changes that allow corrupt behaviour, and I have suggested two explanations: (i) many in the civil service have been corrupted inwardly—weakened by dazzling inequality, divided loyalties, and disorienting urban life, and (ii) the fragmentation of political life in Nigeria continues to channel loyalty away from the policy process and the abstract state back to self and tribe.

THE FUTURE FOR GOOD GOVERNMENT IN NIGERIA

If the analysis of the causes of Nigerian corruption presented above is accurate, then time favours good government. As development progresses, the élite will grow broader, and so less alienated and less driven to ostentation. Nepotistic and party-building corruption will diminish as opportunities outside the state expand. As government becomes more effective, national identity will become stronger, and the parties more issue-oriented. These trends—correlated by Wraith and Simpkins with the reduction of corruption in nineteenth-century England—already appear in the Second Republic.

The expansion of the private economy is

the key, both to the reduction of nepotism and to the broadening of the élite. Value-added in Nigerian manufacturing more than doubled in real terms between 1970 and 1977, and construction tripled.[82] This development was fuelled by oil revenues which increased by a factor of 13 in nominal terms over the same period. (By comparison, manufacturing in Ghana actually declined over the same period and increased by 57 per cent in Cameroun.) The percentage of the labour force employed in manufacturing increased from 10 to 17 from 1960 to 1978, services increased from 19 to 27, while agriculture declined from 71 to 56.[83] One observer has noted the arrival of a new non-industrial bourgeoisie composed of traders and speculators "riding the oil boom."[84]

The likely consequence of the expansion of the private economy is that Nigerians will enter government who have already fulfilled their material ambitions. Moreover, they will identify not with an alienated élite of bureaucrats, but with the process by which they built their lives; they may be conservative, but not corrupt. While old names dominated the national election campaigns in 1979, a number of young Nigerians were seeking regional governorships: "These are not men motivated by the old chop-chop politics . . . they are in it for what they can give rather than what they can get." They are men who have already achieved success in private enterprise or in a profession.[85]

The Nigerian political environment is also changing: ethnic narrownesses are yielding to national loyalty and identification with issues. Ethnicity is still vital politically, as the recent moves to bring the total number of States to 40 prove, but it is less divisive in national politics. This change may be due, in part, to the 1979 election regulations that now force presidential candidates to seek votes outside their ethnic base.[86] Other major factors are the period of military rule, and the exponential increase in economic development spending from oil revenues,[87] both of which raised the stature of the central government and so increased national identification.[88] Also, the fragmentation into smaller States may in itself strengthen the government in the federal system.

Identification with issues is increasing and beginning to displace ethnic loyalty. Shagari was attacked as a conservative, not as a Northerner, during the 1979 elections,[89] and again in 1983. The shift to issues/class politics follows from the diversification and organisation of interest groups in society, an example of which would be the increased activity of the labour unions. They were consolidated by the Federal Military Government in 1975, and Nigeria has witnessed more labour unrest since then than at any time since independence.[90]

On the cultural level, one phenomenon deserves mention: the Maitatsine rioting. These Muslim fundamentalists reject the materialism of all political parties[91]—presumably the same corrupt benefits which almost all national leaders are busy vocally rejecting. Is this extremism only the product of a radical personality? Does it point to the failure of the politicians to go beyond corrupt self-seeking? Or could it be another sign of a new puritanism actually shared to a degree by the political leaders, which will further the cause of development as the Reformation did in Europe?

I have been tracing shadows in this article, and only much more work and the passage of decades will clarify the real dynamics of corruption in Nigeria. I have suggested that in the long run the development of a vital, differentiated private economy, with a broader, better, more patriotic élite, will reduce corruption. However, the most important short-run variable is unknowable: Who will come to power, and how aggressively will they enforce the tough anti-corruption laws already on the books? None of the theories of corruption that I have discussed forces the conclusion that the phenomenon will not wither if attacked systematically. Most Nigerian observers seem to agree that it should be so attacked,[92] arguable benefits notwithstanding.

NOTES

1. Carl J. Friedrich, *The Pathology of Politics* (New York, 1972), p. 161. See also T. M. Ocran, *Law in Aid of Development* (Accra, 1978), p. 116, and J. S. Nye, "Corruption and Political Development: a cost-benefit analysis," in *American Political Science Review* (Washington), 56, 1967, p. 417.

2. James C. Scott, "The Analysis of Corruption in Developing Nations," in *Comparative Studies in Society and History* (Ann Arbor), 2, June 1969, reprinted in Monday U. Ekpo (ed.), *Bureaucratic Corruption in Sub-Saharan Africa: toward a search for causes and consequences* (Washington, D.C., 1979), pp. 29–61. In some cases, developing countries have very strict laws: Nigeria's 1975 Corrupt Practices Decree puts a heavy burden on defendants by creating a presumption that favours received by officials were in return for corrupt acts. *Supplement to Official Gazette Extraordinary* (Lagos), 2 December 1975, A172, Section 4.

3. The Spaniards actually auctioned colonial posts; see Scott, loc. cit. p. 29 in Epko (ed.), op. cit. For other examples of public office as property, see Morton Keller, "Corruption in America: continuity and change," in Abraham S. Eisenstadt et al., *Before Watergate: problems of corruption in American society* (Brooklyn, 1978), p. 9 (sale of office in eighteenth-century Britain); Ronald Wraith and Edgar Simpkins, *Corruption in Developing Countries* (London, 1963) (sale of British parliamentary seats by voters); and Theodore M. Smith, "Corruption, Tradition and Change," unpublished, p. 25 (feudal offices in Indonesia). I link these examples together as involving public office where the holder's primary duty is understood to be to himself.

4. See Ocran, op. cit. p. 119, fn. 10 (love of ostentation as cause of corruption, especially common in West Africa). Wraith and Simpkins, op. cit. p. 40 (love of ostentation as traditional in African society).

5. E.g. Lincoln Steffens, *The Shame of Cities* (New York, 1957 edn., first published in 1904), pp. 43ff. (corrupt government clique in virtuous city of Minneapolis).

6. Compare P. S. Muhar, "Corruption in the Public Service in India," Presidential Address to the Indian Political Science Association, 26 December 1954, as cited in Friedrich, op. cit. pp. 138 and 150 (bribes as offerings to deity in India), with Wraith and Simpkins, op. cit. p. 152 (Quaker style of business dealings—no bargaining, set prices—a religious injunction).

7. E.g. John William Ward, "The Common Weal and the Public Trust, Politics and Morality," Harvard Institute of Politics, 1981, p. 6 (corruption contrasted with contractarian, rationalist ideology); Wraith and Simpkins, op. cit. pp. 159ff. (rise of science generally as related to waning corruption in Britain); and Ralph Braibanti, "Reflections on Bureaucratic Corruption," in *Public Administration* (London), 40, 1962, p. 357 (diffusion of bureaucratic norms as part of solution to corruption).

8. See P. C. Lloyd, *Africa in Social Change* (Baltimore and Harmondsworth, 1967), p. 246 (unrealistic aspirations of most youths in West Africa); and the novel by Chinua Achebe, *No Longer at Ease* (New York edn. 1961), wherein a young civil servant ends up in debt from poor planning and is driven to corruption.

9. Colin Leys, "What Is the Problem About Corruption?" in *The Journal of Modern African Studies* (Cambridge), 3, 2, August 1965, p. 215; Smith, op. cit. p. 31 (low salaries as cause of corruption most often identified by Indonesian public officials in survey); and Ocran, op. cit. p. 120.

10. Nye, loc. cit; Ocran, op. cit. p. 118; and also M. McMullan, "A Theory of Corruption," in *Sociological Review* (Keele), 1961, pp. 181 and 196.

11. On tribal demands, see Wraith and Simpkins, op cit. p. 42; also Achebe, op. cit. and McMullan, loc. cit. p. 196.

12. See Scott, loc. cit. and "Corruption, Machine Politics and Political Change," in *American Political Science Review*, 63, 1969, p. 1142. Also Braibanti, loc. cit. (depoliticisation of the civil service as important to eliminating corruption); and McMullan, loc. cit. p. 195 (non-availability of private funds for party building in developing countries).

13. Ocran, op. cit., p. 119; and Steffens, op. cit. pp. 19ff. (railroad and other entrepreneurs corrupting St. Louis city councillors).

14. Samuel P. Huntington, *Political Order in Changing Societies* (New Haven and London, 1968), ch. on "Modernization and Corruption," reprinted in Ekpo (ed.), op. cit.; and Victor Levine, *Political Corruption: the Ghana case* (Stanford, 1975), p. 5.

15. Leys, loc. cit. and Ronald Cohen, "Corruption in Nigeria: a structural approach," in Ekpo (ed.), op. cit. (only 300 auditors in the Nigerian Government in 1973).

16. Compare the methods of the various Nigerian "Assets Commissions" with Abscam.

17. Braibanti, loc. cit. p. 369, quotes Bentham ("Publicity is the very soul of justice. It is the keenest spur to exertion and the surest of all guards against improbity."). See also A. J. Heidenheimer, "Political Corruption in America: is it comparable?" in Eisenstadt et al. op. cit.

(rôle of American press in battling corruption).

18. Wraith and Simpkins, op. cit. pp. 190ff.

19. McMullan, loc. cit. p. 194 ("climate of corruption" affecting cabinet ministers as well as policemen).

20. As, for example, Indians in East Africa; Nye, loc. cit. p. 420.

21. Scott, 'The Analysis of Corruption in Developing Nations', p. 39—multinationals.

22. Wraith and Simpkins, op. cit. pp. 77ff.

23. Scott, "The Analysis of Corruption in Developing Nations," p. 35, makes the distinction between legislation and enforcement and the kinds of pressure operating at the two levels. See also McMullan, loc. cit. p. 196, and Nye, loc. cit. p. 420.

24. This concept is fully developed in Scott's two articles, cited above. See also Nye, loc. cit. pp. 420–1.

25. Scott, "Corruption, Machine Politics and Political Change."

26. While Nigeria is an obvious example of this in the developing world, it is interesting to note that in England the same kind of parochial warfare was also replaced by corrupt administration in the Settlements of 1660 and 1688. Wraith and Simpkins, op. cit. p. 60. This phenomenon of corruption replacing violence follows generally from Scott's analyses.

27. Nye, loc. cit.

28. Ibid. See also Henry Jones Ford, "Municipal Corruption in America: a comment on Lincoln Steffens," in Political Science Quarterly (New York), xix, 1904, p. 673: "future anthropologists to 'rejoice' that 'men of affairs in [post-Civil-War America] corrupted government in securing opportunities of enterprise,' because 'slackness and decay are more dangerous to a nation than corruption,' " as cited in Heidenheimer, loc. cit.; Friedrich, op. cit. p. 164; and Nathaniel Leff, "Economic Development Through Bureaucratic Corruption," in American Behavioral Scientist (Princeton), 8, 3, 1964, reprinted in Epko (ed.), op. cit. pp. 325–40.

29. Leff, loc. cit. and "Emergence of Black Market Bureaucracy: administration, development and corruption in the new developing states," in Public Administration Review (Chicago), 28, 1968, p. 437.

30. Herbert H. Werlin, "The Consequences of Corruption: the Ghanaian experience" in Political Science Quarterly, 88, 1, March 1973, p. 171, reprinted in Ekpo (ed.), op. cit. pp. 247–60; and Commonwealth of Massachusetts, Final Report to the General Court of the Special Commission Concerning State and County Buildings (1980).

31. See, for example, the inter-boss conflicts of Pennsylvania chronicled by Steffens, op. cit. pp. 101–61.

32. This is emphasised by Leys, loc. cit.

33. According to Robert Caro, The Power Broker (New York, 1975), Robert Moses corruptly induced support for the creation of the Long Island park system.

34. For example, Nye, loc. cit., posits that under favourable conditions—essentially, those auguring for stability in government and a sense of security among the corrupt élite—high-level corruption is likely to have a net positive impact on capital formation. The argument is that (i) if corruption is at a high level, it will put funds in the hands of those likely to save, and (ii) if they feel secure, they will save by putting the funds into investment within the country.

However: (i) even if the corrupt officials are at the top of the government, there is no reason to assume that they will put less of their income into consumption than the bribe payers; and (ii) even if these officials do feel secure, there is no reason to expect that their savings will benefit economic development—they may speculate in land, or they may find that overseas investments offer higher returns. Nye's matrix is suggestive, not probabilistic.

35. Scott uses the terms "market" and "parochial," in "The Analysis of Corruption in Developing Nations," loc. cit.

36. Chinua Achebe, Things Fall Apart (Greenwich edn. 1959), pp. 21–2.

37. Obafemi Awolowo, Awo: the autobiography of Chief Obafemi Awolowo (Cambridge, 1960), pp. 12–13.

38. Monday U. Ekpo, "Gift-Giving and Bureaucratic Corruption in Nigeria," in Ekpo (ed.), op. cit. pp. 161–88.

39. On this arrangement generally, see Louis J. Munoz, "Traditional Participation in a Modern Political System—the Case of Western Nigeria," in The Journal of Modern African Studies, 18, 3, September 1980, pp. 443–68, although he does not discuss corruption.

40. A. O. Obilade of the University of Lagos argues in conversation that polite corruption was prevalent in, and only in, this context.

41. Munoz, loc. cit.

42. Awolowo, op. cit. p. 8.

43. Ibid.

44. Adrian Peace, "Prestige, Power and Legitimacy in a Modern Nigerian Town," in Canadian Journal of African Studies (Ottawa), 13, 1–2, 1979, pp. 25–51. See generally, Victor T. Levine, "African Patrimonial Régimes in Comparative Perspective," in The Journal of Modern African Studies, 18, 4, December 1980, pp. 657–73.

45. E.g. Wraith and Simpkins, op. cit.

46. E.g. Robert L. Tignor, "Colonial Chiefs in Chiefless Societies," in The Journal of Modern African Studies, 9, 3, October 1971, pp. 339–59, reprinted in Ekpo (ed.), op. cit.; Lloyd, op. cit. p. 250; Wraith and Simpkins, op. cit. p. 37. See

also McMullan, loc. cit. p. 186 (gift-giving as only one of many factors).

47. Peace, loc. cit. p. 41.

48. Compare *Things Fall Apart* with *No Longer at Ease*, pp. 90–94.

49. See M. G. Smith, "Historical and Cultural Conditions of Political Corruption Among the Hausa," in *Comparative Studies in Society and History*, 6, 1964, p. 164, reprinted in Ekpo (ed.), op. cit. pp. 211–60.

50. E.g. Leys, loc. cit.; Ward, op. cit. p. 7 (primary loyalty of new arrivals in America to their family, etcetera, as factor in corruption); and Ocran, op. cit. p. 122 ("overpowering allegiance to primordial groups."

51. Awolowo, op. cit. pp. 33ff. Awolowo was deprived of his father's hard-earned wealth by the succession law of the area (siblings before offspring), and in the years that followed, his relatives, though financially able, never paid for him to be educated, instead seeking to use his labour in one way or another.

52. Cf. LeVine, *Political Corruption*, pp. 58–9, where a Ghanaian ex-official confided in a scholar that among those he had regularly done business with, 21 were members of his extended family, while 22 were non-family major clients, such as contractors. Obviously these numbers are only suggestive.

55. Wraith and Simpkins, op. cit. p. 35.

54. *Africa Now* (London), November 1982, p. 55.

55. *Fortune* (Chicago), July 1979, p. 147.

56. *Africa* (London), April 1979, p. 25.

57. Quoted by Maxwell Owusu, *Uses and Abuses of Political Power: a case study of continuity and change in the politics of Ghana* (Chicago and London, 1970), p. 332.

58. Organisation of African Unity, *What Kind of Africa by the Year 2000? Final Report of the Monrovia Symposium* (Addis Ababa, 1980).

59. E.g. LeVine, op. cit. p. 87; Hugh H. Smythe and Mabel M. Smythe, *The New Nigerian Elite* (Stanford, 1960), pp. 131–3.

60. McMullan, loc. cit. p. 194.

61. Lloyd, op. cit. p. 250.

62. Conversation with A. O. Obilade, University of Lagos.

63. There is ample literature on the weakness of African administrative practices: see particularly, A. L. Adu, *The Civil Service in New African States* (New York, edn. 1965), p. 12, who argues that around independence the civil services in all British territories were overwhelmed by the simultaneous obligations to indigenise, and to take on the tasks of creative national government (as opposed to basic police administration). Similar arguments are advanced by Gatian Lungu and John Oni, "Administrative Weakness in Contemporary Africa," in *Africa Quarterly*

(New Delhi), 18, 4, 1979, p. 3; and Cohen, loc. cit.

64. The World Bank, *World Development Report, 1980* (Washington, D.C., 1980), Annex Table 20.

65. Awolowo, op. cit. pp. 12 and 37. Of his country boyhood views of the District Administrative Officer, he recalls: "What a mighty man I thought he was, so specially favoured by God to have a white skin and occupy such a position of exalted superiority." After Awolowo had visited a nearby town, and seen white men walking around on their own legs as opposed to being carried by hammock, they became more human for him.

66. Ibid. pp. 49–51.

67. Achebe, *No Longer at Ease*, p. 78.

68. Smythe and Smythe, op. cit. pp. 132–3.

69. Awolowo, op. cit. p. 92. See also Wraith and Simpkins, op. cit. p. 45 (debt as antecedent of corruption).

70. E.g. Ocran, op. cit. and Wraith and Simpkins, op. cit.

71. Lloyd, op. cit. p. 250, regards unrealistic aspirations more broadly as the "inevitable concomitant of rapid economic development." See also *No Longer at Ease*, p. 21, for Obi's explanation (before his own downfall) of corruption in the civil service as the product of men of inferior education trying to advance themselves.

72. One could point, for example, to the elaborate hierarchies of the Ibo chiefs, with their associated dress codes. See George T. Basden, *The Ibos of Nigeria* (Philadelphia, 1921), ch. 24. See also Wraith and Simpkins, op. cit. p. 40.

73. Awolowo, op. cit. p. 70.

74. Smythe and Smythe, op. cit. p. 120.

75. Cyprian Ekwensi, *Lokotown and Other Stories* (Ibadan, 1966). See also the plot line of *No Longer at Ease*—Obi's fall into corruption follows debt, but perhaps more importantly, the failure of a traditionally forbidden romance, ostracism by his kinsmen, and general bitterness and inner confusion.

76. *World Development Report, 1980*. Nigerians are moving in search of high-paying jobs. See generally, Barry Riddell, "The Migration to the Cities of West Africa: some policy considerations," in *The Journal of Modern African Studies*, 16, 2, June 1978, pp. 241–60.

77. Lloyd, op. cit. pp. 313ff. I have argued above that the government élite was extremely conscious of its class. This is consistent—only mass identification changes the character of politics. Élites manipulate non-class notions in their political leadership of the masses. Cf. Lawrence P. Frank, "Ideological Competition in Nigeria: urban populism versus élite nationalism," in *The Journal of Modern African Studies*, 17, 3, September 1979, pp. 433–52.

78. Richard Harris, "Nigeria, Crisis and Compromise," in *Africa Report* (Washington, D.C.), March 1965, p. 25.

79. Conversation with Obilade, University of Lagos.

80. Lloyd, op. cit. p. 312.

81. Nigerian G.N.P. *per capita* lies at about the median for free-world countries, but 32 per cent of this is new oil wealth (1977), and Nigerian health, diet, and education indicators all are below the average for the 38 *lowest* G.N.P. countries. See *World Development Report, 1980* and *World Tables, 1980*. However, in 1965, the salary scale for Nigerian civil servants began at £336, 50 per cent above the average wage for coal miners, and ran to over £1,000 in most job categories, £2,000 in some. See Nigerian Government, *Staff List* (Lagos, 1965), and Federal Republic of Nigeria, *1966 Yearbook* (Lagos). From 1974 to 1975, the Gowon Government handed out huge raises to civil servants, in order to secure their continued political support. See Richard A. Joseph, "Affluence and Underdevelopment: the Nigerian experience," in *The Journal of Modern African Studies*, 16, 2, June 1978, pp. 221–39.

82. World Bank, *World Tables, 1980* (Washington, D.C., 1980).

83. *World Development Report, 1980.*

84. Joseph, loc. cit.

85. Eddie Iroh, "Age of the New Breeds," in *Africa*, 97, September 1979, p. 42.

86. U.S. Department of State, *Background Notes—Nigeria* (Washington, D.C.), August 1982.

87. *World Tables, 1980;* 14-fold increase from 1973 to 1977.

88. Frank, loc. cit.

89. "Style and Strategy in the Presidential Campaign," in *Africa*, 91, March 1979, p. 16; "From Competition to Compromise," in ibid. 97, September 1979; Peter Pan, "Special Interview," in *Africa Now,* November 1982, p. 50; and *Africa Confidential* (London), 18 July 1979.

90. *Africa*, 128, April 1982.

91. *Africa Confidential,* 20 October 1982.

92. See generally the tenor of remarks quoted on p. 225, above. Also interviews with Shagari in *Africa Now,* November 1982, p. 55, and with five presidential candidates in 1979, "47 million Voters ÷ 5 = 1 President," in *Africa*, 92, April 1979, pp. 12 and 24–5.

Unit IV

DEVELOPMENT

The concept of development is multifaceted and consequently subject to a variety of interpretations, depending on the standards and perspectives of the analyst. Some scholars dealing with development regard *modernization* as the major key to growth and well-being, and thus concentrate on internal or domestic socioeconomic processes of modernization, including social mobilization, as the major determinants of a society's development. Critics of modernization theory, on the other hand, point out that rapid social and economic change is as likely to lead to instability, or what Samuel Huntington refers to as "political decay,"[1] as it is to development. A different "school" of commentators focuses on the state's external *economic* links on which the country often appears to depend for its growth and stability; however, these analysts are often critical of such ties and predict negative outcomes if the nature of the economic linkage and dependence is not radically changed.[2] Yet other interpretations of development amount to advocacy of one or another ideological position, such as African Socialism, Afro-Marxism, or capitalist-oriented behavior. However, at its heart, resources themselves often dictate economic behavior. As Crawford Young has noted: "Ideology does make certain choices more likely . . . but within each framework, a very wide margin of difference arises from the skill, competence, and rationality with which a given strategy is pursued."[3]

Still another perspective on development refers to *political* behavior; that is, the extent to which citizens come to regard governmental structures (e.g., legislative bodies) or independent centers of power (e.g., political parties or trade unions) as *legitimate* methods of political activity and decision making. This outlook is premised on the notion that legitimacy leads to governmental effectiveness, which in turn leads to economic development and political stability. Indeed, some analysts see economic and political forces as having a synergistic effect on development, although different analysts often follow rather different paradigms in arriving at this conclusion. For example, Warren Weinstein argues that "development is not merely growth; it involves . . . improvement in the economic and social circumstances of all members of the society as well as the right to *participate* in the political process."[4] On the other hand, I. L. Markovitz sees the linkage of political and economic development as a means of *changing* the "lifestyles of people and the economic forces of production that have existed for

149

centuries" and creating political structures that will guarantee an equitable distribution of the rewards in the new system.[5]

Whatever methods or channels of development African governments use, it is clear that most African citizens see development as *economic* in character, and they assume that it is the government's responsibility to initiate, promote, and underwrite policies that lead to economic growth. Such expectations, however, are not generally matched by governmental performance. Even in countries where the potential for economic growth is high, the general level of economic development is usually low. Dependent in many ways on foreign capital, multinational corporations, and foreign aid, African states have not been able to establish sufficiently strong economies that can function independently of external influences. In some cases states lack managerial and technical skills and suffer from bureaucratic corruption and mismanagement of national resources, thereby realizing only a fraction of their development potential. In other situations agriculture has often been devastated by natural disasters, or by agriculturalists making poor choices about crops. Alternately, national economies based on a single crop (e.g., coffee) or a single industry (e.g., mining copper) are inevitably vulnerable to periodic gluts on the market or wide variations in international prices.

Statistical "averages" give some idea of the continent's poverty. In mid-1984 the *average* per capita GNP in Africa was $810, and as varied as $140 in Ethiopia and $2,670 in South Africa. Birthrates outnumbered death rates by 45 to 18; population rates expanded by an annual average of 2.9 percent. The estimated population of the continent for mid-1984 was 531 million, with a projected population of 855 million by the year 2000—that is, before most students reading this book are middle-aged! An average of 45 percent of the continent's population is under age fifteen, a good portion of whom will enter the labor market in the near future.[6]

By any standard, these are enormous problems and obligations for any society to face. They are doubly difficult for African governments, which must concurrently cope with the "revolution of rising expectations" that was kindled during the nationalist period and continues to be fanned by politicians seeking popular support for fragile political systems, and with modernization pressures, which increasingly stimulate population movements from underdeveloped rural areas to overcrowded urban centers. Economic development may not ensure a society's advance to modernization, but without it modernization will be difficult, if not impossible. But how should an African country promote its own development most efficiently? Since the achievement of independence, political leaders in Africa have sought both the technical means to develop their economies rapidly and the ideological supports necessary to justify the public sacrifices needed for economic growth.

While some African states, such as the Ivory Coast or Kenya, have followed capitalist-oriented policies, most of the African states profess adherence to African Socialism as the theoretical framework for their development strategy. Various leaders, such as Léopold Senghor and Julius Nyerere, tried to codify this doctrine at an early stage in the process of developing their national economic policies. But two decades later, there is little agreement among African leaders on the specific content of African Socialism, despite attempts to establish such agreement. And, more serious, the most hopeful attempt to construct African Socialism—President Nyerere's pursuit of *Ujamaa* in Tanzania—has foundered on the shoals of overzealous administrators, unreconstructed peasant farmers, and disastrous weather conditions. Other leaders, such as Robert Mugabe of Zimbabwe or Samora Machel of Mozambique, adopt the rhetoric of Marxist economic policies, but they cannot quickly alter their states' economic infrastructures, which are closely tied to external capitalist socioeconomic forces and thus beyond their capacity to influence easily. And where states such as Zambia attempt to direct their economy through widespread state control, these efforts are commonly checked or minimized by external dependence and bureaucratic confusion and mismanagement, let alone the sheer enormity of the task. Nonetheless, all of these variants of African Socialism serve as something more than a philosophy of redistribution; they express a commitment to development and the aim of minimizing dependence on industrialized nations and creating national solidarity.

Beyond this, there are recurring themes in the policy statements of African leaders on the problems of development that suggest that they share a general orientation toward their mutual dilemma. They cite colonial exploitation as the origin of their poverty. They call for citizens to recognize their social obligations by working for the improvement of their community. They urge citizens to be productive and to convert their subsistence activities into cash enterprises. They charge labor unions with the task of giving production rather than consumption first priority. And they denounce "class struggle" in Africa as a pernicious hindrance to growth and as divisive of traditional African communities. Despite all these urgings, however, the economic development that has occurred since independence continues to be outpaced by both population growth and public demands for policy "outputs."

There are also recurring analytical themes regarding the causes of and solutions for the development dilemma. We offer three rather different ones that are critical but also constructive analyses of specific aspects of the problem. One of these examines ethnicity as a factor in the modernization process, another examines the implications of "dependency theory" for economic development, and a third takes a critical look at explanations for the failure of development in rural areas.

Ethnic competition continues to have a serious impact on African states because they must expend energy and resources managing conflict or distributing rewards among ethnic groups. As the earliest organizing force for political mobilization, ethnicity casts a culturally exclusive and wider net of influence than functional groups such as trade unions or "petty bourgeois" class formations. In consequence, ethnicity imposes a signficantly durable polarizing effect on African political systems. In his article in this section, Robert H. Bates examines the extent to which ethnic competition is intensified by the modernization process, and identifies not only the rewards for which they compete but also some of the modes, channels, and consequences of that competition.

For its part, dependency theory postulates that the cause of African underdevelopment is not traditional or inherited backwardness but rather the continent's continuing dependent relationship with the global capitalist economy. The hallmarks of underdevelopment include African economies oriented to exporting primary commodities to the West, domestic inequalities of wealth, "inappropriate" (capital-intensive) technologies, "unequal exchange," and a corrupt *comprador* class. This theory is a fundamentally different explanation for underdevelopment from modernization theory, and provides an original prescriptive orientation toward the future. Colin Leys's article in this section traces and analyzes various thematic explanations of dependency, identifies and criticizes some of their flaws, and offers realistic insights that suggest that the possibilities for development in Africa may not be as bleak as they sometimes seem.

The final selection is an analysis of one of Africa's most serious socioeconomic problems—the crisis of food production with its concomitant threat for widespread hunger and malnutrition. Michael F. Lofchie and Stephen K. Commins offer a critical examination of four explanations of food deficits in African agriculture—i.e., theories of underdevelopment and comparative advantage, environmental constraints, and flawed Western aid programs—with recommendations for reform that might alleviate or avert future crises. This article provides an excellent opportunity to test the value of alternative theoretical explanations against a specific African development problem.

NOTES

1. Samuel P. Huntington, "Political Development and Political Decay," *World Politics* XVII, no. 3 (April 1965), 386–430.

2. See, for example: Walter Rodney, *How Europe Underdeveloped Africa* (London: Bogle L'Ouverture Publications, 1974), or Patrick J. McGowan and Dale L. Smith, "Economic Dependency in Black Africa: An Analysis of Competing Theories," *International Organization* 32, no. 1 (Winter 1978), 179–235.

3. Crawford Young, *Ideology and Development in Africa* (New Haven: Yale University Press, 1982), p. 326.

4. Warren Weinstein, "Human Rights and Development in Africa: Dilemmas and Options," *Daedalus* 112, no. 4 (Fall 1983), 172. Italics added.

5. I. L. Markovitz, *Power and Class in Africa* (Englewood Cliffs: Prentice-Hall, Inc., 1977), p. 324.

6. Statistics extracted from *1984 World Population Data Sheet* (Washington, D.C.: Population Reference Bureau, Inc., 1984).

Modernization, Ethnic Competition, and the Rationality of Politics in Contemporary Africa

Robert H. Bates

Theories of modernization imply the demise of ethnic competition. This is true of sociological theories, in which specific, differentiated, "rational" interests are held to displace generalized, diffuse, "primordial" ties. It is also true of Marxist theories, in which horizontal class cleavages are held to displace vertical segmentary ties as markets broaden and as social relations become organized about the capitalist means of production. A consensus exists, then, that ethnic competition belongs to the premodern era; insofar as it persists, it is an irrational form of behavior or a form of false consciousness.

Despite the predictions of these theories of social change, ethnic competition strongly endures. It is a feature of politics even in the most modern of nation-states. More relevant to the subject of this essay, in contemporary Africa, the levels of ethnic competition and modernization co-vary. Awareness of these facts must provoke a reappraisal of modernization theories, and this essay joins with my own earlier work and the recent work of others in stressing the weakness of classical expectations concerning ethnic behavior.[1]

Where this essay differs from the work of others is in emphasizing the rational basis for ethnic competition. For what I argue is that ethnic groups represent, in essence, coalitions which have been formed as part of rational efforts to secure benefits created by the force of modernization—benefits which are desired but scarce.

DEFINITIONS

The major terms of the argument are "modernity," "ethnic competition," and "ethnic group."

In keeping with conventional usage, I define modernity operationally and call those societies more modern which attain higher levels of the following variables: education, per capita income, urbanization, political participation, industrial employment, and media participation. In practice, I will restrict my attention to the first three of these variables. I feel justified in using a single term—"modernity"—to refer to these distinct variables, for it has been repeatedly demonstrated that they are highly interrelated and that their interrelation derives from their tapping a single underlying dimension.

By ethnic competition, I mean the striving by ethnic groups for valued goods which are scarce in comparison to the demand for them.

The definition of an ethnic group is, perforce, complex. Like all groups, ethnic groups are organized about a set of common activities, be they social, economic, or political; they contain people who share a

From *State Versus Ethnic Claims: African Policy Dilemmas*, edited by Donald Rothchild and Victor A. Olorunsola (Boulder: Westview Press, 1983), pp. 152–71, by permission of the author. This paper is a further development of ideas initially developed by the author in presentations to the Program of Eastern African Studies at Syracuse University and later published in *Comparative Political Studies*, vol. 6, no. 4 (January 1974), pp. 457–84.

conviction that they have common interests and a common fate; and they propound a cultural symbolism expressing their cohesiveness. The primary factor that distinguishes ethnic groups from other kinds of groups is the symbolism which they employ. The symbolism is characterized by one or more of the following: collective myths of origin; the assertion of ties of kinship or blood, be they real or putative: a mythology expressive of the cultural uniqueness or superiority of the group; and a conscious elaboration of language and heritage. In addition, ethnic groups differ from other groups in their composition; they include persons from every stage of life and every socioeconomic level.[2]

It is important to note that ethnic groups need not be tribes. The term "tribe" denotes a group, generally rural, which is bound by traditional political structures to which people are linked by the mechanisms of traditional political obligation. Ethnic groups need not be based on traditional political institutions; rather, many are based upon newly created organizations, forged in the competitive environment of modern nation-states. And the ties that bind the members of ethnic groups are often material interests, and not traditional obligations. Ethnic groups may expand into the rural sector and gain the backing of tribes; this in fact can be a politically dangerous stage in their evolution, and this paper will examine some of the circumstances that can promote such urban-rural linkages. But, nonetheless, ethnic groups should be distinguished from tribal groups, and the origins and dynamics of the former should be considered independently of what is known and asserted about traditional political behavior in Africa.

THE ARGUMENT AND EVIDENCE FOR ITS PLAUSIBILITY

Modernity is a cluster of desired goods. This is not to state that it is uncritically accepted, nor that African people do not decry the costs of modernization. The development of such philosophies as Negritude, Humanism, and the multitudinous versions of African Socialism by African intellectuals, and the spread of urban prophet churches and antiwitchcraft movements among some of the African masses, suggest the sensitivity of many to the costs of modernization.[3] Nevertheless, it is obvious that the components of modernity are strongly desired.

Not only is modernity desired, but the goods it represents are scarce in proportion to the demand for them. The inevitable result is that people compete. This competition is best illustrated in the struggles over income and for several of the resources which create it: land, markets, and jobs.

Land

In the agricultural societies of Africa, particularly where the population is dense, the penetration of a money economy gives rise to an intense competition for land. As Colson states: "By themselves such changes had an impact on local systems of land rights as men began to evaluate the land they used in new ways. They also led to an increasing number of legal battles over land; for men were encouraged to establish long-term rights in particular holdings either for immediate use or for subsequent gain."[4] While much of the competition for land is intraethnic, much of it is interethnic as well. Hill has published accounts of several major interethnic land disputes in Ghana.[5] The dispute between the Kikuyu and Masai over control of the former White Highlands has created a major cleavage in the political life of Kenya. And a major source of urban conflict is the tension between those indigenous ethnic groups who have alienated their lands and those immigrant groups who have benefited from the occupation of urban real estate.[6]

Markets

The competition for control of markets is equally intense. One of the best analysts of this phenomenon is Cohen, who documents the intensive rivalry between the Yoruba and Hausa for control over trading routes to the interior along the southern coast of Nigeria.[7] Lloyd documents the rivalry between Itsekiri and Urhobo for marketing facilities in Warri. Such conflicts characterize Eastern Africa as well.[8]

Jobs

Equally as pervasive is the competition for jobs. Parkin discusses the rivalry between Luo and Baganda for employment in the industrial and service sectors of Kampala; Grillo, in his analysis of the East African Railways, notes a similar rivalry between Luo and Abaluhya.[9] Competition for employment has been noted between the Bamileke and Douala in the Cameroun, between Nyanja and Bemba speakers on the copper belt of Northern Rhodesia, between indigenous Africans and strangers in Abidjan, and between Kasai Baluba and Bena Lulua in Kasai province in the Congo.[10] Exacerbating these tensions has been the expansion of the production of educated employables at a rate in excess of the expansion of job opportunities, a phenomenon that has been studied in Ghana, Nigeria and elsewhere.

Modernity and Stratification

Not only does modernization thus create competition; but because the elements of modernity are valued and scarce, they form the basis of a new stratification system in Africa. This is not to state that traditional criteria of social ranking are totally relinquished; indeed, all evidence is to the contrary, and we shall later argue that the interplay between the two stratification systems is in fact crucially important. Nonetheless, those who possess the attributes of modernity can more successfully claim higher social rank in contemporary African society than can those who do not.

The creation of new stratification systems is documented in studies of occupational prestige in Africa. These studies find that modern roles, such as those of the teacher or clerk, are given high prestige and that in fact they are generally ranked higher than the roles of traditional societies, such as those of craftsman or hunter. The results of these studies go beyond suggesting that

modern occupations are prestigious, however, to emphasizing that modern conceptions of stratification are being utilized by African peoples. Thus, studies report a close correspondence between the ranking of occupations by Africans in the Congo and those produced in the more developed countries.[11] Hicks, in a study of occupational prestige in Zambia, finds the criteria for the rankings to be similar to those reported in industrialized societies.[12] The prestige of an occupation can largely be accounted for, he indicates, by the degree of responsibility, service value, income, education and the nature of the working conditions associated with it.

The numerous studies of elite formation in Africa also suggest that those who possess the attributes of modernity can successfully lay claim to high status in many indigenous societies. Thus, Lloyd in a series of articles notes the rise of wealthy traders and educated clerical workers as a new elite in Yoruba society; Austin discusses the same phenomenon among the Ashanti and, like Lloyd, documents the conflicts between the new elite and the traditional ruling classes.[13] The same pattern has been reported in East Africa. Studies of the Gisu, Chagga, Luo, and Abaluhya describe how the spread of education and cash cropping generated new groups of literates and wealthy traders and how these new segments of the population successfully lay claim to elite status.[14]

Stratification and Competition

Crucial to the emergence of ethnic competition is that societies as well as individuals tend to be evaluated along the dimension of modernity. Those groups which are wealthier, better-educated, and more urbanized tend to be envied, resented, and sometimes feared by others; the basis for these sentiments is the recognition of their superior position in the new system of stratification.

In Calabar, for example, the indigenous Efik took readily to education, while the immigrant Ibo lacked both education and the wealth which would follow; the result was tension and hostility, sentiments which were exacerbated by the Ibos' attempts to close the gap.[15] This case finds its parallel in the famed rivalry between the Ibo and the Yoruba. So too with the northern peoples of Nigeria: their fear of the superiority of the southern peoples in the modern social and state system led them to an explicit policy of "northernization" whereby they gave privileged access to educational and employment opportunities to residents of the north. Their unequal status led to another point of conflict with the southerners, this time over the date of self-government in Nigeria. As related for the Birom of northern Nigeria, "Birom leaders expressed unease at the thought of rapid achievement of selfgovernment—in fact at the idea of selfgovernment before the Birom have produced enough professional men and traders and artisans to be able to claim all the occupations of control which exist in their Division."[16] As a result, the Birom aligned with the Northern Peoples Congress instead of with one of the several Southern parties which were competing for their allegiance, for the Congress favored a later date for self-government.

This pattern is also found in East Africa. In Kenya, for example, the less modernized pastoralists feared the perpetuation of the disparity between themselves and the more educated, urbanized, and wealthy agriculturalists which would result were Kenya to become independent under the political control of the agriculturalist peoples. As a result, the pastoralist groups less fervently pressed for self-government in Kenya than did the agriculturalists; and when they saw that their efforts were to fail, they sought to fragment power through a federal constitution. This conflict provided a major basis for the political competition between KANU and KADU in Kenya.[17] As Zolberg succinctly states, in the case of the Ivory Coast: "Many [of the changes introduced under colonial rule] have reinforced old differentiations between tribes by adding to them new ones based on modern attributes, such as wealth and education."[18] And as one Nigerian commentator states, ethnic competiton breaks out when "groups must compete for places in the class, status and power systems of the new nation. In a manner of

speaking . . . it is a form of social indecision regarding the strategy of equitable distribution of . . . advantages available to people in the new African nations."[19]

BASIS FOR THE FORMATION OF ETHNIC GROUPS

The basic question that arises from this discussion is: why should the competition for the components of modernity and for status positions as defined by modernity involve ethnic groups at all? At least three answers can be given to this question. The first is that the distribution both of modernity and of ethnic groups tends to be governed by the factor of space. *Where* modernization takes place often largely determines *who* gets modernized. The second is that administrative and ethnic areas often coincide. And the third is that it is often useful for those engaged in the competition for modernity to generate and mobilize the support of ethnic groupings.

The Factor of Space

It is the geographers who most forcefully portray the spatial patterns of modernization. Originating in "nodes" or "central places," modernity then spreads or "diffuses" into the more remote regions of the territory, they report. They also demonstrate that the level of modernity slopes downward with distance, with the central places being the most modernized, the proximate areas being the next most developed, and the hinterlands lagging behind.[20] While there is considerable debate over whether territoriality is a required component of the definition of an ethnic group, there is no denying that the members of an ethnic group tend to cluster in space; nor can it be questioned but that colonial policy made every attempt to assign ethnic groups to stable and rigidly defined areas. One result of this correspondence in spatial orderings is that members of ethnic groups will tend to have preferences with respect to allocational decisions which are homogeneous and well defined. This is particularly the case with respect to siting decisions, i.e., choices as to where to locate specific facilities or projects. The benefits from such decisions accrue to those who are most proximate and they diminish monotonically with distance from the project. Insofar as a group occupies a specific area, then, its members would have a uniform preference with respect to sites; they would prefer that resources be devoted to constructing projects that are in or near "their" area and they would rank alternative locations in the order of their proximity.

Many ethnic conflicts in fact take the form of locational disputes. A major reason for the split between the Bemba-speaking and other factions in Zambia, for example, was that the Bemba-speaking areas appeared to derive disproportionate benefits from projects built in response to Rhodesia's UDI; a railway and pipeline were constructed in the northeast and the main road in the area upgraded to provide Zambia with a life line to the sea. Ethnic competition takes the form of regional conflict in other nations as well; and this, of course, is what one would expect, given the locational feature of allocational decisions.

Another result of the correspondence of spatial orderings is that groups are differently advantaged in terms of their attainments. Soja, in his analysis of "modernization" in Kenya, finds that the Kikuyu, being proximate to Nairobi and the highlands, are the most urbanized and educated, and among the wealthier, of the ethnic groups in Kenya.[21] Similarly, Coleman and Abernethy argue that the initial advantage of the Yoruba in Nigeria derived from their proximity to Lagos and from the early establishment of missions in Lagos and Abeokuta.[22] The Ibo, being more remote from these areas, were initially less exposed to the centers of modernization; and being less proximate to the locus of mission activity, they lagged badly in the attainment of education and well-paying jobs. The pre-eminence of the Baganda, and the tensions which have resulted, have also been explained in terms of their proximity to the administrative capital and largest town in Uganda. As one analyst reports:

In Uganda (with the possible exception of the southeastern area) geographical distance from the capital city is sufficient to provide a rough indicator of the degree of modernity. Most Ugandans are fully aware that the Baganda profited more than others from their close proximity to the administrative center of the country.[23]

So pervasive a phenomenon does this appear that spatial proximity is sometimes offered as an alternative to classic notions of "cultural receptivity" in explaining differing rates of change. Thus, Kasfir, discussing Apter's structural-cultural theory of modernization in Buganda, notes that given the proximity of the Baganda to Kampala, the "argument . . . cannot be proved or disproved."[24] And Gugler, in discussing the general resistance of pastoralists to the forces of change, comments that "the underlying more general factor [is] probably that many of these are difficult of access to schools and administration alike."[25]

Space, Administration, and the Incentive to Organize

Local administration serves as one of the primary agents of modernization in Africa. And the colonial powers, by delineating administrative boundaries along "tribal" lines, made it in the interests of their subjects to organize ethnic groupings so as to gain control over the administrative mechanisms which themselves controlled the modernization process.

This assertion is best demonstrated in the studies of one of the primary sources of income in Africa—land. Colson notes that colonial policy produced two contradictory developments in land law. On the one hand, the growth of the cash economy furnished an incentive for individual ownership; on the other hand, the dominant mythology of the colonial administration, that land was "communally owned," restricted permanent rights to land to the members of the local ethnic group.[26] A clear implication of Colson's analysis is that as the benefits of land ownership increased, as they did with the spread of cash cropping, so did the importance of retaining and affirming membership in ethnic groups. The political consequences of this rapidly became evident in the conduct of the local councils in which jurisdiction over land rights had in part been vested. The local councils began to function as ethnic organizations, legislating so as to restrict ownership to members of local ethnic groups and to divest "strangers" of rights of permanent tenure. In this way, the material benefits to be derived from land ownership were purposefully restricted to local residents.[27]

The power of the local administration over economic resources extended beyond the control of land tenure to such other matters as access to markets and market stalls, the regulation of crop production and animal husbandry, the construction of roads for the export of produce, and the like. At the behest of those who had the greatest stake in the modern economy, often organized in "improvement unions," many councils acted so as to bias the distribution of these programs for the benefit of the local population and away from immigrant strangers. La Fontaine reports that local leaders in Mbale sought to distribute roads and payments to coffee growers so as to benefit GiSU cash croppers exclusively. Lonsdale documents the attempts by the Kavirondo local councils to restrict access to markets to Abaluhya and Luo cash croppers. And Lloyd, in his discussion of Urhobo and Itsekiri rivalry in municipal elections in Warri, notes that "it was said during the 1955 election campaigns that whichever tribe won the election would restrict the lease of stalls to its own members and thus give them a monopoly of the trade in the town."[28]

Given that power over the distribution of many of the benefits of modernity is vested in the local administration, and given the correspondence between administrative and ethnic boundaries, it is natural that persons would create politically cohesive groups and utilize these to restrict the degree to which the administration could compel the sharing of benefits with others. The demand of ethnic groups for their own districts and councils represents a logical continuation of this process, for by securing this demand they could more perfectly exclude others from such benefits and thereby reserve to themselves a larger portion.

The Behavior of the Moderns

A third major class of reasons for the formation of ethnic groups is that in the competition for the benefits of modernity, it has been in the interests of the most modern elements to sponsor the growth of "traditional" consciousness in Africa.

Before explaining why this is so, it is instructive to indicate the extent of the evidence for the major role that moderns have played in organizing "traditional" groupings. The "educateds" often were the founders of ethnic unions. Thus Lonsdale speaks of "the Christian establishment" of mission-trained literates who helped to form the Kavirondo Taxpayers Welfare Association.[29] Twaddle writes of the "'new men' created by missionary education" who helped to form the Young Bagwere Association.[30] And the role of the former mission students in organizing the independent schools among the Kikuyu and promoting ethnic consciousness in that tribe has been discussed by many authors.[31] In terms of income, it is often those who are better-off by dint of their occupations in the modern sector—the clerks, cash croppers, and traders—who form ethnic unions. Ottenberg, for example, notes that it was those who "work as clerks for the local British Administration, who teach in local schools, who work for traders, or who are traders themselves" who founded ethnic unions among the Afikpo Ibo.[32] Sklar notes that both the Egbe Omo Oduduwa and the Ibo State Union "were created by representatives of the new and rising class—lawyers, doctors, businessmen, civil servants."[33] And Bennett notes that the Bahaya Union was led largely by relatively prosperous cash croppers and members of cooperative societies whose economic interests were threatened by the government's policies toward coffee cultivation and land management.[34]

The role of urban dwellers in the formation of ethnic unions stands out most clearly in the literature from West Africa. There, ethnic unions were most often formed in urban centers and only later exported to the rural areas whose names they often bore. As stated by Offodile: "It is significant to observe that almost all the tribal unions now existing in Nigeria were found, not in the very towns of the tribes represented, but outside their own villages, and sometimes outside their own tribal territories."[35] Thus it was in Lagos where the Ibo came into competition with the Yoruba and where Ibo tribal consciousness was formed. It was in Leopoldville that Abako was founded; only later was it exported to the majority of the Bakongo in the surrounding rural territories.[36] And even in the case of such minor tribal unions as the Afikpo Town Welfare Association, the origin of the organization lay in the city: "An educated Afikpo man working at a trade-union post in Aba, who had traveled widely in the course of his work . . . realized the need for a protective union to aid Afikpo people. . . . At his own expense he had 400 membership cards printed to organize Afikpo people."[37]

In explaining the behavior of the moderns, we can note numerous motivations for the formation of these unions, but one stands out above all others: the perception by the moderns that they must organize collective support to advance their position in the competition for the benefits of modernity. To this we now turn.

Social and Economic Competition and the Formation of Groups

We have noted that there are good reasons for one ethnic group to be more advanced than another; in part, the spatial diffusion of modernization makes this inevitable. The members of an advantaged ethnic group are motivated to defend their leading position; they devise methods for retaining their privileged positions, such as biasing local council legislation in the ways we have described. Moreover, because modernity is desired, the less favored members of a privileged ethnic group place immense pressure on their more advantaged brothers to share the benefits derived from their advanced positions. Thus, family loyalties are activated to secure jobs; the income of the more prosperous is claimed by kin, often to meet school fees that will in turn secure future prosperity; and urban dwellers find their households being used by country folk in search of urban employment.[38] Under the pressure of the less advantaged, a sense of obligation resembling that usually extended to immediate kin is thus broadened to include fellow village dwellers and even persons from other villages and districts; and the language of relationships, such as the use of putative kin terms, is broadened to suggest this expansion. The result of these pressures is that the more advantaged members of the group are forced to draw into their sphere others of their kind. And the social-climbing less advantaged generate a mythology of consanguinity in search of modern benefits. The initially advantaged group thus consolidates and comes to view itself as an ethnic grouping in the process.

A major result is to create among the members of other groups a sense of threat and disadvantage. In the competition for jobs, it is the more modern elements of these groups who most directly experience this threat and perceive it in ethnic terms. They come to understand that they are placed at a disadvantage by their inability to activate the sense of ethnic obligation so as to gain access to the modern sector. Moreover, they perceive that their individual progress is closely determined by the collective standing of their group; they therefore initiate programs of collective advancement in response.

The creation of ethnic support by the competitors for jobs has been noted by Grillo in his analysis of the Railway African Union in Uganda. High office in the union often led to promotion to more advanced jobs in the railway company, and so was much desired by railway employees. In order to enhance their mobility prospects by gaining union office, contenders for advancement would sometimes make appeals to tribal loyalty. As stated by Grillo, "Although those seeking office . . . may have little sense of tribal interest, tribalism may be one of the weapons used in the struggle."[39] A similar pattern has been noted in Kenya, where accusations are made regarding the "Kikuyuization" of the government services and ethnic pressures are mounted by the leaders of the less advanced groups in protest over job discrimination.[40] However, the most striking illustration of the creation of ethnic action is to be found in West Africa. Perceiving that their individual fates in the struggle for modernity were tied to the collective standing of people from their own areas, the most modern members of the less modernized groups organized large-scale programs of advancement among their people. Abernethy furnished the best discussion of the phenomenon:

The struggle for employment was bound to produce frustration, and those not chosen for the best jobs found it easy to blame their plight on the advantages possessed by members of other groups. Of course, different groups clearly did have differential access to education, which in turn was the key to job mobility. . . . What was the best course of action open to the urban migrant who was acutely concerned lest his ethnic group fall behind others in the struggle . . . ? Certainly the rural masses had to be informed of the problem. If the masses were not aware of their ethnicity, then they would have to learn who they really were through the efforts of "ethnic missionaries" returning to the homeland. These "missionaries" would also have to outline a strategy by which the ethnic group, once fully conscious of its unity and its potential, could compete with its rivals. Clearly the competition required enrolling more children within school, particularly at the secondary level for the graduates of a good local secondary school would be assured of rapid . . . mobility within modern society.[41]

In this manner, Abernethy accounts for the formation of ethnic unions among the Ibibio, Ibo, and Urhobo in Nigeria.

Political Competition

A similar pattern obtains in politics. In the political arena, it is not just power that is at stake, but also the benefit which power can bring: control over the distribution of modernity itself.

There can be no doubt but that electoral competition arouses ethnic conflict. The tensions arising from the 1964 elections in Nigeria were one of the precipitates of civil war in that country. The primary instruments of the virulent ethnic conflict in the Congo were the numerous political parties formed by politicians to contest the 1960 elections. And it was elections, or the anticipation of them, that precipitated ethnic conflict in Zanzibar, Rwanda, and Ghana.[42]

Perhaps the main reason for these conflicts is that in the competition for power, ethnic appeals are useful to politicians. Given that most constituencies tend to be dominated by the members of one ethnic group—a result of the politics of apportionment and delimitation—an ethnic appeal is an attractive and efficacious weapon in the competition for office. Moreover, because ethnic groups contain persons of all occupations, socioeconomic backgrounds, lifestyles, and positions in the life cycle, the appeal of common ethnicity can generate unified support where other issues would be divisive. As a result, in the competition for power, and for the benefits of modernity and the prestige which it confers, politicians stimulate the formation of competitively aligned ethnic groups. As stated by Sklar: "Tribal movements may be created and instigated to action by the new men of power in furtherance of their own special interests."[43]

Naturally, this is not to state that the politicians are alone to blame for the rise of ethnic conflict. Indeed, while they do instigate ethnic conflicts, they often behave like captives of the forces which they helped to create. This leads us to the last question with which we plan to deal in this paper: having accounted for the formation of ethnic groups, how can we explain their persistence?

THE PERSISTENCE OF ETHNIC GROUPS

Ethnic groups persist largely because of their capacity to extract goods and services from the modern sector and thereby satisfy the demands of their members. Insofar as they provide these benefits to their members, they are able to gain their support and achieve their loyalty.

The capacity of ethnic groups to extract benefits from the modern sector is best demonstrated in their relationship with those who have achieved positions of prominence in that sector. Ethnic groups exert powerful social pressures upon the modern elite in order to satisfy the demands of their members. Perhaps the most persuasive evidence for these assertions is the reaction of the modern elite itself. Its members experience their positions not only as privileged but also as onerous; they feel that they are at the center of tremendous social pressures. As Uchendu states: "My town demanded leadership from me. But this leadership is a trying as well as a thankless experience. My town has a passionate desire to get up."[44] Chona, once vice president of the Republic of Zambia, argues the same point: modern leaders are subject to concerted pressures and forced to act as spokesmen for ethnic interests. Rather than blaming members of the national elite for instigating "tribalism," he states, the citizens of Zambia should blame the "local leaders in the villages and towns" who "travel . . . to Lusaka to meet leaders" in order to urge them to serve parochial interests. Chona concludes, "Unless the local leaders in the villages and towns stop being competitive against other groups and begin to regard top leaders as national leaders we shall not find a lasting solution to [the problem of ethnic conflict]."[45]

The demands upon the modern elite are predictable. Characteristically, they include demands for material resources: financial contributions from the moderns for the construction of new facilities and for the creation of educational funds. Some groups even levy taxes upon their more prosperous urban members.[46] The demands of ethnic groups are also for service: the use of the skills of the moderns, be they technical, educational, or political, on behalf of "their people."

The capacity of ethnic groups to extract goods and services from the modern elite derives from several sources. They control the allocation of strong inducements. For example, because elite skills are a desired commodity, ethnic groups are able to win the use of these skills by making their acquisition contingent upon ethnic service. Thus Lloyd reports for the Itsekiri that "several lawyer-politicians who were sent to England with community funds are expected on their return to repay the debt either in cash . . . or by winning tangible benefits for their people."[47] Other inducements include prestige: symbols of status are conferred or withdrawn by ethnic groups in recognition of services performed for the group. Plotnicov documents the conferring of status by ethnic groups in Jos; members of the modern elite, he writes,

have the skills for dealing with government and the wider community. Their knowledge in legal and economic matters, secretarial and bookkeeping procedures, and their general sophistication in modern and urban affairs is indispensable. Their value to the ethnic group . . . [is] recognized through the granting of high . . . offices . . . and sometimes . . . titles as well, which further reinforce the modern elite's powers.[48]

Ethnic groups also possess strong sanctions, most notably the capacity to withdraw elite status. This is vividly revealed in the political sector, where, for example, the Luo, Sukuma, and Lozi turned out of office several of their most renowned political leaders, some of cabinet rank. The reported reason for the imposition of these sanctions was the elite's failure to serve local interests.[49]

There is another reason for the ability of ethnic groups to extract goods and services from the incumbents of the modern sector. For many moderns, what is prestigious is still defined in terms of traditional criteria. For many, modernity becomes a resource which they utilize to attain prestige within the traditional sector.

Evidence for the continued presence of traditional notions of stratification is contained in the very studies which emphasize the pre-eminence of modern stratification systems. Hicks, for example, finds that the standard deviation of the rankings of modern occupations by Africans is higher than that of the rankings by Europeans; he attributes this in part to the use by Africans of two sets of stratification criteria, one traditional and the other modern.[50] Similarly, Foster found that Ghanaians give higher ranks to traditional political offices—chiefs and councilors—than they give to many modern occupations "despite the fact that often holders of these [offices] had little education and received little . . . pay. Clearly the respondents in Foster's study were using at least two dimensions to rate the full list of occupations: one being the western dimension and the other a traditional dimension."[51]

The acceptance of traditional stratification patterns leads many moderns to convert their success in the modern sector into prestige in the traditional order by utilizing their wealth to obtain prestigious positions in their ethnic groupings. Many studies cite the purchasing of traditional titles by the successful entrants into the modern sector. Others note the use of wealth to purchase traditional offices. Still others record the use of income derived in the modern sector to practice clientage and to finance ceremonies so as to enhance social standing in the traditional order. As Balandier states:

> [A wealthy person] can . . . make "sociological investments"; in this case, he uses new economic conditions to achieve or to reinforce a traditional type of prominence. The size of his "clientele" and the extension of his generosity will reveal his degree of success; his profit will be expressed in prestige and authority . . . the economic "game" is still only a method to achieve goals determined by the old social and cultural system.[52]

Ethnic groups are thus able to extract investments from persons seeking access to elite positions in the "modern" order. Moreover, the "moderns" need, and seek to elicit, the support of ethnic groupings. Forces thus promote the supply and demand of services between the ethnic groupings and the most "progressive" elements of modernizing societies.

Conclusion

Theories of social change predict the demise of ethnic grouping. A major contribution of the study of African politics is to document the falseness of this prediction. Modernization and ethnic conflict do intersect, both empirically and intellectually. In this essay I have examined this point of intersection and tried to explain how the process of modernization can promote ethnic group formation.

It is precisely the rationality of ethnic behavior that has eluded the modernization theorists of both the sociological and political-economic persuasion. Because they failed to perceive the usefulness of ethnic organization, they failed to predict the efflorescence of ethnic competition. Ethnic organization is a means of organizing so as to attain the benefits of modernization; it is a form of coalition-building in the rational pursuit of specific objectives. In this conclusion I wish to amplify this argument with special reference to politics.

Political systems allocate resources. In particular, they make decisions regarding the location of wells, clinics, schools, roads, markets, and other facilities. The location of such facilities determines who gets the benefits. If a clinic, for example, is located in district A, it is *not* located in district B. In the parlance of game theory, the political process determining the allocation of such facilities is simple: the outcome is either 1 (if you win and get the project) or 0 (if you do not).[53]

In the competition for benefits, it is obviously useful for groups to be "bigger"; in most forms of political competition groups do better if they are larger in size. But it is also true that it is useful to limit the size of groups and to restrict the number of beneficiaries. Exclusion is desirable if the benefits are fixed in size; a budgetary allocation or a capital fund will produce greater benefits per capita if spread over fewer people. Exclusion is desirable even when the benefits are nonmonetary. If there are, say, a fixed number of classrooms or scholarships or jobs at a project site, then, once again, individuals do better if there are fewer claimants for these benefits. While there are forces which make it desirable to expand the number of people in a coalition competing for favorable allocational decisions, there are thus also strong forces promoting the restriction of these benefits. For the benefits are subject to dilution or crowding, and rational actors will therefore seek to confine them to as few people as possible.[54]

We have noted that because the incidence of the allocation of benefits and ethnic group membership are both a function of spatial location, it is natural that those seeking benefits should have preferences which are organized along "ethnic" lines. Further considerations promote such behavior. Institutions—such as local governments, "traditional" political systems, kinship ties, markets and trading networks—are likely already to exist in specific locations; their pre-existence reduces the cost of organizing. Moreover, the uniformity of language within groups and the difficulty of communicating across linguistic lines means that, for a limited set of resources, organizers will prefer intragroup organizing to organizing across groups. Not only the incidence of the benefits but also the incidence of the costs of organization therefore correspond to spatial boundaries.

As a consequence of these considerations, I argue, actors, in the rational pursuit of benefits, will organize competitive groupings and these will take ethnic form. Ethnic groups are, in short, a form of minimum winning coalition, large enough to secure benefits in the competition for spoils but also small enough to maximize the per capita value of these benefits.[55]

It should be noted that this analysis provides a rational grounding for one of the major interpretations of ethnic group behavior: that of situational analysis. Situational analysis stressed that ethnic groups often lack an "objective" basis. It also stressed that they are dynamic. Ethnic groups, it noted, were in fact sometimes "invented," forged out of cultural materials which had lain latent until mobilized in efforts to organize. Situational analysis also stressed that the boundaries of ethnic groups were subject to repeated redefinition. When opposed to another major group, then group membership would be defined inclusively; in other situations, the group would be internally divided and ethnic membership would then be more restrictively defined.[56] The analysis which I advance furnishes an explanation for the patterns highlighted by situational analysis. For depending upon the issue and the competitive arena, the size of the coalition which would insure maximum individual benefits to its members would vary; and

different criteria of inclusion and exclusion would therefore be invoked as groups formed in efforts to reap maximal benefits in the competition for scare resources. The dynamics underscored by situational analysis thus became predictable corollaries of an approach based upon the assumption of rational behavior.

What are the implications of this analysis? One, of course, is that ethnic competition will not disappear as modernization proceeds; the very purpose of this paper is to show the weakness of such reasoning. Nor will it decline as people are subject to higher levels of education; clearly, the behavior is not atavistic or "prerational" and so it will not diminish as people acquire more sophisticated training. Rather, it would appear, what is required is a form of correction which exploits the very properties which generate the phenomenon in the first place: the desire for benefits and the capacity to act rationally in pursuit of them.

The appropriate response, then, is one of institutional design. Efforts should be devoted to creating institutional environments which alter incentives so that persons organize coalitions of a different nature when in pursuit of their interests. Attempts should focus on exploiting the very nature of ethnic competition so as to channel and diffuse it.

Examples of such attempts come from Nigeria, where constitutional designers created new electoral rules in an effort to decouple the desire for office from the making of political appeals to ethnic consciousness. New states were created in an effort to reduce the expected value of attempts to organize regional blocs; as each state included a smaller proportion of the electorate and controlled a smaller proportion of governmental delegates, each had less reason to aspire to be winning in the competition for public benefits.

Moreover, the founding fathers of the new Nigerian republic required political parties to draw a fixed minimum proportion of votes in a designated proportion of separated and widely scattered jurisdictions. The purpose was to reduce the attractiveness of narrow ethnic appeals; such appeals, while mobilizing some, would alienate others and so reduce the capacity of the parties to fulfill their distributional quotas.

Current political events in Nigeria leave open the question of the effectiveness of these measures. Nonetheless, they underscore that those most affected by ethnic conflict recognize the rational wellsprings of ethnic behavior and seek to control it by designing institutional environments wherein persons, in the rational pursuit of their own best interests, will have reason to behave in ways consistent with the maintenance of political order.

In conclusion, in this essay I should note that I have taken what can be termed an instrumentalist view of ethnic behavior. Others, most notably Geertz, have established a consummatory interpretation.[57] Consummatory behavior would lead to ethnic conflict over issues other than material advantage. Moreover, it would lead to ethnic conflict even when it "didn't make sense," i.e., when the costs exceed the benefits to the parties concerned.

It is important to realize that both principles are at work. And it may well be the case that while instrumentalist behavior may lead to the formation of ethnic groups, consummatory behavior is important in explaining their persistence; as I have stressed, people who organize ethnic groups are often captured by the forces they set in motion. Nonetheless, for two major reasons, I feel that instrumentalist considerations are paramount. The first is that the consummatory model makes ethnic behavior constant, whereas as a matter of empirical fact ethnic behavior has been found to be variable. The second and related point is that ethnic behavior is controllable. Just as ethnicity can be organized, it can be disorganized. The rise and fall of ethnic consciousness marks the history of almost every nation-state; and efforts to create political institutions to contain, to ameliorate, and to defuse ethnic self-assertion mark the constitutional histories of many political communities. Theories of ethnic behavior based upon the power of primordial sentiments suggest the futility of such efforts. What should be suggested, rather, is their difficulty. For the rational component of ethnic behavior

clearly exists and it has been and should be exploited so as to direct political choice-making into less explosive channels.

NOTES

1. See, for example, Stanley Greenburg, *Race and State in Capitalist Development* (New Haven and London: Yale University Press, 1980); and Crawford Young, *The Politics of Cultural Pluralism* (Madison: University of Wisconsin Press, 1976).

2. For discussion of the definitional problem of the term, see Robert Melson and Howard Wolpe, "Modernization and the Politics of Communalism: A Theoretical Perspective," *American Political Science Review* 64 (December 1970): 1122–1130; Pierre L. van den Berghe, "Introduction," in Pierre L. van den Berghe, ed., *Africa: Social Problems of Change and Conflict* (San Francisco: Chandler, 1965), pp. 1–11; Paul Mercier, "On the Meaning of 'Tribalism' in Black Africa," in van den Berghe, ed., *Africa: Social Problems of Change and Conflict*, pp. 483–501; and Abner Cohen, *Custom and Politics in Urban Africa* (Berkeley and Los Angeles: University of California Press, 1969). To be noted is that to affirm the reality of ethnic groups is not to ignore their internal divisiveness. Conflicts between major segments and areal groups, between commoners and persons of royal blood, and between clans and villages—all these cleavages do exist. Nonetheless, internal conflicts do not necessarily weaken the capacity of the larger ethnic groups to mobilize their members for collective purposes; the conflict-laden, internally divided Ibo are a case in point. The fact of internal division and conflict should therefore not be taken as evidence of the absence of effective ethnic collectivities nor discredit the validity of our enterprise.

3. One of the major social costs of modernization is the development of new stratification patterns, and thus inequality; another is the generation of new individual opportunities, and thus the promotion of individual self-interest at the expense of traditional social obligations. At the elite level, African Socialism, and its other variants, represent an attempt to speak to these problems. At the mass level, witchcraft and anti-witchcraft movements represent parallel attempts to deal with these problems. For analyses of the relationship between social change and attempts to control witchcraft, see the contributions in John Middleton and E. H. Winter, eds., *Witchcraft and Sorcery in East Africa* (London: Routledge and Kegan Paul, 1963).

4. Elizabeth Colson, "The Impact of the Colonial Period on the Definition of Land Rights," in Victor Turner, ed., *Profiles in Change: African So-*

ciety and Colonial Rule (Cambridge: Cambridge University Press, 1971), p. 194.

5. See Appendix 3 in Polly Hill, *The Migrant Cocoa-Farmers of Southern Ghana* (Cambridge: Cambridge University Press, 1963). See also the cases reported in L. T. Chubb, *Ibo Land Tenure* (Ibadan, Nigeria: Ibadan University Press, 1961); and Michael Twaddle, "Tribalism in Eastern Nigeria," in P. H. Gulliver, ed., *Tradition and Transition in East Africa* (Berkeley and Los Angeles: University of California Press, 1969), pp. 193–208.

6. See, for example, the discussion of the politics of Mbale contained in J. S. LaFontaine, "Tribalism among the Gisu," in Gulliver, ed., *Tradition and Transition in East Africa*, pp. 177–192; and the analyses of the politics of urban Nigeria contained in Richard L. Sklar, *Nigerian Political Parties* (Princeton: Princeton University Press, 1963).

7. Cohen, *Custom and Politics in Urban Africa.*

8. P. C. Lloyd, "Tribalism in Warri," in West African Institute of Social and Economic Research, *Fifth Annual Conference Proceedings* (Ibadan, Nigeria: University College, 1956), pp. 78–87. See also J. M. Lonsdale, "Political Associations in Western Kenya," in Robert I. Rotberg and Ali A. Mazrui, eds., *Protest and Power in Black Africa* (New York: Oxford University Press, 1970), pp. 589–638; and Dharam P. Ghai, "The Bugandan Trade Boycott: A Study in Tribal Political and Economic Nationalism," in Rotberg and Mazrui, eds., *Protest and Power in Black Africa,* pp. 755–770.

9. David J. Parkin, "Tribe as Fact and Fiction in an East African City," in Gulliver, *Tradition and Transition in East Africa*, pp. 273–296 and R. D. Grillo, "The Tribal Factor in an East African Trade Union," in Gulliver, *Tradition and Transition in East Africa*, pp. 297–321.

10. See Willard R. Johnson, *The Cameroon Federation* (Princeton: Princeton University Press, 1970); Chapter 10 of Gwendolen M. Carter, *Independence for Africa* (New York: Frederick A. Praeger, 1960); and C. W. Anderson et al., *Issues of Political Development* (Englewood Cliffs, N.J.: Prentice-Hall, 1967).

11. N. Xydias, "Prestige of Occupations," in Daryll Forde, ed., *Social Implications of Industrialization and Urbanization in Africa South of the Sahara* (Paris: UNESCO, 1956), pp. 458–469; J. Clyde Mitchell and A. L. Epstein, "Occupational Prestige and Social Status among Urban Africans in Northern Rhodesia," *Africa* 29, 1 (1959): 22–39; and J. C. Mitchell and S. H. Irvine, "Social Positions and the Grading of Occupation," *Rhodes-Livingstone Journal* 38 (1965): 42–54.

12. R. E. Hicks, "Occupational Prestige and its Factors: A Study of Zambian Railway Workers," *African Social Research* 1 (1966): 41–58.

13. Lloyd's articles are referenced and summarized in P. C. Lloyd, *The New Elites of Tropical Africa* (London: Oxford University Press, 1966); Dennis Austin, *Politics in Ghana 1946–1960* (London: Oxford University Press, 1964).

14. J. S. LaFontaine, *City Politics: A Study of Leopoldville, 1962–63* (Cambridge: Cambridge University Press, 1970); Lonsdale, "Political Associations in Western Kenya"; Twaddle, "Tribalism in Eastern Nigeria."

15. W. T. Morrill, "Immigrants and Associations: The Ibo in Twentieth Century Calabar," *Comparative Studies in Society and History* 5 (July 1963): 424–448.

16. T. M. Baker, "Political Control Amongst the Birom," in West African Institute of Social and Economic Research, *Fifth Annual Conference Proceedings*, pp. 88–94.

17. See, for example, the discussion in Fred G. Burke, "Political Evolution in Kenya," in Stanley Diamond and Fred G. Burke, eds., *The Transformation of East Africa* (New York: Basic Books, 1966); and Donald Rothchild, "Ethnic Inequalities in Kenya," *Journal of Modern African Studies* 7 (December 1969): 689–711.

18. Aristide R. Zolberg, *One Party Government in the Ivory Coast* (Princeton: Princeton University Press, 1964; rev. 1969), p. 5.

19. A. A. Akiwowo, "The Sociology of Nigerian Tribalism," *Phylon* 23 (Summer 1964): 162.

20. See, for example, the analyses by Peter R. Gould, "Problems of Structuring and Measuring Spatial Changes in the Modernization Process: Tanzania 1920–1963." Paper presented at the annual meeting of the American Political Science Association, Washington, D.C., September 2–7; and by Edward W. Soja, *The Geography of Modernization in Kenya* (Syracuse, N.Y.: Syracuse University Press, 1968).

21. *Ibid.*; see also Rothchild, "Ethnic Inequalities in Kenya," pp. 689–711.

22. James S. Coleman, *Nigeria: Background to Nationalism* (Berkeley and Los Angeles: University of California Press, 1958); and David B. Abernethy, *The Political Dilemma of Popular Education: An African Case* (Stanford: Stanford University Press, 1969).

23. Nelson Kasfir, "Cultural Sub-Nationalism in Uganda," in Victor A. Olorunsola, ed., *The Politics of Cultural Sub-Nationalism in Africa* (Garden City, N.Y.: Anchor, 1972), pp. 47–148.

24. *Ibid.*, p. 76.

25. Josef Gugler, "The Impact of Labour Migration on Society and Economy in Sub-Saharan Africa: Empirical Findings and Theoretical Considerations," *African Social Research* 6 (December 1968): 465.

26. Colson, "Impact of the Colonial Period on the Definition of Land Rights," p. 194.

27. See also the discussion in Coleman, *Nigeria: Background to Nationalism*, p. 59, and Chubb, *Ibo Land Tenure*, p. 25.

28. Lloyd, "Tribalism in Warri," p. 86; also, LaFontaine, *City Politics: A Study of Leopoldville, 1962–63*; and Lonsdale, "Political Associations in Western Kenya."

29. Lonsdale, "Political Associations in Western Kenya," p. 628.

30. Twaddle, "Tribalism in Eastern Nigeria," p. 197.

31. See, for example, Carl G. Rosberg and John Nottingham, *The Myth of "Mau-Mau": Nationalism in Kenya* (New York: Frederick A. Praeger, 1966), pp. 105–135.

32. Simon Ottenberg, "Improvement Associations Among the Afikpo Ibo," *Africa* 15 (January 1955): 4.

33. Sklar, *Nigerian Political Parties*, p. 72.

34. George Bennett, "Tribalism in Politics," in Gulliver, ed., *Tradition and Transition in East Africa*, p. 80.

35. E. P. O. Offodile, "Growth and Influence of Tribal Unions," *West African Review* 18 (August 1947): 937.

36. An excellent discussion is contained in LaFontaine, *City Politics: A Study of Leopoldville.*

37. Ottenberg, "Improvement Associations Among the Afikpo Ibo," pp. 15–16.

38. Relevant materials include Grillo, "The Tribal Factor in an East African Trade Union," pp. 297–321; Jean L. Comhaire, "Economic Change and the Extended Family," in van den Berghe, ed., *Africa: Social Problems of Change and Conflict*, pp. 117–127; and John C. Caldwell, *African Rural-Urban Migration: The Movement to Ghana's Towns* (New York: Columbia University Press, 1969). Particularly germane are the discussions of "the failure of class formation" in Africa which underscore the extent of the use of kinship networks to extract the benefits accruing to the more modern elements of society. Good examples are provided in P. Mercier, "Problems of Social Stratification in West Africa," in Immanuel Wallerstein, ed., *Social Change: The Colonial Situation* (New York: John Wiley, 1968), pp. 340–358; and in Arthur Tuden and Leonard Plotnicov, eds., *Social Stratification in Africa* (New York: Free Press, 1970).

39. Grillo, "The Tribal Factor in an East African Trade Union," p. 318.

40. Rothchild, "Ethnic Inequalities in Kenya," pp. 689–711. See also Gavin Kitching, *Class and Economic Change in Kenya* (New Haven and London: Yale University Press, 1980).

41. Abernethy, *Political Dilemma of Popular Education*, pp. 107–108.

42. See the discussion in Austin, *Politics in Ghana 1946–1960*; Crawford Young, *Politics in the Congo* (Princeton: Princeton University Press,

1965); Michael F. Lofchie, "The Zanzibari Revolution," in Rotberg and Mazrui, *Protest and Power in Black Africa*, pp. 924–967; and René Lemarchand, "The Coup in Rwanda," in Rotberg and Mazrui, *Protest and Power in Black Africa*, pp. 924–967.

43. Richard L. Sklar, "Political Science and National Integration—A Radical Approach," *Journal of Modern African Studies* 5 (May 1967): 6.

44. Victor G. Uchendu, *The Igbo of Southeast Nigeria* (New York: Holt, Rinehart and Winston, 1965), p. 9.

45. Mainza Chona, "Who is Responsible for Tribalism?" *Zambia News*, May 5, 1968.

46. For example, see Offodile, "Growth and Influence of Tribal Unions," p. 937, for a description of the levying of educational funds by the Ibo State Union; for an analysis of the contribution of urban dwellers to the construction of civic facilities in rural villages, see A. F. Hershfield, "Ibo Sons Abroad: A Window on the World." Paper presented at the annual meeting of the African Studies Association, Montreal, October 15–18, 1969. See also the discussion of the impact on rural development of financial contributions from urban dwellers in Caldwell, *African Rural-Urban Migration*, pp. 161ff.

47. Lloyd, "Tribalism in Warri," p. 86.

48. Leonard Plotnicov, "The Modern African Elite of Jos, Nigeria," in Tuden and Plotnicov, eds., *Social Stratification in Africa*, p. 289.

49. *Africa Report* 15, 4 (1970): 8–9; *Africa Diary* 10, 3 (1970): 4788–4789; Ruth S. Morgenthau, "African Elections: Tanzania's Contribution," *Africa Report* 10, 11 (1965): 12–16; and Ian Scott and Robert Molteno, "The Zambian General Elections," *Africa Report* 14, 1 (1969); 42–47.

50. R. E. Hicks, "Occupational Prestige and Its Factors: A Study of Zambia Railway Workers," *African Social Research* 1 (1966): 213.

51. *Ibid.*, p. 219.

52. Georges Balandier, "Traditional Social Structure and Economic Changes," in van den Berghe, ed., *Africa: Social Problems of Change and Conflict*, pp. 392–395.

53. More formally, a game is simple if $V(B) = 0$ or 1 for all $B \; P(N)$, where B is a coalition or subset of N, the set of all players; where $P(N)$ is the power set of N; and where V is the characteristic function.

54. The process, in short, is subject to decreasing returns to scale. More formally, if for all $T \leq S \leq N$, then a game is subject to decreasing returns to scale if $\dfrac{V(S)}{|S|} < \dfrac{V(T)}{|T|}$.

55. More formally, where the competition for spoils can be represented as an N person game in characteristic function form, where we restrict ourselves to the space of coalitionally rational payoff configurations, and where payoffs are subject to decreasing returns to scale, then, if a

coalition is winning, it is minimally winning. See Richard McKelvey and Richard Smith, "A Comment on the Debate Over Riker's Size Principle," unpublished, and William Riker, *The Theory of Political Coalitions* (New Haven and London: Yale University Press, 1962).

56. See Anderson et al., *Issues of Political Development;* also, Young, *Politics of Cultural Pluralism.*

57. Clifford Geertz, "The Integrative Revolution: Primordial Sentiments and Civil Politics in the New States," in Clifford Geertz, ed., *Old Societies and New States* (New York: Free Press, 1963).

African Economic Development in Theory and Practice

Colin Leys

The character of African economic development in the past twenty years is strangely obscure. This has a good deal to do with the size and diversity of the continent—Nigeria is booming, Ethiopia starving, and so on—but it is due even more to the filtration of the African experience through successive layers of interpretative theory. One can see this from the sort of questions people ask: Have the African economies become less or more "dependent" or "externally oriented"? How far is their new technology "appropriate"? Are they less vulnerable than formerly to "unequal exchange"? How far have "basic needs" been met? These are not primarily factual questions. They testify to the extraordinary degree to which African reality has been overlaid by theory. It is as if the poverty of so many millions in Africa were too painful to contemplate without being immediately set in the context of a theory that can somehow explain it, and at the same time show the way to ending it. The motive is good, but the pitfalls are many. Today, the prevailing view of African economic development is pessimistic—profoundly disappointed at the postindependence record, and gloomy about future prospects. This view, however, is a reaction to a previous moment of exaggerated optimism. Neither really helps us to understand what is happening in Africa. To be able to come a little closer to that reality, we need to stand back somewhat from the interplay of hopes and fears and theories that reflect and may so easily amplify them.

Reprinted from *Daedalus*, Journal of the American Academy of Arts and Sciences, Cambridge, MA, "Black Africa: A Generation After Independence," vol. 111, no. 2 (Spring 1982), 99–124, by permission of the journal.

THE PHASE OF OPTIMISM

It is easy to forget just how unqualified was the optimism about African development that reigned in the early 1960s, just as the formal decolonization of Africa was being completed. Ten newly independent African countries were among the eighteen UN delegations that persuaded the General Assembly to declare the goal of the UN Development Decade to be "the attainment in each less developed country of a substantial increase in the rate of growth, with each country setting its own target, taking as the objective a *minimum* annual rate of growth of aggregate national income of 5 percent at the end of the decade."[1] For the Second Development Decade (1970–80), the target was raised to 6 percent, and in both decades, ambitious targets for industrialization were also set. These targets were far higher than the historical achievement of most of the industrialized countries; Britain's growth rate, for example, never reached a 2 percent average from 1853 to 1913, and even the U.S. and German rates of growth of gross national product (GNP) down to World War II were well below 5 percent a year on average.

What accounted for this optimism? Partly it was a result of the general optimism caused by postwar economic recovery, the unprecedented growth rates of Germany, France, and Japan, and the belief that in Keynesian demand management, combined with sound international monetary arrangements, a technique had at last been found that could maintain a permanently rising volume of international trade. There was also the example of the Soviet Union's spectacular growth between the wars, based on five-year plans, a technique also adopted by India after its independence. And there was the African leaders' keen sense of the waste of their peoples' human potential under colonialism, and the ambition to catch up with the industrial countries, by taking advantage of their technology and of the aid that was expected to flow from them in growing amounts.

The results of the two "development decades" in Africa have certainly belied this optimism. More than four-fifths of the sub-Saharan African countries still fall in the low-income category of developing countries (with annual per capita incomes of less than $360 in 1978), and their average rate of growth per capita of 0.9 percent over the two decades was the lowest of all the regions of the Third World.[2] Worse, the World Bank's most optimistic forecast is that the African countries will experience only a one percent average annual per capita growth rate in the 1980s; more likely, they will on balance experience a slight decline, with a growing number of people in "absolute poverty."[3] It is true that gross rates of growth (undivided by population growth) were on average quite strong (though not up to the "development decade" targets): for the low-income African countries, the average annual growth of gross domestic product (GDP) was 4 percent in the sixties and 2.4 percent from 1970 to 1978. For the eight African middle-income countries (above $360 per capita GNP), the figures were 4.4 percent and 3.7 percent.[4] Given the world recessions of the 1970s, these figures were not unimpressive; and there were great individual variations, with some African countries—not all of them oil exporters—enjoying much more rapid rates of growth. But there were also many countries that stagnated, and others that regressed disastrously—for instance, Angola and Uganda. In any case, given annual population growth rates closer to 3 than to 2 percent in most African countries, economic growth rates needed to be very high, by world standards, if Africans were to become better off. Moreover, statistical averages conceal severe inequalities, as seen in Table 1. Food production per capita has declined, and in the Sahel region, stricken by war and drought, aid

agencies estimated that a million people would die of hunger and malnutrition in 1980 alone. Meantime, development aid has declined steadily from the levels of the sixties—especially U.S. aid, which fell from 0.53 percent of U.S. GNP in 1960, to 0.18 percent in 1980, compared with the Second Development Decade target of 0.7 percent. At the same time, African indebtedness rose. By 1990, the World Bank predicts, repaying and servicing old debt will use up over 80 percent of all new borrowing by the African countries. Grim scenarios prevail for the future of African resource depletion, pollution, regional cooperation, and the like.[5]

THE PESSIMISTIC REACTION—FROM "MODERNIZATION" TO "DEPENDENCY" AND "BASIC NEEDS"

Instead of leading to a systematic theoretical critique of the basis for the earlier overoptimism, the gap between those expectations and experience led to an equal and opposite tendency to pessimism. The optimism had been rationalized by theories of "modernization." The pessimistic reaction was rationalized in terms of "underdevelopment" and "dependency," and given a practical expression in poverty-oriented development programs. It is necessary to place these successive theoretical systems in perspective.

Modernization theory was the outgrowth of a gradually expanding perception of the obstacles in the way of rapid growth in the ex-colonies. At the end of World War II, the emphasis was heavily, if not exclusively, on the shortage of capital. By the mid-1950s, it was recognized that the problem of capital absorption—that is, effective use of capital—was, if anything, more serious than the problem of capital supply. This view lay behind the increasing emphasis on development planning in the late 1950s. Experience with planning soon revealed, however, that implementing plans was more difficult than drawing them up. This led to increased concern with development administration, administrative and management training, and even to experiments with "infecting" Third

World businessmen with "achievement motivation."[6] By the mid-1960s, it was apparent that none of these sectors could be isolated from the total social milieu, and there developed a concern with altering traditional values, attitudes, and social practices. Modernization theory denoted the sum of these perspectives. The mid-1960s were its high point. Social scientists working in Africa were among the most influential exponents of the modernization approach, according to which development consisted of a complex transition from traditional primordial society, based on multiplex, affective, and ascriptive relationships, to modern society, based on role separation, rational relations, and achieved statuses. At a certain stage in this transition, a "take-off" into sustained economic growth would become possible.

The main tenets of economic theory that belonged to this general outlook have been summarized by Killick:

- Economic development is a discontinuous process of structural transformation.
- National poverty is self-perpetuating, with low income countries caught in a vicious circle of poverty. But, with the savings ratio as a rising function of income, growth tends to become self-sustaining above a certain critical level of income *per capita*.
- A "big push" or "critical minimum effort" is required to break out of the "low-level equilibrium trap" and achieve self-sustaining growth. . . .
- While the "big push" requires many inputs, its single most important ingredient is a massive increase in the ratio of investment to national income.
- Development entails industrialisation which, by choice or necessity, will concentrate on satisfying the home market for manufactures by substituting for imports.

Killick adds:

With the probable exception of [the first] item, not one of these propositions would today command general assent among Western-based or trained economists. The evidence has refuted the ideas of a "poverty trap" and that high incomes automatically ensure sustained growth. Faith in the efficacy of a big push engineered by development planners and fuelled by massive investments in fixed capital has similarly faded. Both planning and import-substituting industrialisation are now regarded as having failed to deliver the benefits they seemed to offer.[7]

This tells us that these theories were wrong, but not why. It is commonplace to say that they were "Eurocentric," wrongly assuming that European (or Western) experience was valid for Africa—for instance, they tended to be obsessed with scale and with industry, neglecting the possibilities of small economic units and the centrality of agriculture. They were also excessively economistic—preoccupied with capital-output ratios, but incapable of analyzing the noneconomic determinants of such ratios, such as education and training, state administrative competence, or ethnic rigidities in labor markets. But a more fundamental weakness was that they rested on

Table 1. Inequality in Africa

	GNP per capita	Proportion of GNP received by		
		Lowest 40 percent	Middle 40 percent	Top 20 percent
Tanzania (1967)	89	13	26	61
Uganda (1970)	126	17	36	47
Kenya (1969)	136	10	22	68
Sierra Leone (1968)	159	10	22	68
Ivory Coast (1970)	247	11	32	57
Zimbabwe (1968)	252	8	23	69
Gabon (1968)	497	9	24	67

Source: M. S. Ahluwalia, "Income Inequality," in H. Chenery et al., *Redistribution with Growth* (London: Oxford University Press, 1974), p. 12.

certain illusions that modernization theory made into an explicit doctrine. They assumed that the "backwardness" of the Third World was an "original" backwardness, a primeval backwardness that had once been universal and could be overcome by the transmission of capital and know-how from the industrial West. But this was profoundly misleading. The backwardness of Africa was a new form of backwardness, the product of colonialism. The technological backwardness of African agriculture, for example, had been *shaped* and even *developed* by colonialism. In the mid-nineteenth century, for instance, before colonial rule, H. Kjekshus estimates that the interior of what is now mainland Tanzania carried at least 4.5 million cattle; with regard to the coastal region, he cites a German officer writing in 1891 that "the still widespread opinion in Germany that you need only step outside of your door to shoot an antelope or a pheasant anywhere in Africa is based on a complete misunderstanding. The entire coast is as poor in game as can possibly be imagined." It was poor in game because it was supporting a rich agricultural and pastoral economy. Kjekshus adds, "Similar reports abound from areas that are today the country's major game sanctuaries"—areas now infested with the tsetse fly, where no cattle can live.[8] It was only after the introduction, under colonization, of rinderpest, smallpox, jigger fleas, and other scourges, followed by the retreat of people, the advance of the tsetse, and the forced development of export crops in the remaining areas of cultivable land, that Tanzania's agricultural backwardness acquired its modern form. And what development was achieved was done with virtually no new technical or capital inputs. Walter Rodney's comment that "the vast majority of Africans went into colonialism with a hoe and came out with a hoe" contains a very large element of truth. Similar observations could be made for African trade, African manufacture, and African administration in many parts of the continent. This is not to say that colonialism cut off a development that would otherwise have made Africa into a region of advanced industrial societies. It is only to say that, to an embarrassing degree, not only did modernization theory fail to see that African backwardness was shaped by colonialism, but it also failed to see how far the postindependence pattern of trade and investment, the patterns of aid given to local "elites," or the transfer of Western tastes, reinforced the backward, inegalitarian structures of the ex-colonial African economies.

In Africa, the theoretical reaction to modernization, strongly inspired by Latin American "dependency" writers—the *dependentistas*—began in the late 1960s, particularly after the Arusha Declaration of 1967 in Tanzania. The essence of this reaction was to shift from ignoring many of the external determinants of African development to seeing them as primary, and as almost wholly negative, inspired as they were by the interests of foreign capital and foreign states, not the interests of the population concerned.[9] In this view, the result was an "external orientation" of the African economies (geared to exporting primary commodities of low value and importing manufactures of high value); a process of "unequal exchange," which limited the development of "internal linkages"; and severe inequalities of income and wealth, which further limited the development of the domestic market, reinforced the political power of comprador ruling classes, and gave rise to chronic corruption, political instability, military coups, and so forth. And this process was aggravated, not relieved, by industrialization undertaken by multinational corporations, leading, among other things, to high rates of surplus transfer, the rising use of imported inputs, and capital-intensive industrial technology.

Out of the critique of modernization theory and the apparent ineffectiveness of many of the economic development policies associated with it, there emerged the so-called poverty-oriented, or "basic needs" approach to development. Developed largely within the International Labour Organization (ILO) and the World Bank, it was strongly influenced by a group of thinkers especially concerned with Africa (notably Hans Singer, Dudley Seers, Richard Jolly, and others), and popularized by Robert McNamara during his middle years as the Bank's president. Behind this line of thought lay an acceptance, though usually tacit, of much of the dependency viewpoint. The approach seeks to raise the living standards of the poorest inhabitants of Third World countries by means of policy packages—rural development, aid to the so-called informal sector, and so on—that will directly benefit them, without challenging the basic structures of the economy or the balance of political power (although it is sometimes implied that the relief of poverty will lead to both of these results), either because these are seen as unalterable, or because the proponents of such an approach are not enthusiastic about changing them. These thinkers are, however, distressed by the human costs of the present situation. "Redistribution with growth" (as an early version of this line of thought was aptly titled) represents the unhappy consciousness of international development orthodoxy. It is interesting to contrast the standpoint of this approach with the views of Paul Prebisch after more than half a century of work on the development of Latin America: "You cannot produce . . . fundamental transformation without changing the power structure. You cannot take the surplus from the private hands that have appropriated it without subduing their power. . . . In my view the fundamental thing is to change the power structure in the country."[10]

The dependency theorists and their epigones have undoubtedly identified many of the forces that explain the pattern of modern Africa's development. Case studies in virtually every African country testify to the reality of the structures to which dependency theory points, and the basic needs approach, which is so deeply indebted to dependency theory, has become a new orthodoxy. Contemporary views of African development are overwhelmingly colored by these orientations. Yet there is little doubt that they too obscure as much as they reveal. To read the African record, it is now necessary to remove this theoretical envelope in its turn.

The most important shortcoming of dependency theory is that it *implies* that there is an alternative, and preferable, kind of development of which the dependent economies are capable, but which their de-

pendency prevents them from achieving—when this alternative does not in fact exist as an available historical option. The core meaning of "dependent development," or "underdevelopment," is that "the economies of one group of countries are conditioned by the development and expansion of others" in such a way that the development of the former is blocked.[11] But this blockage is not held to be absolute; after all, there has been some growth in almost all of the Third World countries, including the African countries. So what is said to be thwarted is some supposed alternative course of development, which would be followed if the countries were not dependent. This, however, is never specified—and for a good reason. Either what is implied is a superior (autonomous, inward-oriented) kind of *capitalist* development; for this to be helpful it would then have to be shown how an autonomous capitalist development could be expected to unfold without the inequalities and unevenness, the instability, crises, unemployment, and wars that have characterized early capitalism elsewhere—and to do it much faster than has ever been achieved before. Or the implied suppressed alternative is a *socialist* path of development: in this case, it would be necessary to show the social and political forces capable of carrying through such a strategy, and that it could reasonably be expected to be superior. In most African countries, this would be difficult, to say the least. There has to be something wrong with a conceptualization, the import of which is that the world should be other than it can be. This manifests itself in a radical ambiguity. Concerning Niger, for example, R. Higgot writes:

> groundnut production accounted for 65 per cent of all Niger's very feeble external revenue during the first decade of independence. As of 1976, however, uranium was accounting for the same percentage but of a larger absolute volume. . . . While this revenue bonanza makes Niger more solvent, and able to overcome some of the distress of the drought period of the early 1970s, it also ties it much more firmly into a dependency situation within the world economy.[12]

One sees what the author is getting at. But, given that he does not see any alternative way of producing the uranium ore, or any alternative means of starting to raise the level of Niger's productive forces, is Niger's new *dependency* on the French Atomic Energy Commission, the Pechiney Mokta group, and others (which also became to some extent *dependent* on the government of Niger) a good thing or a bad thing? What is gained by focusing the discussion around the concept of dependency?

Dependency theorists have performed an important task of demystification. It was important to insist that all development has a definite historical and social character—that there is no such thing as development *sans phrase*, and that the development experienced in Africa is capitalist. It is important to avoid romanticizing a manufacturing development that consists of spending large sums on advertising to persuade Africans to eat Weetabix, costing twenty times as much and being one twentieth as nourishing as the maize meal they used to eat.[13] It is necessary to be alert to the multiple ways in which "periphery capitalism" involves economic, social, and political costs for periphery populations the loss of surplus through unequal exchange in monopolistic markets or through transfer pricing, the hidden costs of "aid," the suborning of national leaders by foreign capital, and so on. But it is another matter to elevate a catalogue of periphery capitalism's many shortcomings into a doctrine of its *inability to develop* the periphery—relative to an implied alternative way of going about it, which is not in fact available.

This is not to say that there *are* no other options. The point is rather that dependency theory implies that there is some option, superior to what at present exists, when this is often not the case. Because of this, it fails to recognize that *some* of what is happening under dependent development is, after all, still development: painful, wasteful, and ruthless, like early capitalism everywhere, but development nonetheless. In some areas, exchange has been more or less generalized, production has been at least partly reorganized, wage labor has been increasingly detached from the land. In the sufferings of the masses—not just from famines and wars, but also from forced migration, cultural deprivation, hu-

miliation, extortion, and insecurity—there is also a certain potential for advance. The failure to recognize and grapple with this renders dependency theory misleading and hence impotent in relation to those areas where the advance has occurred.

Three other shortcomings of the dependency approach also deserve emphasis. First, like any structuralist theory, dependency theory has tended to be historically weak. It is true that dependency theorists correctly reproached modernization theorists with being ahistorical, but the "history" to which the *dependentistas* themselves appeal is typically very linear and general, not to say universal. It presents the influence of the industrialized countries on the tropical world as a broad and continuous process of surplus extraction that has merely taken successive forms— from primitive accumulation through colonial monopolies, to sophisticated practices such as transfer pricing and monopoly pricing for technology transfers. In this perspective, little distinction is made between the different stages of development of capitalist countries at the "center," and the effects of these differences on relations with the periphery; or between the different resource endowments, scale, geopolitical significance, and above all, preexisting social structures of the various periphery countries. Today it seems clear that every country must be understood in the uniqueness of its own historical development and its own distinctive relations with the metropolitan powers if its development potential is to be understood.

Second, dependency theory has tended to neglect the significance of the cyclical nature of capitalist accumulation on the world plane. Dependency theory was in itself a product of the "long boom" from 1940 to 1970—or rather, of a particular phase of it. Between 1958 and 1965, a net flow of capital ran from the Third World to the United States, of the order of $16 billion, while there was also a growing net flow of funds out of the United States into Western Europe. From the standpoint of Latin America, where dependency theory was first developed, this seemed to portend a permanent exclusion from the industrialization process. This was theorized by A. G. Frank as merely an acceleration of the inveterate process of surplus transfer ("the contradiction of expropriation/appropriation"), and by Emmanuel as the "inevitable" movement of capital toward geographic areas of high demand for final products. It fell to Latin American writers such as F. H. Cardoso and O. Sunkel to point out, from the vantage point of Brazil in the late 1960s, that there had to be something wrong with this, because a veritable boom of mainly American private investment was occurring there. Cardoso, however, was too committed to the dependency framework to abandon it, coining the singularly unexplanatory term "associated dependent development" to deal with the reality that Brazil and other rapidly industrializing Third World countries seemed to represent.[14] But the truth was that Brazil represented a phenomenon that would become much more common as the European investment boom spent itself, and as Japanese competition in manufactures—coinciding with the first internationally synchronized recessions of 1970–71 and 1974–75—created excess capacity, a surplus of investable capital, and an attempt to restore profitability by shifting investment to areas that had higher rates of exploitation. In Africa, this tendency seems so far only to have affected significantly the Ivory Coast and South Africa, but there seems to be no absolute reason why it should stop there.[15]

Third, dependency theory has not been much more alert to the active principles of imperialism than modernization theory had been. Although anti-imperialist in intention, its focus on the structures of economic subordination tended to direct attention away from the impact of great power military and geopolitical intervention. This may well have been more decisive, especially economic and military support for political clients, and economic and military intervention against anti-imperialist forces, encouraging high levels of military spending and fostering military coups and wars. For instance, for the twenty-eight sub-Saharan African countries (excluding South Africa) for which estimates can be made, the real level of military spending rose *fourfold* between 1965 and 1977. In 1976 twenty sub-Saharan Af-

rican countries were spending an average of 3.1 percent of GDP on their armies—not far below the level of the rich West European NATO countries.[16] For countries that were mainly among the poorest in the world, these were crippling expenditures. An important part of this expenditure was directly due to imperialist military threats, as in post-1974 Mozambique and Angola, or was the outcome of complex great power maneuvers, as in Ethiopia and Somalia. Mauritania was nearly crippled by its abortive colonial war in ex-Spanish Sahara, and Morocco may yet be.[17] Fourteen of the thirty-six sub-Saharan African countries have fought wars—civil or external—during the last twenty years; twenty (including some that have had wars) have experienced coups (some several).

All these considerations do not yield a more optimistic picture than that of the *dependentistas*, but one that is more complex and less generalized. The insights of dependency theory must never be forgotten, but must be separated from the utopian framework in which they have been cast. We must assess the African record in the context of the actual historical options; we must consider the actual historical forces—internal and external—at work in each country and region; we must take into account the cycle of accumulation and the reality of imperialist interventions of all kinds. The general result is likely to be much more complex, more diverse, and much more dynamic than most scenarios in vogue today suggest.

This does not mean that no general patterns are to be found, although the variety that constitutes the African reality emerges from almost any classification one cares to make. In 1972 Samir Amin classified the African economies into three groups—colonial trade economies, plantation economies, and labor reserve economies. For all its oversimplification, this schema had the great merit of grasping some essential distinctions between the different kinds of impact of colonialism on Africa, differences that imparted distinctively different dynamics to the development of the colonial economies, and it has been widely referred to since.[18] It is difficult to propose any simple typology that will be as serviceable in the 1980s. Table 2 classifies the African economies by two very rough measures of "endowment," and by the broad principles on which their development policies are based—the latter being important in themselves, and also a rough indicator of the actual balance of social forces at work in the countries concerned.

AFRICAN CAPITALISM

If dependency is a new utopianism, a new "philosophy of poverty" based on a preoccupation with the "bad side" of periphery capitalism, does periphery capitalism have a "good side" that has been neglected? This is the essential argument of one of the earliest and most consistent critics of dependency, the late Bill Warren. In his posthumous book, *Imperialism, Pioneer of Capitalism,* he developed the argument he had first advanced in 1973, that the postwar development of the Third World has actually been a case of *successful capitalist development*—more rapid than in the industrialized countries, either historically or in

the same postwar period; that the benefits of this capitalist growth have not been restricted to the richest minority; that unemployment has not on the whole increased; that "marginalization" is only a pejorative word for the process of increasing *integration* of new segments of the population into capitalist relations of production; that, in short, periphery capitalism has been performing its historic task of rapidly developing the productive capacity of the Third World.[19] What Warren did not stress, but which is equally central to his thesis, is that capitalist development is, and always has been, uneven, contradictory, and costly in human terms. Its historically "progressive" character springs from a "grim, destructive, and oppressive logic."[20] Warren did not argue that the capitalist development taking place in the Third World was "nice" (though he considered that the middle-class anticonsumerist hostility to some of it was misguided and hypocritical).[21] He argued only that it was taking place; that no "nicer" form of capitalist development (free from social dislocation, unevenness, exploitation, unequal exchange, inequality,

Table 2. Development Strategy—A Pattern of African Development

	Sahel Region		Mineral Exporting		Other	
Capitalist	Chad	(−1.4)*	Niger	(−1.3)	Ghana	(−0.8)
	Senegal	(−0.2)	Zaïre	(0.7)	Uganda	(−0.2)
	Upper Volta	(0.3)	Liberia	(1.6)	Sierra Leone	(0.4)
	Sudan	(0.6)	Mauritania	(1.9)	Benin	(0.6)
	Mali	(1.1)	Togo	(3.6)	Central African	
			Nigeria	(3.7)	Republic	(0.7)
					Rwanda	(1.5)
					Burundi	(2.1)
					Ivory Coast	(2.4)
					Cameroon	(2.5)
					Kenya	(2.7)
					Malawi	(2.9)
					Lesotho	(6.0)
Socialist	Somalia	(−0.5)	Angola	(−2.1)	Mozambique	(0.1)
	Ethiopia	(1.3)	Guinea	(0.3)	Tanzania	(2.3)
			Zambia	(0.8)		
			Zimbabwe	(0.8)		
			Congo P.R.	(0.9)		

Source: *Accelerated Development in Sub-Saharan Africa,* World Bank (Washington, D.C.: 1981).
*Figures in brackets refer to average annual rates of growth per capita 1960–79; the table excludes countries with fewer than 1 million population. For the Tanzanian figures, see note 35.

oppression, wars, and so on) has ever occurred or could occur; and that failure to acknowledge what was occurring could only handicap the masses of the Third World in their struggle to improve their lot, and eventually overthrow capitalism and replace it with communism. From this standpoint, dependency theory and the basic needs school appear as modern forms of "critical-utopian" and "bourgeois" socialism.[22]

There are various difficulties with Warren's position, yet it has the great merit of forcing us to look again, as unsentimentally as possible, at the African record, which has caused so much distress to all but the hardest-nosed neoclassical economists working on Africa. If we omit the mineral-exporting economies, where sudden apparent increases in the growth rate may be due (though not necessarily) merely to changes in prices or the level of mining activity, we get the picture in Table 3.

It is first of all clear that the overall real growth of output was substantial even in the 1970s, when world trade was faltering and the import costs of oil were rising so fast. It is true that some of the higher growth rates in the seventies (Malawi's, for example) were due to favorable terms of trade. But this is irrelevant, since unfavorable terms of trade also account for some of the weaker growth rates (Malawi also suffered a 14 percent *drop* in its terms of trade between 1960 and 1970). It is also irrelevant that so much of the growth was in export agriculture, so long as agricultural export markets exist and domestic ones do not; and irrelevant that this expansion was achieved by planting more acreage rather than by higher yields on existing acres, so long as that is the most profitable way to expand output.[23] There was also a significant growth of production in general, and manufacturing in particular (with the exceptions of Sudan and Uganda)—however "inappropriate," dependent, capital-intensive, and import-using it may have been. There were also substantial increases in life expectancy and in literacy, which would have been impossible if all the benefits of the growth that occurred had been entirely confined to the rich minority.

It is true that the levels of income achieved were very modest by world standards. But it is necessary for any Western observer to calibrate his observations of Africa carefully. Although life expectancy at birth in sub-Saharan Africa in 1979 was only about forty-seven years, compared with seventy-four years in the industrialized countries, it was nonetheless eight years higher than in 1960, an increase of more than 20 percent. Literacy registered an even bigger advance, from about 5 percent to about 25 percent of the total adult population over the same period. Millions of Africans remained in abject poverty, yet the poverty of many millions was less abject than it had been twenty years before. As P. Kennedy noted in Ghana in 1976,

What were luxury goods for one generation tend to become subsistence goods, or at least "essential" commodities for the next. In Ghana today, the government is trying to control the distribution and therefore the price of a number of basic goods precisely because they are in such great demand. Some of these now seem to be regarded as "essential" goods, for example, washing powder, toilet soap and tinned milk, whereas this was not the case 20 years ago. Other commodities, too, like transistor radios, bicycles, toothpaste and the possession of good clothes, in addition to every-day clothes, appear to be widely owned and used in the towns by the poorer sections of the community.[24]

It is also important to have an appropriate time frame. The inarticulate premise of too much commentary is that Africa's industrial revolution should be capable of being accomplished in a generation or two. A recent study suggested, for example, that on the basis of recent trends it would take Kenya 201 years to begin to reduce the *absolute* number of people outside enumerated wage employment—with the implication that this showed the "limited dynamism that marks recent Kenyan employment growth."[25] But apart from the fact that "enumerated" employment is probably less than half of total wage employment in Kenya (a fact that itself indicates the spread of capitalist production relations ahead of the capacity of the state statistical service to record it), are two centuries really much

Table 3. Non–Mineral-Exporting Capitalist Countries in Africa

	Population 1979 (in millions)	Average Annual Growth Rate of GDP (percent)		Life Expectancy at Birth (years)		Industry as Percent of GDP		Manufacturing as Percent of GDP	
		1960–70	1970–79	1960	1979	1960	1979	1960	1979
Sahel									
Chad	4.4	0.5	–0.2	35	41	12	11	4	8
Senegal	5.5	2.5	2.5	37	43	17	24	12	19
Sudan	17.9	1.3	4.3	39	47	15	13	5	6
Mali	6.8	3.3	5.0	37	43	10	11	5	6
Upper Volta	5.6	3.0	–0.1	37	43	14	20	8	14
Other									
Ghana	11.3	2.1	–0.1	40	49		21	10	8
Benin	3.4	2.6	3.3	37	47	8	12	3	5
Sierra Leone	3.4	4.3	1.6	37	47		23		5
Uganda	12.8	5.9	–0.4	44	54	13	7	9	6
Rwanda	4.9	2.7	4.1	37	47	7	21	1	15
Burundi	4.0	4.4	3.0	37	42		15		10
Kenya	15.3	6.0	6.5	41	55	18	21	9	13
Ivory Coast	8.2	8.0	6.7	37	47	14	23	7	12
Cameroon	8.2	3.7	5.4	37	47		16		9
Malawi	5.8	4.9	6.3	37	47	11	20	6	12
Lesotho	1.3	4.6	7.0	42	51		15		2

Source: *Accelerated Development in Sub-Saharan Africa,* World Bank (Washington, D.C.: 1981); and *World Development Report,* 1981.

too long for the conversion of the bulk of a country's labor force into wage earners (which, given the expected growth of population, is what this particular measure implies)? It also needs to be repeated that capitalist development is inherently uneven, both geographically and over time. For every success story in the African continent there are several failures. The chronic weakness of most of the Sahel economies, for instance, and their predicted stagnation for most of the 1980s, are as much due to the nature of capitalist development as are the success stories of countries such as the Ivory Coast.[26]

What this implies is that African capitalism has accomplished more than dependency theory allows—though in a limited number of places, and at an immense cost in terms of wars, famines, corruption, oppression, cultural deprivation, militarism, and foreign domination. But even this claim may be questioned. Are the advances that capitalism appears to have made in some places capable of being sustained? Are the best records of the sixties and seventies a reflection of easy options—more extensive agriculture, import-reproducing industrialization, and so on—that are now largely exhausted and that cannot be replaced? Are the gains of these years—such as they are—essentially precarious and about to be swallowed up in the inexorable growth of the African populations?

The debate on this question has so far revolved largely around the two fastest growing African economies (other than those with strong mineral exports), namely, the Ivory Coast and Kenya, the assumption being that if their growth cannot be sustained, the prospects for relatively poorly endowed African economies to develop further within capitalist relations of production must seem slight.[27] Both countries embarked at independence on an explicitly capitalist development policy, though not described as such; Kenya called its strategy African socialism, the Ivory Coast called it "planned, contractual and controlled liberalism."[28] Both opened their doors to foreign investment and encouraged domestic rural and commercial entrepreneurship. Kenya had the advantage of a relatively large settler enclave and

an Asian-owned commercial sector, both of which could be Africanized. The Ivory Coast had received a much more modest stimulus from settler agriculture, but adopted a peculiarly close relationship with France, including very high levels of technical and capital assistance; it was the pivot of France's continuing commercial dominion of the former French West Africa.[29]

Those who see the Kenyan and Ivorian experience as evidence that capitalism can develop Africa, point to the relatively high rates of growth that have been achieved in these countries on the basis of an alliance between a local capitalist class and foreign capital. *Dependentistas*, on the other hand, consider this growth precarious, and as having been achieved partly by extending agricultural production in ways that have reached their limits, and partly by making most of the population pay more for their necessities through the protection given to a highly inefficient and often socially undesirable import-reproducing manufacturing industry. They see industrial employment rising slower than industrial output, and foreign exchange constraints eventually halting the advance that was achieved during the last two decades.

In spite of its interest and importance, this debate has struck many observers as inconclusive. The record of growth does have a lot to do with favorable commodity price movements, the expansion of world markets in the sixties, a French policy favoring Ivory Coast industrialization within the ambit of France's own domestic plan, and high-cost import-reproducing industrialization. On the other hand, it also has to do with increased commercialization of farming, rapidly expanding informal sectors in manufacturing, large transfers of know-how, and so on.

The real issue, however, is whether the capitalist expansion of these economies that has undoubtedly occurred is necessarily fated to come to a halt, not whether it is fated to encounter new problems, as it surely is. The dependency school takes these problems and elevates them to the status of a theory of "blockage." Their opponents see the problems as inherent in capitalist development, but see no reason to suppose that they cannot be overcome. For instance, the fact that imported branch-plant technology tends to minimize the share of manufacturing inputs obtained locally is frequently cited as a major reason industrialization leads to foreign exchange constraints, and not to the expansion of linked domestic industries. This is true, but it is not impossible for African host governments to force such plants to increase progressively over time the proportion of locally produced inputs that they buy, as has been done in Latin America. Another oft-cited problem is the falling rates of growth of agricultural output, leading (as in Kenya and Nigeria today) to rising food imports. This constraint too can be tackled by agricultural reorganization to raise farm productivity. Such possibilities, however, depend greatly on the exercise of state power, and it is here that the question of the class structures of these countries becomes especially important, since the exercise of state power expresses the balance of class forces in the dominant alliance or bloc, and the counterweight of opposing classes.

In this connection, the so-called national bourgeoisie in Kenya and the planter class in the Ivory Coast have been the chief focus of attention. Up to a point, this focus is correct. The nature of the "class of capital" is bound to be important for the nature and rate of capitalist development. Its significance, however, is easily misunderstood. Dependency theorists tend to look at the matter in the following way. Foreign capitalists have no interest in developing the periphery, but only in exploiting it for the profit of their companies at the center. Domestic, or peripheral, capitalists have an interest in developing the periphery (i.e., maximizing investment in their own countries), but lack the means and the know-how. Sometimes it is said that they lack the will as well. This perception of the African businessman as essentially a comprador, content to live parasitically as a commission agent for foreign capital, was crystallized in Frantz Fanon's savage appraisal:

This native bourgeoisie, which has adopted unreservedly and with enthusiasm the ways of thinking characteristic of the mother coun-

try . . . will realize, with its mouth watering, that it lacks something essential to a bourgeoisie: money. . . . If the government gives it enough time and opportunity, this bourgeoisie will manage to put away enough money to stiffen its domination. But it will always reveal itself as incapable of giving birth to an authentic bourgeois society with all the economic and industrial consequences which this entails.[30]

Fanon was referring to something real. But is it *generic*, as he implied? Is it equally true of all African countries? Is it permanently true anywhere? Is it as true today as it was in the Africa Fanon knew at the end of the 1950s? There can be little doubt that in some African countries bourgeoisies have begun to form that have at least some capacity to organize domestic capitalist production. Their emergence, however, was strongly conditioned by the histories of the particular ex-colonies in which they have appeared. It is an oversimplification, but not a very misleading one, to say that in Kenya and the Ivory Coast, their advance was assisted by white settler enclaves, which pioneered a degree of internally oriented development, including the development of a wage-labor force under colonialism. These enclaves forced the more advanced African producers into economic and political competition with them, finally forcing them to take a leading role in their respective nationalist movements. Elsewhere in West Africa, the colonial trade economies produced, from an early stage, indigenous classes of *merchant* capitalists and petty traders. These different trajectories have left their marks on the different African capitalist classes, especially in the degree to which they are oriented to production rather than trade. These differences, however, can be exaggerated; the "logic" of capital probably works fairly quickly to elide them.[31] There seems no good reason to suppose that Nigeria will forever lack for manufacturing entrepreneurs, and Kennedy claims not to have found them scarce in Ghana in the late sixties. It is equally a mistake to think, in any case, that foreign capital is not interested in developing the periphery. What capital is interested in is not development, but its own expansion. When the conditions exist for profitable productive investment in the periphery, both foreign and domestic capital (no longer salivating for lack of money) become interested in it.

The emergence of such conditions has something to do with stages of growth—the commercialization of agriculture, the separation of workers from the land, the expansion of internal demand. But it also has to do with politics, and it is the *political* power of domestic capital that is at least as important as its capacity to organize production on its own. When circumstances permit an indigenous capitalist class to establish itself effectively in power, as, in the Ivory Coast and Kenya, the conditions for capitalist development at the hands of both foreign and domestic capital are enormously enhanced. Such power is, of course, never limitless; in the Ivory Coast, for example, the mutual dependence of the Ivorian plantocracy, French capital, and the French state is reflected in the extremely cautious—but profitable—strategy pursued by Houphouet-Boigny in advancing national interests vis-à-vis French interests. But the emergence of African states capable of sustaining the conditions for capitalist growth—a measure of reliability in public administration, social control without repression so severe as to jeopardize stability, a nonarbitrary application of commercial and criminal law, and so on—is importantly conditioned by the political power exercised by a domestic class with substantial capital of its own at stake.

The real measure of the importance of a politically cohesive production-oriented domestic class of capital is the fate of various countries that for various reasons have lacked one hitherto: Zaïre, for example, and Nigeria, both rescued to a lesser or a greater degree by oil exports; Mauritania and Niger, which seem likely to forfeit much of the benefit that their mineral exports might bring at the hands of an effective local bourgeoisie; above all, Uganda. Here, the African capitalist class was politically divided, and the Ganda, who made up the most important section of it, were fatally ambivalent—economically, in their commitment to accumulation (as a result of the semifeudal relations of production in Buganda), and politically, in their inability

to transcend the parochial confines of Ganda traditionalism, as was needed in order for them to secure a political basis for capital accumulation.

The Ugandan experience under Amin from 1971 to 1979 provides, in fact, a sort of negative objective lesson in the substantiality of capitalist development in Africa. In office was a dictator whose political power rested at first primarily, and later exclusively, on force. Revenues were channeled increasingly into military expenditures, the trading sector was in effect seized and parceled out among army officers, soldiers, and their associates; the civil state apparatus, including its economic management branches, was decimated and demoralized. The conditions for simple reproduction, let alone expanded reproduction, were destroyed. The whole economic structure unraveled. Primary crop production continued, but on a reduced scale, and less and less produce was traded officially. By 1979 prices had risen about 2,000 percent above 1971 levels. Moonlighting and black market trading became essential for salaried workers if they were to stay alive. The advance earlier achieved by capitalism in Uganda—which had an average annual increase of GDP of 5.9 percent, or 2.2 percent per capita, in the 1960s—can be judged from the difference between 1970 and 1978–79 in these figures, as shown in Table 4. At the same time, it was the particular unevenness of capitalist development in Uganda that contributed decisively to the catastrophe of the Amin regime.[32]

Two particular kinds of constraint on future growth loom large in the thinking of most dependency writers on Africa (including the basic needs school): the size of the internal market and agricultural productivity. These constraints are real. The limited size of most African domestic markets—even Nigeria's, after the oil boom—sets severe limits to successful manufacturing development, especially using imported technology geared to large production runs. Food production per capita was also falling in African economies generally in the late 1970s, posing a serious threat to further nonagricultural advance. The Ivory Coast suffered from the first of these con-

Table 4. Output of Selected Products in Uganda 1978–79, as percentage of 1970

Fabrics	55
Soap	9
Matches	16
Cement	38
Corrugated iron sheets	7
Sugar	8
Cotton (officially marketed)	14
Coffee (officially marketed)	45
Blister copper	14
Goods forwarded by rail	13

Source: *The Rehabilitation of the Economy of Uganda,* Commonwealth Secretariat (London: 1979).

straints, Kenya from both. The former tackled the problem of market size by trying to become an exporter (of wood veneers and textiles) to Europe under the terms of the Lomé Convention. Kenya could not easily follow this route, because its textile firms were not European-owned, but largely Japanese and Indian; whereas it suited the French firms in the Ivory Coast to restructure their production there to serve their European markets, as the latter grew more competitive. Does this mean that Kenya's industrial growth will be blocked? To suppose so is to suppose that neither the multinational corporations, nor the Kenyan business class associated with them, are capable of devising new strategies to deal with the problem of market size—from new tax regimes to new foreign policy initiatives to restore the East African regional market, new initiatives in Europe, and so on. It is not obvious that this supposition is well founded.

Similarly in relation to agriculture. The problem of food production is technically soluble: in the opinion of one recent study,

in relative terms, very little irrigation is being used, very few chemical inputs are used and almost no mechanization has taken place in Kenyan agriculture. . . . the easy options of Kenyan agricultural development have still not been fully utilized. High-yielding varieties of maize, millet, and sorghum have still only been adopted by a minority of the peasants. . . . Also, the potential of high-yielding dairy cattle has not yet been fully exploited. . . . The potential of mixed farming

has hardly been realized in Kenya outside Central Province.[33]

What is ultimately in question is the *political* possibility of reorganizing the relations of production in agriculture so as to raise productivity—implying, perhaps, an accelerated process of land concentration in the hands of a few capitalist farmers, and an accelerated increase of landlessness, or the development of state-subsidized irrigation for large-scale agriculture, and so on. There is no question that these are difficult hurdles to jump, but some African countries will find ways of doing so. On the other hand, only a limited number will, at least in the foreseeable future. It would be as mistaken to think that capitalism is in the process of developing all the countries of Africa as it is to suppose that it has not developed, and cannot develop, any of it.

ACTUALLY EXISTING AFRICAN SOCIALISM

Long before the academic debate about capitalism and dependency had even started in Africa, many African countries had come to doubt either their ability to develop within capitalist production relations, or the desirability of doing so, or both. A strong socialist strand existed in the nationalist movements of many, if not most, African countries, and the postindependence experience of Africa has provided it with plenty of reinforcement.

There are at least four different groups of African socialist regimes: (1) the regimes more or less directly descended from the *Rassemblement Démocratique Africain* (RDA), linked to the French Communist and Socialist parties for most of the 1940s—Guinea, Mali (1960–68), and the Congo People's Republic; (2) regimes that chose a "socialist" option out of a conviction, based on postindependence experience, that capitalist development was impossible, or not in the popular interest—Ghana (1960–66), Tanzania, Zambia, Somalia, and Benin;[34] (3) Ethiopia (since 1974), whose "socialist" option is a complex blend of the antifeudal movement, especially among the intelligentsia, and the Russian/Cuban military alliance; (4) regimes formed in anticolonial struggles—Guinea-Bissau, Mozambique, Angola, and Zimbabwe.

Obviously, there is as much variety in African socialism as it actually exists (not as it is hoped to become) as there is in African capitalism; from enormously differing endowments to widely differing conceptions of the transition to socialism; from the rigid centralism of Touré's Guinea (at least until 1979) to the comparatively open and certainly undoctrinaire regime of Nyerere's Tanzania; from Ethiopia's enforced dependence on the USSR to Zimbabwe's current enforced dependence on the West. There remain, however, clear areas of convergence: public ownership of strategic industries; state or cooperative trading; limits on foreign investment; trade and aid orientations that include Comecon economies or China, or both; restraints on the emergence of indigenous capitalism; efforts to equalize private consumption; efforts to promote collective or cooperative farming; and most important of all in the long run, efforts to foster popular power in local as well as national institutions.

The economic growth record of the socialist countries is particularly hard to assess, in view of the additional obstacles placed in their way by imperialism—from France's attempt to sabotage the Guinean economy after 1958 to the subsequent abortive invasion of Conakry in 1970; from the aid penalties imposed on Ghana and Tanzania after their exercise of a "socialist" option to the assassination of outstanding leaders such as Mondlane in 1969 and Cabral in 1973; and the continuing burden imposed on Mozambique and Angola by South African military attacks. In the case of Zimbabwe, the British-dictated constitutional limitations on nationalization, the political power of the white bureaucracy and army units, the economic weight of the white working class and foreign capital, and the South African threat, all combine to make the practical potential of the regime's "socialism" acutely problematic.

But when all allowances are made, the general economic record of the African socialist countries has also disappointed sympathetic observers. Several of them have succumbed to antisocialist coups (Mali,

Ghana, and perhaps Guinea-Bissau). In others, socialism has reduced itself largely to the nationalization of major foreign assets, combined with redistributive, welfarist, and normally agrarian rhetoric, more or less imperfectly matched by performance on the part of the single party or military leadership (e.g., Zambian "humanism"). Others have not yet really emerged from the trauma of the liberation struggle. In the socialist camp, Tanzania stands out, like the Ivory Coast and Kenya in the capitalist camp, as the focus of debate, because of its persisting socialist initiative and a relatively well-sustained growth rate unfavored by natural resource endowment.[35] What light does the Tanzanian debate shed on the possibilities of the socialist option?

As is well known, the Tanzanian initiatives took five principal forms: (1) democratization, (2) nationalization, (3) income equalization and measures to prevent the leadership from turning itself into a bourgeois class, (4) collective farming, and (5) national economic "self-reliance." By the standards of many African countries, Tanzanian efforts at democratic one-party government have been genuine, and the tendency to arbitrary administration has been contained. But only the regime's most uncritical apologists would maintain that elections have offered the voters any serious influence on policy development, or contributed significantly to raising their level of political consciousness; while attempts to introduce worker self-management, in 1971 through plant-level workers councils, and from 1976 through village councils, were largely neutralized by the growing bureaucratism and authoritarianism of the state apparatus. Nationalization has been a mixed success: on balance it seems probable that the state-run industrial sector has been relatively efficient, and the commercial sector rather inefficient (leading to some instances of reprivatization). A "leadership code" successfully blocked senior party and state officials from engaging in capitalist accumulation, income differentials between state employees were strikingly reduced, and the scope for private capital accumulation in commerce and farming was severely limited by the nationalization measures, credit policy, and so on. Socialist farming, however—evidently crucial, politically and socially as well as economically, in a country where 83 percent of the workforce is in agriculture—was unsuccessful as a voluntary program, and in 1973 was largely abandoned, to be replaced by forced "villagization," under—in theory at least—increasingly close state supervision. Combined with severe droughts, this led in 1974 to a catastrophic fall in agricultural output, including food output, from which the economy has not yet fully recovered. Compounded by the oil price increases in 1973, and then by the Ugandan war of 1978–79, this drop in output led to a period of intense austerity, increased reliance on authority to secure agricultural production, and the abandonment of at least a significant part of the hoped-for financial and commercial national self-reliance. As a result, foreign borrowing and technical and policy inputs from the World Bank and Western aid donors increased dramatically.[36]

Two broad schools of thought can be discerned in the debate about this experience. One holds that a society is "in transition to socialism if . . . [it is] . . . deliberately reshaping itself along more egalitarian and more participatory lines and . . . promoting cooperative and non-acquisitive motivations among men and women in their economic and other inter-relationships."[37] In this view, Tanzania is grappling manfully with the irreducible difficulties that stand in the way of all such endeavors. The other school holds that this conception of socialism is idealist—that is, it sees socialism as a matter of values and intentions (in Nyerere's own words, "socialism is an attitude of mind") divorced from the realities of the production relations that actually exist. These relations, inherited from colonialism, are capitalist, and the second school considers that capitalism has a logic that cannot be indefinitely defied without a fundamental crisis of production. It considers also that the crisis of the mid-1970s, while aggravated by the drought, is ultimately attributable to a failure to confront the basic contradiction between two principles on which produc-

tivity can be increased—either the drive for individual accumulation in a competitive market *or* the drive for accumulation by self-determining cooperative groups within a democratic cooperative commonwealth.

The initial form taken by this criticism was that the regime's socialism would prove empty unless it involved the mobilization of the poorest peasants and workers against the rich peasants and their employers, including the state bureaucracy (identified as a bureaucratic bourgeoisie). More recently, S. Mueller, in a forceful critique inspired by the postdependency debate, has emphasized the close parallel between Tanzanian policy and that of the populists (Narodniks) against whom Lenin polemicized at the turn of the century in Russia. The Tanzanian syndrome, she argues, has a distinctive logic: in the name of socialism, the development of an entrepreneurial class, whether in industry or agriculture, is thwarted; but peasant production, the basis of all economic advance, is thereby confined to the household plot and the hoe. No division of labor is possible; no significant productivity increase can be assured by state-provided inputs of seeds or fertilizers, given the heavy disincentives to individual advancement (state control of land and credit, opposition to the expansion of full-time wage labor, and so on). The result is stagnant or declining output, provoking fresh efforts of state control (appointment of village managers and village management technicians, reintroduction of minimum acreage laws from the colonial period, restrictions on population movement, corvée labor, and so on), and leading ultimately to efforts to break the bottleneck by the polar opposite of "African socialism"—large-scale capitalist farming financed by international capital (the World Bank in particular).

Narodism stifles class formation and gives birth to a repressive state. It cannot be the vehicle for a transition to socialism, and no such process of transition is occurring in Tanzania. Narodism in that country has instead been the vehicle for pauperisation both at the economic and political levels. . . . Here, socialism has not triumphed over capitalism. . . . In Tanzania one is only viewing capitalism in its "least developed" and "worst forms." . . . With the extraction of relative surplus value precluded under this system, compulsion is the only way the state can squeeze greater surpluses from its poor and demoralised peasantry. This necessitates an increasingly repressive political and administrative system, which in turn reduces the opportunities for popular expression and political participation.[38]

It is difficult not to accept the main thrust of this analysis, in spite of its polemical tone and rather one-sided character; difficult not to recognize, through it, the theoretical basis for an understanding of "actually existing" African socialism,[39] of culturally and practically diverse experiences, from Tanzania to Guinea and Guinea-Bissau. If the avatar of African capitalism is a corrupt, arbitrary, and despotic regime presiding over economic regression, the avatar of African socialism is an increasingly hollow and parasitic form of domination by the state *apparat*, again leading to economic regression. Just as "in the colonies, there are more bourgeois-minded people than bourgeois," in the African socialist regimes, there tend to be more socialists than there is socialism. And not all that many socialists either, in some cases.[40]

But it is a mistake to dismiss the Tanzanian experience, or any other socialist project in Africa, as no *more* than a mutation of backward capitalism. Any such judgment involves an element of determinism that echoes that of the dependency school and must be rejected. To idealize actually existing socialism is useless; to minimize its significance is an equal and opposite error to that of failing to recognize the development that capitalism, in a few places, has brought about.

The accomplishments of African socialism are not, on the whole, to be measured in terms of growth rates. They are primarily social and political, above all, in having posed the *question* of the form within which development is to occur, in having made it comprehensible to ordinary people that they do have collective historical choices that they may try to exercise if they will. The achievement of the Tanzanians and the Ghanaians in this respect is epochal. One can also say that the accom-

plishments of actually existing African socialism lie partly in its failures: to paraphrase Marx, what succumbed in these failures was not African socialism but the "persons, illusions, conceptions, projects, from which the idea of socialism in Africa was not free, from which it could be freed . . . only by a series of defeats."[41]

As with African capitalism, an adequate perspective on African socialism must be long-term and continental in scope. The Nkrumahist illusions of "state socialist" industrialization, which succumbed to the 1966 coup in Ghana, and the populist illusions of cooperative farming without class conflict, which succumbed to the forced villagization decision of 1974 in Tanzania, are lessons of history that belong to all the African peoples. The immediate beneficiaries of such failures are often implausible collections of military officers, posing as councils of National Redemption; but the long-run legatees are those in all African countries who have contemplated these experiences and are increasingly determined that the people as a whole should profit from them. To doubt this is to ignore the growth that has occurred, in spite of all the setbacks, in the awareness and understanding of labor leaders, students, and farmers in Africa over the last two decades, and to underrate the will and capacity for historical action that has been shown by ordinary people in innumerable boycotts, "holdups," strikes, "riots," and rebellions in all regions of the continent, to an extent that has not yet been adequately documented.

POLITICAL PERSPECTIVES

Implicit in these remarks are analytical and political judgments that should be candidly stated. Analytically, they rest on the assumption, which is still occasionally denied, that classes are forming in Africa, whose struggles will shape the future development of the continent. Politically, what has been said here rests on the view that the underclasses of Africa, whose logical tendency is toward socialism, must be supported in their struggles.

Neither of these judgments can be adequately defended, or perhaps even explained, in a brief compass. The formation of classes is bound up with the mere fact of capitalist penetration throughout the continent. To the extent that this process is incomplete, embryonic, and uneven, the development of the African classes is too. This does not make them less real. Those who doubt the historical significance of classes in Africa tend to contrast them with the classes of Europe, attributing to the latter a homogeneity and cohesion they have never possessed, and which they lacked most spectacularly when Marx first defined the class character of capitalism in the late 1840s. It is true that the African classes differ in many ways from classes in contemporary Europe or North America. The much earlier stage of capitalist development accounts for part of the difference. The specific histories of these countries, the forms taken by the prior stages of class struggle, and the distinctive class cultures and ideologies resulting from them, are equally important.

For example, the central and still very recent role played by the colonial state and foreign capital affected the genesis of the African capitalist, and especially the African industrial capitalist, to the extent that many observers have doubted his very existence—until one day he is encountered, buying out an import agency in Accra, establishing a factory in Nairobi, or owning a block of apartments in London. At the other end of the scale, migrant African workers, such as the cocoa and coffee farm-workers in Ghana, the Ivory Coast, and Buganda, have been "proletarianized" in circumstances that tend to neutralize them politically, like Turkish workers in Germany, or Mexican workers in California. But the increasingly stabilized workforces of the factories in Zaria or Nairobi, or the gold mines in Ghana, have accumulated traditions of political action that correspond very closely to the "corporate" level of consciousness that marked the earliest stage of the formation of the working classes in Europe and elsewhere. The nature of postcolonial electoral mobilization by parochial parties, now largely discredited, has left its mark in a fragmented political culture, in which class ties compete with multiple other forms of consciousness—ethnic, local, religious, and so on. Yet the economic evolution of the African countries has tended to throw their class character into sharper and sharper relief.

The large literature on the development of classes in Africa has not so far yielded much agreement on the specific character and tendency of class formation in Africa generally. The verdict is still open on whether the higher state bureaucracy constitutes in itself a new kind of dominant class; whether state employees as a whole form a distinct, privileged class, or constitute "aristocratic" strata within other classes; under what conditions peasants, who still form the great majority of the African populations, have acquired or may acquire a radical consciousness and the capacity for sustained political mobilization; what forces determine the evolution of the balance between class consciousness and ethnic, regional, or religious consciousness.[42] But few would now deny that class forces are critical for the fate of development in every African country, or that every development strategy has an inescapable class character.

As for the political standpoint from which African development has been considered here, it is, in intention at least, one of solidarity with the African masses who are impoverished and oppressed and who are in various ways struggling to overcome this—a protracted, partly conscious, partly unconscious collective historical aspiration and movement best captured in the expression, the African revolution. The most valid of all insights of the *dependentistas* is the recognition of the immense costs that people in Africa (and other regions of the Third World) have been paying for the capitalist development of at best some parts of the continent, in the interests of a narrow alliance of domestic and foreign capitalists. This process has generated many forms of resistance, and in the long run, this resistance is the basis on which any genuinely popular alternative development strategy will have to be founded. The weaknesses of the first African "socialisms" are, from this point of view, not really so different from those of the early European socialisms.

They are, or were, the product of the masses' first encounters with capitalism, and perhaps were unavoidably conceived and implemented primarily by the educated middle class, whose aspirations on behalf of the masses tended to be counterbalanced by their willingness (often perceived as an inescapable necessity) to decide everything on their behalf. These utopian and often gravely compromised socialisms, I have argued, are not to be dismissed, but they cannot command unqualified support either. A commitment to the emancipation of Africa involves judgments as to the forces and projects that best represent the interests of the masses, that are most democratic, judgments that are as difficult to make in Africa as they are everywhere else. But the mistakes of those who really try to answer these questions will more often than not be generously forgiven.

The Western observer who adopts this position is often challenged to say what he or she would recommend "instead" of what this or that regime, capitalist or socialist, is doing or has done. This sounds like a reasonable demand, designed as it is to curb the pretensions of armchair criticism. Yet what the African revolution needs is not so much recommendations as support. Outsiders can contribute usefully to African policy-making, but too many of these efforts are vitiated by the weakness of the popular forces on which most progressive policies ultimately depend for their success—and this weakness is aggravated by the failure of too many in the West to extend to the African revolution even the most elementary forms of support. How many of these challengers have worked for the release of trade unionists detained in various African countries, or protested the shooting of students in Zaïre, or the hanging of Zimbabwean guerrillas by the illegal Smith regime—or even the lending of their own money by their own banks to the repressive racist state of South Africa?

This discussion may seem to have wandered far from the problem of economic development, but such is not really the case. The African peoples are extremely poor. Even if external conditions are favorable, most African regimes will be unable to do much more than moderate the poverty of most of their populations in the next generation. In reality, it is more likely that their fragile economies will be subjected to new stresses, arising from the global contradictions of capitalism and imperialism. Given that the productive capacity exists in the Western world to relieve this poverty entirely, and to initiate rapid increases in African productivity, this human waste is abominable as well as dangerous.[43] Yet in the last analysis, a solution will not come from anywhere but Africa. Those who envisage only long-term stagnation and decline forget that it is out of the crises and struggles to which these inevitably lead that new social forces, capable of new solutions, are gradually emerging.

NOTES

Thanks are due to the Department of Political Studies, Queen's University, Kingston, Ontario, and the Institute of Commonwealth Studies, London, for help in preparing this article.

1. *Year Book of the United Nations*, 1961, p. 229, italics added.

2. *World Development Review,* World Bank (Washington, D.C.: 1980), p. 85.

3. Ibid., p. 12.

4. Unweighted averages from Ibid., p. 112. The middle income sub-Saharan African countries are: Ghana (per capita GNP $390 in 1978), Cameroon ($460), Liberia ($460), Zambia ($480), Zimbabwe ($480), People's Republic of the Congo ($540), Nigeria ($560), and the Ivory Coast ($840). It should be added that, of course, growth rates are often poor indicators of changes in living standards. Even if we neglect the question of income distribution (which may become more unequal with growth of the GNP), a growth of GNP may have no effect, or an adverse effect, on domestic living standards, as has often been noted, for example, in the case of growth based on mineral exports or tourism. It is also necessary to recognize the dubious basis of many national income statistics. they are cited here because no better indicator of the development of the forces of production is available at present.

5. A compendium of these is T. Shaw and M. Grieve, "the Political Economy of Resources: Africa's Future in the Global Environment," *Journal of Modern African Studies* 16 (1) (1978): 1–32.

6. Some American foundation money was spent in Africa, though more in the Middle East and South East Asia, on training programs founded on the quaintly fantastic ideas of D. McClelland, as developed in *The Achieving Society* (New York: Van Nostrand, 1961).

7. T. Killick, "Trends in Development Economics and Their Relevance to Africa," *Journal of Modern African Studies* 18 (2) (1980): 368–69.

8. H. Kjekshus, *Ecology Control and Economic Development in East African History*, (London: Heinemann, 1977), p. 72.

9. For example, the works of Samir Amin, Roger Genoud, G. Arrighi, C. Meillassoux, J. S. Saul, E. A. Brett, Walter Rodney, M. Mamdani, I. G. Shivji, J. Rweyemamu, P.-P. Rey, M. Cohen, G. Williams, and R. Howard.

10. Interview with E. Crawley, *South*, January–February 1981, p. 32.

11. The quotation is from T. Dos Santos, "The Crisis of Development Theory and the Problem of Dependence in Latin America," in *Underdevelopment and Development*, edited by H. Bernstein (Harmondsworth: Penguin, 1973), p. 76.

12. R. Higgot, "Structural Dependence and Decolonisation in a West African Landlocked State: Niger," *Review of African Political Economy* 17 (January–April 1980): 57.

13. R. Kaplinsky, "Inappropriate Products and Techniques: Breadfast Food in Kenya," *Review of African Political Economy* 14 (January–April 1979): 90–96.

14. F. H. Cardoso, "Dependent Capitalist Development in Latin America," *New Left Review* 74 (July–August 1972): 83–95.

15. On the Ivory Coast, see L. K. Mytelka, "Direct Foreign Investment and technological Choice in the Ivorian Textile and Wood Industries," in "Trends in International Transfer of Technology," special issue of *Vierteljabresberichte der Entwicklungs-landerforschung*, edited by D. Ernst, March 1981.

16. *SIPRI Yearbook* (New York: 1980), pp. 23, 31.

17. By 1978, shortly before abandoning Tiris el-Gharbia to the Moroccans, Mauritania's military spending is said to have accounted for 60 percent of its overall budget (M. Bennounce, "The Political Economy of Mauritania: Imperialism and Class Struggle," *Review of African Political Economy* 12, May–August 1978: p. 50). In 1978 its public debt was 138 percent of GNP. Morocco's was $5.1 billion, up from $711 million in 1970, and equivalent to 40 percent of GNP.

18. S. Amin, "Underdevelopment and Dependence in Black Africa: Origins and Contemporary Forms," *Journal of Modern African Studies* 10 (4) (1972): 503–24.

19. Bill Warren, *Imperialism: Pioneer of Capitalism* (London: New Left Review Editions, 1980), chapters 7, 8; "Imperialism and Capitalist Industrialisation," *New Left Review* 81 (1973): 3–44.

20. B. Beckman, "Imperialism and Capitalist Transformation: Critique of a Kenyan Debate," paper presented to the Conference on the African Bourgeoisie, Dakar, 1980, mimeo, p. 19.

21. See Warren, *Imperialism: Pioneer of Capitalism*, p. 249: "The fact that purchase of consumer durables by low-income households occurs at the expense of public and perhaps other forms of consumption may be regarded as a distortion of resource allocation consequent to Western influence. But when did the poor ever know what was good for them? Would they actually opt for more collective (public) consumption if given the choice? No one knows, but it cannot be denied that most durable consumer goods—such as bicycles, sewing machines, motorbikes, radios and even television sets and refrigerators—significantly enhance the quality of life of poor households. It is only those who already possess such goods in abundance who feel it appropriate to suggest that it is undesirable for others to have them."

22. Of critical-utopian socialists, Marx and Engels wrote: "The proletariat, as yet in its infancy, offers to them the spectacle of a class without any historical initiative. . . . Only from the point of view of being the most suffering class does the proletariat exist for them. . . . they are full of the most valuable materials for the enlightenment of the working class. . . . [But their] proposals . . . are of a purely utopian character"; while the "socialist bourgeois" were "desirous of redressing grievances, in order to secure the continued existence of bourgeois society. . . . They desire the existing state of society minus its revolutionary and disintegrating elements." *The Communist Manifesto*, in Marx, *The Revolutions of 1848*, edited by D. Fernbach (Harmondsworth: Penguin, 1973), pp. 95, 93.

23. Moreover, of the larger African countries, only the Ivory Coast seems to have been very significantly helped by sustained above-average levels of official economic aid.

24. P. Kennedy, "Indigenous Capitalism in Ghana," *Review of African Political Economy* 8 (January–April 1977): 29.

25. S. Langdon, citing F. Stewart in "Industry and Capitalism in Kenya: Contributions to a Debate," paper prepared for the Conference on the African Bourgeoisie, Dakar, 1980, mimeo, pp. 16–17.

26. Capitalism does not cause the rains to fail—as far as we know—but it causes changes in land use that expose people to the risk of disaster when the rains fail, and it finds no profit in most developments that might permit the Sahel populations to reestablish their traditional sym-

biosis with their environment. See C. Meillassoux, "Development of Exploitation: Is the Sahel Famine Good Business?" *Review of African Political Economy* 1 (1974): 27–33; A. Baird et al., *Towards an Explanation of Disaster Proneness*, University of Bradford Disaster Research Unit, Occasional Paper no. 11, August 1975.

27. As testimony to what has been said earlier about the dynamic nature of African development, the Ivory Coast is now expected to become self-sufficient in oil by 1982, and seems likely to become a mineral exporter thereafter.

28. B. Campbell, "Capital Accumulation and the Post-Colonial State in the Ivory Coast," paper presented to the panel in "Bureaucratic Bourgeoisie or Ruling Elite," African Studies Association Conference, Philadelphia, 1980, p. 10.

29. In 1978 gross official aid inflows to the Ivory Coast were $122 per capita, compared with $16 for Kenya, and an average for sub-Saharan Africa of $31.

30. Frantz Fanon, *The Wretched of the Earth* (Harmondsworth: Penguin, 1967), pp. 143–44.

31. Nonetheless, the embodiment of a class's economic and political capacities in its familial and social institutions and culture does exercise an independent influence. Apart from relatively early studies such as those by Samir Amin, P. Marris and A. Somerset, and S. Kaplow, this topic awaits proper investigation in Africa.

32. See E. A. Brett, "The Political Economy of General Amin," *IDS Bulletin* 1 (7) (April 1975): 15–22.

33. John Carlsen, *Economic and Social Transformation in Rural Kenya*, Scandinavian Institute of African Studies (Uppsala: 1980), pp. 223–24.

34. We exclude Sudan, and should perhaps exclude others, whose socialism comes too close to the purely rhetorical variety of Tolbert's Liberia or the last days of Bokassa in the Central African Empire: "The Central African Emperor has decided to adopt the revolutionary and authentically African and nationalist ideas of the Libyan Arab Jamahirya." R. Delpey, *La Manipulation*, cited by M. Boli Richard in the *Le Monde* section of the *Manchester Guardian Weekly*, April 5, 1981.

35. There is an apparent discrepancy between the decline in the volume of agricultural production that occurred in Tanzania in the mid-1970s and the growth rates of GDP shown in the national accounts and recorded in Table 2 above (see *Accelerated Development in Sub-Saharan Africa*, World Bank, Washington, D.C., 1981, p. 187). There may also be other reasons for the high overall growth rates apparently achieved, but it seems more likely that the figures are too high.

36. Tanzania's external public debt rose from $248 million in 1970 to $1,095 million in 1978. *World Development Report 1980*, p. 138.

37. *Towards Socialism in Tanzania*, edited by B. U. Mwansasu and R. C. Pratt (Toronto: University of Toronto Press, 1979), p. 6.

38. S. Mueller, "Retarded Capitalism in Tanzania," Socialist Register 1980, pp. 220–21. Comparisons of any sort between contemporary Africa and late Czarist Russia are apt to seem farfetched at first sight, but the similarities between the thought of the Russian populists on the fate of the peasantry after the emancipation of the serfs, and that of some contemporary theorists of the African peasantry, are striking (for a recent example, see G. Hyden, *Beyond Ujamaa*, Berkeley, University of California Press, 1980). Lenin's study, *The Development of Capitalism in Russia*, provides the starting-point for the critique advanced by Mueller, as it does for the work of M. Cowen and others on the very different political development in Kenya.

39. The phrase is Rudolf Bahro's, in *The Alternative in Eastern Europe* (London: New Left Books, 1978).

40. The saying is quoted in Roger Genoud's important early study, *Nationalism and Economic Development in Ghana* (New York: Praeger, 1969), p. 52.

41. Cf. Marx, "The Class Struggles in France," in *Surveys from Exile*, edited by D. Fernbach (Harmondsworth: Penguin, 1973), p. 35.

42. A leading proponent of the view that the higher bureaucracy of the African state are forming themselves into a dominant class has been J. S. Saul (see, for example, his *State and Revolution in Eastern Africa*, New York, Monthly Review Press, 1980). For convenient references to the now enormous literature on class in Africa, see *Review of African Political Economy* no. 19, September–December 1980, special issue on Consciousness and Class.

43. This is the main burden of the Brandt Commission Report, *North-South: A Programme for Survival*; see pp. 12–17 and passim.

Food Deficits and Agricultural Policies in Tropical Africa

Michael F. Lofchie and Stephen K. Commins

Hunger is the most immediate, visible, and compelling symptom of a continent-wide agricultural breakdown in tropical Africa. The crisis of food deficits has now become so perennial and so widespread that it can no longer be understood as the outcome of particular political or climatic occurrences such as wars, ethnic strife, or drought. Sub-Saharan Africa is the only region in the world where food production *per capita* has declined during the past two decades. As a result, the average calorie intake *per capita* has now fallen below minimal nutritional standards in a majority of African countries. By current estimates, approximately 150 million out of Africa's 450 million people suffer from some form of malnutrition originating in an inadequate supply of foodstuffs. This abysmal picture is further highlighted by the fact that the Food and Agriculture Organisation of the United Nations recently indicated that no fewer than 28 African countries were faced with food shortages so critical that further famine might occur imminently.[1] This stark reality challenges fundamentally our earlier assumptions about the possibility of economic development.

There is every indication that food shortages will become more rather than less severe during the next decade. By 1980, Africa had already become heavily dependent upon food imports, at a time when grain prices were rising and African governments faced acute shortages of foreign exchange. Grain imports tripled during the 20 years between 1960 and 1978, but due to

From *Journal of Modern African Studies*, vol. 20, no. 1 (March 1982), 1–25, by permission of the journal and its publisher, the Cambridge University Press.

price increases, especially during the 1970s, their cost multiplied nearly 12-fold. If current trends continue, Africa's demand for food imports will triple again by 1990, when sub-Saharan countries will be forced to import approximately 17 million tons of grain annually, simply to maintain 1975 levels of consumption. Even this staggering volume of imports would do nothing to reduce the tragic gap between average consumption *per capita* and the amount of food required to provide minimal nutritional standards. A further 13 million tons of imports would be required to alleviate this deficit.[2] Even the most optimistic estimates, which foresee some recovery in the productivity of the food-producing sector of African agriculture, envision the need for a doubling of food imports during the decade of the 1980s.

Food deficits on such a massive scale are a sobering entry point for Africa's third decade of independence. The problem is much deeper than the failure of an agricultural continent to feed itself. It is present in the environmental degradation that afflicts not only the semi-arid areas of western and eastern Africa, but also the high rainfall regions of Zaïre, Zambia, and the West African coast. Desertification, the conversion of once arable soil to desert-like infertility, can be observed in every African country across the equatorial belt from Senegal to Somalia. Soil loss on so appalling a scale reflects both the pressure of increasing population to land ratios, and the imprudent use of capital-intensive temperate-zone technologies on fragile tropical soils. Generations of accumulated wisdom and historically evolved agricultural systems are now rendered largely irrelevant by greatly increased production requirements, and by the pressures of outside markets and political forces.

Africa has been the scene of a bewildering kaleidoscope of experimental strategies for agricultural development. It has become a continental proving-ground for policies ranging from socialist collectivism to free-market individualism, with countless approaches somewhere on the continuum between the two. It would require an encyclopaedic inventory of research even to compile the literature on world hunger, and this would not begin to touch on such sensitive theoretical concerns as the determinants of successes or failures of rural development efforts.[3]

The causes and remedies of food deficits in Africa have been the subject of a wide-ranging debate.[4] This article examines certain of the principal schools of thought which participate in this debate, and assesses the remedial policies which each suggests. Our objective is to help clarify some of the contending analytic viewpoints, to call attention to the bewildering complexity of the problem, and to suggest a framework within which future rural development policies may be considered. It is useful for our purposes to begin with a discussion of two major contending approaches. These might best be identified as the theory of underdevelopment and the theory of comparative advantage. We will then consider the factor of environmental deterioration, and the impact of international food-aid policies, particularly those of the United States.

THE THEORY OF UNDERDEVELOPMENT

The best known and, by a wide margin, most widely discussed analysis of poverty and agricultural failure in Africa is found in the complex of theories concerned with underdevelopment. It would not repay us here to summarise at length the differing analyses of such prolific theoreticians as Paul Baran, André Gunder Frank, Samir Amin, Argihiri Emmanuel, Walter Rodney, and Immanuel Wallerstein.[5] It may suffice to extract from this protean array of literature a common core of presuppositions which bears most directly on the problem

of food deficits, and on the failure of the food-producing sector of African agriculture to provide adequately for the continent's population.

The point of departure from the theory of underdevelopment is the view that the root causes of Africa's economic problems, like those of other developing areas, lie in the nature of the continent's relationship with the global economic system. Underdevelopment theorists normally begin with the presupposition that the world can be divided into the core and the periphery. The core consists of those few countries, principally in North America and Western Europe, which, during the past five centuries, have been able to develop advanced capitalist economic systems. The periphery consists of those countries in Africa, Latin America, Asia, and elsewhere, commonly referred to as the "developing areas," whose economies are, in fact, desperately underdeveloped. The theory of underdevelopment asserts that the core countries have been able to achieve advanced forms of capitalism at least in part because of their capacity to exploit—that is, extract an economic surplus from—the periphery. The peripheral countries, conversely, are poor because their wealth has been drained off to sustain the process of economic growth in the core. In a nutshell, the economic surplus which might have been used to generate development in peripheral areas is used instead to finance further enrichment of already affluent nations.

Peripheral countries find it virtually impossible to transform their status in the world system. For they are highly dependent on the core for capital, technology, and for markets for their products. Moreover, the policies of these countries are formulated by élites, sometimes referred to as "comprador," whose decisions advance the interests of western capital. Although theorists of underdevelopment sometimes acknowledge a degree of mutual independence between core and periphery, they view this as highly asymmetrical because the core countries have far greater discretion over the terms of their participation in the global economic system. The peripheral countries, precisely because they are so poor, are politically as well as economically weak, and must generally accept the terms of trade they are confronted with as a set of "givens" over which they have little or no control.

The theory of underdevelopment attempts to explain the reasons for the failure of the agricultural sector of developing areas to generate an adequate supply of locally needed food items. It is believed that since the economies of the developing areas are fundamentally shaped by their dependence upon the global economic system, there is a pronounced tendency to favour export agriculture over the production of food crops for domestic consumption. Dependency gives rise to a pronounced dichotomy between the export sector and the food-producing sector; the striking contrast between the two has given rise to the concept of "agrarian dualism." For export production is often carried on in large, plantation-sized farms which are highly favoured in terms of agricultural inputs, whereas food crops for local consumption are grown on peasant farms which are badly deprived of needed agricultural supports.

The export-oriented plantations have benefited from a host of supportive inputs not typically available to peasant farmers. They have access to agricultural-extension services which can help to introduce and sustain scientific methods of production, including high-yield seeds, pesticides, and advanced irrigation technologies. They also benefit from the availability of highly developed infrastructures to deal with the transportation, packaging, and storage of their products. Export agriculture is additionally buoyed by a host of private firms and government agencies which provide "soft" services such as credit, insurance, market analyses and, most importantly, which handle the actual sales transactions to foreign purchasers or commodity exchanges.

The peasant sector, where much of the country's supply of foodstuffs is produced, contrasts fundamentally with the export plantations. Units of production are small in scale, and thus are not in a position to take advantage of modern agricultural technologies. As a result the most common

instrument is the hand-held hoe; less frequently, some form of animal-drawn cultivation. Almost never, except in the rarest cases of successful peasant co-operatives, is there any complex machinery. Peasant agriculture is also starved of other vital inputs. Agricultural-extension services are conspicuous by their inadequacy, with the result that there is little or no provision of scientific inputs for the production of locally consumed food crops. Modern varieties of seeds, fertilisers, and pesticides are, similarly, far less commonly available than in the plantation or export areas. Feeder roads tend to be woefully inadequate, as well as other important elements of infrastructure, such as facilities for the storage or preservation of food grains. There are few systematic efforts to organise the supply of food items from the countryside to urban centres, or between different rural areas, with the result that an appalling proportion of the food which is produced goes wasted for want of access to markets. In sum, the shortage of foodstuffs in Africa can be traced directly to the systematic structural neglect of the food-producing sector.

This theory of the roots of Africa's food crisis has proved to be highly compelling because of its sweeping synthesis of historical, political, and economic factors. But its very all-inclusive generality is also the source of considerable doubt about its ultimate utility. For although the theory does illuminate important structural pathologies in African agriculture, it can be deeply criticised on a variety of grounds. Some of the more general judgements are fairly well known.[6] These include: a tendency to challenge the crudely moralistic oversimplification involved in a bimodal division of the world between exploitative core and exploited periphery; a growing realisation that the very term "periphery" is so broad that it impedes an understanding of the considerable economic and political differences between countries in the developing world; and, among some thinkers, a strong conviction that the notion of "comprador" is inadequate as a conceptualisation of class domination in Africa.

It has recently been argued that the theory of underdevelopment also fails to understand the nature of the African peasantry, and the overriding cultural factors which limit their food production.[7] Other critics have called attention to the need for a more sophisticated classification than dependent *versus* non-dependent countries, and for a far more probing treatment of the class factors which inhibit or facilitate food production on the African continent. In the last analysis, a theory which uses identical terms to explain skyrocketing food imports both in Nigeria and Tanzania is seriously lacking in persuasiveness.

Our principal concern is with the limitations of the theory of underdevelopment as it pertains to a strategy of rural development. Here, its shortcomings are particularly acute. A conspicuous feature of the theory's strong condemnation of the global trading system is a call for withdrawal from external markets—a process sometimes referred to as economic closure—and those who lay heavy stress on the exploitative aspects of world trade for underdeveloped countries are especially likely to suggest this as a remedy. The difficulty with this approach is that it leaves a host of critically important practical questions unanswered, especially those that have to do with the acquisition of foreign exchange. While it is absolutely true, as dependency theorists point out, that the terms of world trade have shifted steadily against agricultural countries, it is woefully inadequate to suggest that the solution is to withdraw from world markets, because those who choose to do so must necessarily forego, or reduce substantially, their stocks of innumerable essential commodities. The theory of underdevelopment is regrettably silent on how countries which pursue a policy of closure can equip themselves with the scientific and technological wherewithal of the modern world.

A second shortcoming in the rural strategy of the theory of underdevelopment is its unqualified reliance upon collectivised agriculture. Agrarian socialism tends to be viewed as an integral accompaniment of the policy of closure. The argument advanced for this position by a number of theorists is that unless the capitalist relations of production in the countryside are dissolved, it would be impossible to re-

orient agricultural production away from world trade towards the cultivation of foodstuffs for local consumption. Capitalist farmers would continue to be attracted to the higher levels of profit available in western markets, and their influence over the local state would enable them to influence agricultural policy in such a way as to facilitate production for export.

Our reservation concerning socialist agriculture is essentially pragmatic, and has to do with the fact that it has generally proved incapable of sustaining high levels of agricultural production.[8] For this reason, country after country in Eastern Europe and elsewhere has abandoned collectivised farming in favour of private farming, mixed forms of production, or locally controlled co-operatives. Whatever its attractive theoretical merits, agrarian collectivism in Africa has been consistently unable to transform production levels in the countryside. Indeed, those countries which have sought to implement rural socialism, most conspicuously Tanzania, find themselves today in the midst of calamitous agricultural crises, and they must import enormous volumes of foodstuffs in order to avert starvation in the countryside. The great irony of socialist agriculture in Africa is that it has tended to exacerbate the very dependency it was intended to remove; it has necessitated heightened levels of financial and material dependence on western donors.

In the last analysis, the greatest value of the theory of underdevelopment may lie in the fact that it sounds a persuasive warning about the pitfalls of uncritical dependence upon world trade. It demonstrates graphically the results of a world economy in which relatively affluent nations can afford to outbid local consumers for the use of local agricultural land. However, the theory does not demonstrate the viability of a strategy of "withdrawal" and, indeed, it does not even rebut theories of rural development which call for poorer countries to remain involved in world markets as a partial solution to their food crises.

COMPARATIVE ADVANTAGE

The major alternative to dependency theory is found in the principle of comparative advantage, the view that countries can maximise their economic potential by specialising in the production of commodities at which they are most efficient in terms of such inputs as capital and labour. This concept was originally suggested in the writings of David Ricardo nearly 200 years ago. For Ricardo, the notion of comparative advantage was a powerful argument for free trade since an unrestricted flow of products between countries would enable them to use their productive resources most efficiently:

> It is quite important to the happiness of mankind that our own enjoyment should be increased by the better distribution of labor, by each country producing those commodities for which by its situation, its climate and its natural or artificial advantages, it is adapted, and by their exchanging them for the commodities of other countries, as that they should be augmented by a rise in the rate of profit.[9]

This kind of specialisation, according to Ricardo, would not only lead to more wealth for all nations, but to the greatest possible improvement in living conditions for their people. He believed strongly that comparative advantage must work to the benefit of all concerned, and that the poorer governments would only worsen their economic position by withdrawing from world markets—indeed, there is a strong implication in Ricardo's work that the least-developed nations would be particularly well advised to specialise narrowly in their range of products, since this would enable them to trade in world markets on the most advantageous possible terms.[10]

Writers who followed Ricardo have expanded and altered some of his theoretical ideas, but the basics of the argument have remained the same.[11] Perhaps the most significant addition has been the expansion in the number of factors of production which need to be taken into account to determine a country's comparative advantage. Ricardo gave almost exclusive emphasis to labour as the measuring rod of efficiency in any sphere of production. More contemporary authors have argued the need for land and capital to be taken into account, as well, before a country's comparative advantage can be accurately established. Significantly, however, two of the major premises of Ricardo's thought have remained intact. Modern theorists of comparative advantage tend not to question either his assumption of the mobility of labour between spheres of production, or his conviction that poor and rich countries alike would improve their economic well-being by participating freely in world markets.

Agricultural economists who accept the doctrine of comparative advantage tend to see no fundamental problem in economies which are characterised by agrarian dualism. They see the heavy structural emphasis on export crops as the natural and beneficial consequence of the operation of free-market forces. William O. Jones, for example, has stated that:

> The great African production of coffee, cocoa, tea, peanuts, palm oil, and cotton occurred because these crops could be sold; that is, because consumers in Europe, North America, and elsewhere manifested an economic demand for these commodities, and because a marketing system was developed to communicate the character and magnitude of this demand to African farmers. As a consequence, African producers were able to enjoy more nonfarm goods such as textiles and utensils, than they had before.[12]

According to this perspective, it would be a grave mistake to shift away from export crops to food production as a means of solving the problems of food deficits. If such inputs as capital, land, and labour are more effectively utilised when allotted to the production of export crops, it would, from the standpoint of comparative advantage, be economically imprudent to shift these resources to food production. For the income generated by the sale of export crops, such as coffee, cocoa, or tea, would make it possible to purchase far greater amounts of wheat and corn than could have been produced domestically with the same inputs.

Perhaps the most important contemporary proponent of the theory of comparative advantage for developing countries is Hollis Chenery, an economist with the World Bank. His influence has been based partly on his willingness to challenge certain of the more extravagant claims sometimes advanced by other economists. In particular, Chenery questions the classical assumption that specialisation of production for foreign trade promotes economic growth. He demonstrates a distinction between analyses of comparative advantage (trade theory) and of economic development (growth theory). In his most recent work, Chenery associates himself with a number of important economists, including Joseph Schumpeter, who believe that "comparative advantage is a static concept that ignores a variety of dynamic elements." The elements Chenery refers to, including especially the stimulus that exports provide for the growth of the industrial sector, would be of critical importance for a country seeking overall expansion of its economic system.[13]

For the political leaders of developing countries who require practical guidance in making decisions about how best to allocate their own scarce resources, growth theory would appear to have decisive advantages. It is, for example, far more concerned than is the theory of comparative advantage with changing relationships "over time among producers, consumers and investors in related sectors of the economy." Indeed, if there is one single point of differentiation between growth theory and trade theory, it is the greater concern in growth theory for the expansion of multiple sectors of the economy, not simply the export sector. Chenery is particularly emphatic on this point:

[development requires] much more emphasis on the sequence of expansion of production and factor use by sector than on the conditions of general equilibrium. Growth theory either ignores comparative advantage and the possibilities of trade completely, or considers mainly the dynamic aspects, such as the stimulus that an increase in exports provides to the development of related sectors. . . . With this different point of view, growth theorists often suggest investment criteria that are quite contradictory to those derived from considerations of comparative advantage.[14]

For Chenery, it is axiomatic that a developing country's best long-term economic interests lie in balanced, multi-sectoral de-

velopment. Present market forces, which comparative advantage would rely upon to promote this purpose, are inadequate, since they do not reflect future patterns of consumption and demand.

Given the force of this critique it is rather surprising that Chenery nevertheless continues to advocate a positive rôle for the concept of comparative advantage in the development process. His argument on this point is carefully modulated: if comparative advantage can be modified by taking into account some of the important differing assumptions of growth theory, it can serve as an influential principle of planning. Four such assumptions would need to be incorporated into the theory, namely:

(a) factor prices do not necessarily reflect opportunity costs with any accuracy; (b) the quantity and quality of factors of production may change substantially over time, in part as a result of the production process itself; (c) economies of scale relative to the size of existing markets are important in a number of sectors of production; and (d) complementarity among commodities is dominant in both producer and consumer demand.[15]

By accepting these assumptions, rather than the more pristine doctrine of pure comparative advantage, a developing country can carefully plan its economic policies so as to achieve a judicious balance between emphasis on foreign trade and other strategies which are more likely to promote multi-sectoral development.

Chenery's contribution is of immense value to development scholars. For it establishes the principle that participation in the global trading economy may not by itself enable a developing country to allocate its resources in such a way that the growth of complementary sectors of its economy is promoted. We would identify this principle, for the sake of brevity, as "market failure," and Chenery's theoretical concern about this is well substantiated by the unfortunate experiences of a number of African economies. For countries which have pursued an aggressive strategy of emphasis upon export agriculture have often experienced market failure in its bitterest form. Their earnings from agricultural exports have fallen far short of national needs, and they have been consistently unable to enter the world market to acquire food grains on anything even remotely resembling an adequate scale.

The reasons for this market failure are worth identifying. Contrary to early expectations which saw tropical exports as scarce, high-demand goods, available from only a limited number of suppliers, whereas food grains produced in the temperate zones would be available in abundance, the exact opposite has turned out to be the case. The production of tropical export crops is now an enormously competitive field with new suppliers constantly entering the market,[16] sometimes in response to only modest upward fluctuations in price. Indeed, the market is so competitive that the entry of a single new producer, or the harvest of a bumper crop in one country, can depress prices below their previous level. Coffee provides an excellent example of this situation. African suppliers such as Kenya, Tanzania, Ethiopia, Uganda, and the Ivory Coast compete intensely for market shares against not only each other, but also a host of producers in Latin America, notably Brazil, and Colombia. The dominant tendency during the past decade has been for conditions in the world coffee market to depress prices, and to hold them relatively constant at low levels.

This tendency is strongly reinforced by the nature of the market confronted by tropical producers. For the real market does not consist of large numbers of consumer nations bidding competitively against one another for tropical commodities, but rather of a handful of powerful multinational trading corporations. Companies such as General Foods, Nestles, Lipton, and Brooke Bond often occupy an oligopolistic or, not infrequently, a monopolistic position in the market.[17] If tropical commodities appear expensive on the shelves of western supermarkets, the reasons have less to do with the rate of return to producer countries than with the ability of these processing and trading firms to engage in the time-honoured tradition of purchasing cheap and selling dear. Part of what enables them to do so, in addition to their commanding position in the market-place, is the high degree of elasticity of demand for the products they provide, because this can be used to gain bargaining leverage against the producer nations.

The market strength of the large trading companies—or, more precisely, the weakness of the tropical producers—is further reinforced by such factors as the elasticity of consumer demand and the ready availability of synthetic or substitute products. Since tropical agricultural products are not day-to-day necessities, individual purchasers can quickly alter their consumption patterns in response to price fluctuations. This tends to have a continuously depressing effect on the market. The easy availability of alternatives—synthetic chocolate for cocoa, a coffee-chicory mixture for whole coffee, herb and spice teas for authentic tea, or soft drinks for any of these—has a similar effect. The cumulative impact of these factors has been to make it almost impossible for producers in the developing world to gain price leverage in the international market-place. As a result, tropical agriculture seems perilously unlikely in the future to do any better than it has in the past in generating the levels of foreign exchange necessary to finance a sustained programme of food imports.

Further doubt is cast on the wisdom of any strategy based on the continuation of export agriculture, and the import of food crops, by the nature of the world market for basic grains. Temperate-zone food exporters, in clear contrast to tropical crop exporters, benefit from a highly buoyant market for their products. Countries which can export wheat, corn, rice, and other grains are dealing in day-to-day necessities, and they can be confident that prospective customers do not have substitutes or alternatives readily at hand. Moreover, the world market for these crops is virtually monopolised by the United States, Canada, Australia, and Argentina, the great wheat exporters who can choose from a host of anxious consumer nations in both the developed and developing worlds. They can also depend upon a steady and expanding market for their goods. Not only are massive importers such as China and Russia constantly entering this market to negotiate long-term, high-volume purchase agreements, but there is a rapidly increasing demand for food grains among middle-income developing countries and in Eastern Europe.

The poorer developing nations enter the market for food grain only with the greatest difficulty. They lack adequate reserves of foreign exchange, and in any case these are often committed in large measure to other vital purposes, such as petroleum imports, the financing of foreign debts, and the purchase of raw materials for factories. Because the grain needs of African countries often fluctuate widely from one year to the next, it is impossible to predict import levels over an extended period of time. And since African economies are typically small in scale, their grain purchases do not begin to compare with those of the Soviet Union and China. As a result, they are compelled to enter what amounts to an international grain "spot market." This can be disastrous, as it was during the early 1970s when the famine-struck countries of the Sahel had to enter the international grain market at a moment of critical scarcity, just as soaring purchases by the Soviet Union had driven prices to record levels.

It would therefore appear that an undiluted comparative advantage approach to development is a risky strategy at best. Danger of "market failure" places many developing countries in a highly vulnerable position, especially given their weakness in the international market-place. Inability to provide basic foodstuffs for the local population is all-too-common a result of government decisions which rely heavily on export commodity strategies. Nevertheless, the basic principle of comparative advantage has validity in that Africa does possess highly varied resources and production factors which, at least potentially, would enable a number of countries to compete very effectively on world markets. A strategy of comparative advantage could have considerable utility only if incorporated into a broader approach to agricultural development, one that reflected sensitivity to other important political, economic, and environmental considerations.

ENVIRONMENTAL CONSTRAINTS[18]

In considering the broad framework for strategies of agricultural development in Africa, it is essential to consider the continent's particular environmental constraints. Although these have been well explored in a number of books,[19] the relationship between environmental deterioration and agricultural stagnation is still too often ignored in the formulation of appropriate strategies. The task of doing so is formidable, for Africa is a continent of micro-environments, with great ecological changes often occurring over very short distances. Such variations make environmentally conscious agricultural planning extraordinarily difficult and complex. Yet the necessity for such a strategy is tragically illustrated by the fact that the planned introduction of certain exogenous crops, and of new agricultural techniques, has already led to ecological disasters which, in themselves, make efforts at future development even more daunting.

Underlying the basic difficulties of agricultural production in tropical Africa is the general fragility of most of the soils. African soils vary greatly in depth and initial nutrient content, reflecting differing influences of parent material, vegetation, and climate. But as a general rule, the soil cover of sub-Saharan Africa is not readily suitable for on-going agriculture. The problem, in a nutshell, lies in the fact that "sandy soils deficient in important elements preponderate over clay and limestone soils and there are proportionately fewer young, rich alluvial soils than on any other continent."[20] The principal exceptions are in northern Africa, where the Nile food plain and the lowland regions of the western Mediterranean countries can sustain intensive agriculture over extended periods. Sub-Saharan Africa is not so fortunate. Its soils tend to be highly weathered, relatively poor in humus, and very susceptible to such damaging processes as erosion and leaching.

To understand the nature of the environmental constraints on African agricultural development, it is useful to begin by recalling that the continent was once highly forested, with a rich cover of trees protecting and nurturing the soils beneath. Under this historical condition, in so far as it can be presently reconstructed, its tropical soils were rich and fertile. For the humus content of the soil—which is of vital importance in providing nutrients for plant life, and in retaining moisture near the surface—was constantly replenished by leaf litter from the canopy of trees. Wherever the forest cover has been removed, whether through natural causes such as fires, or as a result of human habitation, the effect has been to set in motion a disastrous cycle of rapid ecological deterioration: without a covering blanket of trees, the soil no longer benefits from the continuous replenishment of its humus content. And, since tropical soils have a high level of micro-organic activity, the residual humus in the topsoil tends to be rapidly depleted by the process of microbial decay. African tropical soils are so unstable in this respect that they can lose their arability almost completely in a matter of years.

Deforestation has other negative consequences as well. Without a layer of humus near the surface, rainfall penetrates rapidly downwards into the sub-soil, leaching the surface of many available nutrients, thereby drastically diminishing its utility for agricultural purposes. In areas where the previous cover consisted of savannah grassland, a comparable cycle of decay can be discerned. The richness of these regions was often reflected, in the past, in the dark, highly organic texture of the surface soils. However, if the natural vegetation of savannah grasses is removed for agricultural or grazing purposes, the soils are also exposed in a rapid process of nutrient removal by a combination of microbial activity and downward leaching due to heavy precipitation.

The tendency for rainfall to penetrate rapidly downwards often leads to an even more serious ecological malaise, because the sub-surface water dissolves the laterite found in many African soils. When the water evaporates, as between heavy rains, these metal deposits precipitate-out, leading to the formation of a stone-like pan beneath the surface of the soil. Once underway, this condition is extremely difficult, if not impossible, to reverse. Deep ploughing, sometimes suggested as the only possible corrective, has not proved to be a solution; this action merely brings fragments of the encrusted iron pan to the surface where they must be laboriously removed by hand. Moreover, without a top blotter of leaf litter or savannah grasses, the first heavy rains merely repeat the cycle. Downward penetration of water once again sends sub-surface metallic deposits into solution, and evaporation then recapitulates the formation of the sub-surface pan.

Contemporary Ivory Coast furnishes a sad example of the ecological and agricultural ramifications of the unplanned removal of the forest cover.[21] The timber resources of the nation's rainforest, once one of the lushest in West Africa, are being rapidly dissipated to help boost the country's exports. As recently as 25 years ago, the Ivory Coast's forests covered approximately 12 million hectares. This has now shrunk to about one-third of that area, and the pace of felling timber is such that little, if any, woodland may remain by the end of the century. Without the protection of the forest canopy, the soils in many southern areas have been exposed to severe processes of nutrient removal, laterisation, and erosion, rendering them virtually useless for agricultural purposes. These vast regions have also lost most of their capacity to retain moisture, depleting the underground reserves and leading to severe water shortages. Even more ominously, these changes have drastically disrupted rainfall patterns in the Ivory Coast's northern neighbours, Mali and Upper Volta. The contemporary intensification of drought conditions in these societies is, in part, traceable to the ecological disruptions in the Ivory Coast.

In the past, traditional patterns of cropping were developed which were adaptive to the difficulties of tropical environment.[22] For example, the forested areas were, in effect, closed communities where plants and animals constantly replenished the nutrients in the soil through their death and decay. Successful farming required that the canopy of forest and bush be continued in some fashion to allow for a return of nutrients to the earth. In dried, more savannah-like areas, "shifting cultivation" evolved as the major agricultural technique: old fields whose fertility was depleted were simply abandoned for varying periods of time (up to 20 years) and new fields were opened up. Shifting cultivation generally differed from "crop rotation," whereby extended land-use was sustained by changing what was planted on a given piece of land from one year to the next, although inevitably both systems tended to overlap in large regions of Africa.

It would be unrealistic to portray traditional agricultural systems as models of pristine harmony, but there is considerable reason to believe that they did work reasonably well when compared with much that has occurred since the colonial era. Since population densities were low, there was little need for intensive cultivation and, therefore, little hardship involved in practising agricultural methods which required farm areas to be left fallow for long periods. Perhaps more importantly, low population pressure meant that very few communities suffered from land scarcity; virtually all members of society could be assured of access to some arable land.

Since land was relatively abundant, traditional methods of agriculture were not accompanied by the extreme socio-economic inequalities that have become commonplace today. Class formation, where it did occur, was of limited proportions, and there were few glaring divisions between landless and landed populations. This probably meant that when calamities of deprivation did occur, they tended to be the result of natural disasters, such as drought or flood, rather than maldistribution in the economic system. Under these conditions, deprivation would have been more equally shared among all members of society. To the extent that the extensive starvation which accompanies contemporary food shortages is a result of social structures characterised by wide gaps between wealth and poverty, this particular aspect of food deficits was, in all likelihood, far less common then than now.[23]

European rule contributed to the decay of Africa's agricultural resources in at least two distinct ways. One was through the imposition of export requirements which involved the introduction of crops and methods of cultivation that were not well suited to the African soil base. Cotton, groundnuts, and tobacco have proved particularly destructive. Their introduction necessitated clearing large areas of the original cover of forest and brush, thereby depriving the soil of its principal source of organic replenishment. These three crops are also especially damaging in that they tend to absorb unusually large quantities of nutrients from the top-soil, thereby contributing to a particularly rapid decline in arability. Moreover, unlike the original cover of forest, grasses, and scrub, these crops are harvested annually, a practice that leaves the ground bare between growing seasons. Stripped of its cover, the top-soil is especially susceptible to erosion and laterisation. The cumulative result has been to launch an apparently irreversible cycle of deterioration, and to convert large areas of Africa from a humanly suitable milieu to desert or semi-desert in less than a century's time.

The second effect of European rule was more indirect and had to do with rapid population growth. The introduction of bio-scientific medicine eventually led to lower death rates and increasing numbers of people. By the early decades of this century, there were simply more people in the rural areas of much of Africa than could be supported by traditional methods of shifting cultivation which required that large amounts of land be left unutilised at any given time. Land areas which had been allowed to regenerate during periods of extended fallow, now had to be cultivated annually with all-too-apparent results in terms of declining soil fertility. Levels of production that could formerly be sustained without the need for exogenous supports, now required greater and greater amounts of fertilisers and other purchased inputs. This has had the effect of tying Africa's rural food producers ever more closely to the urban cash economy, a dependence which can seriously exacerbate the problem of food scarcity in the countryside.

The growth of population has also meant greatly increased pressure on Africa's remaining forest reserves. Vast areas have been cleared to make way for agricultural production, a process which has sometimes occurred even where soil fertility and other determinants of production are so unfavourable that only the most marginal sort of agriculture can be sustained. Forested areas are also denuded as a result of the insatiable demand for charcoal, still the continent's most common cooking fuel and, increasingly, an important source of export earnings for certain countries. The cumulative result of all these pressures is that the forest canopy which was once a major part of the African geographical environment, an invaluable ecological resource, may well have been irretrievably lost.

The portentous implication of environmental deterioration in Africa is that it rules out a return to earlier systems of agricultural production as a solution to the ongoing crisis of food shortages. Not only would these systems be completely incapable of sustaining today's levels of population, but they were, in any case, dependent upon ecological sources of soil replenishment which are no longer part of the natural environment. An agricultural restoration, if it is to occur, will necessarily depend upon artificial methods of providing humus and nutrients to the soil. But the lessons which can be drawn from environmental deterioration are, nevertheless, too important to be overlooked. For even the most agro-scientific approaches to agricultural recovery are unlikely to remedy the crisis of food shortages in the absence of an ecologically conscious response to economic activities which continue to damage the environmental milieu. Under present conditions, it is not at all difficult to envision a future in which agroscientific programmes to rebuild production are dwarfed by the magnitude of the agricultural consequences of environmental damage. Already heavily dependent upon food imports from abroad, Africa conveys an unmistakable impression of a continent moving even further in that direction.

Food Aid

The most common response to the problem of food deficits in Africa has been to import what is most urgently needed from abroad, frequently in the form of food aid. As an immediate remedy for critical emergencies, this "solution" cannot be faulted. Even the most vocal critics of corruption, waste, and inefficiency in food-aid programmes acknowledge that they save lives. If starvation is the result of short-term causes, such as drought, war, or blight, food aid can provide a breathing space until more basic remedies can be introduced, or until natural recovery occurs—as a result, this type of assistance has been virtually immune to fundamental criticism. Of course, some reforms have been suggested in order to improve the delivery of food to the truly needy through the elimination of programmatic abuses.[24] This approach can be of great value, especially when the budgets for such relief work are under political attack in donor countries. But it should not be allowed to obscure the more basic question; namely, do food-aid programmes contribute to the persistence, or even worsening, of the very problems they are intended to alleviate?

The issue is enormously complex. For food assistance can clearly be of some concrete benefit in less-developed countries.[25] It can be targeted specifically towards the most deprived and disenfranchised groups within a society, and can thus provide a modest safety net for the poorest of the poor, a social stratum that has proved maddeningly elusive to a host of other governmental and international development agencies. Food-aid programmes which provide essential nutrition for such vulnerable groups as refugees, women, and children have an especially compelling moral claim to continued support. Moreover, they can provide tangible resources for other, more all-inclusive development projects. Food aid may be employed, for example, to encourage price stabilisation and grain storage, development tasks that are of great importance in rural areas which are affected by cyclical instability in the availability of food supplies. Food aid has sometimes been linked effectively to the improvement of rural infrastructures through "food for work" projects which employ food recipients as labourers for the construction of roads, irrigation systems, and reclaimed land. And, in a context where foreign assistance is declining in real terms, food aid can free scarce governmental resources for other social services.

None the less, serious questions about the ultimate impact of food aid remain. As the Presidential Commission on World Hunger noted in its final report:

At best, there is an inherent contradiction between food which increases the dependency of recipients upon donors, and measures to increase purchasing power and basic food production within developing countries themselves. . . . In some cases, food aid undermines the efforts of recipient nations to develop a more self-reliant base of their own. Food aid has also enabled some recipient governments to postpone essential agricultural reforms, to give low priority to agricultural investment, and to maintain a pricing system which gives farmers inadequate incentives to increase local production required for greater self-reliance in basic foodstuffs.[26]

Comments such as these have helped dispel the mystique of food aid, and have paved the way for searching criticisms about its nature and impact, as well as the policy motivations of the donors. The "Food for Peace" programme of the United States, PL 480, has been the subject of intense scrutiny since it is by far the largest single food-aid scheme in the developing world and, as such, has provided a model for many others. Numerous critics have pointed out, for example, that this programme had its origins in domestic pressures within America, especially the need to solve the problem of growing domestic food surpluses by creating foreign markets for grains. Others have singled out the tendency for food aid to be awarded on the basis of political and military criteria, rather than the needs of the people themselves.[27]

Food aid has also lent itself to serious abuse within the recipient countries.[28] It has provided a source of enrichment for corrupt élites who somehow manage to spirit away an appalling amount of the food intended for the hungry, and who cheat relief organisations by charging exorbitant sums for transportation and storage. Politicians have also taken advantage of assistance programmes by demanding bribes to allow relief organisations to operate, by using food relief as a source of patronage, and by threatening to withhold food relief from potentially disaffected groups. Moreover, food-for-work projects are clearly of much greater benefit to well-to-do landowners—whose holdings increase substantially in value from infrastructural improvements—than to landless and destitute families. Indeed, food-relief programmes have been subject to such a wide variety of forms of corruption that they have helped to widen the gap between rich and poor in virtually every country in which they operate.

The most serious criticisms of food assistance, however, focus on its tendency to act as a long-term disincentive for local agricultural production.[29] Most of what is imported is distributed through the national marketing network, and so often competes directly with locally produced foodstuffs. As a result, in country after country, the availability of concessionally priced food from abroad has fundamentally undermined the price structure of locally produced food items, and has contributed to the further decline of agricultural economies already buffeted by drought, input shortages, and political disruptions. The aid administrators have been chronically unable to remedy this problem. Motivated by the need to make food available as quickly as possible to needy persons, often under extremely difficult conditions, they have not had the opportunity or the authority to introduce methods of distribution that would conserve the economic basis of local agriculture. Even such targeted programmes as food-for-work and maternal-child care are now generally acknowledged to have a measureable disincentive effect on local agricultural production.

As a result, some peasant farmers have actually been driven off the land by this kind of external assistance. Marginal agriculturalists who might otherwise have been able to survive economically have, on occasion, been unable to compete in the market-place with heavily subsidised wheat or rice. Driven from their plots by cheap foreign grains, as well as by the conditions which induced the initial shortages, such farmers have frequently been compelled to join the ranks of those who depend for their survival upon food assistance. In this way, food aid can set up a permanent cycle of deterioration. It can increase the number of dependent persons by diminishing the market for locally produced goods; it can result in the establishment of a price structure which makes it difficult, if not impossible, for peasant producers to recover economically; and it can compete directly against the donor capital that is needed to improve transportation and storage. These tendencies may help explain why so many food-assistance programmes which were initially intended only to provide short-term emergency relief have become almost indelible features of the rural economic landscape.

An equally serious long-term issue is the destruction of initiative at the local level. Peasants who are economically exploited by corrupt food-aid administrators, or who are victimised when assistance programmes are manipulated for political purposes, are hardly likely to emerge as eager participants when called upon to involve themselves in development projects for economic reconstruction. Food aid has also been observed to generate a mentality of dependence. A report on an agro-forestry project in Upper Volta graphically depicts this problem:

> So extensive has this food aid mentality permeated the way of life, that rather than act as an incentive to community improvement, food aid has the opposite effect. It is an assurance that despite bad labor practices that lead to eroded and exhausted soil and marginal harvests, there will be food to eat, there will be food aid. Food aid is an argument *against* the idea that land reclamation and sound agricultural practices are necessary.[30]

It is nearly impossible to discredit the arguments of those who feel that food aid is an unfortunate part of an international system of dependence that casts Africa in the rôle of a continent of begging bowls.

In the final analysis, food aid is not a solution for human misery and malnutrition in Africa. It is essentially a dead-end approach, an entry into a morass of complexities from which there is no apparent exit. Rather than being easily administered—enjoying local political support and targeted towards specific recipient populations—food-aid programmes have become bureaucratic and political nightmares for both planners and project administrators. The ease with which such assistance can be dissipated or spoiled makes for stresses and strains in the body politic that are enduring and difficult to locate—when someone cares to try. And far from alleviating the misery of hunger the net result may be to contribute to its continuation. As a short-term necessity in situations of dire emergency, food aid may well be the only answer; as a strategy for agricultural development it is no solution at all.

The ultimate irony of food-assistance programmes, however, may well lie in the fact that there are often adequate local foodstuffs available in other districts of the recipient country. These are typically prevented from reaching needy areas by a lack of administrative capacity, and by inadequacies in infrastructure and marketing mechanisms. If the resources and human energies allotted to food aid programmes could be channelled towards improving the country's own systems of economic management, transportation, storage, and distribution, this would undoubtedly do more to alleviate hunger on a long-term basis than any quantity of external food assistance.

CONCLUSION

It is clear that no single theoretical perspective adequately explains the decline of food production in Africa, and that there is no single policy which is likely to resolve it. The morass of historical, environmental, and economic factors is so complex as to render the efficacy of any solution problematic. Underdevelopment theory, for example, is helpful in analysing the impact of colonialism and the international economic system on Africa, but it falls far short of suggesting workable solutions. The alternatives it presents presuppose massive and radical changes not only in Africa, but in the West as well. Since theorists of underdevelopment tend to believe that the impoverishment of the less-developed world will continue so long as capitalism determines the international market behaviour of western nations, they tend to remain aloof from discussions of specific projects and policy remedies. For all of its complex historical analysis, then, the theory of underdevelopment in its raw form reduces to an almost absurdly simple policy prescription: end global capitalism.

Much the same can be said of the doctrine of comparative advantage. Since those who hold this position tend to explain any shortages—including food deficits—in terms of governmental interference with the operation of free-market forces, the solution they prescribe tends towards an equally simple, and equally unworkable, remedy: eliminate state-imposed barriers to the operation of the market. Theorists of both underdevelopment and comparative advantage share a disquieting trait in common: they tend to treat evidence of the failure of their strategy as proof of the need for ever greater applications. Thus, in the former, the remedy for failure of socialism becomes—apply more socialism. Just as, in the latter, the solution for the failure of free-market approaches becomes—free the market further.

Both of these approaches tend to be equally insensitive to Africa's immense environmental problems. Workable strategies of agricultural development should take into account the highly delicate and already badly disrupted state of the ecological basis of African agriculture. This would entail working out an extremely difficult balance between the retention of those traditional agricultural systems which can be defended on environmental grounds, and the introduction of modern agricultural practices which would be more responsive to the growing food requirements of rapidly increasing populations. On a continent where about one-half of the land can be classified as arid or semi-arid, the introduction of annual crops can be disastrous. Yet socialist and free-market oriented agricultural planners alike all too often see the remedy for Africa's food deficits in terms of the creation of large-scale, capital-intensive farms.

Additionally, western aid programmes have often run counter to the needs of African peasants, and have thus inhibited rather than encouraged greater local food production. Government-to-government assistance runs a very great risk of supporting corrupt and venal régimes and, to this degree, can be held partly accountable for the growing mood of cynicism and disillusionment with African leaders. This mood has been well expressed by the Ghanaian novelist Ayi Kwei Armah:

> How long will Africa be cursed with its leaders? There were men dying from the loss of hope, and others were finding gaudy ways to enjoy power they did not have. We were ready here for big and beautiful things, but what we had was our own black men hugging new paunches scrambling to ask the white man to welcome them onto our backs. These men who were to lead us out of our despair, they came like men already grown fat and cynical with the eating of centuries of power they had never struggled for, old before they had ever been born into power, and ready only for the grave.[31]

Yet so long as external assistance is given on a government-to-government basis, it is almost impossible to conceive of an aid project which would by-pass an entrenched régime to deal with the agricultural needs of food producers at the local level.

This article has examined four approaches to Africa's food deficits. Combining their positive features we would suggest a series of critically important reforms which can best be understood as broad guidelines for future agricultural development in Africa. These might include:

(1) Genuine empowerment of the peasantry in order to enable rural producers to affect the political process, the character of the market-place, and the administration and implementation of foreign aid. This would be essential in preventing their exploitation by political élites, and in reversing national policies which subordinate peasant needs to the interests of the urban privileged. It could be facilitated by links with trade unions and rural-based co-operatives. One of the most important problems confronting peasant movements in

Africa is to overcome rural-urban conflicts over food policies. The realisation of power by the peasantry would assist in the creation of effective channels of communication with government agencies, and with organisations representing the interests of urban-based social classes.

(2) Land-tenure policies which prevent "the sharks eating the fishes" and which, thereby, preserve the positive features of small-scale peasant agriculture. The shortcomings of both socialist and free-market strategies are instructive on this point. The efforts of governments to create collective agriculture have not only led to the coercion and brutalisation of the peasantry, but to a sharp downward spiral in agricultural production. Large-scale agricultural projects promoted by capitalist interests have also done more harm than good by creating massive numbers of landless and unemployed persons. Small-holder schemes sustained, in part, by governmental limitations on land acquisition and support for agricultural improvements, show great promise in avoiding both these pitfalls.

(3) Freer access to commodity markets through by-passing the large firms which presently dominate the international market-place in Africa's major export products. Without this major external change, internal reforms that lead to greater security of land tenure and increased peasant participation will lose much of their long-term effectiveness. The theory of comparative advantage has much positive merit for developing countries in Africa, but even a carefully planned emphasis on export crops will continue to be disastrous unless there are real prospects of improved price levels for these products. The paramount objective of this reform would be to avoid the extremes of autarky and dependence in international markets, and to generate new and more equitable modalities for trade, transfer of technology, and investment.

(4) Agricultural policies that are more fully influenced by sensitivity to environmental constraints. Far too much of the planning for African agriculture has separated environmental from developmental issues. The result has been agricultural policies which devastate the land and drastically diminish its value as an economic resource for future generations. The measurements of economic output should be revised to incorporate such criteria as long-term sustainability. This might be expected to lead to a fundamental reappraisal of the value of such crops as groundnuts, cotton, and tobacco, as well as agricultural projects which include a much greater emphasis on reforestation.

Reordering paradigms and practices will be a formidable task. Yet the compelling reality of Africa's increasing food deficits requires nothing less than fundamental changes in these areas. To the extent that previous policies have failed to alleviate the severe shortages, a continuation of existing practices seems an exercise in futility. Models of agricultural reform which do not take these guidelines into account offer only the prospect of an ever deepening crisis.

NOTES

1. *Times* (Los Angeles), 9 March 1981.

2. United States Department of Agriculture, *Food Problems and Prospects in Sub-Saharan Africa: the decade of the 1980's* (Washington, D.C., 1981), pp. 1–8.

3. See, for example, Nicole Ball, *World Hunger: a guide to the economic and political dimensions* (Santa Barbara and Oxford, 1981).

4. E.g. Kenneth Anthony et al., *Agricultural Change in Tropical Africa* (Ithaca, 1979), and "The Roots of Famine," in *Review of African Political Economy* (London), 15–16, 1979, pp. 1–74; Raymond Hopkins and Donald Puchala (eds.), *The Global Political Economy of Food* (Madison, 1978); Radha Sinha, *Food and Poverty: the political economy of confrontation* (London, 1976); Lester R. Brown, with Erik P. Eckholm, *By Bread Alone* (New York, 1974); and Susan George, *How the Other Half Dies: the real reasons for world hunger* (Montclair, 1977).

5. Cf. Paul Baran, *Political Economy of Growth* (New York, 1957); Samir Amin, *Unequal Development* (New York, 1976); Immanuel Wallerstein, *The Modern World System: capitalist agriculture and the origins of the European world economy in the sixteenth century* (New York, 1974); Walter Rodney, *How Europe Underdeveloped Africa* (Dar es Salaam, 1972); Arghiri Emmanuel, *Unequal Exchange* (New York, 1972); and André Gunder Frank, *Dependent Accumulation and Underdevelopment* (London, 1978).

6. Nicola Swainson, *The Development of Corporate Capitalism in Kenya, 1918–1977* (London and

Berkeley, 1980); Richard L. Sklar, "The Nature of Class Domination in Africa," in *The Journal of Modern African Studies* (Cambridge), 17, 4, December 1979, pp. 531–52, and "Postimperialism: a class analysis of multinational corporate expansion," in *Comparative Politics* (New York), October 1976, pp. 75–92.

7. Goran Hyden, *Beyond Ujamaa in Tanzania: underdevelopment and an uncaptured peasantry* (London and Berkeley, 1980).

8. René Dumont, *Socialism and Development* (New York, 1973), especially chs. 2 and 4.

9. Pierro Sraffa (ed.), *Works and Correspondence of David Ricardo*, Vol. 1 (Cambridge, 1962), "On the Principles of Political Economy and Taxation," p. 132.

10. Ibid. p. 135.

11. We are indebted to Rhys Payne, "Economic Development and the Principle of Comparative Advantage," University of California, Los Angeles, 1980, for a sweeping survey of the relevant theories.

12. William O. Jones, *Marketing Staple Food Crops in Tropical Africa* (Ithaca, 1972), p. 233.

13. Hollis Chenery, *Structural Change and Development Policy* (Oxford, 1979).

14. Ibid. p. 275.

15. Ibid.

16. Barbara Dinham and Colin Hines, *Agribusiness in Africa* (London, 1982).

17. Ibid.

18. We are indebted to the helpful comments of Dean Freudenberger, Jerry Moles, and Antony Orme in the preparation of this section.

19. Antoon de Vos, *Africa, the Devastated Continent?* (The Hague, 1975); Paul Richards (ed.), *African Environment: perspectives and prospects* (London, 1975); and Michel Frederic Thomas and G. W. Whittington (eds.), *Environment and Land Use in Africa* (London, 1969).

20. De Vos, op. cit. p. 20.

21. Howard Schissel, "Forest Cover Blown," in *The Guardian* (London), 29 April 1981.

22. William Allan, *The African Husbandman* (Edinburgh, 1965), and A. T. Grove and F. M. G. Klein, *Rural Africa* (Cambridge, 1979).

23. Jean Suret-Canale, *French Colonialism in West Africa* (New York edn. 1971); Richard W. Franke and Barbara H. Chasin, *Seeds of Famine: ecological destruction and the development dilemma in the West African Sahel* (Montclair, 1980); Robin Parsons and Neil Palmer (eds.), *Roots of Rural Poverty in Central and Southern Africa* (Berkeley, 1977); and Colin Bundy, *The Rise and Fall of the South African Peasantry* (London, 1979).

24. Report of the Presidential Commission on World Hunger, *Overcoming World Hunger: the challenge ahead* (Washington, D.C., 1980); Mark Schomer, "Can Food Aid and Development Aid Promote Self-Reliance?" Bread for the World Background Paper No. 28, 1978; Brown, op. cit.; and Hopkins and Puchala (eds.), op. cit.

25. Christopher Stevens, *Food Aid and the Developing World: four African case studies* (London, 1979), and S. J. Maxwell and H. W. Singer, "Food Aid to Developing Countries: a survey," in *World Development* (Oxford), 1979, pp. 225–47.

26. Presidential Commission on World Hunger, op. cit. p. 140.

27. Frances Moore Lappé, Joseph Collins, and David Kinley, *Aid as Obstacle* (San Francisco, 1980); Denis Goulet and Michael Hudson, *Myth of Aid* (New York, 1971); Jack Nelson, *Hunger for Justice* (Maryknoll, 1980); and George, op. cit.

28. Betsy Hartmann and James Boyce, *Needless Hunger: voices from a Bangladesh village* (San Francisco, 1979); Barry Newman, "Graft and Inefficiency in Bangladesh Subvert Food-for-Work Program," in *Wall Street Journal* (New York), 20 April 1981; and Geoffrey Lean, "Scandal of UN's Food Aid in Africa," in *The Observer* (London), 17 June 1979.

29. Lean, loc. cit.; Alan Riding, "US Food Aid Seen Hurting Guatemala," in *New York Times*, 6 November 1977; and Tony Jackson, "Statement Before the Committee on Development and Cooperation of the European Parliament," Brussels, 1 April 1980.

30. October 1980 description of the Church-funded Agro/Forestry Project in Ouahigouya, Upper Volta, which has been operational since 1979.

31. Ayi Kwei Armah, *The Beautiful Ones Are Not Yet Born* (New York edn. 1969), p. 79.

Unit V

INTERNATIONAL AFFAIRS

The foreign policy goals of African states are much the same as those of other nations; namely, to preserve their independence and protect themselves against foreign aggression, to gain respect and a degree of influence in world affairs, and to establish friendly and productive relations with other countries. As with other nations, the methods that African states use to conduct their foreign affairs and participate in the international arena are influenced by their ideologies and shaped by their levels of economic development and political stability. However, unlike many of the industrialized nations, African states have had relatively few opportunities for taking foreign policy initiatives, except when dealing with their neighbors on a regional level. Even then, such initiatives are often influenced by external intervention, and African states have been forced to adopt a rather concrete and immediate view of their national interests.

While the basic goals and methods of African diplomacy have not changed appreciably over time, the issues and vocabulary of African international affairs in the mid-1980s are rather different from those that occupied the energies of African leaders in the early stages of national independence. In 1964, for example, most African leaders were concerned with the growth and success of the recently created Organization of African Unity (OAU). Regional federations such as the East African Federation were still effective organizations whose members shared common goals and in the fresh glow of their independence assumed they could work together to achieve them. Pan-Africanist ideology generally provided crucial support not only for entry of African states into the international system, but also as an organizing force on the continental level, as illustrated by the Pan-African Freedom Movement for East, Central and Southern Africa (PAFMECSA) whose concerns focused on freedom for the remaining colonies in that region. Frontier disputes, as between Ethiopia and Somalia, were still seen as manageable, rather than as grave threats to the political and economic life of an entire region, while liberation struggles in Central and Southern Africa were in their earliest stages and posed few adverse consequences for neighboring states. Finally, it appeared that the East-West dimensions of international politics could be contained on the continent within the rhetoric and practices of "nonalignment." However, even in 1964 the crisis in the Congo (now Zaire) demonstrated that political instability and insurrection in an African state could quickly become a focus of global concern.

By the mid-1970s, it was obvious that the character of African foreign affairs had become highly internationalized and increasingly subject to external intervention. This was due in part to the liberation struggle in Southern Africa and the irredentist movement in Somalia, both of which involved hostile and competitive national or ethnic forces, which ultimately fell into the U.S.-USSR competitive orbit. Consequently, as new eras opened up after events such as independence for Mozambique and Angola, or the collapse of Emperor Haile Selassie's ancien régime in Ethiopia, the structures of these situations continued to be marked not only by domestic uncertainty but vulnerability on the international scene as well. Equally important, Pan-Africanism had failed to materialize as a centralizing and guiding force that could override national considerations for the purpose of promoting mutual interests or resolving inter-African differences. As Kenya, Uganda, and Tanzania adopted opposing national ideologies and moved in different economic directions, the influence of Pan-Africanist ideology was insufficient to prevent the dissolution of the East African Community, formerly the East African Federation. Concurrently, internationally oriented political and economic problems, such as increases in the world price for oil or U.S.-USSR rivalry for control of the Indian Ocean, began to intrude on African continental and national affairs. Clearly, the fragility of political as well as economic structures in Africa served not only to weaken many African states, but also to invite intervention.

Events in the early 1980s reflect the continuation and persistence of these basic themes. Pan-Africanist ideology, in particular, has been severely tested. One of its most important tenets was expressed in the OAU's early commitment to honor the sovereignty and autonomy of all its members. Yet this has been seriously eroded by Morocco's persistent claims since 1976 to northern portions of Western Sahara (formerly Spanish Sahara), and the deep divisions within the OAU over recognition of that country's major liberation movement—the Polisario—and its declaration of that state's new status as the Saharan Arab Democratic Republic (SARD). Indeed, the OAU's disarray on such issues during the early 1980s is symptomatic of the continuing internal politicized competition between militants and moderates that has marked the political behavior of the organization since its inception. However, such divisions are not unusual in regional organizations that embrace a large number of countries with diverse economic and political policies. Nevertheless, the net effect results in territorial disputes that are often burdened by fundamental ideological differences and sharp reactions to East-West conflicts that are remote and even irrelevant to the specific issues at hand.

Yet Pan-Africanist sentiments cannot be wholly discounted because they continue to inspire means of promoting economic development of African states. Nowhere is this more evident than in Southern Africa, where members of the South African Development Coordination Conference (SADCC) are attempting to assist each other to minimize their economic dependence on the Republic of South Africa while simultaneously maximizing their own economic development. Even in this endeavor, Pan-Africanist ideology is of limited material value because most of the SADCC states—especially Mozambique, Angola, Botswana, and Zimbabwe—are essentially helpless in the short term against South Africa's military and economic might. As a result, some of these states have been forced to accept restrictive bilateral agreements with the Republic through which South

Africa imposes de facto limitations on their political freedom and ultimately their economic growth.

There are a variety of approaches to the study of African international affairs. One would be to examine these affairs on a regional basis, taking into account, for example, the crises in Southern Africa or the Horn of Africa and looking at their inter-African as well as their international implications. A second approach would be to list and examine the relationships of African countries with major political actors on the world scene, such as the U.S. and the USSR, or with important world organizations such as the United Nations or the European Common Market. Still a third approach would be to analyze economic interrelationships among African states, such as among the members of the Economic Community of West African States (ECOWAS), or the SADCC countries, or with South Africa. One might even take into account the extent to which intra-African affairs, e.g., the Nigerian Civil War, 1967–70, or the Angolan Civil War of 1975–76, shaped African foreign policy-making. For our part as editors, we have tried to take a broad view of common problems that affect African international affairs, although we cite illustrations of more specific concerns in the bibliography. And while African states are not all equally affected by any single political or economic issue, we have tried to illuminate questions that truly affect the continent as a whole. As with many of the other readings in this collection, we note the pessimism of the contributors on various aspects of African international relations. Yet despite persistent pronouncements concerning the collapse, or expected collapse, of African states, there is a degree of hope in these articles—hope that in the face of great odds to the contrary, African states may not necessarily follow all the rules of political behavior previously known in the West but may in fact create new political patterns of their own, which time and circumstances will test.

The topics covered in this section include an analysis of the consequences of foreign intervention in African affairs, changing African leadership styles on the international scene, and international factors contributing to the survival or persistence of weak African states. S. N. MacFarlane's concern is with the extent to which foreign intervention in African states destabilizes and intensifies regional conflicts, and with those factors that render African states particularly vulnerable to such interference. As MacFarlane sees it, political fragmentation, "catastrophic economic performance," and regional disparities in power may, in the future, be greater hazards than outside intervention. In their contribution, Timothy M. Shaw and Naomi Chazan argue that the highly personalistic international leadership that was so significant in earlier stages of African diplomacy has now been replaced by influence based primarily on coalitions and structures. National differences and inequalities in the bases of economic and political power, they say, will continue to reduce the individual influence of political leaders and probably increase the authority of various nongovernmental organizations. In our final selection, Robert H. Jackson and Carl G. Rosberg contend that notwithstanding structural and organizational weaknesses, many African states have survived primarily because of the support they receive from the international society of states, which provides both normative and juridical conditions necessary for their continued existence.

Intervention and Security in Africa

S. N. MacFarlane

The last several years have witnessed a growing number of interventions in internal and regional disputes in Africa. If one begins in 1975, a partial list of such intrusions would include the 1975–6 Angolan crisis, the Shaban (Kantangan) interventions in 1977 and 1978, the war in the Horn in 1977–8, the conflict in the Western Sahara from 1975 to the present, and the crisis in Chad. The frequency of this kind of behaviour by both regional and external actors suggests that intervention is a significant issue of African regional security.

Most studies of intervention in Africa view the issue from the perspective of East-West relations or that of policy-makers in the intervening or in rival states.[1] The validity and utility for certain purposes of this approach cannot be denied, but the discussion of intervention in Africa is incomplete without attention to its impact on regional politics. This article is an enquiry into the relationship between external military interference in civil and regional disputes on the one hand and African regional security on the other. Is intervention regionally destabilizing? Does it hinder development? Does it intensify regional conflict? Is it destructive of national sovereignty?

The geographical focus of this paper is on OAU (Organization of African Unity) Africa. It would be artificial, however, to exclude the Republic of South Africa from a discussion of African security when the internal and external situations of many states in the southern part of the continent are so clearly dependent on the domestic politics and foreign policy of the Republic. Where appropriate, therefore, aspects of

South African policy and behaviour are considered here.

The terms "intervention" and "regional security" are both rather imprecise and contentious. It is accordingly appropriate to indicate how they are being used here. For the purpose of this paper, intervention refers to coercive military involvement in civil and regional conflict, involvement which is intended to, or does, affect internal political outcomes.[2] This includes intrusions not only by actors from outside the region, but also by states and other agents within it. It may be, and has been, unilateral, as in the case of Tanzanian intervention in Uganda; multilateral, as with the joint actions of the United States, France, Morocco and Belgium in Shaba; or collective, as in the case of the recent OAU involvement in Chad. It may involve the regular forces of the intervening power or irregulars dependent upon and acting at the behest of the intervener, as is arguably the case with UNITA–South African cooperation in Angola or MRM–South African collaboration in Mozambique.

Military intervention is of course neither the only, nor necessarily the most significant, kind of external intervention in African affairs. One can speak of covert or economic intervention without doing violence to the basic sense of the term. There is every reason to believe, for example, that CIA involvement in the Congo crisis and in a number of subsequent conflicts,[3] or French investment and assistance programmes in the francophone African countries,[4] have had significant consequences for the internal politics of the target state and for regional security. But the limitation of the discussion to identifiable military action renders the concept of intervention operational in that it allows a relatively un-

From *International Affairs*, vol. 60, no. 1 (Winter 1983/4), 53–73. Reprinted by permission of the journal. Abridged by the editors.

ambiguous distinction between a category of events described as interventions, and a host of other activities the intent or impact of which is to influence political outcomes within other states.

The concepts of national security and regional security are perhaps even more difficult to define with any sharpness than is that of intervention. Those who use these terms tend to employ them in such a way as to further their own interests and policy preferences. When European and American policymakers and writers in the Western strategic literature talk of African security, one suspects that what they have in mind is the security of Western interests in Africa or the importance of Africa to Western security.[5] Likewise, if Soviet writers were to use the term African security, it is probable that they would define it in terms of the expulsion of Western interests and the maintenance and expansion of positions of Soviet influence and "socialist orientation."[6] There does exist, however, in OAU member states, implicitly if not explicitly, an African conception of African security. This is the perspective focussed upon here.

Walter Lippman held that a state is "secure to the extent to which it is not in danger of having to sacrifice core values if it wishes to avoid war and is able, if challenged, to maintain them by victory in such a war."[7] Following this line of reasoning, one can define African security in terms of the ability of states within the region to pursue their core values without internal or external hindrance. It is inevitable that the enumeration of the core values of a group of states as large and diverse as OAU Africa should be somewhat arbitrary. Moreover, in specific instances it is probable that the core values of specific regional actors will be inconsistent with those of its neighbours. In this context, one could cite the Somali commitment to bring the entire Somali "nation" into one state versus the Ethiopian and Kenyan commitments to their own territorial integrity. But it would in all likelihood be accepted by most politically aware people in the region and by a majority of regimes that a list of core values would include internal political stability and national integration, self-determina-

tion and the consolidation of external sovereignty, and economic development.[8] Such a list is not complete. One might also include the termination of apartheid in South Africa, the end of colonial rule in Namibia, and the realization of some form of closer African unity. But these last three do not seem to influence state behaviour to the same degree as the first group does. Many states in the region, for example, while subscribing to the tenets of pan-Africanism, violate its spirit when its dictates run counter to perceived national economic and political interest. Nigeria's recent expulsion of illegal aliens is a case in point. With respect to southern African issues, many black African states, while vociferously condemning South African policy on Namibia and the race question within the Republic itself, maintain wideranging and lucrative economic ties with South Africa. For these reasons, this discussion focusses on the first group of objectives noted above.

The usual ways in which security is pursued are threefold: the creation of military forces sufficient to deter external threats or to beat them off should deterrence fail; adherence to alliances which supplement national capabilities; and the definition of norms of interstate behaviour which diminish or remove external threats. The first two have been common in African politics. With respect to the first, for example, Ethiopia responded to the threats of Somali irredentism and Eritrean secessionism in the 1960s by building—with American assistance—one of the largest, best-trained, and best-equipped military forces in sub-Saharan Africa. The reliance of some French and British ex-colonies on military ties with the metropolitan powers is an illustration of the second. But Africa is usually considered to be exceptional in its development of the third basis of security, the definition of norms of behaviour reducing external threats from both within and outside the region.

William Zartman, in a 1967 article on the African state system, enumerated several such norms, three of which are particularly relevant here. The first was that "intra-system solutions [were] preferable over extra-system solutions."[9] With this went adherence to the principles of non-alignment. In a situation where no African state could hope to compete militarily with the great powers, general acceptance of this norm enhanced regional security by reducing the likelihood that these external actors would involve themselves in African conflicts.

A second was that wars of conquest were not acceptable policy alternatives. The territorial legacy of the colonial period was not to be called into question. A third, mentioned by Zartman and prominent in the OAU Charter, was the principle of non-interference in the internal affairs of member states.[10] More recent authors have also stressed the non-conflictual rule-governed character of interstate relations in Africa.[11]

One need not go far to find violations of all three of these basic norms, even in the first years after independence and the formation of the OAU. The reliance of French ex-colonies on support from their former rulers in dealing with internal and external threats, a reliance which included the basing of several thousand French military personnel in francophone Africa, has already been noted.[12] Moroccan pressure on Mauritania and Somali attacks on Ethiopia and support for insurgency in Kenya in the early and mid-1960s, as well as the Libyan annexation of the Aozou Strip in 1973, may be cited as examples of infringements of the second of these norms. Ghanaian support in the early 1960s of radical opposition to moderate African regimes, Gabonese support of Biafra, and Nyerere's aid in the early 1970s to Obote in the latter's attempts to unseat Idi Amin were all violations of the third.

Nevertheless, these norms reflected, and to an extent governed, state behaviour in OAU Africa to a remarkable degree, with the result that the region was in the 1960s and early 1970s largely free from interstate conflict. The regional organization and its member states were reasonably successful in insulating disputes such as the Nigerian civil war from external military involvement,[13] in preventing disputes between member states from escalating into armed conflict,[14] and in limiting and resolving those conflicts which occurred.[15] It might be argued that low levels of conflict within the region merely reflected an absence of

the means to prosecute war, and, in fact, defence expenditure in OAU Africa was in the 1960s quite low when compared to other regions in the Third World. In 1968, for example, Africa accounted for only 7 per cent of developing country arms imports.[16] However, the failure to acquire the means of self-defence reflected not only the poverty of the region, but the belief that it was unnecessary. This belief was in large part based upon a general acceptance of the normative structure of regional politics, as mentioned above. In short, national elites in the region could on the whole concern themselves, as was their wont, with socialist utopianism, economic development and social welfare, or power-broking and personal enrichment, with little need to preoccupy themselves with questions of external security.

THE IMPACT OF INTERVENTION: NEGATIVE OR POSITIVE?

Within the region, it is generally maintained that intervention has a negative impact on African security,[17] being itself a security problem rather than a solution to problems of security. This conclusion is apparently based upon several implicit or explicit judgements with respect to the effect of external military interference on African core values: that intervention both prolongs and intensifies the conflict which provoked it, increasing the number of casualties and refugees and the level of physical destruction in the target environment; that it thereby jeopardizes economic development; that it erodes national sovereignty; and that it is politically destabilizing.

This assessment is reflected not only in attitudes towards intrusions by non-African actors, but in prevailing African opinion even in instances where the intrusion is undertaken by an African actor in pursuit of objectives which enjoy widespread sympathy in the region. The Tanzanian intervention in Uganda in 1979 in response to Ugandan military provocations and in order to remove a regime widely considered to be destabilizing in the regional context is a case in point. The action met widespread condemnation and received almost no support at the Monrovia OAU summit later in the year.[18]

None of the generalizations upon which this negative assessment of intervention is based stands up to close examination. Moreover, several are rejected, in specific situations where national interests or ideological commitments are at issue, by African states which otherwise subscribe heartily to the condemnation of interventionist behaviour in African affairs. The questionable character of these general assertions about the impact of intervention on African security will be demonstrated primarily with reference to recent cases involving three areas of conflict: Angola, the Horn, and Chad.

The argument concerning intervention and the intensity and duration of conflict runs along the following lines. In principle, the introduction of well-equipped units of an external power increases the quantity of firepower deployed and often alters the quality of the conflict through the deployment of technologically more sophisticated systems. Moreover, such intrusions can draw a conflict out, in that it is often when a local actor is close to exhaustion that he appeals for more considerable external support. Finally, intervention may bring counterintervention in support of other parties to the conflict. The cycle of intervention, counterintervention, and escalation in the Angolan conflict is well known, and it is quite plausible that the result was a far higher intensity of conflict than would otherwise have obtained. In Chad (1978–82), Libyan intervention and the consequent competitive involvement of Sudan, Egypt, and, indirectly, the United States in support of Hissène Habré, significantly enhanced the military capabilities of local actors and widened the scope of the conflict.

But there are also cases in which intervention at a level sufficient to determine the outcome of a conflict terminated hostilities or drastically reduced their scale far earlier than would otherwise have been the case. In such instances, it might well be asked whether a short, relatively intense conflict was not preferable, in terms of total numbers of military and civilian casualties

and displaced persons and of the degree of disruption of national life, to a prolonged conflict at a lower level.

In Angola, for instance, there is good reason to believe that once the Alvor Accords collapsed in early 1975, conflict between the three liberation movements and the ethnic groups supporting each one would have dragged on more or less indefinitely. In the Horn, Soviet and Cuban assistance to the Ethiopians brought the 1977–8 Somali-Ethiopian conflict to an end far earlier than was likely to have been the case in the absence of this intervention. Soviet bloc logistical support, technical advice, and weapons supply also enabled the Ethiopians to contain the Eritrean insurgency at a much lower level than would otherwise have obtained. Generalization about the relation between intervention and the intensity and duration of conflict is, therefore, suspect.

The argument concerning the effects on economic development derives from that concerning the intensity and duration of conflict. The more intense a civil war is, the greater the disruption of agricultural, commercial, and industrial activity. But if the assumption concerning the relationship between external participation and the intensity and duration of conflict is questionable, so too is its implication concerning the effect of intervention on economic activity.

In specific instances, the effects of intervention on economic activity can cut either way. In Angola, for example, the South African incursion in late 1975 resulted in the mining of most roads in southern Angola and in the destruction of almost every bridge in that part of the country. Current South African support of UNITA allows that group to attack the Benguela railroad with impunity, depriving the Angolans of a vital transport artery and an important source of foreign exchange, the railroad in better times serving as a major conduit for Zaïrean and Zambian copper. South African attacks on Kassinga, ostensibly directed at SWAPO camps in the area, have prevented the reopening of the iron ore mines there, with the result that Angola, once a major African producer of iron ore, now produces and exports none.

On the other hand, Gulf's oil production facilities in Cabinda survived the 1975-6 war and subsequent unrest because they were protected by Cuban troops. French and Moroccan intervention in Mauritania in 1977-8 in response to Polisario guerrilla activity in all likelihood prevented serious and prolonged disruption of iron ore production at Zoueraté, the export of which is Mauritania's major source of foreign exchange.[19] The presence of French troops in Djibouti and the virtual certainty that they would intervene actively if the government of that country were seriously threatened from within or without create a favourable climate for the foreign private investment the government is attempting to attract.[20]

In other cases, intervention has no obvious economic effects. Here, one could cite Chad, where what little economic activity there had been in the north and centre of the country had been so disrupted prior to Libyan intervention that the Libyans, even had they desired to do so, could inflict little damage. The production in the south of cotton, the country's major export crop, was little affected by the Libyan action. Again, there would not seem to be any justification here for broad generalizations about the impact of intervention.

The view that intervention compromises national sovereignty and self-determination rests on the argument that intrusion on behalf of a party to a civil war creates a relationship of dependency such that the local client is incapable of independent action in internal and international affairs where his interests or preferences diverge from those of his patron. In other words, intervention constitutes a new kind of colonialism.

This may be true in some instances. French military intervention in Africa comes quickly to mind here, though it is probable that political and economic ties are far more important in accounting for dependency in much of francophone Africa than is French military activity. But this effect of intervention is by no means necessary. British intervention on behalf of Nyerere in 1964, for example, brought little in the way of political reliability.

Nor is it absolute. Both Angola and Ethiopia are governed by regimes which have benefited substantially from Cuban intervention with substantial Soviet support. While they display a tendency to support the Soviet Union on issues which are to them peripheral—for example, their voting on the Afghan and Cambodian issues at the United Nations—on issues more central to their interests, they show considerable independence. Angola has rebuffed Soviet requests for bases and cooperates with the Western contact group's efforts to resolve the Namibian question.[21] Ethiopia refuses to negotiate on the Eritrean issue, engages in intervention of its own in Somalia,[22] and resists Soviet pressure to restructure its political institutions.[23]

Nor is such influence permanent. The removal or disappearance of the threat occasioning intervention removes the source of a regime's dependence, weakening the basis of influence. The case of British intervention in Tanganyika again comes to mind. Elsewhere, it is probable that an accommodation between South Africa and Angola would reduce considerably the level of Cuban and Soviet influence in Angola, a large part of which is derived from the protection provided to the Angolan regime by these two powers against South African aggression and sponsorship of UNITA guerrillas. The availability of alternative sources of external support has the same effect, as is evident from Egyptian behaviour in the aftermath of the 1973 war, or in Goukouni Oueddei's foreign policy in the aftermath of Hissène Habré's expulsion from Chad by Libyan troops in late 1980. The improvement in Franco-Chadian relations in the summer of 1981 made it possible for Goukouni to request the withdrawal from Chad of Libyan forces. Along similar lines, it could be argued that a more receptive American attitude to overtures from both Angola and Ethiopia could do much to undermine the position of the Soviet Union in both these countries.[24]

Moreover, intervention may preserve and enhance sovereignty rather than eroding it. Soviet/Cuban intervention maintained the external sovereignty and territorial integrity of Ethiopia in the face of Somali invasion. It is probable that their intervention in Angola prevented or postponed that country's eventual disintegration or dismemberment. Finally, even those in the region most adamant in their opposition to intervention in African affairs generally accept that the involvement of external actors in the "struggle for liberation" can further the cause of self-determination.[25]

It is clear in this context that underlying the general condemnation of intervention mentioned above is a wide range of mutually incompatible positions on intervention in African conflict. The 1978 Khartoum OAU summit, which dwelt at length on the subject of intervention, was split between, on the one hand, moderate and conservative governments which supported actions, such as those taken by France, Belgium, and Morocco in Shaba, to preserve a weak regime against a "radical" opposition, and, on the other, "progressive" regimes which displayed great reluctance to condemn Soviet and Cuban activities in Africa while bitterly criticizing involvement by Western powers and the position of those African states which cooperated with France and Shaba and in subsequent proposals for a "pan-African peacekeeping force." In this instance too, then, there is little basis for a sweeping condemnation of intervention.

Turning finally to the question of political stability—assuming that the latter term refers principally to a state of affairs in which a regime or political system is free from serious challenge (originating within the country) to its existence in its efforts to cope with and adapt to evolving internal and external political realities[26]—a look at cases of intervention in Africa suggests that such behaviour may in the short term be either stabilizing or destabilizing in both intent and consequences. By way of illustration, there is little to argue with in the assertion that South African intervention in Angola since 1976, and in particular its support of UNITA, has been destabilizing in both intent and consequences, creating severe difficulties for the regime in the Bié, Moxico, Cuando-Cubango, and Cunene districts, fostering dissension within the ranks of the party, and impeding the government in its attempts to meet the needs of the population and to integrate the di-

verse ethnic groups inhabiting the country into one nation.[27]

By contrast, the recent Ethiopian incursions into western Somalia in support of the Somali Salvation Democratic Front were intended to undermine the Siad Barre regime, but in all likelihood have had the opposite effect by mobilizing nationalist support behind the tottering Barre and inducing the northern Isaaq clans to reduce their pressure on the central government.

Another contrasting example is that of Soviet/Cuban intervention in Ethiopia, which was intended to prop up the socialist Ethiopian government and did just that. The intrusion neutralized the principal external threat to the Derg, provided the Ethiopians with the means to contain the Eritrean and Tigrean insurgencies, and gave the regime the breathing space necessary to consolidate its hold on power in the capital and in central Ethiopia.

In the longer term, there are a number of good reasons for expecting that military intervention is unlikely to enhance a target state's stability. While intervention may bring military victory for one of the parties to a civil or regional dispute, so long as the political and social roots of the conflict which occasioned intervention are not addressed, the solution will remain at best a temporary one, and one which is fraught with dangers of deeper entanglement for the external actor.[28]

External interference may in fact reduce the likelihood of conflict resolution. In the Angolan, Ethiopian, and Chadian cases, external assistance convinced its internal beneficiaries that negotiation with their opponents was unnecessary, that military means were sufficient to resolve the civil conflicts in which they found themselves embroiled. In Angola, the Soviet/Cuban presence has apparently strengthened the MPLA's resolve not to share political power with UNITA. In Ethiopia, and despite Soviet and Cuban advice to the Derg to negotiate with and to grant limited autonomy to the Eritreans,[29] military intervention has made it possible for the regime to survive without compromise and to pursue indefinitely its campaign against the Eritrean insurgency. In Chad, Libyan and OAU intervention on behalf of Goukouni Oueddei's transitional government convinced Goukouni that he could consolidate his control of Chad without any attempt to achieve a political solution involving his principal opponent, Hissène Habré.

Moreover, intervention and a sustained foreign role in defending a government against its internal opposition may discredit that government in the eyes of the broader populace, which comes to see the regime as an instrument of a foreign power and as betraying the nation which it purports to serve.[30] In other words, it may undermine further the legitimacy upon which the stability of a government ultimately rests. In Angola, several sources have maintained that the Cuban and Soviet presence has evoked a hostile nationalist reaction within the MPLA and in the population at large.[31] In Chad, Goukouni's recourse to massive Libyan support redounded to Habré's favour, as the latter came to be seen as the repository of Chadian independence in the face of Libyan depredations.[32]

However, it is again not necessarily the case that intervention will have these effects. It may, on the contrary, set the stage for longer-term stability by removing short-lived threats to basically popular and legitimate regimes. British intervention in the face of army mutinies in East Africa in the mid-1960s may be cited in this context. One might also cite here the recent Senegalese intervention in behalf of Gambian President Jawara.

Moreover, foreign intervention and a sustained military presence need not discredit an incumbent government. There is little evidence to support the view, for example, that the French presence in Senegal, the Ivory Coast, or Gabon has rendered the governments of these countries illegitimate in the eyes of their publics. Whether intervention has this impact depends on a number of factors: the comportment of foreign personnel, the degree to which the military involvement is accompanied by economic benefits to the target state, the performance of the incumbent government in meeting the economic and social aspirations of the populace, the degree of political awareness of the indigenous population, the effectiveness of the opposition in mobilizing public opinion, and so on.

In short, it would appear that it is neither easy, nor very productive, to generalize about intervention and its impact on regional security in the senses discussed above. Intervention in Africa is not a homogeneous phenomenon.

REPERCUSSIONS FOR REGIONAL ARMS LEVELS

That having been said, it is possible to accept a number of more careful conclusions about the relationship between intervention and regional security. First, there appears to be a clear connection between intervention and increased defence spending and weapons procurement in contiguous states. The South African defence budget, for instance, doubled and then doubled again in the aftermath of the Angolan affair, going from R335 million in 1972–3 to R1,564 million in 1979–80. While some of this may be accounted for by inflation in military costs, this corresponded to a rise in the defence share of GNP from 2.1 per cent to 4.5 per cent and in the defence share of central government expenditure from 11.8 per cent to 16.8 per cent.[33] It would be inaccurate to ascribe this substantial real increase in defence spending solely to Soviet/Cuban military activities in Angola. The collapse of the Portuguese empire in Southern Africa and the increasing pressure on the Smith regime in Rhodesia would have altered the basis of the Republic's external security whether or not external forces had intervened. But it is true nevertheless that these processes were particularly disturbing from the white South African perspective, given the close involvement in them of communist powers from outside the region. As Robin Hallett has observed, the South African preoccupation with and fear of "the communist menace" should not be belittled, but taken at face value.[34]

The Kenyan response to the growing conflict in the Horn was to increase defence expenditure from $113 million in 1977 to $255 million in 1979.[35] Again, this should perhaps not be ascribed principally to Soviet and Cuban involvement, given the long history of problems in relations between Somalia and Kenya. But as a regional power committed to capitalist development and to close ties with the West, Kenya could not have been indifferent to the rapid growth in the regional presence of the Soviet Union and Cuba.[36] Moreover, the fact that this shift in Kenyan policy was a response primarily to a "Somali threat" does nothing to diminish the causal connection to intervention, for it was a Somali military intrusion into Ethiopia in support of insurgents in the Ogaden which occasioned the Ogaden war and which provided the Kenyans with graphic evidence of continuing Somali irredentism.

Finally, in a direct response to Libyan intervention in Chad and to what the Nigerians believed to be Libyan involvement in sectarian violence in Kano in late 1980, Nigeria adopted a five-year defence procurement plan valued at $6.4 billion and increased its projected defence budget for 1981–2 by 35 per cent.[37] This reversed the post–civil war downward trend in Nigerian defence spending and in the size of the country's defence establishment.[38]

More generally, while it was noted above that in 1968 Africa accounted for only 7 per cent of developing country arms imports, in 1978 the corresponding figure was 32 per cent.[39] This occurred despite a substantial drop in the dollar value of the purchases of Egypt—which in the 1960s and early 1970s had been the continent's largest arms importer—after the October war. African purchases were somewhat lower (around 26 per cent of developing country arms imports) in 1979. This reflected primarily the curtailment in Ethiopian demand for arms[40] rather than any significant improvement in the security situation in the region as a whole. It remained the case that imports were approximately 3.5 times higher in constant dollars at the end of the period than at the beginning, and that regional defence spending had virtually doubled, while there were approximately 2.5 times as many indigenous military personnel in the region in 1979 as in 1970, this again despite declines in the size of the Nigerian and Egyptian armed forces. The recent frequency of intervention in Africa is part of a climate of growing violence to which this shift in resource allocation is a response. While it is perhaps simplistic to maintain without qualification that arms races lead to war, it is nevertheless true that the better armed a state is, the more able it is to contemplate the use of force. The increasing availability in the region of the instruments of violence removes what was an important constraint on intra-African conflict.

The growing prominence of the military in national budgets and of military tasks in national policy diverts scarce resources, human, financial, and material, from the pursuit of other objectives, such as development, health, and welfare, in societies which are already for the most part desperately poor. Moreover, it may result in an even greater role for military personnel in the domestic political process, with attendant effects on prospects for democracy and human rights.

Second, the increasing incidence of intervention in the late 1970s and early 1980s in Africa reflects an erosion of the normative basis of interstate relations in the region. One aspect of this is an apparently greater willingness of regional actors to seek military assistance from external actors.[41] Another is the greater proclivity of regional actors to involve themselves in civil conflicts in other states and to employ force in their relations with each other. The great majority of instances of intervention since the mid-1970s have involved African actions against fellow Africans. In this context, Akinyemi's assertion, questionable in any case, that the OAU, rather than seeking to resolve conflicts, strives to insulate them from "non-African factors," is rather cold comfort.[42]

GROWING REGIONAL DISORDER

The increasing number of interventions in this period not only reflects but fosters this erosion of previously accepted norms, for, in the absence of a supranational authority capable of enforcing rules, compliance is based upon mutual interest and upon the expectation that others will comply. Each violation of these norms challenges this expectation. As the latter becomes increasingly untenable, regional actors will move further towards seeking other means of guaranteeing their security and pursuing their interests.

For these reasons, it is legitimate to question whether the conventional characterizations of inter-African relations in terms of principles such as the non-use of force, non-interference in internal affairs, general acceptance of the territorial legacy of imperialism, the commitment to pan-Africanism, and multilateral conflict resolution are still valid, and, if they remain so, how long this will last. It is not coincidental that this period has witnessed the apparent demise of the OAU. Too many of its member states no longer take seriously that organization's constitutive principles in situations where the latter impinge upon the pursuit of fundamental national objectives.

It is as an element of this growing regional disorder that the impact of intervention on African economic development should be seen. Regional unpredictability and disarray make the continent as uninviting an economic investment for private interests both within Africa and outside it as it is an unpromising political investment for external actors seeking lasting influence and strategic gain.[43]

So far, it has been argued, first, that there is no basis for a general condemnation of intervention in terms of its impact on African core values. To the contrary, in specific instances it may be, and has been, supportive of these ends. However, in the longer term, it may inhibit the emergence of stable political conditions and may encourage higher levels of defence spending and procurement, while, as part of a growing use of force in regional affairs, it both reflects and furthers a corrosion of the normative basis of interstate relations within the region.

If intervention is only one aspect of a general trend in regional politics, it remains to ask what the profound causes of this trend are. In this sense, intervention is more a manifestation of insecurity than a cause of it. There are at least three fundamental problems in African security, leaving aside the issue of apartheid in South Africa.[44]

The first is political fragmentation. There were several apparently promising movements towards national integration in the 1960s and early 1970s. Ghana under Nkrumah and Nigeria in the period of national reconciliation and rapid growth after the civil war are examples. But with the passage of time, it is increasingly clear that the dominant trend in African politics is towards the disintegration of the states created upon the departure of the European colonialists. Evidence for this may be seen in continuing sectarian problems and North-South conflict in the Sudan, in the failure in Ethiopia to extinguish the Eritrean and Tigrean insurgencies, in the continuing ethnic conflict in Chad, in the failure of a non-ethnic party to emerge in Nigerian politics, in the persistent secessionism of the Lunda in Shaba evident in the popular response to the arrival of FLNC forces from Angola in 1977 and 1978, in ethnic strife between Kikongo, Kimbundu, and Ovimbundu in Angola, in the growing violence between Shona and Ndebele in Zimbabwe, in unrest among the Baganda in Uganda, in continuing Kikuyu-Luo tensions in Kenya, and so on. There is hardly a state in black Africa which appears today to be more viable as a national entity than it did on the eve of independence. Several appear much less so, the unifying influence of colonial power long ago having departed, and the concept of neocolonialism being too nebulous to arouse popular enthusiasm. Even those states usually cited as being based upon a strong national identity, Somalia being a case in point, are riven with ethnically and regionally based struggles for power and position, and for the meagre material rewards available to those who possess them. External oppression has been replaced by oppression by indigenous clan and tribal groupings. The consequences are almost inevitably fissiparous. The connection between ethnic conflict and intervention is evident throughout much of the continent—the Zaïrean involvement in northern Angola in support of the FNLA, the Somali link with their ethnic kin in the Ogaden, and the Libyan connection with Chadian Arabs are all cases in point.

This political fragmentation is exacerbated by the catastrophic economic performance of much of the region in the 1970s and early 1980s. At present, almost two-thirds of the states falling into the World Bank's "low income" (*per capita* income less than $370 a year) category are African. GNP growth *per capita* for sub-Saharan Africa (including rapidly growing countries such as Nigeria, Kenya, and the Ivory Coast, but excluding the Republic of South Africa) was 0.8 per cent per year in the 1970s, down from 1.3 per cent per year in the previous decade. The World Bank notes that output per person grew more slowly in sub-Saharan Africa in the 1970s than in any other part of the world. Seven countries in the region had negative growth in total GDP, while fifteen had negative *per capita* rates of growth in GDP.

Volumes of exports in sub-Saharan Africa fell at an annual rate of 1.6 per cent (median for countries in the region excluding South Africa) during the decade. This fall in volume was accompanied by fairly rapid deterioration in the terms of trade for African oil importers late in the decade (a negative shift of approximately 8 per cent in 1978–80). Mineral exporters were particularly hard hit during the decade, despite a number of good years. Their terms of trade dropped between 1970 and 1979 by an average of 7.1 per cent per year. The softening of oil markets in the last two years has extended these effects to African oil exporters such as Nigeria, Gabon, and Angola as well. The financial consequences of these trends are severe. Current account deficits in the region climbed from $1.5 billion in 1970 to $8 billion in 1980. External indebtedness went from $6 billion to $32 billion between 1970 and 1979. The situation has, if anything, deteriorated further since 1979.

Food production in the 1970s in sub-Saharan Africa grew in absolute terms by some 1.5 per cent per year, but, given the regional population growth rate of 2.7 per cent, the *per capita* growth rate in food production was negative, dropping at an annual rate greater than 1 per cent. A conservative estimate of the number of African countries now self-sufficient in food would be around six or seven.[45] Commentaries from around the continent stress endemic shortages of foodstuffs, both in urban areas and in the hinterland, and consequent severe inflation in the price of staples.[46]

Much of this poor economic record may be explained in terms of prior underdevelopment with attendant undercapitalization, absence of substantial domestic markets, and shortages of technically skilled indigenous personnel, the legacies of the precolonial and colonial eras. The inefficiency of many foreign assistance programmes, the result of poor planning and coordination, insufficient attention to the characteristics of the local environment and the constraints these impose on the development effort, and bureaucratization, is another important factor. A third is the relatively low level of the flow of private capital to Africa, and the outward movement of African capital. A fourth is the crippling effect of OPEC oil price increases on the region's oil importing economies. In addition to these, the incompetence, irresponsibility, and acquisitiveness of many of the continent's leading political figures and of the bureaucratic and political elites from which they emerge and which they serve, cannot be ignored.

In periods when the pie is growing, it is possible to contain communal and class tensions by sharing out the benefits of development. When the pie is not growing or is shrinking, while the numbers of those trying to eat it are expanding, communal conflict over resources becomes an ever more serious problem.

This may be of greatest import in those states which have had some economic success, as subsequent failure necessarily involves the disappointment of expectations formed in the good years. In this context, Nigeria, once considered one of Africa's few success stories, seems at the moment to be in a particularly parlous state, given its falling oil revenues, government expenditure cutbacks, and rising unemployment. The recent reduction in the price of Nigerian oil in violation of OPEC price guidelines is an indication of its distress, as is the expulsion early in 1983 of 1.5–2 million illegal aliens.

While the internal consequence of this economic collapse may be an acceleration of political fragmentation, the increasing recourse to force in regional disputes suggests that its external impact may be a proliferation of conflict in OAU Africa, as regimes attempt to compensate for their incapacity to cope with internal problems by success in foreign policy. The Moroccan involvement in Western Sahara is a case in point.

The third factor which deserves mention here is the growing regional disparity in military and other forms of power. Zartman, in the article mentioned above,[47] described the regional configuration of power as one of highly diffused and unhierarchical distribution at uniformly low levels. The past decade, however, has witnessed the emergence of a number of significant regional powers whose military capacity far outstrips that of the majority of smaller states in the region.[48] Libya, Ethiopia, Algeria, Morocco, and Nigeria are all examples of this. At least one of them—Libya—displays a pronounced tendency to employ its new military power to acquire a political position in regional affairs commensurate with its inflated self-image. One might ask whether the prominence of Nigeria in the 1982 conflict in Chad does not demonstrate a similar tendency on the part of that country.

To summarize, the current state of regional politics gives little ground for enthusiasm. Economic decay, political fragmentation, growing disparities in military power, the accelerating import of arms, an increasing tendency to resort to force in regional disputes, the erosion of regional norms governing interstate relations, the manifest incapacity of the OAU to cope with internal and regional conflicts, and the apparent collapse of that organization, all justify this pessimism. Intervention from outside the region is on the whole overrated as a source of insecurity. It is instead largely a manifestation of and a response to deeper regional problems. Intervention by both regional and extra-regional actors does, however, accelerate several of these trends by impeding conflict resolution, drawing into question the legitimacy of internal beneficiaries, and, as a general phenomenon, encouraging arms

spending and further undermining regional norms.

The prospect for OAU Africa is one of increasing frustration, disintegration, and frequent use of force. This will persist until the economic situation improves and a new regional structure emerges.[49] The dynamics of this process are largely internal and not susceptible to control from outside. The fact that Africans themselves seem incapable of producing a rapid, tidy, and lasting solution to their problems does not suggest that outsiders would do any better.

NOTES

1. See, for example, A. J. Klinghoffer, *The Angolan War: a study in Soviet foreign policy in the Third World* (Boulder, Col.: Westview, 1980); G. Bender, "Kissinger in Angola: anatomy of a failure" in R. Lemarchand, *American policy in Southern Africa: the stakes and the stances* (Washington: University Press of America, 1981); the contributions by David Hall and Colin Legum in S. Kaplan, *Diplomacy of power: Soviet armed forces as a political instrument* (Washington: Brookings Institution, 1981); D. Yost, "French policy in Chad," *Orbis*, 1983, No. 1; and I. Greig, *The communist challenge in Africa: an analysis of contemporary Soviet, Chinese, and Cuban policies* (London: Foreign Affairs Publishing, 1977).
2. For a useful discussion of the definition of intervention, see J. Rosenau, "Intervention as a scientific concept," *Journal of Conflict Resolution*, Vol. 23, No. 2, pp. 149–71.
3. See R. Lemarchand, "The CIA in Africa: how central? how intelligent?" *Journal of Modern African Studies*, Vol. 14, No. 3, p. 413.
4. For an enumeration and account of these programmes, see P. Lellouche and D. Moisi, "French policy in Africa: a lonely battle against destabilization," *International Security*, Spring 1979. See also D. G. Lavroff, *La politique africaine du General de Gaulle* (Paris: Pedone, 1980) and E. Kolodziej, *French international policy under de Gaulle and Pompidou: the politics of grandeur* (Ithaca: Cornell University Press, 1974).
5. In this context, the NSSM 39 objective of "stabilizing Southern Africa" has been referred to as no more than a euphemism for "continued US presence" (A. Isaacman and J. Davis, "US policy toward Mozambique, 1946–1976" in Lemarchand, *American policy in southern Africa*, p. 35). See also S. Makinda, "Conflict and the superpowers in the Horn of Africa," *Third World Quarterly*, Vol. 4, No. 1, p. 93; G. Bender,

"Kissinger in Angola," passim, and J. G. Liebenow, "American policy in Africa: the Reagan years," *Current History*, Vol. 82, No. 482, pp. 97, 98, 134, 136. The latter two comment at some length on the "globalist" focus of recent American policy-makers.

6. See D. Volsky, "Local conflict and international security," *New Times*, 1983, No. 5, pp. 5–7 and A. Gromyko, "Soviet foreign policy and Africa," *International Affairs* (Moscow), 1982, No. 2, pp. 30–33. See also S. Nolutshungu, "African interests and Soviet power," *Soviet Studies*, Vol. 24, No. 3, p. 399.

7. Walter Lippman, *US foreign policy: shield of the Republic* (Boston: Little, Brown, 1943), p. 51, quoted in A. Wolfers, *Discord and collaboration* (Baltimore, London: Johns Hopkins University Press, 1962), p. 150.

8. See, for example, the speech of General Olusegun Obasanjo to the Khartoum OAU summit in summer 1978, in which he cited as the "basic African questions" national integration, the consolidation of independence, international peace and stability, and the improvement of the material conditions of life. Reprinted in *Survival*, Vol. 20, No. 6, pp. 268–9. See also I. W. Zartman, *International relations in the new Africa* (Englewood Cliffs, NJ: Prentice-Hall, 1966), ch. 4, esp. pp. 149–51.

9. I. W. Zartman, "Africa as a subordinate state system in international relations," *International Organization*, Vol. 21, No. 3, pp. 559–61; and Zartman, *International relations in the new Africa*, p. 147, where the point is made that external violence in Africa was "minimal."

10. Zartman, "Africa as a subordinate state system," p. 560.

11. See, for example, J. Stremlau, *The international politics of the Nigerian civil war* (Princeton, NJ: Princeton University Press, 1977), p. 375, which emphasizes the non-conflictual, rule-governed character of African regional politics.

12. For an account of the level and distribution of the French military presence in Africa, see Lellouche and Moisi, "French policy in Africa," p. 109.

13. See Stremlau, *Nigerian civil war*, pp. 373–5. Stremlau rightly notes, however, that the OAU position was not the only factor favouring non-interference by extra-regional actors. He also mentions in this connection the absence of ideological cleavage between the two sides, the weakness of formal and informal ties between the belligerents and foreign governments, the international preoccupation at the time with the Middle East, and the thaw in relations between the two superpowers.

14. An example is the OAU role in reducing tensions between Mauritania and Morocco.

Zartman (*International relations in the new Africa*, p. 95), for example, cites the cessation of hostile broadcasts between the two countries in the aftermath of the second OAU summit as "a significant step in easing tensions between the two states."

15. Zartman, *International relations in the new Africa*, pp. 88–90, with respect to the Algeria-Moroccan conflict. See also I. Wallerstein, *Africa: the politics of unity* (New York: Random House, 1967), p. 73.

16. *World military expenditures and arms transfers, 1963–1973* (Washington: Arms Control and Disarmament Agency, 1975), table 4. If one omits Egypt, whose primary security preoccupation was the Middle East and not Africa, the figure would be 3.5 per cent.

17. This sentiment is obvious in the numerous OAU resolutions dealing with intervention in Africa, and in African support for UN efforts to prohibit intervention as a mode of behaviour among member states. For the OAU view, see for example the 1977 summit resolution "On interference in the internal affairs of African states," *Africa contemporary record 1977–1978* (New York: Africana, 1978), p. C4, and the 1978 resolution "On military interventions in Africa and on measures to be taken against neocolonial manoeuvres and interventions in Africa," *Africa contemporary record 1978–1979*, p. C19. Nolutshungu ("African interests and Soviet power," p. 405) refers in this context to a "reflex and often effete imperative against intervention" among African states.

18. For an account of the Monrovia debate on Uganda, see C. Legum and Z. Cervenka, "The OAU," in *Africa contemporary record 1979–1980*, pp. A61–A62. It should be noted, however, that the hostility towards Tanzania evident in the debate stemmed also from solidarity with Amin among Muslim leaders and from pressure exerted on non-Muslim leaders by Muslim elements in their national elites (see in this context General Obasanjo's criticism of the Tanzanian action despite the prior Nigerian approval of the invasion).

19. For an account of French military involvement in Mauritania, see *Strategic Survey 1979* (London: International Institute for Strategic Studies, 1980), pp. 93, 96. Despite this assistance, Polisario succeeded in applying sufficient pressure on the Mauritanian regime to induce the July 1978 coup which toppled the Ould Daddah regime. The successor government accepted a ceasefire with Polisario, requested the withdrawal of Moroccan troops in early 1979, and concluded a peace agreement with Polisario in August of the same year. Mauritania renounced its claims to the southern portion of

Western Sahara and subsequently withdrew its forces from that territory.

20. On this point, see W. Skurnik, "Continuing problems in Africa's Horn," *Current History*, Vol. 82, No. 482, p. 123.

21. On the Angolan attitude towards Soviet bases, see J. Marcum, "Angola," in G. Carter and P. O'Meara, eds., *Southern Africa: the continuing crisis* (Bloomington, Ind.: Indiana University Press, 1979), pp. 193–4. Volsky ("Local conflict," p. 5) gives a succinct Soviet view of the contact group's initiatives on Namibia. On this point, see also R. Jaster, "A regional security role for Africa's front-line states: experience and prospects," Adelphi Paper 180 (London: International Institute for Strategic Studies, 1983), pp. 41–2. Gerald Bender has claimed recently that a February 1982 joint Angolan-Cuban statement on conditions for withdrawal of Cuban forces from Angola drew a "stiff rebuke" from the Soviet Union. G. Bender, "The continuing crisis in Angola," *Current History*, Vol. 82, No. 482, p. 138.

22. There is good reason to doubt Soviet and Cuban complicity in this venture, as it constitutes an assault on Somali territory, thereby risking the alienation of other African states.

23. On Ethiopian independence from the Soviet Union in internal policy, see P. Henze, "Communism and Ethiopia," *Problems of Communism*, Vol. 30, No. 3, pp. 63–4; O. Ogunbadejo, "Soviet policies in Africa," *African Affairs*, Vol. 79, No. 316, p. 125; and Nolutshungu, "African interests and Soviet power," p. 410.

24. For an argument along these lines with respect to Angola, see G. Bender, "Kissinger in Angola," pp. 112, 113, 117–19.

25. See the Nigerian position, as elaborated by Obasanjo in the speech cited in note 8.

26. For the meanings of stability, see S. Huntington, "Remarks on the meaning of stability in the modern era," in S. Bialer and K. Sluzar, *Radicalism in the contemporary age, Vol. 3* (Boulder, Col.: Westview, 1977).

27. See Bender, "The continuing crisis," pp. 125, 128.

28. On the permanence of military solutions in the Horn, for example, see Nolutshungu, "African interests and Soviet power," p. 411.

29. Ogunbadejo, "Soviet policies in Africa," p. 125.

30. Lemarchand ("CIA in Africa," p. 418) makes a similar point with reference to regime dependence on covert assistance.

31. See, for example, *Africa Confidential*, Vol. 23, Nos. 2 and 8 for accounts of the impact of foreign affairs on factional conflict within the MPLA.

32. Several leading officials in Goukouni's transitional government defected in the aftermath of the announcement of the merger be-

tween Libya and Chad in January 1981. Habré repeatedly called attention to Goukouni's tie to the "Libyan conqueror" in order to broaden his base of support. See *Keesing's Contemporary Archives*, 1981, pp. 31161–2.

33. *South African Yearbook 1981*, p. 286.

34. R. Hallett, "South African intervention in Angola, 1975–1976," *African Affairs*, Vol. 77, No. 308, p. 363.

35. *World military expenditures and arms transfers, 1970–1979* (Washington: Arms Control and Disarmament Agency, 1980), p. 64. Figures are in constant dollars.

36. For the perceived link between Kenyan security and the activity of communist powers in the Horn, see *Weekly Review* (Nairobi), 27 Feb. 1978, pp. 8–9, 11.

37. See the article on Nigerian defence expenditure by J. de Onis in the *International Herald Tribune*, 16 Jan. 1981. De Onis ascribes this increase to worries over the Libyan action in Chad and quotes President Shagari as saying that "Nigeria was being forced by recent world events to reassess its security and defence expenditure." In view of substantial shortfalls in oil revenues and cutbacks in government expenditure across the board, it is unclear whether these targets have been or will be met. See also *Times*, 14 April 1981.

38. On the downward trend in Nigerian defence expenditure and military manpower, see E. Kolodziej and R. Harkavy, "Introduction," pp. 2, 7, and J. Ostheimer and G. Buckley, "Nigeria," pp. 285–302, both in E. Kolodziej and R. Harkavy, *Security policies of developing countries* (Lexington, Mass., Toronto: Lexington/Heath, 1981).

39. *World military expenditures and arms transfers, 1970–1979*, table 2.

40. *World military expenditures and arms transfers, 1970–1979*, table 2. Ethiopian imports fell from $1.1 billion in 1978 to $192 million in 1979 (both figures in 1978 constant dollars), which closely parallels the regional decrease of $1.2 billion from 1978 to 1979.

41. This trend was recognized by the OAU in its resolution "On the settlement of intra-African disputes" (Libreville, 1977), reprinted in *Africa contemporary record 1977–1978*, p. C6.

42. A. Bolaji Akinyemi, "Africa: a foreign policy perspective," *Daedalus*, Vol. 111, No. 2, p. 251.

43. On this point, see Xan Smiley, "Misunderstanding Africa," *Atlantic Monthly*, Vol. 250, No. 3, p. 79.

44. I have benefited considerably in this discussion from an informal presentation by Mr. Dragoljub Najman to the Africa Research Programme at Harvard University's Center for International Affairs in February 1983.

45. Liebenow, "American policy in Africa," p.

98. The data in the above paragraphs are taken from *Accelerated development in sub-Saharan Africa* (Washington: World Bank, 1981), pp. 3, 18–19, 45. All statistics concerning Africa are somewhat suspect, given rudimentary and sporadic collection techniques, and the wide variation between sources such as the World Bank, the IMF, and the FAO. Food production statistics are particularly problematic, given the existence of widespread subsistence production and black markets. There is little reason, however, to doubt the gravity of the region's economic problems, or that the World Bank figures are broadly representative of regional realities.

46. See, for example, Bender, "The continuing crisis," p. 128; Skurnik, "Continuing problems in Africa's Horn," p. 121 and J. Kraus, "Revolution and the military in Ghana," *Current History*, Vol. 82, No. 482, pp. 116, 131.

47. Zartman, "Africa as a subordinate state system," p. 550.

48. See Nolutshungu, "African interests and Soviet power," p. 406.

49. In this, too, Africa resembles to an increasing degree the rest of the Third World. For a discussion of the increasing likelihood of higher levels of interstate conflict and the use of force in the Third World as a whole, as states redefine the politics of their regions, altering the configurations of territory and power left by the colonial powers, see J. J. Weltman, "War in international politics today" in R. O'Neill and D. Ball, eds., *Strategy and defence* (London, Boston: Allen & Unwin, 1982), pp. 49–50.

The Limits of Leadership: Africa in Contemporary World Politics

Timothy M. Shaw and Naomi Chazan

> As it enters its third decade of independence, Africa faces a troubled future. Its troubles are directly related to the growing pains associated with attempts to establish polities, economies, and societies under a second and third generation of leadership. . . . The third decade is a time for diplomacy, with all the art and skill that the calling can carry.
>
> I. WILLIAM ZARTMAN

> Ideological considerations, as a result of their domestic power structure, are now dominating the foreign policy of a number of African states. . . . And the myth of an innocent Africa, preoccupied only with economic development, should finally be discarded.
>
> MICHAEL RADU

> The immediate decision making setting of foreign policy is . . . highly personalised. To African leaders, as to Renaissance monarchs, sovereignty is an attribute of foreign policy. . . . International relations offer the chance of an escape into the big time world of global politics, which must be justified rhetorically in terms of world peace or third world development, but in which the activity itself is to a large extent its own reward.
>
> CHRISTOPHER CLAPHAM[1]

The role of African leaders in foreign policy has fluctuated dramatically in the twenty years since the halcyon days of early independence. In the optimistic atmosphere of the early 1960s it was taken to be axiomatic that leadership in Africa mattered. Individuals shaped the character and quality of the national polity and ideology, which were the primary determinants of foreign policy. The mood and mode of those times have been well expressed by J. F. Maitland-Jones: "The conduct of foreign affairs [in Africa], like that of much of the rest of

Reprinted from *International Journal*, vol. 37, no. 4 (Autumn 1982), 543–54, by permission of the Canadian Institute of International Affairs.

government, is too frequently the province of one man, the head of state, whose preoccupation amid the urgencies of one-party, one-person rule must accordingly be many and fleeting."[2]

The impact of the individual in moulding orientation and impact may itself have been a transitional phenomenon, however, for this brief golden age of African diplomacy has been eclipsed by a set of subsequent changes which have undermined confidence in both political and analytic categories. When viewed from Africa, the world of the 1980s is both more ambiguous and less amenable than that of the 1960s.[3] Leaders no longer appear to be more important than the structures in which they operate. Structures, in turn, are far less ephemeral than the hands that have sought to manipulate them. Not that leadership is now irrelevant; it is just less salient. In this essay we seek to trace the emergence of new limits on leaders as Africa becomes a more diverse and divergent continent.

THE ELUSIVENESS OF INFLUENCE

The evolution of diplomatic practice and analysis in Africa has been characterized, then, by a shift from personal to structural bases of influence and a trend towards a more complex, more uncertain, and hence more confounding situation. The current group of leaders faces a considerably less generous and less coherent world system. Although African diplomacy is more mature than before, paradoxically African diplomats are more marginal: leadership alone no longer ensures visibility and effect.[4]

This transition from impact to impotence is divisible into three phases which fall conveniently into three decades: the initial period of considerable individual influence during the first independence decade; an era of collective endeavour during the 1970s; and now, in the eighties, a more complicated milieu involving hangovers from the previous two periods, but also distinctive new factors.

Five elements in this tripartite transition can be identified. This cluster of features ranges from the more to the less specific: (1) generational changes among African leaders; (2) distinctive patterns in the bases and behaviours of interstate coalitions; (3) shifts in the rankings of issue-areas (were political, economic, or strategic issues most important?); (4) structural developments in the global and domestic systems; and (5) analytic tendencies away from a focus on leadership, through coalition politics, to a new concern for the politico-economic bases of foreign policy. In short, each decade represents a unique conjuncture of forces and relations. The present period incorporates not only established interests and outcomes but also novel phenomena: a more problematic and perplexing situation for both statesmen and scholars.

INDIVIDUAL INFLUENCE IN THE 1960S

African presidents were recognized and acclaimed as leading actors on the world stage in the early 1960s; as the opening citation from Clapham indicates, having first achieved attention in the nationalist vanguard of the postwar period, they entered an international arena disturbed by superpower politics yet certain about the prospects for economic opportunities. In an essentially confident and nationalist age, each leader designed and expressed his own development strategy and concomitant foreign policy. From the conscious and pragmatic dependency of Félix Houphouët-Boigny of Ivory Coast through the array of "African socialisms" propounded by Léopold Senghor (Senegal), Modibo Keita (Mali), Kenneth Kaunda (Zambia), and Julius Nyerere (Tanzania), to the supposedly "scientific" socialism of Sékou Touré (Guinea) and Kwame Nkrumah (Ghana), each and every African leader guided the initial form of his nation's non-alignment policy and dictated the range of its operative norms.

This first generation was unencumbered by either doubt or precedent; and at a time when the Organization of African Unity (OAU) was first embryonic and later infantile, interstate coalitions were quite fluid and superficial. The designs of and debates among the Brazzaville, Casablanca, and Monrovia blocs were essentially the preserve of individual leaders. The idiosyncratic was supreme as the system, continentally and globally, was expansive and the major issue-area was diplomatic. So Africa's "resources"—an established oral tradition overlaid by a third of the votes in the United Nations system—were both quite appropriate and not insignificant. Only when the major issue-area changed towards more substantive subjects did the narrowness of this power base become apparent. In the interim, leaders vied with each other in separate attempts to rally support and promote pet conceptions; leadership styles were both individualist and competitive.

If the effectiveness of African diplomacy was not question during most of the sixties, neither was the use of the orthodox mode of analysis to describe and explain it. The role of African leaders, particularly the more interesting and elegant ones such as Léopold Senghor and Julius Nyerere, Kwame Nkrumah and Abdel Nasser of Egypt, was examined by extending established diplomatic historiography to a "new" continent. The focus was on individuality and ideology, rather than on process and structure, whether internal or international. It was simply presumed that Kenya's Jomo Kenyatta and Félix Houphouët-Boigny had influence.[5] The transition from the sixties to the seventies and from an expanding global economy to a contracting one evoked critical reservations regarding such commonplace assumptions as Radu notes.

COLLECTIVE INFLUENCE IN THE 1970S

The second decade of independence was, then, a major watershed for African leaders and their followers. The optimism of the 1960s faded as development promises proved illusory. Many of the first generation of nationalist leaders were either overthrown or replaced by less imposing, less secure, and certainly less familiar heads of state. General Ankrah and Kofi Abrefa Busia came in Nkrumah's stead; Idi Amin followed upon Milton Obote's footsteps in Uganda; Anwar Sadat succeeded Nasser; Mengistu Haile Mariam stood in the place of Emperor Haile Selassie of Ethiopia, Moussa Traore in Keita's, Daniel Arap Moi in Kenyatta's. This new diversity of leadership served to break up old-boy networks. A new fluidity was injected into continental affairs, notwithstanding the continuous presence of Houphouët-Boigny, Kaunda, Nyerere, and King Hassan of Morocco.

Meanwhile, the difficulties confronting this second generation were multiplying: if the United Nations' First Development Decade produced disappointing results, the fruits of the second decade were even more scattered. In response to both economic underdevelopment and diplomatic decline, Africa attempted to forge one cohesive coalition based on the OAU in association with Afro-Arab and Third World alignments. Collective advocacy of a New International Economic Order was a response, then, to diplomatic fragmentation and developmental frustration.

Yet while the continent could mobilize a considerable number of votes on such economic issues, its negligible productive capacity exposed the limits of this sort of power. In a decade during which economic issues became central, the continent's ability to exert influence decreased. Despite the longevity of certain founding fathers and despite the occasional economic success story of a Nigeria, a Kenya, or an Ivory Coast, Africa as a whole became more marginal in the global economy. Its diplomatic maturation could not stem this inexorable tide. Moreover, the incidence and intensity of interstate conflict grew—Chad, Nigeria, Sudan, Somalia, Sahara—so that increasingly scarce resources were spent on strategic rather than on diplomatic or economic pursuits. Benign, intra-continental coalitions were transformed into more malignant extra-continental alliances in which a range of middle powers, from Cuba to France, joined the superpowers in seeking an interventionist role in Africa. In these conditions the essential equality of African states and statesmen began to disappear as a few leaders and producers—of petroleum, minerals, commodities, and services—came to play bigger parts than their less fortunate counterparts.

The role of leaders shifted in turn with these currents. Increased value was placed on arbitration and co-ordination rather than on declaration and determination. Leaders capable of promoting conciliation and advancing compromise assumed prominence at the expense of those who, a decade earlier, held sway because of their originality and vision. Much as the first decade commended foresight and innovation, the second demanded of its leaders the more subtle and less developed skills of mediation and unobtrusiveness.

This quite abrupt shift in the fortunes of the continent's states led, eventually, to a transition in mode of analysis. (Academics are rarely noted for their prescience.) As neither the idiosyncratic nor the diplomatic was dominant any longer, and as global structures began to impinge upon Africa's independence, so notions of political economy and dependence were gradually popularized. The diplomatic history tradition was joined by *dependencia* as a means of explaining the continent's underdevelopment and stagnation. The focus on rhetoric was supplanted by a new realism in which only a few resourceful countries and cadres survived: Algeria and Nigeria in the first category and Kaunda and Sir Seretse Khama of Botswana in the second. Idealistic ideologues, such as Nasser, Nkrumah, and Algeria's Ben Bella, were succeeded by less flamboyant technocrats, such as Bendjedid Chadli in Algeria and Abdou Diouf in Senegal. With inflation and recession the world system evolved towards protectionism as Africa became less able, for reasons of both economic and diplomatic decline, to affect it: despite superpower détente, neither North-South dialogue nor global negotiations could turn around international structures to reverse the apparently ineluctable trend towards inequalities both within the continent and between Africa and the rest of the world.

Uncertain Influence in the 1980s

The new decade of the eighties represents, then, a considerably more sobering environment with which African leaders must contend. First, it is more complicated: strands from the previous two decades, such as coalitions and resolutions, are part of the contemporary web. Secondly, it is much more hierarchical: a few countries continue to grow, while the majority get ever poorer. And thirdly, it is much more dangerous: choices are limited, constraints are multiple, calculations have therefore to be rather fine. The general global depression intensifies continental gloom both at the present time and for the foreseeable future; the golden age of African diplomacy seems to grow more distant.

If the 1960s were characterized by individual influence and the 1970s by collective influence, then the 1980s by comparison seem to be distinguished by minimal and uneven influence. The continent as a whole is marginal in a world of strategic stand-offs and economic stagnation. Individual diplomacy and collective coalitions are no longer particularly salient. A variety of generations and issues competes for attention as Zartman has noted; no single factor or forum is dominant. Meanwhile, economic decline, political decay, and diplomatic demise are suggestive of the continent's return to obscurity relieved only by occasional wars and uneven achievements. Most of the conflicts are of long standing and low intensity (e.g., Ethiopia, Somali, Chad, Sahara) and the successes are of ambiguous consequence (e.g., the rapid rise and fall of oil revenues in Libya and Nigeria).

But if leadership is scarce, issues unclear, and influence problematic, the trend towards inequalities appears irreversible, with profound implications for the future of African diplomacy. For the major feature of the contemporary international division of labour is the rise of new middle powers such as Brazil and Mexico in Latin America and Nigeria and Zimbabwe in Africa. Their relative industrialization and consequent influence is a function of their intermediate status at the crossroads of the industrialized and underdeveloped worlds rather than of their national leadership. In a competitive situation of Realpolitik they alone have the resource bases which matter. So their external influence is related to the character of their political economy rather than to the quality of their leadership. President Shehu Shagari, for example, attracts respect and garners favours because he represents Nigeria rather than for his individual skills no matter how considerable. Conversely, Mwalimu Nyerere is less influential now than ever before because individual pleas for liberation and experiment count for less.

On the one hand, the character of coalitions is beginning to reflect the realities of divergent political economies and, on the other, structural capabilities, global and continental cleavages, are less reflective of the ideological or the idiosyncratic than of differences in performance and absorptive potential. The moderate-radical distinctions of yesteryear were reflections of leadership roles (Nkrumah in Casablanca and Tubman in Monrovia), as were the variations between the reliable and the unpredictable African states of the 1970s (Amin's Uganda versus Kenyatta's Kenya; Houphouët-Boigny's Ivory Coast as opposed to Bokassa's Central African Empire; Senghor's Senegal and Ahidjo's Cameroon but not Macias Nguema's Equatorial Guinea). Current antagonisms are less a product of personalities than of longer-range factors inherent in the anatomy of state structures. Such divisions cannot be readily resolved, as were the more ephemeral disagreements prior to the founding of the OAU in 1963. Preparations for the twentieth anniversary of that oganization are already marked by tensions arising from both interstate conflicts and distinctive development orientations. Leadership style is increasingly unimportant, whereas the differences in structural capacity of member-states have become more salient and more intractable.

The evolution in the continent towards deep-seated and deep-rooted rather than temporary differences between states has profound implications for scholars as well as statesmen; these are beginning to be reflected in innovative modes of analysis which focus on the state and social relations rather than on charisma and integration, on political economy rather than on diplomatic or strategic questions.[6] So foreign policy capability or potential is conceived as a function not only of the national product but also of class interactions and coalitions within each particular political economy. Astute leadership is not enough; degrees of industrialization, of contradiction, and of collaboration and alienation are the crucial variables. It is therefore difficult to accept Christopher Clapham's assertion about the essential commonality of the continent as Africanness is no longer as apparent as diversity:

> The states of sub-Saharan Africa have enough in common to make comparative treatment of their foreign policy making processes a matter of more than simple geographical convenience. Though their place in the international stratification system and particularly their economic underdevelopment make them very much part of the third world, with all the general foreign policy consequences which that implies, they pos-

sess in addition features which are distinctively African.[7]

Contemporary realities serve to undermine similarities and to underline inequalities. Nevertheless, some leaders exert inconsistent influences at the poles. Those representing the emerging regional powers compete for continental visibility and supremacy; those at the helm of collapsing states may have a dubious nuisance value; while most African leaders, together with the states they head, seem to be receding into an unpropitious political oblivion.

ALTERNATIVE EXPLANATIONS OF INFLUENCE

As external influence has become less a function of individual leadership and more a function of structural proficiency, so alternative explanations have been advanced for African foreign policies. The first generation of African(ist) scholars assumed that the first generation of African statesmen achieved influence because of the irresistibleness of their ideologies. However, as the first generation of scholars and statesmen was succeeded by second and third generations, and as the African and global systems became more competitive and hierarchical, so national attributes and structural conditions came to balance the idiosyncratic. The compelling idealism of a Nyerere is now matched by the calculating realism of the Nigerian leadership; the radicalism of FRELIMO leader Samora Machel is balanced by the external openness of an Houphouët-Boigny. Moreover, the ability to put interstate coalitions together, as displayed by, say, Algerian or Kenyan diplomats, enables certain states to exert an influence beyond their objective national capabilities.

In addition to the new diversity in the bases of and centres for African diplomacy, informal associations have joined formal institutions as participants in international relations: intergovernmental and non-governmental organizations, from the United Nations Economic Commission for Africa

(ECA) to the African Bar Association, have widened the scope for both leaders and followers in external affairs.[8] Indeed, outstanding leadership in, for example, the ECA—Professor Adebayo Adedeji[9]—and the All-African Council of Churches— Canon Burgess Carr—has enabled Africans in such transnational organizations to achieve individual and institutional attention at least equal to that of leading heads of state. Such roles and bases add further to the fluidity of current African affairs.

WHAT FUTURE FOR LEADERSHIP IN AFRICA?

Changes in the actuality and analysis of African diplomacy have important implications for the future: will leadership continue to decline in salience relative to structural characteristics? Or might continental conditions change so that individual as well as national qualities will once again come to the fore? Futures studies have improved considerably in scope and sophistication in recent years. Nevertheless, alternative scenarios for the mid-term future— until the end of the century—are still not very rigorous or reliable.

However, in conclusion, there appear to be two sets of predictions and prescriptions for Africa which could be said to constitute broad alternative viewpoints: they imply divergent futures for different types of leadership. First, emerging from Adedeji's ECA in association with the OAU is the *Lagos Plan of Action for the Economic Development of Africa 1980–2000*.[10] The touchstone of this plan is collective self-reliance: the partial and gradual disengagement of Africa from the global economy and concentration on its own resources and needs. If the plan's proposal of an African common market by the year 2000 is to be realized even in part, then the continent's position in the world system will have to change dramatically over the next fifteen years. In this case, the prospects for individual leadership would continue to fade while those for collective action would improve. And if Africa's economy were revived through such an inward-looking ori-

entation, then the bases for certain kinds of diplomatic initiative and influence in the future would be laid.

By contrast, the World Bank perspective, *Accelerated Development in Sub-Saharan Africa: agenda for action*,[11] advocates extended and expanded external incorporation, agricultural commodity production for export, and privatization of the parastatal sector, the ubiquitous state-corporate nexus. If this alternative agenda is adopted, then a few individual leaders in the most incorporated states, such as the Ivory Coast and Kenya, will likely be accorded enhanced external visibility while the prospects for the emergence of either other leaders or a continental caucus will be reduced. Such an approach might mean increased inequalities and vulnerabilities, with especially grim implications for the more marginal and radical states. In this context, quixotic leadership patterns could prevail. In short, Africa's eventual choice between the plan and the agenda—that is, between more co-operative self-reliance and more divisive external association respectively[12]—has implications not only for its development possibilities but also for its diplomatic prospects: the balance between leadership and structure, between national attributes and external situations.

In practice, of course, neither the OAU nor the World Bank proposal is likely to be accepted and implemented either unanimously or in its entirety. Rather, the more peripheral states will tend to prefer the provisions and projections of the plan while more industrialized interests will opt for the agenda, thereby perhaps further intensifying the complexities and ambiguities of the continental condition.

By contrast, the analytic future may be both more clear cut and more encouraging: the emergence of political economy, with its stress on structural continuities and asymmetrical relations, as the dominant mode of analysis. As Zartman notes in his own review of African diplomacy during this decade: "The African state is currently under attack, both from within and without. . . . Problems of succession, secession, and liberation are beginning to swarm. . . . Such problems, combined with those of developing in a stagflating world, have led African states to seek new mixes of unity and independence, particularly in the economic field."[13] These mixes will continue to animate diplomats as well as analysts, as leaders tend to operate more in the constrained social contexts of the present and future than as the distinctive individualists of past times.

NOTES

1. I. William Zartman, "Issues of African diplomacy in the 1980s," Orbis 25 (winter 1982), 1025; Michael Radu, "Ideology, parties, and foreign policy in sub-Saharan Africa," ibid., 992; Christopher Clapham, "Sub-Saharan Africa" in his collection on Foreign Policy Making in Developing States: a comparative approach (Aldershot, 1977), 87.

2. J. F. Maitland-Jones, Politics in Africa: the former British territories (New York, 1973), 191.

3. See Timothy M. Shaw, "Which way Africa? ECA and IBRD responses to the continental crisis," in Timothy M. Shaw and Olajide Aluko, eds., Africa Projected (London, 1983).

4. See Timothy M. Shaw, "Introduction: towards a political economy of African foreign policy" and "Conclusion: the future of a political economy of African foreign policy" in Timothy M. Shaw and Olajide Aluko, eds., The Political Economy of African Foreign Policy: comparative analysis (Aldershot, forthcoming).

5. On these and other leaders, see Ali A. Mazrui, "Nationalists and statesmen: from Nkrumah and De Gaulle to Nyerere and Kissinger," Journal of African Studies 6 (winter 1979/80), 199–205.

6. For overviews of these changes, see Timothy M. Shaw, "Review article: Foreign policy, political economy and the future: reflections on Africa in the world system," African Affairs 79 (April 1980), 260–8, and "Class, Country and Corporation: Africa in the capitalist world system," in Donald I. Ray et al., eds., Into the 1980s: proceedings of the 11th Annual Conference of the Canadian Association of African Studies (2 vols; Vancouver, 1981), II, 19–37.

7. Clapham, "Sub-Saharan Africa," 98.

8. For an introduction and explanation, see Naomi Chazan, "The new politics of participation in tropical Africa," Comparative Politics 14 (January 1982), 169–89.

9. See, in particular, his role in preparing and popularizing the Lagos Plan of Action for the Economic Development of Africa 1980–2000 (Geneva: International Institute for Labour Studies, 1981). One instance of this is his essay on "Development and economic growth in Africa to the year 2000: alternative projections and policies," in Timothy M. Shaw, ed., Alternative Futures for Africa (Boulder, CO, 1982), 279–304.

10. See Lagos Plan of Action.

11. (Washington, 1981).

12. See Timothy M. Shaw, "OAU: the forgotten economic debate," West Africa 3375 (12 April 1982), 983–4, and "World economy: Africans respond to World Bank study," Africa News 18 (10 May 1982), 2.

13. Zartman, "Issues of African diplomacy in the 1980s," 1029.

Why Africa's Weak States Persist:
The Empirical and the Juridical in Statehood

Robert H. Jackson and Carl G. Rosberg

Black Africa's forty-odd states are among the weakest in the world. State institutions and organizations are less developed in the sub-Saharan region than almost anywhere else; political instability (as indicated by coups, plots, internal wars, and similar forms of violence) has been prevalent in the two-and-a-half decades during which the region gained independence from colonial rule. Most of the national governments exercise only tenuous control over the people, organizations, and activities within their territorial jurisdictions. In almost all of these countries, the populations are divided along ethnic lines; in some, there has been a threat of political disorder stemming from such divisions; in a few, disorder has deteriorated into civil warfare. Some governments have periodically ceased to control substantial segments of their country's territory and population. For example, there have been times when Angola, Chad, Ethiopia, Nigeria, Sudan, Uganda, and Zaire have ceased to be "states" in the empirical sense—that is, their central governments lost control of important areas in their jurisdiction during struggles with rival political organizations.

In spite of the weakness of their national governments, none of the Black African states have been destroyed or even significantly changed. No country has disintegrated into smaller jurisdictions or been absorbed into a larger one against the wishes of its legitimate government and as a result of violence or the threat of violence. No territories or people—or even a

segment of them—have been taken over by another country. No African state has been divided as a result of internal warfare. In other words, the serious empirical weaknesses and vulnerabilities of some African states have not led to enforced jurisdictional change. Why not? How can the persistence of Africa's weak states be explained? In order to answer the latter question, we must enquire into contemporary African political history as well as into the empirical and juridical components of statehood. An investigation of this question has implications not only for our understanding of African states and perhaps other Third World states, but also of statehood and contemporary international society.

The Concept of Statehood

Many political scientists employ a concept of the state that is influenced by Max Weber's famous definition: a corporate group that has compulsory jurisdiction, exercises continuous organization, and claims a monopoly of force over a territory and its population, including "all action taking place in the area of its jurisdiction."[1] As Weber emphasized, his definition is one of "means" and not "ends," and the distinctive means for him are force.[2] A definition of the state primarily in terms of means rather than ends—particularly the means of force—emphasizes the empirical rather than the juridical, the *de facto* rather than the *de jure*, attributes of statehood. This emphasis is undoubtedly an important element in the appeal of Weber's sociology of the state to political scientists. To be sure, Weber does not overlook the

From *World Politics*, vol. 35, no. 1 (October 1982), 1–24. Copyright © 1982 by Princeton University Press. Reprinted by permission of Princeton University Press.

juridical aspects of statehood. However, he does not explore what many students of international law consider to be the true character of territorial jurisdiction: the reality that such jurisdiction is an international legal condition rather than some kind of sociological given.

By Weber's definition, the basic test of the existence of a state is whether or not its national government can lay claim to a monopoly of force in the territory under its jurisdiction. If some external or internal organization can effectively challenge a national government and carve out an area of monopolistic control for itself, it thereby acquires the essential characteristic of statehood. According to Weber's *de facto* terms of statehood, two concurrent monopolies of force cannot exist over one territory and population. In situations where one of several rival groups—that is, claimant states—is unable to establish permanent control over a contested territory, Weber would maintain that it is more appropriate to speak of "statelessness."

By Weber's definition, a few of Africa's governments would not qualify as states—at least not all of the time—because they cannot always effectively claim to have a monopoly of force throughout their territorial jurisdictions. In some countries, rivals to the national government have been able to establish an effective monopoly of force over significant territories and populations for extended periods—for example, Biafra in Nigeria and Katanga in the Congo (now Zaire). In other countries—such as Chad and Uganda—some of the territories have not been under the continuous control of one permanent political organization, and a condition of anarchy has existed. Furthermore, the governments of many Black African countries do not effectively control all of the important public activities within their jurisdictions; in some, government is perilously uncertain, so that important laws and regulations cannot be enforced with confidence and are not always complied with. If the persistence of a state were primarily the result of empirical statehood, some sub-Saharan African countries would clearly not qualify as states some of the time. Yet it is evident that all of them persist as members of the international society of states; it is also evident that none of the claimant governments that have on occasion exercised *de facto* control over large territories and populations within the jurisdictions of existing states have yet succeeded in creating new states in these areas.

Definitions that give priority to the juridical rather than the empirical attributes of statehood are employed by international legal scholars and institutionally oriented international theorists. One such definition—which shares a number of characteristics with Weber's, but gives them a different emphasis—is that of Ian Brownlie, a British legal scholar. Following the Montevideo Convention on Rights and Duties of States, Brownlie describes the state as a legal person, recognized by international law, with the following attributes: (a) a defined territory, (b) a permanent population, (c) an effective government, and (d) independence, or the right "to enter into relations with other states."[3]

If the assumption of juridical statehood as a sociological given is a shortcoming of Weber's definition, a limitation of Brownlie's is the tendency to postulate that the empirical attributes of statehood—i.e., a permanent population and effective government—are as definite as the juridical attributes; they are not. What does it mean to say that a state consists, *inter alia*, of a permanent population and an effective government? Our research reveals that within sub-Saharan African states, these empirical properties have been highly variable, while the juridical components have been constant. Kenya's population has been more "permanent" and its government more "effective" than Uganda's; yet both states have survived as sovereign jurisdictions. Moreover, an exclusively legal approach cannot adequately deal with the empirical properties of statehood: "Once a state has been established, extensive civil strife or the breakdown of order through foreign invasion or natural disasters are not considered to affect personality."[4] In the formulation of concepts, empirical properties can be determined only by investigation, not by definition.[5] Although Brownlie recognizes the need to incorporate empirical criteria into a "working legal definition of statehood,"[6] he acknowledges (as do other scholars) that there is considerable difficulty in employing these criteria without specifying them concretely. Nonetheless, his definition enables us to undertake an analysis of the empirical as well as the juridical aspects of statehood—that is, a sociological-legal analysis.

Political scientists do not need to be convinced of the limitations of an exclusively legalistic approach to the state, which is usually summed up as "legal-formalism": an undue emphasis on abstract rules, leading to the neglect of concrete behavior and the social conditions that support or undermine legal rules.[7] What is more difficult is to convince a generation of political scientists whose theories and models were formulated in reaction to legal, institutional, and philosophical studies of the state, of the limitations of an exclusively sociological conception of statehood. However, if one assumes that the state is essentially an empirical phenomenon—as was suggested not only by Weber but also by David Easton in a systems approach that has been very influential—one cannot explain why some states manage to persist when important empirical conditions of statehood are absent, or are present only in a very qualified manner.[8] In sum, one cannot explain the persistence of some "states" by using a concept of the state that does not give sufficient attention to the juridical properties of statehood.

THE EMPIRICAL STATE IN BLACK AFRICA

Weber's and Brownlie's definitions of statehood provide a useful point of departure for examining empirical and juridical statehood in contemporary Black Africa. (Juridical statehood is discussed in the following section.) We shall begin with Brownlie's definition, which is more explicit and current. As we noted above, Brownlie specifies two empirical attributes of the state: "a permanent population [which] is intended to be used in association with that of territory, and connotes a stable community," and an "effective government, with centralized administrative and legislative organs."[9]

Before we can apply Brownlie's empirical attributes to our analysis, we must clarify them. First, what exactly do we understand by "a stable community" and its crucial empirical component, "a permanent population"? In attempting to define these terms in the context of contemporary Africa, we find that political sociology may be of considerably more help than law. In political sociology, societies are seen as integrated or disunited, culturally homogeneous or fragmented—resting on common norms and values or not. If we take "a stable community" to signify an integrated political community resting on a common culture, we must conclude that few contemporary Black African states can be said to possess this attribute. The populations of many Black African countries are divided internally among several—and often many—distinctive ethnic entities by differences of language, religion, race, region of residence, and so forth. Moreover, these ethnic cleavages can reinforce each other, thus aggravating the differences. In Sudan, for example, the racial division between Arabs and Africans is reinforced by geography, religion, and language; it has resulted in bitter conflicts over the control of the state. Furthermore, many ethnic entities are divided by international boundaries, with members residing in two or more countries; however, the social and political boundaries between these ethnic entities may well be more significant in terms of public attitudes and behavior than are the boundaries between the countries. As a result, political tensions and conflicts arising from ethnic divisions can seriously affect national political stability and the capacity of governments to control their territories.

From our discussion, it appears that few African states can qualify as stable communities. Where ethnic divisions have been politicized, the result has been serious civil conflict. Thus, ethnic divisions have been a major factor contributing to extreme disorder or civil war in the following countries: Sudan (1956–1972); Rwanda (1959–1964); Zaire (1960–1965; 1977–1978); Ethiopia (1962–1982); Zanzibar (1964); Burundi (1966–1972); Chad (1966–1982); Uganda

(1966; 1978–1982); Nigeria (1967–1970); and Angola (1975–1982). In other countries, ethnic divisions have been sufficiently threatening to prompt governments to control political participation severely out of fear that they would otherwise jeopardize their command of the state.[10] Recent African politics have been characterized by the opposition of most African governments to competitive party systems, their preference for political monopoly generally, their lack of sympathy for federalism, and their attack on political liberties (among other things). All of these can be explained at least in part by the governments' fear of politicized ethnicity. Efforts by African governments to emphasize the "nation" and "nationalism" at the expense of the "ethnos"—efforts that are evident elsewhere in the Third World as well—indicate their concern about the instability of their political communities and the threat posed by that instability not only to individual governments, but to statehood itself.[11]

Second, by "an effective government" Brownlie means exactly what Weber means by "compulsory jurisdiction": centralized administrative and legislative organs.[12] Such a definition is somewhat Eurocentric because it identifies governing not only with administering, but also with legislating. In contemporary Africa, governments do not necessarily govern by legislation; personal rulers often operate in an arbitrary and autocratic manner by means of commands, edicts, decrees, and so forth.[13] To make this empirical attribute more universal, let us redefine it as a centralized government with the capacity to exercise control over a state's territory and the people residing in it. By "exercise control" we mean the ability to pronounce, implement, and enforce commands, laws, policies, and regulations.

The capacity to exercise control raises the question of means. Analytically, the means of government can be considered in terms of the domestic authority or right to govern (legitimacy) on the one hand, and the power or ability to govern on the other. In Michael Oakeshott's terms, the modern state consists, among other things, of both an "office of authority" and "an apparatus

of power"; the two are analytically different and should not be confused.[14] For example, governmental administration usually involves the (delegated) authority to issue regulations *and* the power to enforce them. A government may possess legitimacy, but have little in the way of an effective apparatus of power; or it may have an imposing power apparatus, but little legitimacy in the eyes of its citizens. Other combinations are also possible.[15]

In our judgment, the capacity of Africa's governments to exercise control hinges upon three factors: domestic authority, the apparatus of power, and economic circumstances. First, political authority in Africa (and in other parts of the Third World as well) tends to be personal rather than institutional. Geertz has commented:

Fifteen years ago, scholarly writings on the New States . . . were full of discussions of parties, parliaments, and elections. A great deal seemed to turn on whether these institutions were viable in the Third World and what adjustments in them . . . might prove necessary to make them so. Today, nothing in those writings seems more *passé*, relic of a different time.[16]

Constitutional and institutional offices that are independent of the personal authority of rulers have not taken root in most Black African countries. Instead, the state and state offices are dominated by ambitious individuals, both civilian and military. Post-independence rulers of Africa and Asia, Geertz writes, "are autocrats, and it is as autocrats, and not as preludes to liberalism (or, for that matter, to totalitarianism), that they, and the governments they dominate, must be judged and understood."[17] Wherever African governments have exercised substantial control, strong personal rulers have been firmly in the saddle. This has been the case in regimes that are primarily autocratic—such as Félix Houphouët-Boigny's Ivory Coast, H. Kamazu Banda's Malawi, Omar Bongo's Gabon, Ahmadou Ahidjo's Cameroon, and Gnassingbé Eyadéma's Togo. It has also been the case where regimes are primarily oligarchic—such as Léopold Sédar Senghor's Senegal, Jomo Kenyatta's Kenya, and Gaafar Mohamed Numeiri's Sudan—

and where they are primarily ideological—such as Julius Nyerere's Tanzania and Sékou Touré's Guinea (which exhibits features of despotism as well). Where African governments have not exercised control, it has often been because no personal leader has taken firm command; alternatively, it has been as a result of excessively arbitrary and abusive personal rule, as was the case in Uganda under Idi Amin. In the most unstable African regimes, the military has repeatedly intervened in politics—as in Benin from 1960 to 1972 and in Chad from 1975 to 1982.

Related to the problem of institutional weakness in African states is the disaffection of important elites from the government. The frequency of military coups is perhaps the best indication of elite alienation and disloyalty. Between 1958 and the summer of 1981, more than 41 successful coups had taken place in 22 countries of Black Africa; in addition, there had been many unsuccessful ones.[18] Gutteridge has noted that, "by 1966, military intervention in politics in Africa had become endemic. . . . Even the smallest armies [had] carried out successful coups."[19] There is little doubt that the internal opponent most feared by African rulers—both military and civilian—is the military. Indeed, military rulers have themselves been the victims of military coups—for instance, Yakubu Gowon of Nigeria, and Ignatius Kutu Acheampong and Frederick Akuffo of Ghana in the 1970s. It should be noted that, although Africa's military formations are called "armies" and their members wear uniforms and display other symbols of state authority, they cannot be assumed to be loyal to the government. A military career is sometimes a promising avenue for political advancement; soldiers in Black Africa have become not only government officials, but also rulers of their countries.

Second, the apparatus of power in African governments—the agents and agencies that implement and enforce government laws, edicts, decrees, orders, and the like—can in general be considered "underdeveloped" in regard both to their stock of resources and to the deployment of these resources. In proportion to their territories and populations, African governments typically have a smaller stock of finances, personnel, and materiel than Asian or Western governments, and their staffs are less experienced and reliable. As a result, the concept of governmental administration as a policy instrument bears less relation to reality. Governmental incapacity is exacerbated by overly ambitious plans and policies that are prepared on the assumption that underdevelopment is a problem of economy and society, but not of government. In fact, it is also African governments that are underdeveloped, and in most countries they are very far from being an instrument of development.[20] The modern "administrative state" image of government is of questionable applicability in many parts of the world, but Black African governments are even less likely than others to be rational agencies.

Undoubtedly the biggest problem of both civilian and military administrations in Africa is the questionable reliability of staffs. In a famous phrase, Gunnar Myrdal characterized the governments of South Asia as "soft states."[21] The term can be applied equally to many governments in Black Africa which must operate amidst corruption and disorder. The problem of inefficient staff has rarely been as candidly exposed as in a 1977 report by Julius Nyerere on socialist progress in Tanzania. He noted that ministries were overspending in disregard of severe budgetary restraints; the Rural Development Bank was issuing loans that were not being repaid; state enterprises were operating far below capacity—sometimes at less than 50 percent; "management" was preoccupied with privilege and displayed little enterprise; and "workers" were slack, incompetent, and undisciplined.[22]

Of course, there is considerable variation in the administrative capacity of African governments, and Tanzania is by no means the country most seriously affected by an inefficient state apparatus. While the comparative effectiveness of the Ivory Coast, Kenya (at least under Kenyatta), and Malawi is striking, Benin, Congo-Brazzaville, Mali, Togo, and Upper Volta are infamous for their swollen bureaucracies and administrative lethargy. Once relatively efficient Ghana and Uganda are examples of marked deterioration, the origins of which are perhaps more political than economic and relate to a failure to establish an effective and responsible ruling class. One of the worst cases of administrative decay is Zaire, where the state's resources have been plundered and regulations abused by government officials at all levels. President Mobutu Sese Seko has identified abuses such as the case of army officers who divert for "their own personal profit the supplies intended for frontline soldiers"; the refusal of rural development officials to leave their air-conditioned offices in Kinshasa; and the "misuse of judicial machinery for revenging private disputes, . . . selective justice depending upon one's status and wealth."[23] So extreme is the corruption that observers have had to invent new phrases to describe it; Zaire has been referred to as "an extortionist culture" in which corruption is a "structural fact" and bribery assumes the form of "economic mugging."[24] It has been estimated that as much as 60 percent of the annual national budget is misappropriated by the governing elite.

As we have noted, the inefficiency of African governments extends to the military as well as the civilian organs of the state. As in the case of civilian maladministration, military ineffectiveness stems from socio-political as well as technical-material factors; the size and firepower of the armed forces can also play a role. Typically, military forces in African countries are small in relation to the size or population of a state; however, they are considerably larger than the colonial armies they replaced. Over the past two decades, the size of African armies has increased (primarily for purposes of internal security), and their equipment has been upgraded. As early as 1970, Gutteridge commented that "there is no doubting a general upward trend in the numbers of men under arms in regular forces";[25] there have been no significant developments since 1970 to suggest any change in what appears to be military "growth without development."

In practice, most African armies are less like military organizations and more like political establishments: they are infected by corruption, factionalism, and patterns of authority based not only on rank, role, or function, but also on personal and ethnic loyalties. The ability of African armies to deal with internal conflicts is dubious. Despite overwhelming superiority in men and equipment, the Nigerian Federal Army had great difficulty in defeating the forces of Biafra in the late 1960s; according to Gutteridge, "there were times when the Federal Army seemed to have lost the will to win."[26] Moreover, the state's apparatus of power may be not only aided and supported by the solicited intervention of a foreign power in the form of troops, military equipment, advisers, and so forth, but such intervention can be essential to the survival of a regime. In a number of French-speaking countries, a French military presence has enhanced the power of the African government; in Angola and Ethiopia, Cuban soldiers and Soviet arms and advisers have made a decisive difference to the power and survival of incumbent African regimes in their conflicts with both internal and external powers. The lethargy of African armies has sometimes been acutely embarrassing. When Zaire's copper-rich Shaba Province (formerly Katanga) was invaded by Katangan forces from neighboring Angola in 1977 and again in 1978, President Mobutu's army proved incapable of stopping them; Mobutu had to call upon friendly powers (Morocco, Belgium, France, and the United States) to save his regime.

Third, governmental incapacity in Black Africa is affected by economic circumstances, which are exacerbated by the small size of the skilled work force. African economies are among the poorest and weakest in the world: in 1978, 22 of them had a per capita GNP below $250; throughout the 1970s, the Black African countries had the lowest worldwide rates of growth. Of the world's poorest countries—those with per capita incomes below $330—the 28 that were African had the lowest projected growth rates for the 1980s. In many of these countries, absolute poverty is increasing as birthrates continue to exceed economic growth rates.[27]

Many African countries are highly dependent on a few primary exports for their foreign exchange earnings. They are therefore vulnerable to uncontrollable fluctuations in world commodity prices and, in the case of agricultural commodities, unpredictable changes in weather conditions and harvest returns. The countries without petroleum resources have had to face dramatically increased prices for oil imports, resulting in very severe balance-of-payments problems. In some countries, more than 50 percent of scarce foreign exchange had to be used to pay for imported oil. Moreover, 27 countries had a shortfall in their production of food crops—principally maize—in 1980; they were therefore forced to import food, which resulted in a further drain of scarce foreign exchange. (South Africa became an important supplier of food to Angola, Kenya, Malawi, Mozambique, Zaire, and Zambia, among others.) Lacking industrial and manufacturing sectors of any significance and being highly dependent upon imports, most African countries are caught between the certainty of their demand for foreign goods and the uncertainty of their ability to earn the foreign exchange to pay for them. In many (if not most) of these countries, inflated and consumption-oriented government administrations—whose members enjoy a standard of living far in excess of the national average—weigh down the already overburdened and sluggish economies; in many, the economy is simply exploited to support the political class. The hope that intelligent government planning might effect a substantial economic transformation has long since faded.

It is evident that the term "empirical state" can only be used selectively to describe many states in Black Africa today. With some notable exceptions—for example, Kenya and the Ivory Coast—it seems accurate to characterize Africa's states as empirically weak or underdeveloped. If we adopted a narrow empirical criterion of statehood—such as Weber's monopoly of force—we would have to conclude that some African countries were not states, and that statehood in others has periodically been in doubt. In 1981, the governments of Angola, Chad, Ethiopia, and Uganda could not claim a monopoly of force within their jurisdictions. Furthermore, these countries and some others— for example, Nigeria, Sudan, and Zaire— have exhibited *de facto* statelessness in the past, and there are reasons to believe that they might do so again. Yet it is unlikely that any of their jurisdictions will be altered without the consent of their governments. Jurisdictional change by consent has happened, however. In 1981, The Gambia was forced to call upon neighboring Senegal for troops to put down an armed rebellion by a substantial segment of its own field force under the leadership of leftist militants. The episode undermined the security of the Gambian government to such an extent that it consented to a form of association with Senegal which resulted in a new confederation: Senegambia.

THE JURIDICAL STATE IN BLACK AFRICA

Before we investigate the significance of the juridical state in Black Africa, let us emphasize that "juridical statehood" is not only a normative but essentially an international attribute. The juridical state is both a creature and a component of the international society of states, and its properties can only be defined in international terms. At this point, it is important to clarify what is meant by "international society."[28] It is a society composed solely of states and the international organizations formed by states; it excludes not only individuals and private groups, but also political organizations that are not states or are not composed of states. The doctrine of "states' rights"—that is, sovereignty—is the central principle of international society. It often comes into conflict with the doctrine of international human rights, but international society does not promote the welfare of individuals and private groups within a country or transnational groups among countries; nor does it protect individuals or private groups from their governments.[29] Rather, international society provides legal protection for member states from any powers, internal and external, that seek to intervene in, invade, encroach upon, or otherwise assault their sovereignty.[30] A secondary but increasingly important goal—one that is linked to the emergence of Third World states—is to promote the welfare and development of member states.

According to Brownlie, the juridical attributes of statehood are "territory" and "independence" (as recognized by the international community). In international law, a demarcated territory is the equivalent of the "property" of a government—national real estate, including off-shore waters and airspace; international boundaries are the mutually acknowledged but entirely artificial lines where one government's property rights end and another's begin. Determinate and recognized frontiers are therefore a basic institution of the state system and an essential legal attribute of any state. A government recognized as having political independence is legally the equal of other independent governments, and is not only the highest authority within its territorial jurisdiction but is under no higher authority.[31] It has the right to enter into relations with other states and to belong to the international society of states.

A political system may possess some or all of the empirical qualifications of statehood, but without the juridical attributes of territory and independence it is not a state. Furthermore, these attributes—which constitute territorial jurisdiction—serve as a test of a government's claim to be a state; there is no empirical test. For example, the Transkei, Bophuthatswana, Venda, and Ciskei—black "homelands" in South Africa—are as much empirical states as some other territories in Africa, but they lack statehood because they are not recognized by any state except South Africa and enjoy none of the rights of membership in international society. Since they are creatures wholly of South Africa's apartheid regime, their political survival is probably tied to the survival of apartheid. On the other hand, the former British territory of Lesotho, which is also an enclave within South Africa, but was never ruled by Pretoria and has gained its independence from Britain, is a recognized state and exercises full rights of membership in international society, which are not likely to be threatened in this way precisely because it is independent.

The juridical state in Black Africa is a novel and arbitrary political unit; the territorial boundaries, legal identities, and often even the names of states are contrivances of colonial rule. Only rarely did a colonial territory reflect the shape and identity of a preexisting African socio-political boundary, as in the cases of the British Protectorate of Zanzibar (formerly a sultanate) and the High Commission Territories of Swaziland and Basutoland (Lesotho), which had been African kingdoms. (Under British rule, the *internal* administrative boundaries of a colony were often drawn to conform with indigenous borders where these could be determined.) During the European colonization of Africa in the late 19th century, international society was conceived as a "European association, to which non-European states could be admitted only if and when they met a standard of civilization laid down by the Europeans."[32] With the exceptions of Ethiopia and Liberia, which escaped colonialism and were treated as states, Black African political systems did not qualify as states, but were regarded as the objects of a justified colonialism.

At independence (beginning in the late 1950s), there were therefore very few traditional African states to whom sovereignty could revert.[33] Consequently, there was little choice but to establish independence in terms of the colonial entities;[34] in most cases, a colony simply became a state with its territorial frontiers unchanged. Most attempts to create larger political units—usually conceived as federations—failed, as happened in the cases of the Mali Federation and the Central African Federation.[35] Kwame Nkrumah's vision of a United States of Africa received virtually no support from his counterparts in the newly independent states. Instead, the Organization of African Unity (O.A.U.), formed in May 1963, fully acknowledged and legitimated the colonial frontiers and the principle of state sovereignty within them. As President Modibo Keita of Mali put it: although the colonial system divided Africa, "it permitted nations to be born. . . . African unity . . . requires full respect for the frontiers we have inherited from the colonial system."[36]

It is a paradox of African independence that it awakened both national and ethnic political awareness. In almost every Black African country there are ethnic groups that desire to redraw international boundaries in order to form independent states. Self-determination, which accelerated after World War I and reached its peak in the years after World War II with the independence of numerous colonies, came to a halt in Black Africa at the inherited (colonial) frontiers. The movement, which is still alive sociologically among millions of Africans and within many ethnic communities, is unlikely to make further political-legal progress. The opposition of existing African states and of international society has reinforced the legitimacy of the inherited frontiers and undermined that of the traditional cultural borders. One of the exceptions to ethnic Balkanization has been Somali irredentism in Ethiopia and Kenya, which has sought the creation of a greater Somalia defined by cultural rather than colonial boundaries. But so far, Somali irredentism—as well as Biafran nationalism, Katangan separatism, and Eritrean secessionism—has failed to win international legitimacy. When the claims of Somali cultural nationalists were debated at the founding meeting of the O.A.U. in 1963, the argument advanced by the Kenyan delegation represented the view of the vast majority of African governments: "If they [the Somalis] do not want to live with us in Kenya, they are perfectly free to leave us and our territory. . . . This is the only way they can legally exercise their right of self-determination."[37] When the Kingdom of Buganda—an administrative region within the colony of Uganda and a traditional African state—declared itself independent in 1960 after realizing that the British authorities were going to give independence to Uganda, no other state recognized the declaration. Buganda failed to achieve juridical statehood; it remained a region—albeit a troublesome one—of the new Ugandan state, which became independent in 1962.

African decolonization—like decolonization elsewhere—demonstrated that it is impossible to have rational empirical qualifications for statehood. Many colonies became states although the viability of their economic bases and their developmental potentiality were questionable. Some of the new states had minuscule populations and/or territories: Cape Verde, the Comoros Islands, Djibouti, Equatorial Guinea, Gabon, The Gambia, Sao Tome and Principe, the Seychelles, and Swaziland. Empirically these entities are really microstates, but juridically they are full-fledged states.[38] Their independence reveals the assumption of the contemporary international community that even countries of very questionable viability and capacities can be preserved by a benevolent international society. In other words, international society has become a global "democracy" based on the principle of legal equality of members. Even the most profound socioeconomic inadequacies of some countries are not considered to be a barrier to their membership: all former colonies and dependencies have the right to belong if they wish. The existence of a large number of weak states poses one of the foremost international problems of our time: their protection and preservation, not to mention development. The survival of states is not a new issue; indeed, it is the historical problem of international relations, which has served to define traditional international theory as "the theory of survival."[39] What is new is the enlarged scope, added dimensions, and greater complexity and delicacy of the problem in contemporary international society.

INTERNATIONAL SOCIETY AND THE AFRICAN STATE

The juridical attributes of statehood can only be conferred upon governments by the international community. The Transkei is not a state because South Africa alone does not have the right to confer statehood, whereas Lesotho is a state because the international community accepted—indeed encouraged—British decolonization in Africa. Even though a state's jurisdictions and boundaries often appear to be "natural" phenomena and sometimes correspond with natural land forms, they are political artifacts upheld by the international community. Among other things, the international society of states was formed to support the doctrine of states' or sovereigns' rights as a cornerstone of international order. Basically, it involves mutual rights and obligations—for example, the right of a country to exist and not to have its jurisdiction violated, and its duty not to violate the rights of others.

In this section we offer an explanation as to why the existing pattern of juridical statehood has been maintained in Africa. The most important conditions that have contributed to this phenomenon appear to be: the ideology of Pan-Africanism; the vulnerability of all states in the region and the insecurity of statesmen; the support of the larger international society, including particularly its institutions and associations; and the reluctance, to date, of non-African powers to intervene in the affairs of African states without having been invited to do so by their governments. We will briefly discuss each of these conditions.

First, unlike any other continent except Australia, "Africa" is a political idea as well as a geographical fact with a distinctive ideology: African nationalism. This ideology emerged largely as a result of the universal African experience of colonial domination. European colonialism and its practices fostered the reactive ideology of African nationalism, which was directed at political independence and the freedom of the continent from European rule. Colonialism was the experience of Africans not only as individuals or as members of subordinated communities, or even as members of particular colonies; it was also their experience as Africans—a common political experience. As long as any country on the continent remains dominated by non-Africans, Pan-Africanism means the liberation of the continent in the name of African "freedom." Almost without exception, the Pan-Africanists came to realize that freedom could in practice only be achieved within the existing framework of the colonial territories that the Europeans had es-

tablished. The European colonies were the only political vehicles that could give expression to African nationalism; as a consequence, these artificial jurisdictions acquired a vital legitimacy in the eyes of most knowledgeable Africans. Politicians in particular have maintained that, whatever the size, shape, population, and resources of these jurisdictions, they have a right to exist because they are the embodiment of the African political revolution. The only practical way of realizing the goal of African freedom was through the independence of the colonial territories. By this process, the successor states were made legitimate—not one, or several, or many individually, but all equally. Moreover, it is consistent with the ideology of Pan-Africanism that until Namibia—and perhaps even South Africa—are free, "Africa" is not yet free.

Therefore, however arbitrary and alien in origin the inherited state jurisdictions might have been—and however far removed from traditional African values—they have been endowed with legitimacy. The ideology of Pan-Africanism that has gained historical expression in this way is a fundamental bulwark within Africa against the violation of existing, inherited state jurisdictions. At the same time Pan-Africanism disposed the new African statesmen to associate in a common continental body whose rules would legitimize existing jurisdictions and specify any international actions that would be considered illegitimate. As a result, the principles of the O.A.U., as set down in Article III of its Charter, affirm: the sovereign equality of member states; non-interference; respect for sovereignty; peaceful settlement of disputes; and the illegitimacy of subversion.[40] In sum, the ideology of Pan-Africanism has been expressed in the acceptance of the inherited colonial jurisdictions and the international legitimacy of all of the existing African states.[41]

Second, there is a common interest in the support of international rules and institutions and state jurisdictions in the African region that derives from the common vulnerability of states and the insecurity of statesmen. This approach would appear to be a variant of Hobbes's explanation of why rational individuals would prefer subordination to Leviathan as against freedom in the state of nature: general insecurity. "Since many are vulnerable to external incitement for secession it was obvious to most of the O.A.U. Members that a reciprocal respect for boundaries, and abstention from demands for their immediate revision, would be to their general advantage."[42] In order to survive, weak African governments had to be assured of the recognition and respect for their sovereignty by neighboring states, as well as any other states in a position to undermine their authority and control. Regional vulnerability and the general apprehension of externally promoted interference and subversion have disposed African governments to collaborate in maintaining their jurisdictions.

From a balance-of-power perspective, it might be objected that, in actual fact, the roughly equal powerlessness of African governments is what upholds state jurisdictions by making violation very difficult and therefore unlikely. But military weakness did not prevent the Tanzanian army from invading Uganda and overthrowing Amin's tyranny, and it did not prevent the Katangan rebels from invading Shaba province in Zaire on two separate occasions. To the contrary, the civil and military weakness of most African governments disposes them to fear international subversion by neighboring states and others who may support their internal enemies. Consequently, it is weakness that induces all of them to support the rules and practices of the O.A.U. which are intended to uphold existing state jurisdictions. African international society—specifically the O.A.U.—is intended to provide international political goods that guarantee the survival, security, identity, and integrity of African states, which the majority of African states cannot provide individually.

The O.A.U. is less an "organization" with its own agents, agencies, and resources than it is an "association" with its own rules: a club of statesmen who are obligated to subscribe to a small number of rules and practices of regional conduct, and to which every state except South Africa belongs. It is evident from the rules of Article III that the O.A.U. is very much a traditional association of states. But the O.A.U.'s effectiveness, like that of other successful international associations, probably owes less to its formal procedures than to its internal political processes. According to a leading student of the association, its main source of strength is the way in which it fosters the peaceful settlement of disputes.[43] Conflict resolution has often taken place outside the Commission of Mediation, Conciliation, and Arbitration—which was specifically set up for the purpose. Most statesmen involved in disputes have resorted to mediation or conciliation by the O.A.U. Chairman, who is elected annually by the members, or by another respected member who is not involved in the disputes. The success of the O.A.U. is indicated by the fact that the majority of the numerous disputes among its members have been contained through its internal political process. Its only significant failures to date have been the wars in the Horn of Africa prompted by Somalia's attempts to claim border territories in Ethiopia and Kenya (challenging the inherited boundaries as well as a fundamental principle of the O.A.U.) and the Uganda-Tanzania war of 1978–1979, which resulted in the overthrow of Idi Amin's tyranny.[44]

Third, the African states all became independent at a time when international society was highly organized and integrated. Its elaborate framework of international associations of both a worldwide and a regional or functional kind includes bodies that are important for African states: the United Nations (and its numerous specialized agencies that deal in whole or in part with Africa), the Commonwealth, Francophonie, the Lomé Convention of the European Economic Community (EEC), and so forth. Membership in such associations is an acknowledgement of the existence of the member states and of their international rights and duties, including the right not to be interfered with. Their membership in international society acknowledges the legitimacy and supports the independence of African states. Indeed, the states' rights that derive from membership in the United Nations and other bodies are commonly used by African governments—sometimes with considerable skill and success—to secure both material and non-material benefits from the international system.

International society is a conservative order. Any international actor that seeks to interfere by force or any other illegitimate means in the affairs of a member state is almost certain to be confronted by a condemnation of its actions by most other states. The only interventions that are acceptable under present international rules and practices are those to which the legitimate government of the target country has consented. Imposed or unsolicited interference is difficult to justify; in Africa, the attempts by Kantangan rebels, Biafran secessionists, Eritrean separatists, and Somalian and Moroccan irredentists to alter existing jurisdictions by force have to date not only been roundly condemned, but successfully resisted. Moreover, external powers that have been in a position to assist African claimant or expansionist states in their attempts at forced jurisdictional change have usually been loath to do so. For example, in 1977 the U.S.S.R. switched its military support from Somalia to Ethiopia when the Somalis seized Ethiopian territory by force. The Ethiopian army did not invade Somalia after it had expelled the Somali forces from Ethiopia's Ogaden region (with major Cuban as well as Soviet assistance). When external powers have intervened in Africa, they have usually respected existing state jurisdictions: most such interventions were in response to solicitations by African governments or revolutionary regimes fighting against colonial or white minority regimes.

The rare interventions in independent African states that were not solicited by a sovereign government, and thus did not respect existing state jurisdictions, can—with two exceptions involving France—be explained by the intervening power's status as an international outcast. In southern Africa, there have been numerous armed intrusions by the South African army into Angola to destroy, harass, or contain forces of the South West Africa People's Organization (SWAPO), and at least one dramatic raid into Mozambique to punish or destroy anti-apartheid movements in their sanctuaries. They can be accounted for by Pretoria's outcast status and preoccupation

with political survival. The military interventions by the Rhodesian armed forces into Zambia and Mozambique toward the end of the Rhodesian conflict can be understood in similar terms, as can the 1970 raid by Portuguese soldiers and African collaborators on Conakry, the capital of independent Guinea. The only interventions that cannot be explained in this way were made by France: in Gabon (1964) to restore a regime that had been overthrown, and in the Central African Republic (1979) to overthrow a government and to impose a new regime. In the first case, France had entered into an international agreement to protect the M'Ba government; in the second, it appears that other African states had given their tacit consent to the action, and may even have solicited it.

CONCLUSION

We have argued that juridical statehood is more important than empirical statehood in accounting for the persistence of states in Black Africa. International organizations have served as "post-imperial ordering devices" for the new African states,[45] in effect freezing them in their inherited colonial jurisdictions and blocking any post-independence movements toward self-determination. So far, they have successfully outlawed force as a method of producing new states in Africa.

Membership in the international society provides an opportunity—denied to Black Africa under colonialism—to both influence and take advantage of international rules and ideologies concerning what is desirable and undesirable in the relations of states. The impact of Third World states on those rules and ideologies is likely to increase as the new statesmen learn how to take advantage of international democracy. They have already been successful in influencing the creation of some new ideologies. For example, the efforts of the Third World have led to the formation of the North-South dialogue which would legitimate an international theory of morality based on assumptions of social justice that have heretofore been largely confined to internal politics.[46] The states of the

South—supported by some Northern statesmen—have asserted a moral claim on the actions and resources of the North; international society is not only being subjected to demands for peace, order, and security, but for international social justice as well. This radical new development in international relations is associated with the emergence of the Third World. If it succeeds, a revolutionary change in international morality will have been brought about.

The global international society whose most important institutions have been established or expanded since the end of World War II has been generally successful in supporting the new state jurisdictions of independent Africa; thus, the survival of Africa's existing states is largely an international achievement. Still, international effects on empirical statehood are ambiguous. International society has legitimated and fostered the transfer of goods, services, technology, skills, and the like from rich to poor countries with the intention of contributing to the development of the latter. But there are definite limits to what international society can contribute to the further development of the capabilities of African states. A society of states that exists chiefly in order to maintain the existing state system and the independence and survival of its members cannot regulate the internal affairs of members without the consent of their governments. It is therefore limited in its ability to determine that the resources transferred to the new states are effectively and properly used. In spite of a strong desire to do so, there is no way to guarantee such transfers against the wishes of a sovereign government without interfering in its internal affairs. Consequently, the enforcement of state jurisdictions may be at odds with the effort to develop the empirical state in Africa and elsewhere in the Third World. By enforcing juridical statehood, international society is in some cases also sustaining and perpetuating incompetent and corrupt governments. Perhaps the best example in sub-Saharan Africa is the international support that has gone into ensuring the survival of the corrupt government of Zaire. If this relationship is not an uncommon one, we must conclude that international society is at least partly responsible for perpetuating the underdevelopment of the empirical state in Africa by providing resources to incompetent or corrupt governments without being permitted to ensure that these resources are effectively and properly used.

State-building theories which assume that empirical statehood is more fundamental than juridical statehood, and that the internal is prior to the international in state formation and survival, are at odds with contemporary African experience. To study Black Africa's states from the internal perspective of political sociology is to assume that the state-building process here is basically the same as it was in Europe (where the political sociology of the modern state largely developed). In Europe, empirical statehood preceded juridical statehood or was concurrent with it,[47] and the formation of modern states preceded (and later accompanied) the emergence of a state system. European statesmen created jurisdictions over the course of several centuries in Machiavellian fashion—by dominating internal rivals and competing with external rivals—until the international system had attained its present-day jurisdictions.[48] However, as Tilly points out: "The later the state-making experience . . . the less likely . . . internal processes . . . are to provide an adequate explanation of the formation, survival or growth of a state."[49] In Black Africa (and, by implication, in other regions of the Third World), external factors are more likely than internal factors to provide an adequate explanation of the formation and persistence of states. State jurisdictions and international society, which once were consequences of the success and survival of states, today are more likely to be conditions.

Arnold Wolfers pointed out that in the Anglo-American conceptualization of the international system versus the nation-state, the most persistent image has been one of international discord versus internal order and civility.[50] In contemporary Black Africa, an image of international accord and civility and internal disorder and violence would be more accurate. At the level of international society, a framework of rules and conventions governing the relations of the states in the region has been founded and sustained for almost two decades. But far less institutionalization and political order has been evident during this period at the level of national society: many African countries have been experiencing internal political violence and some internal warfare. Insofar as our theoretical images follow rather than precede concrete historical change, it is evident that the recent national and international history of Black Africa challenges more than it supports some of the major postulates of international relations theory.

NOTES

1. Weber, *The Theory of Social and Economic Organization*, ed. by Talcott Parsons (New York: Free Press, 1964), 156.

2. *Ibid.*, 155.

3. Brownlie, *Principles of Public International Law*, 3d ed. (Oxford: Clarendon Press, 1979), 73–76.

4. *Ibid.*, 75.

5. See Giovanni Sartori, "Guidelines for Concept Analysis," in Sartori, ed., *Social Science Concepts: A Systematic Analysis* (forthcoming).

6. Brownlie (fn. 3), 75.

7. See Harry Eckstein's brilliant critique, "On the 'Science' of the State," in "The State," *Daedalus*, Vol. 108 (Fall 1979), 1–20.

8. Easton avoids the concept of the "state" in favor of that of the "political system"; see *The Political System: An Inquiry into the State of Political Science* (New York: Knopf, 1953), 90–124.

9. Brownlie (fn. 3), 75.

10. See Nelson Kasfir, *The Shrinking Arena: Participation and Ethnicity in African Politics, with a Case Study of Uganda* (Berkeley, Los Angeles, London: University of California Press, 1976).

11. See Clifford Geertz, "The Judging of Nations: Some Comments on the Assessment of Regimes in the New States," *European Journal of Sociology*, XVIII (No. 2, 1977), 249–52.

12. Brownlie (fn. 3), 75; Weber (fn. 1), 156.

13. See Robert H. Jackson and Carl G. Rosberg, *Personal Rule in Black Africa: Prince, Autocrat, Prophet, Tyrant* (Berkeley, Los Angeles, London: University of California Press, 1982).

14. See Michael Oakeshott, "The Vocabulary of a Modern European State," *Political Studies*, XXIII (June and September, 1977), 319–41, 409–14.

15. The legitimacy of a government in the eyes of its citizens must be distinguished from its legitimacy in the eyes of other states; it is international legitimacy that is significant in the

juridical attribute of statehood. A government may be legitimate internationally but illegitimate domestically, or *vice versa*. An instance of the former is Uganda during the last years of Idi Amin's regime; of the latter, the Soviet Union in its early years.

16. Geertz (fn. 11), 252.

17. *Ibid.*, 253.

18. There is a wealth of literature on military intervention in Africa. Two outstanding accounts are Samuel Decalo, *Coups and Army Rule in Africa: Studies in Military Style* (New Haven: Yale University Press, 1976), and Claude E. Welch, Jr., ed., *Soldier and State in Africa: A Comparative Analysis of Military Intervention and Political Change* (Evanston, Ill.: Northwestern University Press, 1970). Both have excellent bibliographies.

19. William Gutteridge, "Introduction," in Richard Booth, "The Armed Forces of African States, 1970," *Adelphi Papers*, No. 67 (London: International Institute for Strategic Studies, 1970), 4.

20. Jon R. Moris, "The Transferability of Western Management Concepts and Programs, An East African Perspective," in Lawrence D. Stifel, James S. Coleman, and Joseph E. Black, eds., *Education and Training for Public Sector Management in Developing Countries* (Special Report from the Rockefeller Foundation, March 1977), 73–83. For Ghana, see Robert M. Price, *Society and Bureaucracy in Contemporary Ghana* (Berkeley and Los Angeles: University of California Press, 1975); for Kenya, Goran Hyden, Robert Jackson, and John Okumu, eds., *Development Administration: The Kenya Experience* (Nairobi: Oxford University Press, 1970).

21. Myrdal, *Asian Drama: An Inquiry into the Poverty of Nations* (New York: Twentieth Century Fund, 1968).

22. Nyerere, *The Arusha Declaration Ten Years After* (Dar es Salaam: Government Printer, 1977), esp. chap. 3: "Our Mistakes and Failures," 27–48.

23. Independence Day Speech of President Mobutu Sese Seko, July 1, 1977, typescript, translated from the French by James S. Coleman.

24. See *West Africa*, No. 3255 (December 3, 1979), 2224; and Ghislain C. Kabwit, "Zaire: The Roots of the Continuing Crisis," *Journal of Modern African Studies*, XVII (No. 3, 1979), 397–98.

25. Gutteridge (fn. 19), 1.

26. *Ibid.*, 3.

27. *Africa Contemporary Record*, 1979–80, p. C 109.

28. The concept of "international society" is explored in Martin Wight, *Power Politics*, ed. by Hedley Bull and Carsten Holbraad (London: Royal Institute of International Affairs, 1978), 105–12. Also see Hedley Bull, *The Anarchical So-*

ciety: A Study of Order in World Politics (London: Macmillan, 1977), 24–52; and Alan James, "International Society," British Journal of International Studies, IV (July 1978), 91–106.

29. In considering the issue of human rights in Africa, the O.A.U.'s Assembly of Heads of States stressed the equal importance of "peoples' rights," and recently recommended that an "African Charter on Human and Peoples' Rights" be drafted. Peoples' rights are the rights of a sovereign people and can only be claimed and exercised by state governments. See Africa Contemporary Record, 1979–80, p. C 21.

30. Bull argues that the primary historical goal of international society has been to preserve the society of states itself; but it is difficult to see how this can be accomplished in the long run without first guaranteeing the sovereignty of member states. See The Anarchical Society (fn. 28), 17.

31. This is essentially the Austinian concept of "sovereignty." See John Austin, The Province of Jurisprudence Determined, ed. by H. L. A. Hart (London: Weidenfeld and Nicolson, 1954).

32. Bull (fn. 28), 34.

33. For an argument that at least in some cases "independence" was a "reversion" to sovereignty, see Charles H. Alexandrowicz, "New and Original States: The Issue of Reversion to Sovereignty," International Affairs, XLVII (July 1969), 465–80. For an opposing view, see Martin Wight, Systems of States, ed. by Hedley Bull (Leicester: Leicester University Press, 1977), 16–28.

34. French West Africa rather than its constituent units—Senegal, Mali, Upper Volta, Ivory Coast, etc.—could have been one state had Africans been able to agree to it; Nigeria could have been more than one.

35. At the time of independence in 1960, British-governed Somaliland joined the Italian-administered trust territory to form the Somali Democratic Republic. In October 1961, the Federal Republic of Cameroon came into being, composed of East Cameroon (formerly a French Trust Territory) and West Cameroon (part of a former British Trust Territory). Independent Tanganyika joined with Zanzibar to form the United Republic of Tanzania in April 1964.

36. Quoted in Robert C. Good, "Changing Patterns of African International Relations," American Political Science Review, Vol. 58 (September 1964), 632.

37. Quoted in Ali A. Mazrui, Towards a Pax Africana: A Study of Ideology and Ambition (Chicago and London: University of Chicago Press, 1967), 12.

38. According to the United Nations, in 1978 there were 13 African countries (8 on the continent and 5 island countries) with a population of less than one million. Nine of these had populations of 600,000 or fewer. See Africa Contemporary Record, 1979–80, p. C 107.

39. Martin Wight, "Why is there no International Theory?" in Herbert Butterfield and Martin Wight, eds., Diplomatic Investigations (London: George Allen & Unwin, 1966), 33.

40. Zdenek Cervenka, The Organization of African Unity and its Charter (New York and Washington: Praeger, 1969), 232–33.

41. Martin Wight defined "international legitimacy" as "the collective judgement of international society about rightful membership in the family of nations." See his Systems of States (fn. 33), 153 (emphasis added).

42. Cervenka (fn. 40), 93.

43. Zdenek Cervenka, The Unfinished Quest for Unity: Africa and the OAU (New York: Africana Publishing Co., 1977), 65.

44. As of March 1982, it was unclear whether the war between Morocco and the Polisario over the former Spanish Sahara could be considered a failure for the O.A.U., since it was uncertain whether the Sahrawi Democratic Republic (SADR) was as yet a legal member of the organization. See "The OAU's Sahara Crisis," West Africa, March 8, 1982, p. 639.

45. Peter Lyon, "New States and International Order," in Alan James, ed., The Bases of International Order: Essays in Honour of C. A. W. Manning (London: Oxford University Press, 1973), 47.

46. Independent Commission on International Development Issues, North-South, a Programme for Survival (Cambridge: MIT Press, 1980); Roger Hansen, Beyond the North-South Stalemate (New York: McGraw-Hill, 1979); Robert L. Rothstein, Global Bargaining: UNCTAD and the Quest for a New Economic Order (Princeton: Princeton University Press), 1979.

47. Charles H. McIlwain has noted that "Independence de facto was ultimately translated into a sovereignty de jure." Quoted by John H. Herz, "Rise and Demise of the Territorial State," in Heinz Lubasz, ed., The Development of the Modern State (New York: Macmillan, 1964), 133.

48. See Wight (fn. 28), chaps. 1 and 2.

49. Charles Tilly, ed., The Formation of National States in Western Europe (Princeton: Princeton University Press, 1975), 46. Unfortunately, Tilly tends to neglect the international dimension of European state making. For two excellent essays on this topic, see Martin Wight, "The Origins of Our States-System: Geographical Limits," and "The Origins of Our States-System: Chronological Limits" (fn. 33, 110–52).

50. "Political Theory and International Relations," in Wolfers, Discord and Collaboration: Essays on International Politics (Baltimore and London: The Johns Hopkins University Press, 1965), 239–40.

Bibliography

This bibliography is a selected list of periodical literature on subjects related to the five units of this reader. On the whole, the articles focus on topics or processes rather than on specific countries; a few country studies are included to illustrate the general questions under consideration. These titles were culled primarily from articles indexed in the *International Political Science Abstracts* for the years 1972–83, and they reflect the kinds of issues that concerned Africanists during that period as well as the range of interpretations and methods that they used for their analyses.

We must point out, however, that this bibliography is by no means exhaustive, nor does it necessarily represent every possible interpretation or method of analysis used by Africanists. While the bibliography—and the footnotes in this collection of scholarly articles—provides sources for research materials, students should be aware of the number of different types of sources available for their research purposes. Operating on the maxim that "half of knowledge is to know where to find it," we offer the suggestions below for research resources. Most of them are specifically Africanist-oriented, but we also include generalist or multidisciplinary sources that should be of particular assistance for students whose libraries do not contain many specialized area studies sources. The use of both types of sources will maximize access to a wide range of research evidence.

For *retrospective* bibliographies, see:
Africa South of the Sahara: Index to Periodical Literature, 1900–1970. Boston: G. K. Hall, 1971.
CAMP Catalog. Chicago: Center for Research Libraries, 1977. Supplements issued from time to time to update.
Duignan, Peter, and L. H. Gann, eds. *A Bibliographical Guide to Colonialism in Sub-Saharan Africa.* Cambridge: Cambridge University Press, 1973.

International Africa Institute, London. *Cumulative Bibliography of African Studies.* Boston: G. K. Hall, 1980.
Scheven, Yvette, comp. *Bibliographies for African Studies, 1970–1975.* Waltham, Mass.: Crossroads Press, 1978. See also her volumes for *1976–1979* (1980) and *1980–1983* (1984).
Witherell, Julian W., comp. *The United States and Africa: Guide to U.S. Official Documents and Government Sponsored Publications on Africa, 1785–1975.* Washington, D.C.: Government Printing Office, 1978.

For *United Nations* documents, consult:
I.B.I.D. (International Bibliography, Information, Documentation). New York: Unipub, since 1973, issued quarterly.
United Nations Documents Index. New York: United Nations, since 1950, issued monthly. Superseded by *UNDEX*, 1974–79; superseded by *UNDOC: Current Index, United Nations Documents Index,* since 1979.

For sources that focus exclusively on Africanist material, see *current bibliographies,* such as:
Africana Journal: A Bibliographic and Review Quarterly.
A Current Bibliography on African Affairs.
International African Bibliography: Current Books, Articles and Papers.
Joint Acquisitions List of Africa (JALA).
Readers should also consult the generalist bibliographic serials in the social sciences, such as:
International Bibliography of the Social Sciences, which includes series on economics, anthropology, sociology, and political science.
Public Affairs Information Service Bulletin (PAIS).
Social Sciences Index.

For students who need timely summaries and commentaries, or to track a series of events to set them in chronological order, yearbooks and news digests are especially useful. The best yearbook is *Africa Contemporary Record* (New York: Africana Publishing Company), which has been published annually since 1968; it provides a country-by-country survey of major political events and socioeconomic policies; features a number of essays on the major issues of the year; and records some of the major political and economic documents of each year. Students might also refer to *Africa South of the Sahara* (London: Europa Publications), issued since 1971, for similar, although not as detailed, evidence. There are numerous news digests, although the foremost one for African evidence is the *African Research Bulletin* (Exeter, England: Africa Research Ltd.) issued monthly since 1964. Other news digests include (1) *Africa Confidential*, (2) *Africa News, Weekly Digest of African Affairs*, (3) *African Index*, and (4) *SADEX* (Southern Africa Development Documentation Exchange). Students might also consult *Keesing's Contemporary Archives*, which has been published since 1931; its worldwide coverage includes Africa.

PERIODICALS DEVOTED PRIMARILY TO AFRICAN AFFAIRS

Listed below is a selection of journals devoted primarily to social science evidence about African affairs; on the whole they are indexed in leading current bibliographies on Africa, as well as the major social science current bibliographies. (The list includes date of origin, institutional affiliation, if any, and location)

Africa. London: International African Institute, 1926. Quarterly.
Africa Quarterly. New Delhi, 1960. Quarterly.
Africa Report. New York: African-American Institute, 1965–. Monthly.
African Affairs. London: 1901–. Quarterly. Formerly *Journal of the Royal African Society.*

African Economic History. University of Wisconsin, 1974–. Semiannual. Formerly *African Economic History Review.*
African Perspectives. Leiden, 1976–. Semiannual.
African Social Research. University of Zambia, Lusaka, Zambia, 1944–. Semiannual. Formerly *Rhodes-Livingstone Journal, Human Problems in Central Africa.*
African Studies. Witwatersrand University Press, 1921–. Quarterly. Formerly *Bantu Studies.*
African Studies Review. University of Florida, African Studies Association, 1958–. Formerly *African Studies Bulletin.*
American Universities Field Staff Report Service, Africa Series. Hanover, New Hampshire, 1951–. Issued irregularly.
Canadian Journal of African Studies. Loyola College, 1967–. Triannual.
Economic Bulletin for Africa. UNECA, 1961–. Quarterly.
Genève-Afrique. Institut Africain de Genève, 1962–. Semiannual.
International Journal of African Historical Studies. Boston University, 1968–. Semiannual. Formerly *African Historical Studies.*
Journal of African History. University of London, School of Oriental and African Studies, 1960–. Quarterly.
Journal of African Studies. University of California at Los Angeles, 1974–. Quarterly.
Journal of Asian and African Studies. York University, 1965–. Quarterly.
Journal of Modern African Studies. Cambridge University Press, 1963–. Quarterly.
Journal of Southern African Studies. Oxford University Press, 1974–. Semiannual.
Politikon: South African Journal of Political Science. University of Pretoria, 1974–. Afrikaans and English. Biannual.
Présence Africaine. Paris, 1947–. Quarterly.
Rural Africana. Michgan State University, 1967–. Quarterly.
South Africa International. Johannesburg, 1970–. Quarterly.

MULTIDISCIPLINARY JOURNALS

Listed below is a selection of multidisciplinary journals that frequently publish articles about Africa; almost all of them are indexed in leading social science current bibliographies.

American Journal of International Law
British Journal of International Studies
Canadian Journal of Political Science
Civilisations
Comparative Political Studies
Comparative Politics
Current History
Economic Development and Cultural Change
Ethnic and Racial Studies
Foreign Affairs
Foreign Policy
International Affairs
International Organization
Journal of Commonwealth and Comparative Politics
Journal of Developing Areas
Journal of Development Studies
Journal of International Affairs
Objective: Justice
Orbis
Parliamentary Affairs
Plural Societies
Political Quarterly
Race
Round Table
World Marxist Review
World Politics
World Today

SELECTED PERIODICAL LITERATURE

Determinants of Political Behavior

Davis, R. Hunt, "Interpreting the Colonial Period in African History," African Affairs 72, no. 289 (October 1973), 383–400.

Eker, Varda, "On the Origins of Corruption: Irregular Incentive in Nigeria," Journal of Modern African Studies 19, no. 1 (March 1981), 173–82.

Kirchnerr, Eugene C., "Towards an Explanation of the Transitionary Nature of the Political Map of Africa in the Period 1950–1978," Africa Quarterly 21, nos. 2–4 (1982), 5–22.

Kofele-Kale, Ndiva, "The Problem of Instrumental Leadership in Contemporary African Political Systems," Journal of

Asian and African Studies 13, nos. 1–2 (January and April 1978), 80–94.

LeVine, Victor T., "African Patrimonial Regimes in Comparative Perspective," Journal of Modern African Studies 18, no. 4 (1980), 657–73.

Lonsdale, John, "States and Social Processes in Africa: A Historiographical Survey," African Studies Review 24, nos. 2–3 (June–September 1981), 139–225.

Nkemdirim, Bernard A., "Reflections on Political Conflict, Rebellion, and Revolution in Africa," Journal of Modern African Studies 15, no. 1 (March 1977), 75–90.

Samoff, Joel, "Class, Class Conflict, and the State in Africa," Political Science Quarterly 97, no. 1 (Spring 1982), 105–27.

Sklar, Richard L., "The Nature of Class Domination in Africa," Journal of Modern African Studies 17, no. 4 (December 1979), 531–52.

Southall, Aidan W., "The Illusion of Tribe," Journal of Asian and African Studies 5, nos. 1–2 (January–April 1970), 28–50.

Uchendu, Victor C., "The Cultural Roots of Aggressive Behavior in Modern African Politics," Journal of Asian and African Studies 12, nos. 1–4 (January–October 1977), 99–108.

Young, Crawford, "Patterns of Social Conflict: State, Class, and Ethnicity," Daedalus 111, no. 2 (Spring 1982), 71–98.

Participation

Auma-Osolo, Agola, "Objective African Military Control. A New Paradigm in Civil-Military Relations," Journal of Peace Research 17, no. 1 (1980), 29–46.

Berg-Schlosser, Dirk, "Modes and Meaning of Political Participation in Kenya," Comparative Politics 14, no. 4 (July 1982), 397–415.

Bienen, Henry S., "Military Rule and Military Order in Africa," Orbis 25, no. 4 (Winter 1982), 949–65.

Blunt, Peter, "Social and Organisational Structures in East Africa: A Case for Participation," Journal of Modern African Studies 16, no. 3 (September 1978), 433–49.

Chazan, Naomi, "African Voters at the Polls: A Re-examination of the Role of Elections in African Politics," Journal of

Commonwealth and Comparative Politics 17, no. 2 (July 1979), 136–58.

Doro, Marion E., "'Human Souvenirs of Another Era': Europeans in Post-Kenyatta's Kenya," *Africa Today* 26, no. 3 (Winter 1979), 43–54.

Elaigwu, J. I., "Military Intervention in Politics. An African Perspective," *Genève-Afrique* 19, no. 1 (1981) 17–38.

Joseph, Richard A., "Democratization Under Military Tutelage: Crisis and Consensus in the Nigerian 1979 Elections," *Comparative Politics* 14, no. 1 (October 1981), 75–100.

Khapoya, Vincent B., "Determinants of African Support for African Liberation Movements: A Comparative Analysis," *Journal of African Studies* 3, no. 4 (Winter 1976), 469–89.

Killick, Tony, "Development Planning in Africa: Experiences, Weaknesses and Prescriptions," *Development Policy Review* 1, no. 1 (May 1983), 47–76.

Mazrui, Ali A., "Soldiers as Traditionalizers: Military Rule and the Re-Africanization of Africa," *World Politics* 28, no. 2 (January 1976), 246–72.

Mbilinyi, Marjorie J., "The 'New Woman' and Traditional Norms in Tanzania," *Journal of Modern African Studies* 10, no. 1 (May 1972), 57–72.

McKown, Robert E., and Robert E. Kauffman, "Party System as a Comparative Analytic Concept," *Comparative Politics* 6, no. 1 (October 1973), 47–52.

Mueller, Suzanne D., "The Historical Origins of Tanzania's Ruling Class," *Canadian Journal of African Studies* 15, no. 3 (1981), 459–97.

Ross, Marc H., and Veena Thadoni, "Participation, Sex, and Social Class," *Comparative Politics* 12, no. 3 (April 1980), 323–34.

Rouyer, Alwyn R., "Political Recruitment and Political Change in Kenya," *Journal of Developing Areas* 9, no. 4 (July 1975), 539–62.

Sandbrook, Richard, "The Political Potential of African Urban Workers," *Canadian Journal of African Studies* 11, no. 3 (1977), 411–33.

Southall, Aidan W., "Social Disorganization in Uganda: Before, During, and After Amin," *Journal of Modern African Studies* 18, no 4. (1980), 627–56.

Structures and Processes of Government

Goldsworthy, David, "Civilian Control of the Military in Black Africa," *African Affairs* 80, no. 318 (January 1981), 49–74.

Hayward, Fred M. "A Reassessment of Conventional Wisdom About the Informed Public: National Political Information in Ghana," *American Political Science Review* 70, no. 2 (June 1976), 433–51.

Huntington, Samuel P., "Reform and Stability in South Africa," *International Security* 6, no. 4 (Spring 1982), 3–25.

Luke, Timothy W., "Angola and Mozambique: Institutionalizing Social Revolution in Africa," *Review of Politics* 44, no. 3 (July 1982), 413–36.

Lungu, Gatian F., and John O. Oni, "Administrative Weakness in Contemporary Africa," *Africa Quarterly* 18, no. 4 (April 1979), 3–16.

Martin, Robert, "Legislatures and Economic Development in Commonwealth Africa," *Public Law* (Spring 1977), 48–83.

Mazrui, Ali A., "The Cultural Fate of African Legislatures: Rise, Decline and Prospects for Revival," *Présence Africaine* no. 112 (1979), 26–47.

Munslow, Barry, "Why Has the Westminster Model Failed in Africa?" *Parliamentary Affairs* 32, no. 2 (Spring 1983), 218–28.

Ojwang, J. B., "Legislative Control of Executive Power in English and French-Speaking Africa: A Comparative Perspective," *Public Law* (Winter 1981), 511–44.

Panter-Brick, S. K., "Four African Constitutions: Two Models," *Government and Opposition* 14, no. 3 (Summer 1979), 339–48.

Rothchild, Donald, and Michael Foley, "The Implications of Scarcity for Governance in Africa," *International Political Science Review* 4, no. 3 (1983), 311–26.

Samoff, Joel, "The Bureaucracy and the Bourgeoisie: Decentralization and Class Structure in Tanzania," *Comparative Stud-*

ies in Society and History 21, no. 1 (January 1979), 30–62.

Subramaniam, V., "Politicized Administration in Africa and Elsewhere: A Socio-historical Analysis," *International Review of Administrative Sciences* 43, no. 4 (1977), 297–308.

Uzoigwe, G. N., "Uganda and Parliamentary Government," *Journal of Modern African Studies* 21, no. 2 (June 1983), 253–71.

Development

Adams, John, "Economic Development in the Small Economies of Southern Africa: Contrasting Currents in the BLS Countries and the Homelands," *Journal of Asian and African Studies* 13, nos. 3–4 (July and October 1978), 244–55.

Adedeji, Adebayo, "Africa and the South: Forging Truly Interdependent Economic and Technical Links," *Africa Quarterly* 20, nos. 1–2 (1981), 5–29.

Amin, Samir, "Underdevelopment and Dependence in Black Africa–Origins and Contemporary Forms," *Journal of Modern African Studies* 10, no. 4 (December 1972), 503–24.

Bratton, Michael, "Development in Zimbabwe: Strategy and Tactics," *Journal of Modern African Studies* 19, no. 3 (September 1981), 447–75.

Curry, Robert L., Jr., and Donald Rothchild, "On Economic Bargaining Between African Governments and Multi-National Companies," *Journal of Modern African Studies* 12, no. 2 (June 1974), 173–89.

Freund, W. M., "Class Conflict, Political Economy and the Struggle for Socialism in Tanzania," *African Affairs* 80, no. 321 (October 1981), 483–99.

Greenberg, Stanley B. "Economic Growth and Political Change: The South African Case," *Journal of Modern African Studies* 19, no. 4 (December 1981), 667–704.

Hazelwood, Arthur, "Kenya: Income Distribution and Povery—An Unfashionable View," *Journal of Modern African Studies* 16, no. 1 (March 1978), 81–95.

Jeffries, Richard, "Political Radicalism in Africa: 'The Second Independence,' " *African Affairs* 77, no. 308 (July 1978), 335–46.

Jones, R. J. Barry, "International Political Economy," *Review of International Studies*, Part I, "Problems and Issues," 7, no. 4 (October 1981), 245–60; Part II, "Perspectives and Prospects," 8, no. 1 (January 1981), 39–52.

Martin, Guy, "Africa and the Ideology of Eurafrica: New-Colonialism or Pan-Africanism?" *Journal of Modern African Studies* 20, no. 2 (June 1982), 221–38.

McGowan, Patrick J., "Economic Dependence and Economic Performance in Black Africa," *Journal of Modern African Studies* 14, no. 1 (1976), 25–40.

Samoff, Joel, "Crises and Socialism in Tanzania," *Journal of Modern African Studies* 19, no. 2 (June 1981), 279–306.

Shafer, Michael, "Capturing the Mineral Multinationals: Advantage or Disadvantage?" *International Organization* 37, no. 1 (Winter 1983), 93–119.

Shaw, Timothy M., "From Dependence to Self-Reliance: Africa's Prospects for the Next Twenty Years," *International Journal* 35, no. 4 (Autumn 1980), 821–44.

Shaw, Timothy M., and Malcolm J. Grieve, "Dependence or Development: International and Internal Inequalities in Africa," *Development and Change* 8, no. 3 (July 1977), 377–408.

Stultz, Newell M., "Bridging the Black-White Gulf in Africa," *Orbis* 25, no. 4 (Winter 1982), 881–902.

Vengroff, Richard, "Dependency and Underdevelopment in Black Africa: An Empirical Test," *Journal of Modern African Studies* 15, no. 4 (December 1977), 613–30.

International Affairs

Aluko, Olajide, "African Response to External Intervention in Africa Since Angola," *African Affairs* 80, no. 319 (April 1981), 159–79.

Bienen, Henry S., "Perspectives on Soviet Intervention in Africa," *Political Science Quarterly* 95, no. 1 (Spring 1980), 29–42.

Bissell, Richard E., "African Power in International Resource Organizations," *Journal of Modern African Studies* 17, no. 1 (March 1979), 1–13.

Bowman, Larry W., "The Strategic Importance of South Africa to the United States: An Appraisal and Policy Analysis," *African Affairs* 81, no. 323 (April 1982), 159–91.

Brayton, Abbott A., "Soviet Involvement in Africa," *Journal of Modern African Studies* 17, no. 2 (June 1979), 253–69.

Brind, Harry, "Soviet Policy in the Horn of Africa," *International Affairs* 60, no. 1 (Winter 1983/4), 75–95.

Bull, Hedley, "The West and South Africa," *Daedalus* 111, no. 2 (Spring 1982), 254–70.

Coker, Christopher, "Adventurism and Pragmatism: The Soviet Union, COMECON, and Relations with African States," *International Affairs* 57, no. 4 (Autumn 1981), 618–33.

Crocker, Chester A., "South Africa: Strategy for Change," *Foreign Affairs* 59, no. 2 (Winter 1980/81), 323–51.

Foltz, William J., "United States Policy Toward Southern Africa: Economic and Strategic Constraints," *Political Science Quarterly* 92, no. 1 (Spring 1977), 47–64.

Houbert, Jean, "Africa in the Structure of International Politics," *Current Research of Peace and Violence* 3, nos. 3–4 (1980), 177–215.

McGowan, Patrick J., and Klaus-Peter Gottwald, "Small State Foreign Policies: A Comparative Study of Participation, Conflict, and Political and Economic Dependence in Black Africa," *International Studies Quarterly* 19, no. 4 (December 1975), 469–501.

Sesay, Amadu, "Comparative Study of Foreign Policies: A Critique," *International Studies* 19, no. 2 (April–June 1980), 221–41.

Shaw, Timothy M., "International Organizations and the Politics of Southern Africa: Towards Regional Integration or Liberation?" *Journal of Southern African Studies* 3, no. 1 (October 1976), 1–19.

Zartman, I. William, "Issues of African Diplomacy in the 1980's," *Orbis* 25, no. 4 (Winter 1982), 1025–43.

Table of African States*

Name[1]	Capital	Area (thousands of square miles)	Population[2] (Millions)	GNP per capita	Year of Independence
Algeria	Al Djazir (Algiers)	920	21.4 (3.3%)	2,350	1962
Angola	Luanda	481	8.2 (2.5%)	470	1975
Arab Republic of Egypt	Cairo	387	47.0 (2.7%)	690	1922
Benin (Dahomey)	Porto Novo	45	3.9 (3.0%)	310	1960
Botswana (Bechuanaland)	Gaberone	231	1.0 (3.5%)	900	1966
Burkina Faso (Upper Volta)	Ouagadougou	106	6.7 (2.6%)	210	1960
Burundi (Urundi in Ruanda-Urundi)	Bujumbura	11	4.7 (2.6%)	280	1962
Cameroon	Yaoundé	184	9.5 (2.7%)	890	1960
Central African Republic (Ubangi-Shari)	Bangui	240	2.6 (2.6%)	310	1960
Chad	N'Djamena (Fort-Lamy)	496	5.0 (2.1%)	80	1960
Congo, People's Republic of the (Middle Congo)	Brazzaville	132	1.7 (2.6%)	1,180	1960
Djibouti (French Territory of Afars and Issas)	Djibouti	9	0.3 (2.6%)	480	1977
Equatorial Guinea (Spanish Guinea)	Malabo (Santa Isabel)	11	0.3 (2.5%)	180	1968
Ethiopia	Addis Ababa	471	32.0 (2.4%)	140	c.1040
Gabon	Libreville	103	1.0 (1.5%)	4,000	1960
Gambia, The	Bathurst	4	0.7 (2.1%)	360	1965
Ghana (Gold Coast)	Accra	92	14.3 (3.2%)	360	1957
Guinea (French Guinea)	Conakry	95	5.6 (2.8%)	310	1957
Guinea-Bissau (Portuguese Guinea)	Bissau	14	0.8 (2.0%)	170	1974
Ivory Coast	Abidjan	125	9.2 (2.9%)	950	1960
Kenya	Nairobi	225	19.4 (4.0%)	390	1963

Country	Capital				Year
Lesotho (Basutoland)	Maseru	12	1.5 (2.8%)	510	1966
Liberia	Monrovia	43	2.2 (3.0%)	490	1847
Libya	Tripoli	679	3.7 (3.3%)	8,510	1951
Madagascar	Antananarive	227	9.8 (2.8%)	320	1960
(Malagasy Republic)					
Malawi (Nyasaland)	Zomba	46	6.9 (3.2%)	210	1964
Mali (Sudan)	Bomako	479	7.6 (2.4%)	180	1960
Mauritania	Nouakchott	397	1.8 (2.8%)	470	1960
Morocco	Rabat	172	23.6 (2.9%)	870	1956
Mozambique	Maputo (Lourenço Marques)	309	13.4 (2.7%)	270	1975
Namibia (South West Africa)[3]	Windhoek	318	1.1 (2.9%)	1,410	
Niger	Niamey	489	6.3 (3.0%)	310	1960
Nigeria	Lagos	357	88.1 (3.2%)	860	1960
Rwanda	Kigli	10	5.8 (3.1%)	260	1962
(Ruanda in Ruanda-Urundi)					
Senegal	Dakar	76	6.5 (3.0%)	490	1960
Sierra Leone	Freetown	28	3.9 (2.6%)	390	1961
Somali Republic	Mogadiscio	246	5.7 (2.6%)	290	1960
(Somalia and Br. Somaliland)					
South Africa, Republic of	Pretoria	472	31.7 (2.5%)	2,670	1926
Sudan (Anglo-Egyptian Sudan)	Khartoum	967	21.1 (3.0%)	440	1956
Swaziland	Mbabane	7	0.6 (3.2%)	940	1968
Tanzania	Dar es Salaam	365	21.2 (3.2%)	280	1961
(Tanganyika & Zanzibar)					
Togo (French Togoland)	Lomé	22	2.9 (2.9%)	340	1960
Tunisia	Tunis	63	7.0 (2.6%)	1,390	1956
Uganda	Kampala	91	14.3 (3.1%)	23	1962
Western Sahara[4]	El Ayoun	106	0.08 (n.a.)	n.a.	1976
Zaire	Kinshasa	906	32.2 (2.9%)	190	1960
Zambia (Northern Rhodesia)	Lusaka	291	6.6 (3.2%)	640	1964
Zimbabwe (Southern Rhodesia)	Harare (Salisbury)	151	8.3 (3.4%)	850	1965

See notes on following page

Notes to Table of African States

*Statistics compiled from (a) Arthur S. Banks and William Overstreet, editors, *Political Handbook of the World: 1982–1983—Governments and Intergovernmental Organizations as of January 1, 1983* (New York: McGraw-Hill Book Co., 1983); (b) Colin Legum, editor, *African Contemporary Record*, Volume XV (New York: Africana Publishing Co., 1984), p. C-34; and (c) *1984 World Population Data Sheet*, of the Population Reference Bureau, Inc., Washington, D.C. Note: For all sources, the effective dates of statistics vary from 1980 to mid-1984, and in most cases are regarded as estimates. Each of these sources is published annually, and students are advised to consult current editions for the most recent evidence. This table does not include the offshore islands of Cape Verde, Comoros, Mauritius, Réunion (which remains an Overseas Department or French Territory, as of late 1984), São Tomé and Principe, and the Seychelles.

1. Former name in parentheses.

2. Annual growth rate in parentheses.

3. Negotiations since 1968 have failed to resolve issues regarding Namibia's independence from the Republic of South Africa.

4. After Spain's withdrawal from Western Sahara in 1976, Morocco and Mauritania attempted to partition their neighbor, despite the independence proclamation by the Liberation of the Saharan Population, POLISARIO, establishing the Saharan Arab Democratic Republic (SADR). Mauritania withdrew its claims to part of Western Sahara's territory in 1979, but Morocco continues its military efforts to establish sovereign control over the northern area of the country. The SADR was admitted to the Organization of African Unity in 1982, following a controversial and bitter debate; by mid-1984 more than fifty states had recognized the Western Sahara/SADR as independent. All statistical data are estimated.

252

About the Contributors

Robert H. Bates is professor of social science at the California Institute of Technology.

William N. Brownsberger is an associate in the public finance department at Morgan Stanley & Co., Inc., in New York City.

Naomi Chazan lectures in political science in the Harry S. Truman Institute at the Hebrew University of Jerusalem.

Ruth Berins Collier is a lecturer in the Institute of International Studies at the University of California, Berkeley.

Stephen K. Commins is coordinator of the food and agriculture project of the African Studies Center at UCLA.

Samuel Decalo is professor of politics at the University of the West Indies, Trinidad.

Fred M. Hayward is professor of political science at the University of Wisconsin at Madison.

Rhoda Howard is a sociologist at McMaster University in Hamilton, Ontario.

Robert H. Jackson teaches political science at the University of British Columbia.

Nelson Kasfir is in the government department at Dartmouth College.

Colin Leys is professor of political science at Queen's University in Kingston, Ontario.

Michael F. Lofchie is professor of political science at UCLA.

S. Neil MacFarlane teaches government at the University of Virginia.

Carl G. Rosberg teaches political science and directs the Institute of International Studies at the University of California, Berkeley.

Timothy M. Shaw teaches political science at Dalhousie University in Halifax, Nova Scotia.

Richard L. Sklar is professor of political science at UCLA.

Lanciné Sylla is professor of sociology at the National University of the Ivory Coast in Abidjan.